BBP STANDARD MANUAL

FOR SUPERVISORS

BUREAU OF BUSINESS PRACTICE
PRENTICE HALL, WATERFORD, CT 06386

About BBP

BBP is a division of the Prentice Hall, Inc. publishing information services group, the largest of its kind in the world. All of the companies and divisions in our group are leaders in their field—Prentice Hall in college texts, and professional tax & legal services; J.K. Lasser for personal tax planning; Ginn & Co. in basic reading skills; and BBP in multimedia management, supervisory and employee training, to name but a few.

Serving your needs is the largest, most skilled staff of editors, authors, business experts and education specialists ever assembled to bring you the most effective information and training available anywhere. We use the latest technologies to interchange this information so that when you use any of our services you use all of our services—you have access to the united strength and resources of the entire group. You will never find a more dedicated or more technically skilled organization in which to entrust your critical training needs.

Copyright © 1988, Bureau of Business Practice, Inc.
All rights reserved. This book may not be reproduced in part or in whole by any process without written permission from the publisher.
Printed in the United States of America.

ISBN 0-87622-072-3

TABLE OF CONTENTS

INTRODUCTION
Your Role as a Supervisor 1

CHAPTER ONE: HOW TO BE AN EFFECTIVE LEADER
Determining Your Leadership IQ 3
Making the Transition to Supervisor 6
Leadership Without Pain 8
It's Your Decision 10
Delegating Effectively 12
Promotion Decisions Made Easy 15
Second-in-Command 16
Conquering a Crisis 19
Work in Balance 22
A Need to Plan 24
Scheduling for Efficiency 26
Build Motivation Through Goal-Setting 29

CHAPTER TWO: YOUR ROLE IN COST CONTROL
Commit Yourself to Cost Control 32
How to Encourage Cost-Saving Suggestions 34
Make Habitual Tardiness a Thing of the Past 37
Take a Firm Approach to End Chronic Absenteeism 40
How to Turn the Tables on Turnover 43
How to Avoid Unnecessary Overtime 46
Maintain High Productivity for Effective Cost Control .. 50
Teach Your People the Importance of Quality 53
Using Preventive Maintenance to Control Downtime Costs . 55
Strive for Improved Materials Handling 59
Prevent Theft From Impairing Cost-Effectiveness 62
Energy Conservation Helps Keep Costs in Check 65

CHAPTER THREE: THE SUPERVISOR'S TRAINING RESPONSIBILITY

Training Is an Investment 69
Instill Confidence in Your Trainees 73
Proper Orientation Is Important 76
Assessing Training Needs 78
Put Training Instructions in Writing 82
Build Worker Skills With Coaching and Counseling 85
Developing Employee Trainers 89
Make the Most of Your Training Dollar 94
Promote Continuing Education 97

CHAPTER FOUR: SAFETY AND THE SUPERVISOR

A Safe Workplace Begins With You 101
Make Safety Come Alive 103
What OSHA Expects 105
Safety, Workers, and You 107
How to Prevent Accidents and Injuries 110
Machine or Man-Eater? 116
Corralling Horseplay 118
How to Be Prepared for Disasters 121
Train Workers to Be Safety Experts 124

CHAPTER FIVE: YOUR ROLE IN HUMAN RELATIONS

Developing Human Relations Skills 127
Get Acquainted With Your People 130
How to Get Along With Your Peers 132
Build Productive Relationships With Your Superiors 135
The Importance of Recognition 138
PM for People: How to Prevent People Problems 141
How to Handle Employee Complaints 144
Coping With Conflicts 147
How to Help Your People Adjust to Change 149
Older Workers: Make the Most of Their Experience 153
How to Integrate Disabled Workers 156
Think Before You Discipline 160
Evaluating Employee Performance 163
How to Handle Employee Substance Abuse 167

The Issue of Sexual Harassment 170
Avoid Workplace Discrimination 174
Employment-at-Will: Here's What You Need to Know 176

CHAPTER SIX: HOW TO BE AN EFFECTIVE COMMUNICATOR

Make It Your Business to Be Understood 181
Praise and Criticism 184
Giving Effective Orders 186
Communicating Company Policy 188
The Value of Listening 191
Feedback: A Communication Essential 193
Closing Down the Rumor Mill 195
How to Hold Meetings That Work 197
Member of the Meeting 200
Write to Be Understood 203
Before You Interview 205
Interviewing for Best Results 208
Integrating Non-English-Speaking Employees 210

CHAPTER SEVEN: DEVELOPING YOURSELF AS A SUPERVISOR

Rising to Continuous Challenge 212
Planning Your Advancement 214
Managing the Special Project 217
Harness Your Creativity 219
Winning the Race Against Time 222
Less Stress 224

CONCLUSION
Self-Appraisal: Gauging Your Expertise 227

INTRODUCTION

YOUR ROLE AS A SUPERVISOR

The supervisor's role in the company is an important one. You are the essential communication link between top management and plant personnel. Employees look to you for guidance and leadership, while higher management depends on you to convey the company's needs and wants to workers.

Your main role is to get subordinates to do the job effectively and productively. To accomplish this, you must achieve a balance between working alongside your people and standing back and managing—between being a "player" and being a "coach."

If you're like most supervisors, you've gotten a promotion by doing technical work exceptionally well. You're used to doing a job yourself, and probably doing it better than anyone else. Then, all of a sudden, you are a supervisor, and you have to figure out just how much "playing" and how much "coaching" to do.

If you've come from a background of producing results, you're going to have a "doing" type of mentality. You'll tend to do more playing than coaching. But if you take this approach, you will finally get to the point where the daily work of getting the product out the door is interfering with your real job, which is thinking and planning, and doing things other than directly producing results.

What can you do? Understand and use the principles of effective supervision. This will help you gain control of your time and become more efficient in your job.

The seven chapters in this book cover the most basic—and the most crucial—aspects of effective supervision. You should turn to this book whenever you are looking for ways to improve your employees' performance, your department's productivity, or your own abilities. Here's an overview of information provided in this manual:

Effective leadership is the foundation upon which your success as a supervisor is built. In **Chapter One**, you'll learn what the key traits of an effective leader are and how you can mesh these skills with your personality to create your own supervisory style. You'll review planning and scheduling techniques that can help your department run more efficiently. And you'll learn ways to make your job easier through delegation and decision-making.

Controlling costs is as important a supervisory duty as leading your subordinates. **Chapter Two** focuses on ways to reduce unnecessary costs in your department. You'll discover methods for streamlining production, reducing labor and equipment costs, and conserving energy. Best of all, you'll find out how to keep costs in check and still put out the highest quality product.

Indoctrinating new hires is a costly endeavor. It is also a time-consuming one. But, as **Chapter Three** illustrates, breaking in new people—and keeping veteran workers updated—is too important to leave to trial and error. In this chapter, you'll learn how to set up training programs that will get new hires off on the right foot—and keep seasoned employees sharp and productive.

Training employees to work smart is important. But you must also train them to work safely. Being a supervisor puts you in the position of carrying out your company's safety and health policies. And this is one of your most vital duties. In **Chapter Four**, you will review some essential safety facts and learn ways to improve your safety sense.

A safe environment ensures the physical well-being of your workers. But your employees have psychological needs, too. How would you rate your skill at handling the "people side" of your work? **Chapter Five** gives you tips on how to create a climate of harmony and cooperation in your department. It also contains important information on some of the touchiest workplace issues—issues like sexual harassment, drug and alcohol abuse, and employment-at-will.

Mutual understanding is the cornerstone of a well-run department. This give-and-take of information is achieved by your ability to speak and to listen effectively. Are you as good a communicator as you could be? Sharpen your skills by following the advice contained in **Chapter Six**. It will help you make the transmission of policies and ideas—in person, on paper, and in meetings—as seamless as possible.

Motivating workers is a big part of your job. But of equal importance is knowing how to motivate yourself. In **Chapter Seven**, you will learn how to keep yourself motivated by looking for new challenges in your job. You'll discover ways to control stress and make the most of your time—enabling you to focus your energies on special projects and new ideas.

You will notice that at the close of every topic discussion there is room for an **Action Plan**. On these lines, you can jot down specific actions that you might take to implement suggestions, people you might contact for help or advice, questions that must be answered before you can take action, and any other notes that pertain to your particular needs.

The notes you take, in conjunction with the information contained in each section, will guide you toward creating an effective Action Plan—and toward becoming the most expert supervisor you can be.

CHAPTER ONE
HOW TO BE AN EFFECTIVE LEADER

DETERMINING YOUR LEADERSHIP IQ

Of all the persons in a business organization needing a leadership personality, front-line supervisors head the list—for they are the cornerstone upon which the entire management process rests...

Have You Got What It Takes?

Are you a good leader, an average leader, or not much of a leader at all? Many supervisors assume they are leaders because they've been put in charge of a department and have a certain number of subordinates who answer to them. But it's easy to confuse a supervisory position with leadership.

Although it's possible to be a good leader without being a good supervisor, it's difficult to be a good supervisor without being a good leader. The distinction is significant. It shows that leadership is an important part of a supervisor's job. You just cannot be a good supervisor unless you have good leadership abilities.

Here are ten qualities you need to be an effective leader. Although they are listed in numerical order, each is as important as the others in building sound leadership:

1. *Dynamic personality*
2. *Competence*
3. *Salesmanship*
4. *Planning ability*
5. *Organizing ability*
6. *Teaching skill*
7. *Fairness*
8. *Initiative*
9. *Decisiveness*
10. *Enthusiasm*

You may want to substitute other terms for some of the qualities listed. For instance, you may prefer *knowledge* or *skill* for *competence*. And you may think that *honesty* or *integrity* is a better description of the needed characteristic than *fairness*. But regardless of what you call them, you cannot afford to overlook any of these qualities if you sincerely want to develop your leadership ability.

Three Types of Leadership

Few people are born leaders. Leadership takes thought, practice, and constant attention to basic human relations. To a great degree, leadership is the art of influencing people—and there are many types of people. That's why Dave Heimburg, quality control supervisor at the Department of Refuse Removal (Orlando, FL), believes that trying different leadership approaches will be more effective than using just one.

"I know from my own dealings with *my* superiors that I respond well to some types of supervision, but not as well to others. The same holds true for my employees. No one wants to work for a Captain

Bligh, but by the same token, employees don't get much work done when they are working for a wimp. The secret is to combine several types of supervision and to know when to adjust the mixture."

There are three basic leadership styles:

★ **Authoritative**—The leader exercises maximum control and simply tells workers what to do.

★ **Democratic**—The leader encourages subordinates to participate in the decision-making process.

★ **Laissez-faire**—The leader tells workers what is required and lets them make their own decision.

Let's take a closer look at each style.

The Authority Is Yours

"Authoritative supervisors believe that when you *must* get results, you have to impose strict leadership," Heimburg says. And there are times when they're right. But will this approach work well *all* of the time? Heimburg doesn't think so: "This style cannot work over the long haul—you can really use authority only to correct short-term problems."

Authoritative supervision is also useful at two other times, adds Bob Hipp, formerly associate supervisor in operations for Dayton Power & Light Company (Dayton, OH). The first is when you are giving instructions regarding safety. Here there's no room for argument. Simply lay out the safety rules your company has developed, and make sure those rules are obeyed at all times.

An authoritative style is also most desirable during an emergency, Hipp continues. If the building's on fire, there's no time to conduct a meeting. The supervisor must take charge and issue direct, explicit instructions.

A Democratic Approach

"Democratic supervisors look for group decisions. They allow the employees more freedom to make their own decisions, and they maintain only loose control over employees," explains Heimburg.

"The democratic approach," says Hipp, "is useful when you are developing a new technique, instituting a new job sequence, or using new materials. Here, everyone can sit down together before starting the procedure. The supervisor outlines what must be accomplished, and then allows employees to express any ideas they might have.

"Naturally, you're going to end up with some ideas that are impractical," Hipp continues. "However, someone just might come up with a better or easier way to do the job than you had initially planned."

The democratic approach is also useful if some task has been done the same way for a number of years. The routine of doing the job may have perpetuated itself, even if there really is a better way to perform the task. But you can't get any improvements if you use the authoritative approach when assigning that particular job. Instead, be open to suggestions about possible ways the job can be enhanced.

Hands Off

Laissez-faire supervisors maintain little or no control over their people. They look for workers to supply their own goals and motivations. Heimburg believes that a strict laissez-faire approach is a poor way to supervise. While some workers need little motivational help, leaving them too much freedom can kill productivity.

There are times when a laissez-faire approach will work, however. Heimburg notes that it is most successful after the other two styles have been used successfully. "It's the next step in development—especially in building trust between employee and supervisor. The idea is to obtain results without having to be directly involved in how the employee does the day-to-day work."

It's a Matter of Orientation

Now that you are familiar with the different leadership styles, how do you decide which approach to use *when*? The trick is to tailor your approach to the people you supervise as well as to the circumstances at hand.

For example, if you want to be a leader respected by workers who are on repetitive jobs, you must be *task oriented*. That is, you must know all there is to know about how each part of the job is done and be able to demonstrate and answer questions about it.

On the other hand, to be a successful leader of the more creative worker, you must be *people oriented*. The reasoning behind this theory is quite simple: The more skills people bring to their jobs, the more you should depend on their initiative.

Take these two examples:

Suppose you're a supervisor of a production assembly department in a plant that makes small water pumps. Most of the work is done along a conveyor-type assembly line. Each worker is assigned a specific station along the line and performs a single task. One installs diaphragms; another sets gaskets; a third bolts down the pump housings.

This is a situation that calls for a tight ship and an authoritative style of leadership. You tell your people exactly what they have to do and how to do it. You have to establish rules and enforce them. The reason is obvious. One deviation from normal procedures and the entire line would grind to a costly halt.

But what will you do if you are transferred to head a maintenance crew? Will you continue to use the same supervisory methods you used in Assembly? If you do, you're liable to fall flat on your face. The maintenance craftspeople work under far different conditions and require a different type of supervision. Usually, they have many skills and are required to make many decisions on their own. They don't need, and probably will not tolerate, someone looking over their shoulders every minute and telling them which nut to turn next. In this situation, a democratic approach is more reasonable.

It boils down to this: Maintaining a middle course between too much and too little authority is the essential ingredient for effective leadership.

I Like Your Style!

How much time have you spent thinking about your leadership style? Maybe not as much as you should. Some supervisors—naturally enough—develop one style that evolves from their experience and personality. Unfortunately, they never think to try any other approach with their workers—no matter how different those individuals, or the circumstances, may be. But changing your style to meet the situation can be a much more effective way to lead your people.

Keep in mind that changing style doesn't mean changing personality. Nothing is more self-defeating than trying to act like someone you aren't. The change is one of approach, not personality.

It's natural for you to be more comfortable with one style than with another. For example, if you can easily discuss problems and can listen to your employees' side of things, you are probably most comfortable with variations of the democratic style. But whichever style is most comfortable, look for opportunities to practice the other approaches. At some point, *each* leadership style is needed.

▶ WHAT YOU CAN DO → *You can increase your leadership if you...*

1. Become familiar with the different types of leadership styles: Authoritative, Democratic, and Laissez-faire.

2. Review your many duties to determine which leadership style is required to accomplish them all successfully.

3. Develop a leadership style that feels natural to you, but stay on the lookout for times to practice other styles.

Good leadership takes many forms, and the correct form for a particular operation depends on the individual, the type of work being performed, and the situation at hand.

ACTION PLAN:

_____
_____
_____
_____
_____
_____
_____
_____
_____

MAKING THE TRANSITION TO SUPERVISOR

Whether you are new to the job or are a veteran, perhaps the hardest transition you have had to make was your promotion to new supervisor. Do you wish you had known then what you know now? Are there still some situations you wish you knew how to handle better? If so, here's your chance to look objectively at your supervisory practices and . . .

Take a Fresh Approach

If you had to do it all over again, would you take on the responsibility of new supervisor differently? Did you know then *all* the leadership tools you would need on your job? How did you respond to your old peers and your new ones—and how do you handle those relationships now?

Whether you are a recent promotee to supervision or have years of experience under your belt, you can improve your supervisory techniques by examining your job from the point of view of a raw newcomer.

Dealing With Former Co-workers

Once you were one of the troops, but now you've attained your stripes. That means that relationships with former co-workers can become frayed or threatened—especially for those supervisors who once worked side by side with the people whom they now oversee.

One of the biggest hurdles new supervisors face is the resentment of former co-workers. Hard feelings make for uncomfortable relations between you and the involved workers; they can also have a devastating effect on morale and productivity. Here's an example of how this kind of resentment develops:

"I heard Mike Fleming was just promoted to Production Supervisor," John Williams told his friend Mark Buchanan at lunch one day.

"What?" said Buchanan. "We're just as qualified as he is for that position!"

"That's what I thought too," replied Williams. "But look at it this way. Mike is one of the gang. He'll give us all the easy assignments."

"That's true," said Buchanan, brightening a little. "We can take our time on our breaks now. Mike won't care if we're late getting back to work."

If you get promoted over co-workers who were once your friends on the job, don't be surprised if they exert pressure on you to give them the red-carpet treatment. Like Buchanan and Williams, they may assume that you'll hand them the easiest assignments and overlook their disciplinary infractions.

What can you do? Try taking this approach:

▶ Tell your former co-workers that you intend to treat everyone in the department alike—and that rules and policies will apply to all equally.

▶ Strive to establish positive relationships with everyone in your department—even those with whom you have not enjoyed a good rapport in the past.

▶ Create a sense of team spirit—share your departmental goals with your people and ask for their assistance in meeting those goals.

Remember, you're now the person in charge. If workers think you're still at their level on the job, they won't take your word seriously. On the other hand, if you choose to deal with people on a "business only" level, you might end up alienating your workers. Avoid being one of the gang, but don't neglect the importance of positive feedback and reinforcement.

Learn From Others

Employees and former co-workers aren't the only people you must deal with. Now, too, you'll work with other supervisors and with different departments in the company. This interaction is an important part of your supervisory role and will tell a great deal about your chances for success.

Make yourself important to the entire company—not just your own department. Don't take refuge in your office. Learn about the rest of the company, and you'll find other supervisors will come to you for advice, suggestions, and knowledge. The best supervisors look for peers who can help them do their jobs.

Trading information will also give you broad knowledge of the company. And the more you know about your company, the more you'll be privy to—in meetings, in committee memberships, and in other areas.

Reviewing Your Performance

Keeping up with the responsibilities of supervision takes work. You can make the job easier on yourself—and your people—if you review your own performance from time to time. Here are some steps you can take:

★ **Be receptive.** Ask for comments and suggestions from your workers. Encourage them to come forward with ideas for improvement. And when they do, listen and act on the suggestions whenever possible. If it isn't a good idea, explain why to encourage input in the future.

The same holds true for criticism, whether or not it comes in the form of a complaint. Don't feel that because you've been promoted, you have to know it all. You don't. But train your people to present their complaints with a suggestion on how to fix what's wrong.

★ **Set a good example.** Coming in late and leaving early will give workers the impression that you're not serious about your new role. People may even begin to ask why you received the promotion in the first place—and they'd be right to wonder.

Setting a good example sets the pace for the rest of the department—and provides your superiors with a measure of your performance. The attendance records of your subordinates could indicate how effective you are as a supervisor. Besides, how can you discipline for lateness when you yourself arrive late?

★ **Accept accountability for your people.** This is essential if you expect them to work hard for you. When something goes wrong and the flak begins to fly, you can't stand aside and let your people take the punishment. Since they work under your direction, you have to take the responsibility. And if people know that you'll go to the wall for them, you'll have their loyalty in return.

★ **Communicate honestly with your boss.** Be willing to accept responsibility for your actions. If you goof, admit it. Don't be afraid of failures. The most successful supervisors have all had failures, but they've used them as learning experiences. There's truth in the adage that if you haven't had any failures, you haven't been trying very hard.

▶ **WHAT YOU CAN DO** → *Whether you are a new supervisor or an experienced one, you can improve your performance if you . . .*

1. Take steps to see that relations between you and former co-workers are free from jealousy and favoritism.

2. Keep a professional distance from employees, but retain regular friendly conversation to strengthen relations.

3. Learn from fellow supervisors to make yourself valuable to the entire company.

4. Develop your leadership skills by being receptive, setting a good example, accepting accountability, and communicating honestly.

Reviewing your performance from the vantage point of a newcomer can help you grow and improve as a leader.

ACTION PLAN:

_____
_____
_____
_____
_____
_____
_____
_____
_____
_____
_____

LEADERSHIP WITHOUT PAIN

Leadership can be a painful experience: If you bully people into doing what you want, then your leadership is painful to your workers and fellow supervisors. If you let other people walk all over you, your leadership is painful to you. Fortunately, there is a painkiller you can use to become a more effective leader, and it's called ...

Assertive Supervision

Some supervisors are too aggressive. They place unreasonable demands on their people and insist on special favors from their colleagues. Other supervisors are too passive. They let employees get away with everything short of staging a coup. Colleagues, too, often take advantage of a passive supervisor by shifting work to that person's department or by getting new assignments that aren't deserved.

Between these two extremes lie assertive supervisors. These leaders:

- Can talk with people on all levels.
- Are goal directed and make things happen.
- Demonstrate self-respect *and* respect for others.
- Express feelings openly—but in a constructive manner.
- Make firm decisions, but change direction when it becomes necessary.
- Take responsibility for their own actions and behavior.
- Take and give criticism constructively.
- Neither downplay nor overstate their abilities.

As you can see, assertiveness allows you to get your way, but without hurting the feelings of others. Chances are that you agree that this is a goal worth striving for, and would like to give it a try. Let's take a closer look at the problems caused by passiveness and aggressiveness, and then discuss how *you* can start supervising assertively.

The Supervisor as Doormat

In a department led by a passive supervisor, the problems are myriad. First, employees aren't likely to put forth their best effort at all times. They know the supervisor isn't going to criticize them, so they do just enough work to get by.

Employees in this situation also make it a practice to flout the rules. Tardiness, absences, and extended breaks can become the norm when a supervisor fails to enforce departmental regulations.

Another problem is that innovation may pass these supervisors by. If they discover some new equipment or technology that could help their workers perform better, they may be reluctant about asking management to approve the purchase. And even if management is willing to spend money, passive supervisors are frequently left out in the cold because another supervisor spoke up sooner—and louder—then they did.

What causes a supervisor to be passive? For many, a lack of confidence lies at the root of the problem. For others, passivity is due to sheer laziness. But whatever the reason, a passive supervisor might just as well not be a supervisor at all.

The Supervisor as Monarch

"Just go do it," says the supervisor.
"Why?" asks the employee.
"Because I said so!" comes the shouted reply.

Is this your usual method of making job assignments? If so, you're an aggressive supervisor. And like most other aggressive supervisors, you probably have a workforce that's completely demoralized, performs grudgingly, and avoids you at all costs.

There's never any harm in explaining to workers *why* they have to perform a certain way. It may take a few extra minutes, but the employee will have a clearer understanding of what must be done and will likely turn out better work as a result.

There are also dangers in being aggressive with other supervisors. The easiest way to lose the cooperation of your colleagues is to run roughshod over them whenever it suits your purposes. For instance, if your department falls behind in its work, you may think nothing of borrowing workers from another group—without asking that group's supervisor for permission. Needless to say, your presumptuousness will offend and anger the supervisor, whom you may have to rely on for help in the future.

Basically, most aggressive supervisors mistrust other people and their intentions. They believe that they have to stand up—and then walk over others—for their rights.

Yes and No

By now, you're probably convinced that aggressiveness and passivity aren't for you. So what can you do to become assertive? Generally speaking, the keys to assertiveness are learning how to to say no when it's necessary, and learning how to get others to say yes.

Saying no isn't a problem for aggressive supervisors. They say no whenever they feel like it—and often simply *because* they feel like it. Saying no is a bigger problem for passive supervisors. They don't want others to see them as uncooperative, and they're frequently afraid that others will refuse to help them when they need assistance. Worst of all, they may believe that they don't have the right to say no.

Remember, you can and should say no to people who request special favors of you—as long as you genuinely don't have the time or the resources to help them. And even if you can't perform a favor for someone right at the moment, you can stave off any ill feelings by letting the other person know that you'll be willing to help as soon as possible. In addition, you can politely refer them to other sources of work.

When you must say no to a request from an employee, always back up your refusal with an explanation of your decision. If your answer appears arbitrary, the worker may become upset with you, which could affect his or her work.

The Path to Yes

On the face of it, learning to say no seems pretty easy. A greater challenge lies ahead: getting workers and fellow supervisors to say yes when you must make a special request of them.

First things first: The path to yes will be a lot smoother if you've made a practice of saying yes to others whenever possible. Beyond that, you'll have to:

★ **Speak their language.** If you can use the lingo and buzzwords of another department when you're speaking to the supervisor of that group, he or she is more likely to see you as a kindred spirit. Thus, that individual may be more inclined to help you out of a tough situation.

With your own employees, speaking their language means knowing which approach is likely to get you what you want—with the least resistance. If you need greater output, for instance, you must know which employees need to be asked for their help, as opposed to those who will increase their efforts simply because you order them to.

★ **Expect a yes.** The way you make a request for help may imply that you expect no for an answer. Instead of saying "Can you help me?" make it a practice to say "Will you help me?"

By asking in the latter manner, you're soliciting a yes or a no response, not a litany of excuses. And since the person can't use excuses to run interference, he or she may just go ahead and say yes.

★ **Ask, don't demand.** You must be willing to ask for what you need or for what is rightfully yours. At the same time, you can't *demand* these things. You have to present the other party with an option.

The reason for this is simple: No one likes to be backed up against the wall. When you give others the option of helping you, and can give good reasons for needing their assistance, you'll be surprised how often they'll be willing to give you assistance.

▶ **WHAT YOU CAN DO** → You can become an assertive supervisor by . . .

1. Making a commitment to getting what you want—without stepping on the toes of your colleagues or browbeating your employees.

2. Learning to say no when you genuinely can't agree to the request of an employee or a fellow supervisor.

3. Saying yes whenever possible.

ACTION PLAN:

_____
_____
_____
_____

4. Asking for what you need in a sincere and reasonable manner.

Leading your people—and dealing with your colleagues—assertively will pay off in heightened morale and a spirit of teamwork among those you work with.

IT'S YOUR DECISION

When you run into a situation where action is required and there's nobody to tell you what to do, or it's not covered by a company policy, you have to make a decision. You can't count on your assistant, another supervisor, or any of the other workers involved. It's up to you and you alone to . . .

Keep Work Running Smoothly

Indecision can destroy your effectiveness as a supervisor. When your workers stand idly by as you struggle over what action to take, the cost of your hesitancy can mount up quickly—not only in terms of lost productivity, but also in terms of your people's morale. After all, who has much respect for a supervisor who can't make up his or her mind?

But before any intelligent decision can be made, you need to understand certain principles. Keep in mind that a decision is a choice between neutral alternatives; it is rarely a choice between right and wrong. Then, too, a supervisor's function is to select that action that gets the most done, at the least cost, and with the fewest disadvantages. Finally, remember that one decision often impacts upon or dictates many subsequent ones.

A Four-Step Process

Some decisions obviously require more time and study than others. However, no decision should be made without appropriate consideration of its effects and consequences. Four steps are essential in developing correct decisions—ones that will keep your department running smoothly. These are:

1. **Gathering information**
2. **Listing alternatives**
3. **Taking action**
4. **Reviewing the course of action**

Let's take a closer look at each step.

Getting the Facts

The first step is to gather as much relevant information as time and circumstances permit. It has been said that people's decisions can be no better than their information. You can't hire a research crew to dig up all the relevant information about each problem you face, but you can gather all the data available to you.

Remember, you can make a wrong decision because you know too little about something, but you seldom make a wrong decision because you know too much. Therefore, ask yourself these questions about the problem at hand:

★ **What is the real problem?** Is it based on fact or opinion? Is your information truthful or does it stem from bias?

★ **How did it come about?** Is it unique or common to others? Will it solve itself?

★ **Is the stated problem the real problem**—or only a symptom? Has it been defined in too-narrow terms?

★ **What is the critical issue involved?** Should we tackle only this part of the problem at this time?

★ **What is the real goal,** purpose, or objective we're trying to achieve? Is it critical to the department's or company's goals or plans—or only incidental?

Weighing the Alternatives

You've gathered all the available information about the problem and analyzed all aspects of the particular situation. Now you're entering the creative phase of decision-making. What are your possible courses of action?

The first that occurs to you probably represents your usual approach to this type of situation. But it may not offer the best possible solution. Only by considering all the possible alternatives can you be confident you will not overlook any opportunities to get the results you want.

Here is a checklist to use for weighing the alternatives:

- Have only the usual alternatives been considered?

- Are there unusual or creative possibilities to consider?

- Are reasons you have for discarding alternatives sound?

Taking Action

Now you must make a decision by selecting the best alternative available. You've analyzed all the information you were able to gather. You've considered several possible decisions. Now you must narrow your choice to one decision that your judgment and experience tell you offers the best chance for success.

So you convert your decision into action. See to it that the decision is put into effect at the proper time. Supervise very carefully how it is being carried out, and document everything connected with your decision so that you can evaluate it later.

Let all concerned know what your decision is. Make sure they understand it completely, and answer any questions that may arise. Listen to any suggestions about, or objections to, your decision. Evaluate these with an eye to improving future decisions.

A Dirty Decision

There's no question that decision-making involves an element of risk. What should you do if something goes wrong and your decision turns out to be a mistake? Consider the following situation:

"How come I always get the dirtiest job?" protested Jack Conley. "That's the third time this month you've put me on cleanup. My back aches for a week every time I do it. Give me a break!"

"That's really tough," Mark Griffin, the floor supervisor replied unsympathetically. "But someone has to do it and you're the one. There's no one else available."

Conley shook his head. "I won't do it again. Give someone else a turn. It's just not fair to give me that job again."

"So what? Life isn't fair, either," said Griffin. "I want you to get on that job *now*."

Thinking the matter had been settled, Griffin went about his business. An hour or so later, Griffin's immediate supervisor, Mike O'Hare, called him into his office.

"Jack Conley came to see me this morning, and he gave me his version of what happened between you two. Look, I don't want to tell you how to run your crew. But I think you were out of line in assigning Conley cleanup again. What about Michaelson or Winters? They're both available, and according to Conley, they haven't performed cleanup for three months."

Fuming, Griffin left the office. But by the time he got back to his department, he realized he'd made the wrong decision. He had acted out of anger and had overlooked the other employees. He decided to apologize to Conley.

When You're in the Wrong

As a general rule, most people would agree that it is a good idea to stand by your decisions once you have made them—unless, of course, a particular decision turns out to be a bad one. Then there usually is no option: A reversal is essential.

It isn't possible to predict the outcome of every action; therefore, skilled decision makers always review each decision they make to determine whether it was the best one. Had Griffin reflected on his decision, he probably would have realized he hadn't considered other alternatives.

If you find yourself in a similar boat, ask yourself if you really had all the information you should have had. What possibilities did you overlook? Did

11

you consider a number of alternatives or did you take the easy way out?

Remember, you learn from each decision how to make a better and wiser one the next time around. In this way, you learn to avoid mistakes and to neutralize the element of risk.

> ▶ **WHAT YOU CAN DO** → *You can improve your decision-making skills if you . . .*
>
> 1. Gather as much data as possible under the circumstances and size up the problem at hand.
>
> 2. Come up with possible solutions to your problem and then decide on one course of action.
>
> 3. Put your decision into action, being sure to inform everyone involved.
>
> 4. Review your decision to make sure it was the right one. If you made a mistake, admit it. Then set things straight.
>
> *Decision-making is a risk-taking venture, but by following certain principles and practices, you can be confident that your decision is the best possible one.*
>
> **ACTION PLAN:**
> _____
> _____
> _____
> _____
> _____
> _____
> _____
> _____

DELEGATING EFFECTIVELY

Most supervisors know that delegating can save them time, build employee skills, and get results. But how many actually delegate? Often, supervisors find it hard to get started because they don't know what to delegate or to whom. But you should have no difficulty delegating if you . . .

Determine What Only You Can Do

Consider the case of Supervisor Kim Garfield. According to her, the days were just too short for everything she had to do. She frequently worked overtime in order to catch up—writing memos, finishing reports, preparing merit ratings. And during the past few weeks she had been busier than usual.

Under the pressure of a large work load, Garfield tried to keep her spirits up and continued to plug away at all the paperwork on her desk. As she looked up at the wall clock to check the time, she saw her department manager, John Warren, walking toward her with a sour expression on his face.

"Kim, I've been waiting for that production report for over a week now. Why haven't you finished it?" Warren asked. "And what about the list of cost-cutting suggestions that you were supposed to have in at the end of last month? What ever happened to that?"

"I'm working on the production report right now," the supervisor said, "but I haven't had a minute to spare to prepare those cost-cutting ideas that you wanted."

"Let me ask you something," Warren said. "Do you ever delegate any of your more routine chores to give yourself time to handle the really important projects?"

"No, I guess I don't," Kim Garfield admitted. "I always figured that if you want a job done right, you have to do it yourself."

"A lot of people feel that way," Warren assured the supervisor. "But you have to learn how to delegate in order to get things done. We all like to think that we are indispensable. However, when we try to do all of the work ourselves, we're only wasting our valuable time. Limit yourself to the tasks only *you* can handle and leave most of the details to other people in your department."

Reliable Delegates

Manager John Warren has had ample experience with delegating, and he has just explained the easiest way for supervisors to begin delegating. As you now know, the trick is to determine the tasks only you can do. Once you've done this, you know exactly what to delegate—all the rest.

But how do you decide who will do what tasks? As Supervisor Kim Garfield has shown, supervisors are sometimes unsure of whom they can trust to do a good job. That's a valid concern. If you're going to hand over some work that you are ultimately responsible for, it's wise to spend a little time deciding who should do it.

So, before handing out any assignments, take a moment to carefully consider who can successfully complete which tasks. To help you think the matter through, ask yourself the following list of questions:

■ **Which employees want more responsibility?** Maybe 75 percent of your workers will welcome new duties—leaving 25 percent that will not. It's best to identify these groups at the start.

■ **Which employees can spare the time?** Some of your best employees may already be loaded down with work. You may have to bypass these individuals or redistribute some of their routine tasks to give them time to handle greater responsibility.

■ **Who can do the job best?** Depending on the task to be accomplished, you might need a candidate who possesses technical expertise, personal interest in the project, or leadership abilities.

■ **Who can do it most economically?** Try to recall which employees have come up with ways to boost efficiency and cut costs in the past.

■ **Who can save the most time?** Think about who tends to work fastest with a minimum of errors.

■ **Who would gain the most in growth from this assignment?** Focus on employees who could benefit from the learning experience.

■ **Can we redesign the task so that a less experienced person can handle it?** If so, who?

Once you've answered these questions, you should have narrowed things down to a core group of employees from which to make your choice. Now, revise your list of candidates, placing the most capable at the top. If you haven't already pinpointed the most appropriate employee for a particular job, you can simply choose a worker from the top of your newly revised list.

Assignments to Results

Now that you've decided what to delegate and whom to delegate to, it's time to assign tasks. Be sure that you present these opportunities in a positive fashion. Show employees that you have confidence in their ability, that you are willing to offer any help, and that you will forgive minor mistakes. You can accomplish all of this by following these steps:

◆ **Explain the assignment.** Describe the job to be done, and let the employee know why it is important—to the company, to the operation, and to the worker. Give the worker a written description as well—one that breaks the procedure down into logical steps and spells out the correct method of accomplishing it.

However, if you want the project to be done differently than it has been in the past, now is the time to say so. You might ask the assigned employee how he or she would do it. In this way, you'll encourage the worker to think independently from the start.

◆ **Create a climate of trust.** Let the employee know exactly why you've selected him or her for the job. You might say, "You're well organized, and that's what this job calls for," or "This assignment is similar to another job you did with terrific results."

This approach builds trust between you and the employee. It says that you think the individual has a lot to offer and deserves the chance to excel in a special assignment.

▶ **Read the person's reactions.** You may find that the employee isn't as enthusiastic about the assignment as you had hoped he or she would be. What should you do about it?

Ask questions. Find out what the worker's concerns and anxieties are. If there is some misunderstanding, try to clear it up. There may be good reasons why the first person on your list can't accomplish the assignment. For instance, the person's existing work load may make it impossible to take on an extra assignment and do it well. If this is the case, go to the next person on the list.

▶ **Set up checkpoints.** Once the job has been officially assigned, make certain that you don't lose sight of it. Set up a time frame for completion of small portions of the job so that you can keep tabs on the work and offer help if it's needed.

You can keep on top of the worker's progress by telling that person to report to you at specific times. You might say, "Check with me on Wednesday and let me know how things are going," or "I'll need a report on this by Friday." In this way you can have a definite follow-up without having to badger the employee.

▶ **Offer your support.** Let the employee know that you're available for help. Also, be tolerant of occasional mistakes. These are part of the learning process. Try not to interfere unless the error will be costly or will affect other operations.

▶ **Measure results.** Since you've set up proper controls, measuring results should be simple. Each time a worker checks in, assess his or her progress and performance. If there is any problem, this is the time to offer additional help. If things are going well, you can relax a bit.

And when the finished product is presented for your approval, you'll see that you have a reliable "delegate" who can either handle that particular task from now on or remain available for special projects in the future.

▶ **WHAT YOU CAN DO** → *You can delegate tasks to lighten your work load, challenge workers, and improve your department's productivity if you . . .*

1. Realize that all supervisors must delegate to give themselves time to accomplish more important tasks.

2. Ask yourself what portions of your work can be done by only you. Then delegate the rest.

3. Determine which employees are willing to handle extra assignments. Then draw up a list of the most capable workers, and assign tasks to people who top the list.

4. Explain each assignment in detail, and tell the worker why he or she was chosen to do the job. Take some time to clear up any misunderstandings.

5. Have the person check in periodically so that you can check progress and offer help when needed.

If you select the right people, offer training, and follow up, you can delegate tasks with a minimum of hassle and save your energy for more important responsibilities.

ACTION PLAN:

PROMOTION DECISIONS MADE EASY

Supervisors who provide opportunities for their employees to get ahead are the ones who attract and keep high-caliber individuals. There's no better tool for building morale, increasing productivity, and making the best use of manpower than an effective . . .

Promote-From-Within Policy

Promotion decisions are rarely easy ones. Naturally, you want to pick the best qualified individual, but that may be difficult to determine under certain circumstances. It takes both judgment and courage to make the right decision.

Judgment, because supervisors must be able to pick out the employees who have the ability and temperament for promotion; courage, because they must pass over the unqualified employees regardless of how nice they are or how long they've been on the job.

Good Old Charlie

Take the case of Charlie Miller, who had worked in the toolroom for 15 years. When Charlie's boss retired, the superintendent got together with two production supervisors to discuss a replacement.

"How about Charlie?" asked the superintendent. "He's been in the toolroom for 15 years and at the pay ceiling for five years now. I think it's time we did something for him."

"It's an idea," one of the supervisors said. "He's easy to get along with and everyone likes him. It would sure prove that we mean what we say about promoting from within if we give Charlie the job."

The other supervisor was outspoken in her objection to Charlie. "Sure, he's a nice fellow," the supervisor said. "But I don't think he has the administrative ability to handle the job. Running the toolroom today is a lot tougher than it was when Charlie started. How about putting that Sloan kid in charge?"

"How long has he been on the job?" the superintendent asked.

"A little over a year," the supervisor said. "But he's sharp. He's the one who set up the color codes to make sure gages are calibrated on schedule."

"I have heard good things about him," the superintendent said. "But he's young and has a lot of time left. I'd like to see Charlie get the chance. What have we got to lose?"

As it turned out, they lost plenty. Two months after Charlie had been promoted, his department was in such a mess that the staff had to go on overtime to straighten it out. Charlie was returned to his job as assistant, and Sloan took over. But Charlie was resentful and claimed the "brass" hadn't give him enough time to make good. Eventually, the superintendent had to let him go. Incidents like this prove the old maxim—you never do people a favor by promoting them into a job they can't handle.

Three Reasons Promotions Backfire

Most promotions that backfire can be traced to one of the following three reasons:

1 Promoting employees merely because they have been around for a long time. Often the old-timers are set in their ways and tend to block or oppose new methods for getting out the work, or else they find it difficult to cope with human relations problems.

2 Selecting the best craftspeople, or the most skilled persons in the department, to supervise the work solely on the basis of skill. Too frequently this approach results in the company's losing good craftspeople and gaining a poor supervisor. A requirement of knowledge or skill in the work to be supervised is significant but not to the point where leadership ability, or the lack of it, is ignored.

3 Choosing the most popular members of a group to be supervisors on the theory that their ability to get along well with people is a crucial factor. Popularity is no guarantee of supervisory success and usually disappears in the heat of management difficulties.

No Hurt Feelings

So far, we've examined scenarios that are apt to arise with a promotion-from-within policy—and ways to deal most effectively with those situations. But there will also be occasions when it is not possible to promote from within. One supervisor who was forced to go outside his department for a qualified assistant reported this experience.

"My assistant left for another job, and I had to find a worker to replace him in a hurry. Even my most experienced people didn't have the experience the job demanded. I had to ask Personnel to look for a replacement. They found one; I interviewed and hired him. When he came to work, he got the cold shoulder from my group.

"I got it, too, but not to the same extent. The staff held me responsible. But they knew I was still boss, and they had to cooperate with me. However, the new assistant was just that—new. They resented his presence, and his giving orders, and sulked about 'never being promoted even though the company is supposed to promote from within.'

"I called a meeting of my workers. I explained to them that my hiring of a new assistant did not reflect on their abilities to perform their own work, and that it did not mean we would always go outside to fill a job opening. I accepted some of the blame for not having trained any of them to be my assistant.

"But I also told them they couldn't expect to advance if they didn't show an interest in the functionings of the department as a whole. And I told them that the way in which they had been doing their work since the arrival of the new staff member certainly did not indicate that interest. I asked them to meet the newcomer halfway; it wasn't his fault that they resented his presence.

"After some mutterings, they agreed. It took another few days for my words to really sink in—but eventually they came around."

▶ **WHAT YOU CAN DO** → *You can make your promotion decisions easier on yourself—and your employees—if you . . .*

1. Promote on the basis of qualifications—not just because "they've been here so long."

2. Look for and develop leadership skills.

3. Have the courage to turn down the popular but unqualified.

4. Explain why when you find it necessary to go outside your department for qualified people.

While it's a good idea to maintain a policy of promotion from within whenever possible, the most important thing is to find the most qualified people for the job—in or out of the company.

ACTION PLAN:

_____
_____
_____
_____
_____
_____
_____
_____

SECOND-IN-COMMAND

You've got your desk all cleaned off, and it's finally time to take your annual vacation. When you return in two weeks, you'll want to find things still running smoothly in your department. However, if you haven't left someone in charge during your absence, you may return to something that falls just short of chaos. Then you'll wish you'd taken steps to . . .

Groom an Assistant

Vacations are only one of the reasons you should have a designated assistant. There's also the possibility that an illness or injury could keep you out of the workplace for a time. On the more pleasant side, you may receive a long-awaited promotion or transfer, and you won't want to leave your department in the lurch.

No matter what the reason for your absence is, you should have already designated an assistant to cover for you, or someone whom you'll want to recommend to upper management as your successor. If you just leave employees to fend for themselves when you're not around, they may not know what to do in an emergency—or they may not be able to get vital questions answered.

"Hiring" Your Assistant

A good way to select an assistant is to act as if you were hiring someone. Of course, the job candidates will be limited to the people you supervise, but you can still employ hiring techniques to judge which of your people is deserving of the post.

Begin by creating a job description—not for the assistant's position, but for your own. After all, the assistant will be taking on all your tasks and responsibilities when you're not around. Some of the things you'll want to list on the job description will be:

- **Paperwork.** Are there any confusing forms to be filled out or reports that must be made? If so, your assistant should be able to work his or her way through the muddle and complete the paperwork properly.

- **Job knowledge.** Your assistant should have a working knowledge of all the jobs in your department. Cross-training is a good way to ensure that employees are well-rounded, and it can help you evaluate who among your workers can learn quickly.

- **Company rules and policies.** If you're not around, you won't want the company rulebook left open to interpretation. Because you're ultimately responsible for what goes on in your department, you must make sure your assistant knows what the rules are and how to apply them correctly in your absence.

- **Open-Mindedness.** An employee who can thoroughly consider evidence, then analyze it and come to a conclusion, is a person you'll want in a position of authority when a problem needs solving. Personal prejudices and inflexibility are *not* the qualities you want your assistant to bring to the job.

- **Personality.** Employees who are congenial and get along well with others are good choices. For example, Bob may know the work inside out, but he doesn't get along well with his co-workers. It might be a better idea to go with Jill as your assistant if she's a little less skilled but more diplomatic. Tact and a balanced disposition are important qualities to look for in choosing an assistant.

This is by no means a complete list of the aspects of your job an assistant will have to have a foundation in; you can probably think of many more. You might list these qualities on a piece of paper. Once you've done that, you can figure out who fills the bill.

Simply go down a list of your employees and ask yourself which of them possess the necessary qualities to be your assistant. You can probably drop several from consideration right away, and can eventually whittle the list down to your final choice.

Now check with your boss to make sure you've made the right decision. Lay out your reasoning and criteria, and ask him or her to verify that the proper selection was made.

Spreading the Word

Once you've made your decision, spread the word as quickly as possible. To begin, of course, inform the employee you've chosen that you would like him or her to act as your assistant and to fill in for you if you must be absent from the workplace.

You may be surprised to hear that some workers will shy away from the job. They may not want to step into the limelight, or they may be afraid that their fellow employees will resent their new status. In any event, move down to the next name on your list if your first choice turns you down.

In the vast majority of cases, however, you won't have to worry about the chosen assistant refusing the post. Most employees will welcome the added responsibility because it's likely that additional rewards will follow from the increased workload. Other employees may be interested in a supervisory career, and a stint as your assistant can help them sharpen the skills they need to run a department of their own some day.

As likely as an employee is to appreciate your offer of becoming the assistant, it's just as likely that there will be other employees who resent your decision. These people may not see the need for you to have an assistant, or they may not be pleased with the selection you made.

The best way to deal with resentful employees is to clearly explain why you believe you need an assistant. Cite some of the possibilities: that things must run smoothly while you are on vacation or absent because of illness, for example.

As far as the selection itself is concerned, be open about the criteria you used in making your decision, and describe how you arrived at it in the end. Stress that everyone was considered, but that the candidate who was selected just seemed to possess most of the qualities needed for the position.

The Importance of Training

"Okay, Jill, you're going to be my assistant. I want you to do what I do, but do it only when I'm not here." That statement may characterize your understanding of the role your assistant will play. If that's the case, you won't be utilizing the full potential of your second-in-command.

In order to "do what you do," your assistant will first have to be thoroughly trained in most of the aspects of your job. And if your assistant exercises his or her skills only when you're not around, he or she is not likely to be proficient at running the department.

So immerse your assistant in the role: Keep the person filled in about upper management's latest memos and directives, discuss departmental problems as they arise, and seek his or her input about any changes you are considering.

Most important, provide training in the day-to-day activities every supervisor carries out. Show him or her where forms and important papers are kept, and outline the chain of command that should be followed if he or she must seek a solution to a problem further up the company ladder.

The crucial aspect of your training will be instruction in how to make decisions. Give your assistant hands-on experience by allowing him or her to make decisions under your guidance. You can provide the options available along with a little input, but place the responsibility for the final decision squarely on the shoulders of the assistant. In time, he or she will be making sound judgments, and will have developed confidence in his or her ability to do so.

After You've Gone...

Having an assistant can be a real boon when you must be away from work for a short period of time. The real payoff for your company comes, however, when you've prepared someone to take over for you permanently. Management won't have to spend valuable time finding someone to take your place.

In fact, having a potential successor already in place can hasten your climb up the company ladder. Look at it this way: Even if management desperately wanted to promote you to a higher position, they may hold back awhile if it seems you can't be replaced. Groom your own replacement, and you can start your climb that much sooner.

▶ **WHAT YOU CAN DO** ➡ *When selecting your second-in-command, be sure to ...*

1. Draw up a job description. Analyze your own position to determine what characteristics your assistant must possess.

2. Match your employees against your ideal of a second-in-command. Narrow your list down and then select the person who meets most of your criteria.

3. Take personality into account. A person can have all the skill in the world as a worker but may not get along with others. This would probably rule out him or her as your assistant.

ACTION PLAN:

_____
_____
_____
_____
_____
_____

4. Provide lots of training and hands-on experience. Explain how you make your decisions, and then allow your assistant to make some on his or her own.

If you follow this advice, you'll be able to take a vacation without worrying about what you'll find on your return. You'll also provide management with the replacement they'll need should you be promoted.

CONQUERING A CRISIS

No one likes to work under pressure, but sometimes there's no alternative. Your department may be asked to produce on the double for a seasonal rush or to jump into action to replace defective parts on a key order. Whatever the crisis, if you keep calm and quickly assess the problem, you can alleviate it. To do this, start by . . .

Acknowledging the Problem

"We'll never meet the deadline now!"

Supervisor Bob Lorenzo looked up from his paperwork to see Tom Hughes, an employee, standing beside his desk. "What's the problem, Tom?"

"The computers just went down," Hughes sighed. "By the time the vendor has the system up and running again, we're sure to lose two days of work. And we have to finish this project for a customer by next week. We'll *never* get it done in time!"

Lorenzo had to admit that the situation looked grim. The deadline was tight to begin with and now this! Lorenzo tried to calm down and think. Before long, he saw a way out of the dilemma.

"I'll talk to some of the other supervisors and see if they can help us," he told Hughes. "Maybe their people can chip away at our project during the lulls in their schedule."

"We could put in some overtime, too," Hughes suggested. "I wouldn't mind staying late, and I'm sure the others would be willing to pitch in."

Lorenzo decided to shoot for cooperation from his fellow supervisors first. The other approach—working overtime—would serve as a strong backup plan in case his first choice failed.

Managing Your Emotions

A computer failure is just one example of a crisis that can occur without warning. A supervisor can be faced with any number of problems on the job that require a quick decision and immediate action.

When faced with a crisis, people often bring on disaster by wasting valuable time on negative emotions. Supervisors are no exception. Under pressure, they can fall victim to three typical stages: panic, anger, and then a desire to blame others.

The problem is that these three stages take up time, and they don't do any good in solving the crisis. Just think what might have happened if Supervisor Lorenzo had panicked. He probably would have accepted defeat, missed the crucial deadline, and lost a valuable customer.

But instead, Lorenzo put his negative emotions on hold for a while. He realized that crises are part of the job. And in a crisis, a calm, rational approach is what's needed.

No matter how urgent matters may seem, you need to take a minute to regain your composure so that you can calmly assess the situation. Follow these guidelines before you act:

▶ **Keep your cool.** Don't escalate the situation into a disaster. Concentrate on taking care of the crisis. It might help to compare a crisis to being under fire. If you're under attack and the sentry didn't warn you, now is not the time to find out why. While you're being attacked—while you're

19

having the crisis—you have to keep a cool head and face the situation.

▶ **Practice stress management techniques.** Deep breathing is a great way to keep from panicking. All you have to do is breathe in slowly though your nose for a count of ten, and breathe out slowly through your mouth for a count of ten. Do this ten times. The less stress you feel, the more effective you'll be in handling the crisis.

▶ **Have a positive attitude.** If you keep telling yourself that there is a crisis and that you can't handle it, you won't be able to. That's why you should eliminate negative self-talk and tell yourself, instead, that you can solve the problem. You can't erase the crisis that occurred, but you can control it by controlling your attitude.

Manage the Crisis

Once you set your emotions aside, you'll be better prepared to handle a crisis. Now is the time to think things through.

Here's a series of steps you can follow to help you come up with a plan of action that will bring any crisis under control. These steps are:

1 Define the problem. In your mind, quickly outline the problem. Or, if you have enough time, consult fellow supervisors or your employees. It's good to go over the basic facts and get input from others so that you don't feel as if you're facing an impossible problem all alone.

2 Come up with three or four solutions. To develop ideas on how to solve the crisis, simply brainstorm. Think of every possible answer to your problem, and make sure you don't eliminate any suggestions at this point. For example, don't say "We tried that one already" or "That will never work." That's the surest way to inhibit people from offering innovative ideas—one of which might be the answer to your dilemma.

3 Quickly look at the pluses and minuses of each alternative. This is the time to go over each idea and look closely at its advantages and disadvantages. If you have many alternatives or some additional time to spare, it's helpful to keep track of this information on paper.

4 Arrange your alternative solutions. At this point, consider combining alternatives. Or if your alternatives seem overwhelming, think about dividing them into smaller and smaller parts. Look for the one that seems to be the most beneficial *and* the most expedient. Then rank your alternatives from the best to the least favored.

5 Implement your first solution now. Don't sit around waiting for that perfect opportunity that may never come. You've defined the problem, developed alternative solutions, checked the pros and cons, and thought things through. So act promptly.

When It's Over

You may bring a crisis under control, but that doesn't mean you're all finished. Once it's over, you should look at the results, learn from them, and congratulate yourself. Do this by:

● **Analyzing** the success and the failure of your final solution. Write down what went well and what you could have improved on. Then keep that piece of paper so that you can see it during the crisis.

● **Discussing** what you've learned. It's the best way to be sure you enjoy success the next time around.

● **Patting** yourself on the back. You can't expect perfection and you can't dwell on your failures. Instead, compliment yourself on a job well done—you deserve it.

Doing Your Best

Ultimately, there's not much that you or anyone else can do to prevent most crises from occurring in the workplace; they are an inevitable part of every job.

But that doesn't mean you should just throw up your hands and give in to the difficulties that assail you on the job. At these times, you are needed more than ever. As a supervisor, you must analyze the problem, find a solution, and put it into action as quickly as possible. If you don't take the reins, no one else will.

Because there are variables involved in every job, any supervisor can be faced with a crisis. There are some situations that you just can't anticipate. But remember, crises are not beyond your control if you resist the temptation to panic and take time to think things through.

> **WHAT YOU CAN DO** → *You can overcome even the most threatening crisis if you . . .*

1. Keep your emotions in check. You can't afford to waste precious time by panicking, getting angry, or blaming others.

2. Acknowledge the crisis and define the problem. Outline the problem and go over the basic facts.

3. Come up with three or four solutions from your colleagues and employees in a brainstorming session.

4. Choose your best solution and rank the others as backups, in case your first choice fails.

5. Put your solution into effect.

Supervisors who are prepared to solve problems and implement their decisions quickly should have no trouble doing their jobs—even during a crisis.

ACTION PLAN:

_____
_____
_____
_____
_____
_____
_____
_____
_____

WORK IN BALANCE

How smoothly does your department run? Are there frequent bottlenecks? Does the work flow follow a feast-or-famine pattern? Do petty bickering, jealousy, and lack of cooperation keep some employees from getting their work done? If this sounds ominously like your department, it's time to consider how well you are . . .

Balancing Work Loads

Good balance of work loads provides even distribution and flow of work among employees and between departments. The symptoms of imbalance are usually right on the surface—but a supervisor may be prone to attribute them to something else. For example, the following productivity slowdowns can be traced back to improperly balanced work loads in many cases:

- Inadequate worker performance
- Poor work procedures
- Congested work areas
- Persistent equipment breakdowns
- Frequent absenteeism and rising quit rates
- Shortages in supplies

If any of these danger signs are flashing in your department, you should turn a critical eye on the way you've been placing job demands on your employees.

Look Around

The only way you can really tell if work load imbalance is causing these and other problems is to pay close attention to what's going on around you. For instance, what did you see when you arrived at your workplace this morning? Was everything running smoothly in a very short time, or did you see signs like these:

■ **Uneven staffing.** Were some people still sipping

coffee and finishing up the sports pages while others were already going flat out? Were some people missing, and if so, why?

■ **Close quarters.** Were certain workstations hard to maneuver around because a lot of supplies were stacked nearby? Were idle employees getting in the way of those who were working at top speed?

■ **Supply shortages.** Were certain employees running out of forms, supplies, or other items—well before their co-workers did?

Situations like these frequently point to unbalanced work loads. But a supervisor can also discover work imbalance when an employee comes to him or her to complain.

"No More Mr. Nice Guy"

"I'm sick and tired of doing all the work around here," said Bob Howard as he stood in front of Supervisor Debbie Webster's desk with his hands on his hips. "Half the clowns in this department hide out in the rest rooms, and the other half talk about their bowling scores. I don't know how they can find the time to slack off, while I'm lucky if I can finish all my assignments in one day. Something's got to be done."

Debbie Webster didn't have much to say—mostly because she had a sinking feeling that she was the cause of the problem. Howard *was* an outstanding performer, and Webster had a tendency to load him up with more work than the others. Any time there was a rush job or an especially crucial task to be done, she was sure to turn to Howard.

Fortunately, something good came of Howard's complaint: Webster made a personal commitment to improve the way she made work assignments in her department. After careful observation, she decided to take some positive steps. Let's take a closer look at what she did—and what you can do—in order to balance work loads once again.

Check On Output

Webster found that certain employees produced far more than other workers—and discovered she had known that all along without feeling bothered by it. In other words, the supervisor had recognized the limitations of certain workers and was willing to live with them.

When you give up on workers who are a bit below average, you're telling them it's okay to do less than their best. At the same time, you will likely begin to put more responsibility on the shoulders of your more capable employees. Neither of these situations is acceptable if you wish to balance work loads among your people.

The answer may lie in productivity quotas. Set the same reasonable standard for each employee, and then make a point of spending time with those workers who fall short. Take any steps necessary to bring their output up to par. Also, be sure to give a word of thanks to those employees who exceed the quota. A bit of recognition can encourage them to continue working to the best of their abilities.

And Check On Input

Input, in this area, means the information you give and the signals you send when making job assignments. Perhaps you are vague about how a particular task is actually carried out. Perhaps you assign the same job to two different employees, which implies that you don't trust either of them to complete the assignment on his or her own. Or perhaps you spend a lot of time with particular employees and give the rest of your people virtually no input at all.

When Webster took stock of her method of giving input to employees, she found that she spent a disproportionate amount of time with two employees whom she had been friendly with before she was promoted to supervisor. These individuals didn't really need any extra coaching; Webster simply liked talking to them and occasionally used them as sounding boards for new ideas.

Of course, other workers resented the fact that these two employees took up most of the supervisor's time. And a work load imbalance was created because, while the good workers were getting their work out, Webster wasn't available to others who needed help getting their jobs done.

Like Webster, you should evaluate your own behavior to see if you are giving employees enough input about their jobs—and enough of the kind of input that will help them stay up with their peers in terms of output. After all, if an employee takes a long time to finish a job, he or she will not be able to move on to another assignment right away, and that assignment may have to be given to another, faster employee who finishes tasks quickly.

Handling Reverse Seniority

Webster also discovered that because trainees in her department were routinely assigned the disagreeable tasks, the company's training program was getting a poor reputation. Because of this, turnover of trainees was unusually large. The complaint heard most frequently? "Trainees get all the dirty jobs." Webster had to admit that this was true. "I always put newcomers on those jobs. Why should I use my top hands to do the dirty jobs? Besides, if a trainee does an unpleasant task without complaining, I know I've got a good worker." That may sound like good reasoning. But she had made two basic mistakes:

★ She never explained the reasoning to the trainees. That's why they frequently got the idea that they'd spend the rest of their careers doing all the dirty work.

★ She never asked seasoned workers to pitch in, thereby overlooking an important morale factor. The trainees would be a lot more receptive to unpleasant tasks if they saw that the experienced staffers were willing to give them a hand.

Actually, a lot of supervisors use this system successfully, but they take the trouble to explain. Newcomers are told they will be asked to do certain jobs that are below the skill level of experienced workers. But they are assured that the number of unpleasant jobs will decrease.

Encourage Ideas

When Webster made it known that she was seeking to eliminate work load imbalance, she was surprised at the reaction of many of her employees. Though they had been reticent about offering improvement ideas in the past, they were more than willing to suggest ways to spread work around equally.

Work load imbalance touches every worker personally, so it shouldn't be a shock that they will want to help you clear it up. Try then to create an environment that fosters freedom of ideas and suggestions for improving the work flow. Because your people are so close to the situation, their solutions are likely to be very usable—and successful.

Once you've implemented their ideas and your own, you'll probably note a drop-off in complaints and an increase in departmental productivity. Instead of having a few shoulder the burden for many, you'll have a work group that pulls together. Every employee will contribute his or her fair share to the overall output of the department, and the renewed spirit of teamwork will be a pleasant experience for all.

▶ **WHAT YOU CAN DO** → *You can achieve balanced work loads—and, in turn, higher productivity—in your department if you make it a point to . . .*

1. Look for the symptoms of imbalance. Problems that seem attributable to something else can frequently be traced to imbalanced work loads.

2. Rely on all workers equally. Don't load up one employee because he or she has proven to be a top performer.

3. Give low achievers the input they need to bring their work speed up to par.

4. When using reverse seniority, explain the reasoning behind it and give assurance that it won't last forever.

5. Solicit employee ideas for balancing work loads. Their hands-on knowledge can provide valuable insights.

In short, keep your eyes open and act on imbalances promptly. Your employees will appreciate it, and your efforts will be rewarded with improved morale and productivity.

ACTION PLAN:

A NEED TO PLAN

Planning is essential to the continued success of your company. Yet, some supervisors don't plan. How do they keep their departments functioning? Usually, they rely on luck, hard work, or a good staff. They might get along by riding luck's coattails for a while, but one day lack of planning will catch up with them. And when it does, the negligent supervisor will wish that he or she had taken the time to . . .

Plan Ahead

What exactly is planning? This seems like a simple enough question, but planning does have a variety of definitions. In general, planning means setting goals and priorities that must be met within a specified time period. It also means:

- Directing your people to perform a specific task.
- Explaining how they can achieve the goal.
- Giving them information so that they can complete it within a specified time.

The definition that sums it up best, however, is this: Planning means taking action that is not trial and error, but purposeful and well thought out.

Plot a Course of Action

How do you respond if something happens to upset the balance in your department? Many supervisors react by improvising their way out of the problem. This works fine for some people, but not everyone is good at spur-of-the-moment decision-making, and these decisions don't always point out the best direction to take.

This is where contingency planning comes in. If you exercise foresight as well as hindsight, you'll have an advantage over those who don't. Surprises won't throw you off balance or force you into making a panicked decision.

You can learn to be contingency conscious by following these four steps:

1 Be Aware. Before you even begin to consider what to do when a problem crops up, you should know:

- the full extent of your workers' capabilities
- why procedures are set up
- the goals of your company
- why changes are taking place

You need to know what is happening now and what *may* happen in the future to affect the present situation.

2 Think Ahead. When you dream up contingency plans, let your mind wander—even among the most outlandish possibilities. Build scenarios in your mind of what *could* happen, given the facts you now know.

3 Expect the Worst. If you're going to stay on your toes, it's better to expect the worst to happen than to hope for the best. For instance, what if a power outage interrupted some of your most important work? How would you make up for lost time? Coming up with an answer to a question like this now will save you from panic if the situation does arise.

4 Take Nothing for Granted. Don't get too comfortable with the "foolproof" plans you've worked out for emergencies. Update them often because too many supervisors have been caught off guard when they thought they had everything down pat.

Getting Organized

Many supervisors find this the hardest part of planning. Yet we all need to control our own time before we can start planning bigger things.

To get organized, first trim procrastination by being aware of different "time-wasters" such as interruptions, unwanted visitors, telephone calls, and distractions. To sharpen your awareness, you might prepare a daily priority. Simply go over your goals for the day and arrange them in priority order. By knowing what must be completed first, you have a greater chance for accomplishing your daily tasks.

Once you conquer this part of planning, move on to the next step—getting your department organized. A good way to start is to draw up an organization chart that illustrates how your department meshes with others (see Figure 1-1). It also gives you a clearer picture of how the work flows from one department to the next, thereby identifying any weak links that could affect the planning chain.

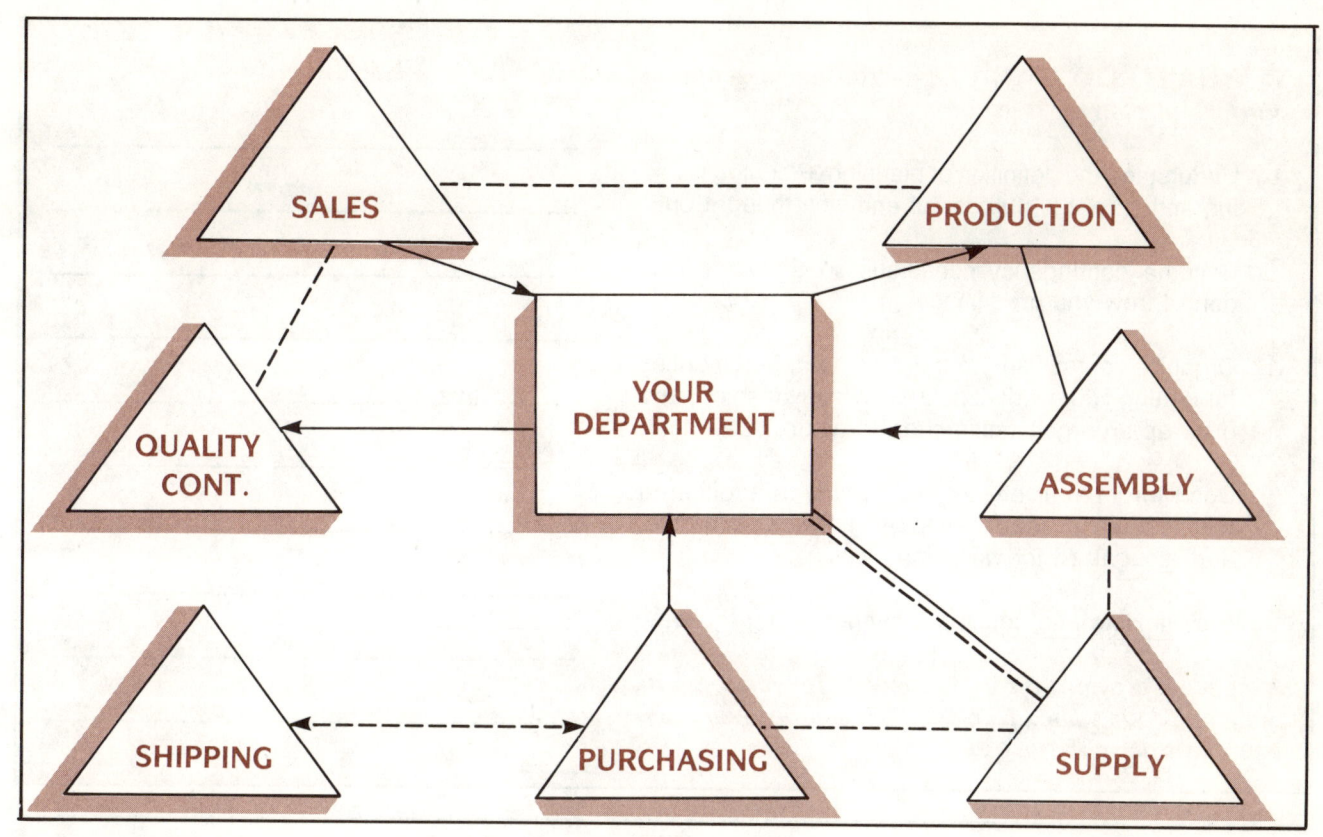

(FIGURE 1-1)

This is also the time to consider the strengths and weaknesses of your employees. Deciding who will perform what jobs is an integral part of your plans. If you assign jobs that fit people's abilities, you'll have a better chance for success.

People Make Plans Work

Every plan has its limitations. Perhaps the biggest one is that things can't happen without the full cooperation of other people in your company. Yet this is one basic fact that many supervisors forget—usually because they get carried away with the act of planning.

Plans may be solid, on target, and so forth, but they don't necessarily recognize the needs of the people who will carry them out. When their needs are ignored, you weaken your planning strategy.

What are these needs? You already know most of them, although you may not think of them as *needs* per se.

First, your people depend on you for *leadership* so that they will have the drive and confidence to carry out your plans. Workers also need to be *motivated*. Of course, having a plan is itself a powerful motivator. But this doesn't mean you can sidestep your responsibilities to get people revved up to perform. The best way to do this is to fully explain the plan's objective and its methods.

Communication has got to be tight, too. Therefore, give employees *feedback*. The give-and-take of information will keep everyone alert. *Recognition* is also essential. Be sure to show employees that their hard work is appreciated.

Finally, workers need to participate. After all, everyone wants to feel that he or she is part of the action. This is especially important during the beginning stages of your plan. Ask for their help then, and you'll have no trouble enlisting their cooperation right on through to the plan's completion.

Plans Must Be Flexible

One last point to consider when you plan is this: Planning is a flexible, ongoing process. Many things can impinge on a job. When changes occur, adjust to meet them. Your plans should not be chiseled in stone.

Then, too, the expectations and needs of your people constantly change. Since they are the fuel that takes your plans from the drawing board to real life, recognize their changing needs in your planning process. By staying flexible, you'll be able to make accurate and effective plans—ones that will get the job done well and on time.

> **WHAT YOU CAN DO** → *You can become a purposeful planner if you...*

1. Understand the definition of planning. Planning is taking action that is purposeful and well thought out.

2. Become contingency conscious so that surprises don't throw you off balance.

3. Organize yourself and your department. Set priorities for getting your work done in an orderly fashion, and draw up an organization chart for your department.

4. Don't forget your employees' needs. In addition to your leadership, they need to be motivated, informed, and recognized for work done well.

5. Stay flexible and adjust to changes along the way.

Because it provides a solid framework for your department and your company, planning is a supervisory skill you can't do without.

ACTION PLAN:

_____
_____
_____
_____
_____
_____
_____
_____
_____

SCHEDULING FOR EFFICIENCY

Juggling everything that goes into the smooth operation of a department is no easy trick. Some days, you may feel that even three hands wouldn't be enough. But planning for the smooth flow of work is one of your most important tasks. It is also one of the hardest. Fortunately, there are methods to help supervisors ...

Schedule Successfully

Scheduling is simply a matter of placing one step after another. No problem, right?

Wrong. Unless you review your schedule from time to time, your people may be carrying out steps that are no longer necessary or that can be streamlined to save time.

Another problem is that your regular daily schedule may not be adaptable enough if your department has to handle a special project or implement a major new program. You may be required to come up with an entirely new system for getting the work done.

Scheduling may not be as simple as it first appears, but it doesn't have to present a huge problem, either. Let's take a look at two different methods that can make it easier for you to determine the best schedule for you: flowcharts, which you can use to improve daily scheduling, and PERT diagrams, which can help you handle special projects in a timely manner.

Go With the Flow

A flowchart is simply an outline of the way work progresses. Each stage that must be passed through to get the work out falls into one of these five categories:

■ **Operation.** An operation is something that advances the work that must be done. It can be as simple as initialing a piece of paperwork or as involved as entering a program into a computer.

■ **Transportation.** This means moving from one point to another an item or a person necessary for the performance of a task.

■ **Inspection.** When the work at hand must be examined for flaws or errors, it is in this stage.

■ **Delay.** When the work process stops temporarily, for any reason, it falls into this category.

■ **Storage.** This is when an item is removed from the process and stored to prevent unauthorized use, or because it is simply not needed at the time.

Remember, only one of these stages—Operation—is truly productive. So the key to a smooth work flow is limiting the amount of time your workers have to spend on the other four categories. To do that, you have to take a careful look at all the steps they're carrying out now to see where you can make improvements. That's where a flowchart can come in handy.

To make a flowchart for your department, record each step your workers perform to do their jobs. Place the steps in the order in which they take place, and note which one of the above categories they fall into.

Once you've categorized each function, take a look at your flowchart to see where you can simplify processes or eliminate those that don't really contribute to the completion of the task. Having the steps down on paper, in black and white, will help you find ways to use your workers' time better.

A Special Plan for Special Programs

While flowcharts will help you plan your day-to-day work schedule, special projects and programs may require more exacting attention to work flow. For example, when a new procedure is being implemented, you'll want to know where you stand in the implementation process at all the key points. And that means you have to know what the key points are. One method for determining them is known as PERT.

PERT is an acronym for Program Evaluation and Review Technique. It was originally designed for use by the U.S. Navy, but is now used effectively in many businesses and industries. The biggest benefit of PERT is that it helps you find the *critical path*, the series of steps that takes the longest and that cannot be delayed.

A PERT diagram is begun in much the same way as a flowchart: Every step that must be carried out to complete a task is written down. In the example of implementing a new procedure, your list of steps might look something like this:

1 Formulate a rough plan for implementing the new procedure.

2 Get management approval for pursuing your idea.

3 Refine your plan.

4 Consult other departments to get ideas about making the implementation go smoothly.

5 Draw up a final implementation program, and make it known to all who will be working on it.

6 Order materials necessary for carrying out the new procedure.

7 Determine new work assignments for your employees, based on the change in work methods.

8 Train employees so that they thoroughly understand how the procedure works.

PERT Preparation

After you've completed the list of major steps, you can prepare the PERT diagram. Begin by writing the major objective of your program on the right-hand side of a piece of paper. In our example, the objective is to implement a new procedure; to do that, employees must be trained in how to carry out that procedure. The last step consists of training employees.

So, to the immediate left of "Implement New Procedure," write "Train Employees." You now continue to work backwards, listing the steps that must take place before the next can be carried out. In some cases, tasks can be taken care of simultaneously—such as consulting other departments as you refine your rough idea. List those steps one above the other.

For a better idea of the diagram-making process, take a look at Figure 1-2. It illustrates a PERT network based on the list of steps necessary for implementing a new procedure.

When you have each step in order, you can move

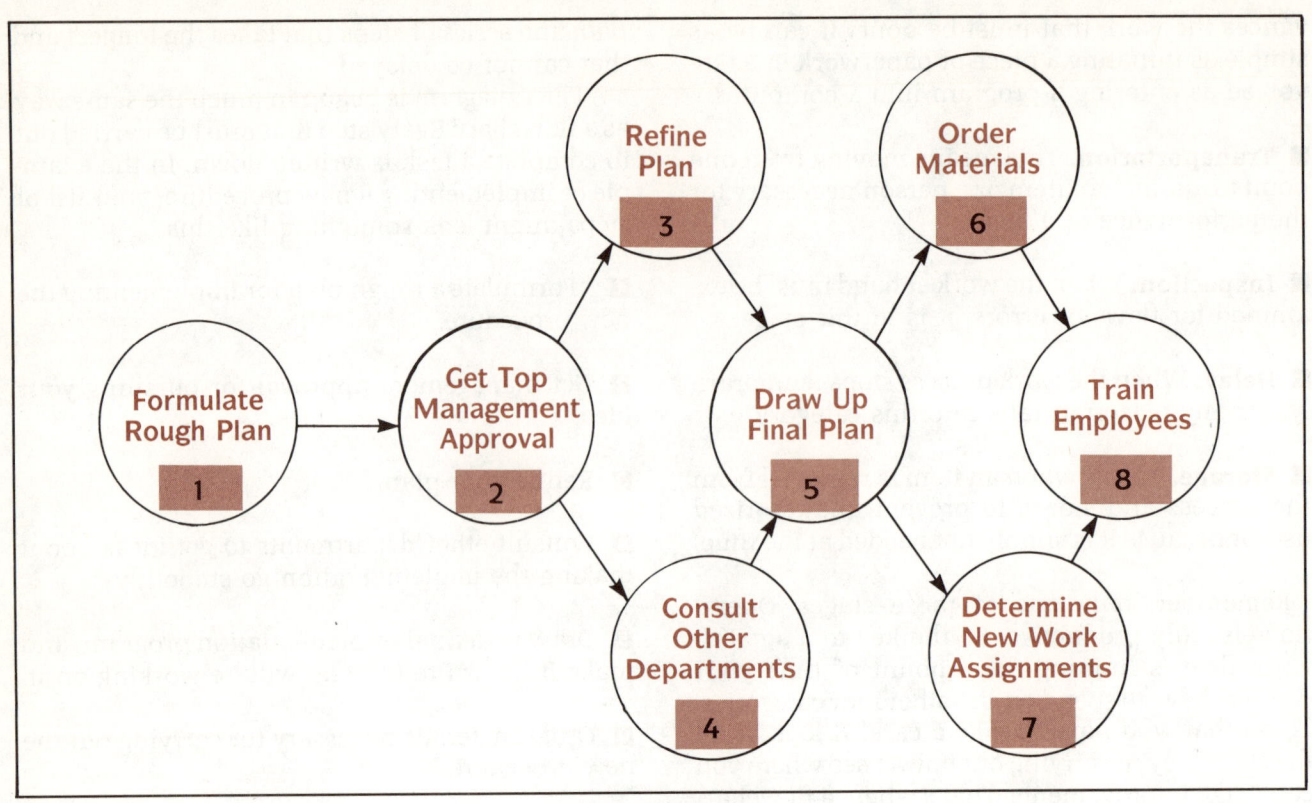

(FIGURE 1-2)

on to the most important part of the PERT process—finding your critical path.

On the Trail of the Critical Path

Take another look at the PERT diagram in Figure 1-2. As you can see, there are two occasions when steps can be carried out simultaneously. Keep in mind that even though these steps can take place at the same time, it's not likely that they'll take the same *amount* of time.

For example, it may take you just one week to decide what work assignments your employees will have under the new procedure. But you may have to wait four weeks for ordered material to arrive. It may take you two weeks to refine your plan, but only one week to consult with other departments. Since path 1-2-3-5-6-8 will take longer to complete than the other, it is your critical path.

Why is it important to know your critical path? Every flow of work—except for the critical path—will have some slack time in it that you can use to deal with crises. If management came to you with a rush job while you were at Steps 6 and 7, you could put off determining the new work assignments for a bit and turn your attention to the new task. Why? Because the materials you ordered won't be arriving for four weeks, and you can't move on until both Step 6 and Step 7 have been completed.

The PERT diagram example we've looked at is a simplified version. Your diagram may have three or more steps happening simultaneously. The important thing to remember is that no matter how many components your diagram has, there is only one critical path. And that's the path you have to pay the most attention to. There can be no delays along it, or the completion date of your project will have to be pushed back. If an emergency comes up, you can look for slack time along the other paths in order to handle it.

You Can Make the Difference

Remember, you play a major role in making flowcharts and PERT diagrams work for you. You have to collect information, develop steps, put them in order, and analyze the results.

Flowcharts and PERT diagrams aren't magical solutions to your work-planning problems. But they can help you pinpoint areas where you have some leeway should a problem occur, and they can help you see where your scheduling can be improved. Best of all, judicious use of PERT and flowcharts can help you prevent scheduling snafus in the first place.

> **WHAT YOU CAN DO** → *Your schedules will be more flexible and efficient if you . . .*

1. Analyze the jobs your employees perform, and list each task they must carry out step by step.

2. Use your task list to draw up a flowchart, which can help you determine the process you can streamline or eliminate.

3. Create a PERT diagram to locate the critical path your work flow takes.

4. Concentrate on meeting all your intermediate deadlines along the critical path.

Using flowcharts and PERT diagrams will help you solve your problems—rather than simply react to them—and make more efficient use of time.

ACTION PLAN:

_____
_____
_____
_____
_____
_____
_____
_____
_____

BUILD MOTIVATION THROUGH GOAL-SETTING

It seems so simple on the surface: You set goals, and your employees meet them. Nothing could be easier, right? Not so fast. There's a lot more involved in goal-setting than meets the eye, and the effective supervisor would do well to . . .

Dig Beneath the Surface

Every department must set goals in order to be productive. Your work group is certainly no exception. The goals you and your people must meet include completing tasks, meeting deadlines, working up to standard, and working within an established budget.

In these terms, a goal is the object of an employee's efforts on the job. If workers don't know where to focus their energies, you're not likely to get the positive results you're looking for. One of your most important supervisory tasks is helping workers focus those energies by setting goals with them and then helping them meet their objectives.

Goals are important for other reasons, too. Goal-setting provides you with a valuable opportunity to communicate positively with your people. It enables you to find out how employees perceive their jobs and what you can do to help them become more effective workers.

Measuring Tasks

Goal-setting begins with work measurement. After all, you can't ask employees to meet goals for improvement if you're not sure what areas need it.

For supervisors whose people perform tangible work (such as assembling a product or resolving customer complaints), it's relatively easy to measure work. In any given period (a day, a week, a month), you simply total up the number of items produced by the employee, or the number of customers dealt with, and so on.

By averaging the output of all your employees,

29

you can determine what a reasonable work rate is. Also, by comparing each individual's output against the departmental average, you'll be able to tell which of your subordinates are most in need of improvement.

It's a bit more difficult to measure the output of employees whose work is intangible. One good way to quantify the results of intangible work is to set a standard by using a "best results" measure. Here's an example of how that works:

Patricia is an employee in your department. She has been in the department longer than anyone else, so one of her most important responsibilities is helping you train new hires. If you want to know how successful she is at that intangible task, your standard should not necessarily be how many people she trained over a certain period of time. She may have trained dozens of people who later left the job because her instruction was poor.

For that reason, a better measure would be how many of her trainees stayed in the department and for how long, or perhaps what the new hires' production rates were after they'd been working for a period of time. These numbers (her "best results") then become the standard by which you judge her work. No matter what method of work measurement you finally develop, you may be surprised to learn that work measurement alone—without the setting of goals—often leads to improvement in employee motivation and productivity. Once your people know that their output is being observed and measured against a standard, they frequently try harder to meet or exceed that standard.

More important, however, work measurement lays the foundation for the goal-setting process. It provides you and your employees with the basis against which success in meeting goals will later be judged.

Goal-Setting Is Now in Session

Once you've assessed where your people stand now, you can hold a goal-setting session with each of your employees. You may already have a good idea about what type of goals you want to set for your employees. But remember that the most effective goal-setting sessions are joint efforts. Employees must play an active role in determining their goals, or they won't be as motivated to achieve them.

Like any other type of meeting, a successful goal-setting session requires careful preparation. In fact, it's a good idea to set goals for the meeting itself. For example, decide that you will not end the session until you and the employee have agreed on goals in all the areas brought up for discussion.

The six steps outlined below should guide you in conducting a goal-setting session. Remember that while these guidelines are geared to you, the supervisor, the employee must be given a chance to contribute ideas and suggestions and to ask questions during the session.

1 Present general objectives. Tell the employee in general terms what you want him or her to accomplish. This means outlining the improvements you're looking for, whether it's reducing costs, increasing production, improving customer service, or cutting down on absenteeism and tardiness.

2 Explain how improvements—or the lack of same—will be measured. Ideally, measurements will be made the same way you determined which standards were appropriate (using techniques such as those presented in the preceding section). In any case, let the employee know how you plan to measure how well goals are being met.

3 Decide on specific goals—together. This is where employee participation is most important. For one thing, each worker knows his or her own limits, and can tell you if a proposed goal is unreasonable when those limits are taken into consideration. Employees are also more likely to be familiar with the day-to-day pressure of the job, another factor to consider when you're setting goals.

In the final analysis, this step is best carried out by combining your judgment and experience with any knowledge the employee has that is relevant to the goals you'd like to set.

One last point here: Remember to take external pressures into account when deciding on employee goals. If other departments must be relied on to meet objectives, you can't set goals so high that they would be impossible to meet if the other department didn't pull its weight.

4 Set a deadline for goal achievement. Of course, a goal must have a deadline in order to have value. If the worker is given an unlimited amount of time to meet objectives, you're hardly in a position to determine if progress is being made.

The goal deadline depends on the nature of the goal involved. For example, a reasonable productivity-improvement goal can probably be reached in a month or so. But it's usually trickier to set objectives involving things like cost savings or better response to customer complaints. The results of an employee's efforts in areas like these may not be apparent for several months or more, and this should be taken into account when you're establishing the goal deadline.

5 Set goal priorities. For all but the most routine, repetitive jobs, multiple goals will probably be desirable. For instance, you may want a worker to simultaneously improve the quality of his or her work while cutting down on absenteeism. Or a worker already trying to meet productivity goals will be asked to help meet the goals created by a special project.

Whether an employee has two goals to work toward or ten, it's important that he or she know which are the most important ones. Otherwise, efforts may become confused, and the worker may neglect crucial goals in order to work on some that are not as critical.

6 Discuss the need to work with others. This is a point we touched on, in part, in Step 3. Employees should recognize that they may have to rely on other people to accomplish their goals. An employee in a shipping department, for example, cannot be expected to ship items more efficiently if deliveries from the warehouse lag behind schedule.

Just as important, employees should be reminded that others are counting on them to help those others meet their goals. Stress that by being cooperative when necessary, workers can win that same cooperation for themselves when they need it.

Finally, Feedback

Your last step is to provide employees with feedback on the progress that has or hasn't been made. Feedback should be given while the worker is trying to achieve the goals and when a task is completed.

Employees should be made aware that their work is being measured, and should know how close their production levels come to the predetermined standard. But a casual mention every now and again that the worker is "doing just fine" isn't enough. Effective feedback must be:

- **Frequent.** The more frequently employees hear about their production, the better.
- **Immediate.** There should be as little delay as possible between performance and feedback.
- **Specific.** Feedback should focus on the productivity of individuals or small groups, not on the department as a whole.
- **Clear.** Employees should understand unit values and any other factors that are used in measuring work.
- **Positive.** Feedback should stress performance goals and standards, rather than emphasizing the negative consequences of failing to achieve those aims.

▶ **WHAT YOU CAN DO** → *To increase motivation through goal-setting . . .*

1. Measure the work that is being done now. You can't plan for the future if you don't know where employees stand in the present.

2. Hold a goal-setting session. Call each employee in and work out a list of objectives that all parties can agree on. Then set priorities so that the worker knows which goals are most important.

3. Stress cooperation. Explain to employees that in order to get the aid of others in meeting goals, they must provide assistance to colleagues when it is requested.

4. Provide ample feedback. It's the best way to keep employees on the road to achieving their goals.

Remember, goal-setting is something you do with employees—not to them. You'll get the best results by asking employees for their input every step of the way.

ACTION PLAN:

CHAPTER TWO
YOUR ROLE IN COST CONTROL

COMMIT YOURSELF TO COST CONTROL

As a supervisor, you're probably well aware of the need to keep departmental costs under control. You realize that when labor, materials, and time are all being used in the most economical manner possible, the company—and all those who work for it—will profit. However, finding surefire ways to rein in expenses can seem like an impossibility, especially when your department is already operating on a shoestring. It can be done, however, if you're willing to make the effort.

Take the Initiative

If your company is like most, its top management is forever on the lookout for effective ways to control expenditures and increase profits. But when the word comes down that some cost savings would be greatly appreciated, do you wonder where on earth you'll be able to find anything to cut back on? *My department's budget is already at rock bottom,* you may think. *Short of cutting back on materials, supplies, or labor, there's not much I can do.*

According to Philip Beckwith, Plant Manager for Binney and Smith (Easton, PA), there are *always* better ways to make use of the money being spent in your department. Strictly speaking, departmental budgets vary little from month to month. But there are often golden opportunities to reduce expenses right under your nose.

Beckwith believes that no production department ever reaches maximum efficiency. Each one has a number of "problem areas" that, when treated correctly, will improve both productivity and boost cost-effectiveness.

Peter Grefe, Manager of Manufacturing at Shur-Lok (Irvine, CA) heartily agrees. "Improving cost-effectiveness and productivity is possible in any industrial operation—but well-organized, systematic procedures are needed," he adds.

"There are different ways to attack problem areas," says Beckwith. "The more effort you are willing to put into it, the better your chances of success." He suggests concocting your cost control prescription by combining the following four ingredients:

- Worker input
- Responsibility
- Improved production efficiency
- Stock control

Now that you know the ingredients, let's learn the directions for combining them into a winning formula for maximum economy.

Step #1: Start With Worker Input

"You can acquire a number of different perspectives on cost control by using one important ingredient—worker input," says Beckwith. Once employees become involved in just about any effort, viable solutions are usually quick to follow. Why?

Because workers are experts in their field, and thus their advice is valuable. And the solutions that they select and implement are usually successful; workers tend to be extremely motivated to back their own ideas and do what is necessary to see that they work—and work well.

"But first, you must show workers that their input for cost control suggestions is wanted and needed," Beckwith emphasizes. "Help them to understand that your company's interests and their interests are the same. Let them know that, in effect, they *are* the company.

"Don't miss any opportunity to remind your people that the company's success and their personal goals are tied together. Both can be achieved by reducing costs, increasing productivity, and improving profits."

Peter Grefe is another advocate of involving employees in cost reduction efforts. "When you encourage workers to look for a better way, they will usually come up with one," he notes.

Step #2: Stir in Responsibility

One tried-and-true way to cut costs is to reduce rejects. And of course, the best way to reduce rejects is to make sure that all work is done correctly the first time.

Beckwith says this can be achieved by giving workers more control of the inspection process. "The idea is to give every worker on the production line maximum responsibility for quality control.

"You'll probably find, as I did, that once your people begin to take responsibility for the product, they also begin to feel a sense of 'ownership' for it. Our people felt this so strongly that they became more critical than even I had imagined. They often surpassed established standards—and that was good. It changed them from clock-punchers to members of the corporate team!"

Step #3: Add a Dash of Production Efficiency

There is a lot of lost production time spent on setup. And wasted time means company money down the drain. That's why it's a good idea to have your people address this area when trying to find ways to reduce costs. They may arrive at a number of viable ideas that will improve efficiency.

"Our workers certainly did," Beckwith asserts. "It used to take a great deal of time to change production lines. We had what we call an 8- or 9-hour surge capability—the ability to change from one operation to another.

"Employees took over. They began looking for ways to do things better and quicker. And they found them. Now, we can change lines in 2 or 3 hours!"

Grefe cites similar successes. "In my department, we start by listing all of the operations performed in the production of a particular product. Next, we carefully assign a cost to each operation, concentrating our efforts on the highest costs first. Finally, we ask ourselves these five questions:

- What can we do to reduce the cost?
- Which operations can we combine, automate, or eliminate?
- Are we limited by cutting feeds and speeds?
- Can we use different, more cost-effective materials?
- How much can we spend to make an improvement?

"Almost invariably, the answers to these questions add up to increased productivity and efficiency," he says.

How? "In one instance, we were looking for a way to reduce the cost of changing dies," relates Grefe. "My employees addressed each of the five questions, and determined that they could combine one of their products with the die-changing process.

"One toolroom machinist was given permission to modify one of our expandable-diameter fasteners so it could be used to hold a die to a die shoe. Before we began using this fastener, it took operators 15 to 20 minutes to take the die out of the press, and another 30 minutes to accurately fit in the new die.

"However, our new method, now called the 'Slide-Di System,' enables the operator to change the dies in just two minutes!" he points out enthusiastically.

Step #4: Include a Pinch of Stock Control

Many departments keep an excess of stock on hand in anticipation of rush orders. And there is a certain logic to this. It would be unprofitable for a company to have people and machines idle because they're waiting for material.

But too much inventory invites misuse and

waste. And there's always a certain amount of inventory that's lost due to spoilage.

You can reduce these losses by maintaining the optimum level of inventory for your operation. Set aside enough stock for normal use, with a slight margin for when there is a heavy work load.

"But be prepared," Beckwith warns. "Once inventories are trimmed, you may discover problems in the production and distribution chain." For example, if a run gets misplaced or you fall behind schedule, you won't have a reserve to draw from to meet demands. But don't panic—it's healthy to expose the flaws in your system," he advises. "Just see these incidents as opportunities to tighten things up. As each weakness is exposed, make sure you create a policy to prevent a reoccurrence."

> **WHAT YOU CAN DO** → *To help your operation meet maximum cost-effectiveness:*

1. Realize that cost control is as important a supervisory duty as overseeing employees.

2. Explain the importance of cost control to your employees, illustrating how their goals for financial security go hand in hand with company profit objectives.

3. Ask your people for input on ways costs might be reduced in your department. Assure them that their feedback is both wanted and needed.

4. Make your workers responsible for conducting their own quality inspections. This will help keep waste due to rejects in check.

5. Look for ways in which production operations might be streamlined and made more efficient. Ask the five questions to help pinpoint problem areas.

6. Maintain an optimum stock inventory at all times; manage supplies economically.

When the above ingredients are combined, you're going to find that you've created a cost control formula that works—and that's good news for your department and your company.

ACTION PLAN:

HOW TO ENCOURAGE COST-SAVING SUGGESTIONS

Companies always need fresh input to reduce costs and improve the efficiency and quality of the work produced. And sometimes the best source of profitable ideas for making things work better is the workforce itself. As a supervisor, you're in an ideal position to flush those ideas out by encouraging cost-saving suggestions in your department. Start by asking . . .

What Is My Attitude?

What is your attitude toward suggestions from your employees? Do you welcome worker ideas with open arms, or turn your back to them? If you take the latter stance, you're cheating yourself—and your company—out of a wealth of productivity-improving ideas.

Many supervisors fear that if an employee comes up with an excellent suggestion, top management will wonder why the supervisors themselves didn't think of it first, and regard them as ineffectual. In reality, however, effective supervisors believe that "all our heads are better than one." They realize that if they encourage their people to think about ways to do their jobs more efficiently, they're running a productive, cost-conscious operation—and management will appreciate their efforts.

So don't be afraid to tap your workers for improvement ideas. Just because you don't come up with *every* idea for bettering operations don't feel that you're slacking off in your role as a supervisor. Quite the contrary—you're simply acknowledging that those who are closest to the job—your people—may have some of the best answers to its problems.

Stimulating Suggestions

Too often, employees feel that their ideas count for very little. They are hesitant to offer recommendations for operational improvements. They may believe that it's their job to keep their mouths shut and do the work—they fear that you will respond angrily to their criticisms of the job.

That's why your first step in stimulating workers to submit suggestions is to call them together and let them know that you welcome their ideas. Then, get the ball rolling by providing them some grist for the "idea mill."

For example, you might throw out some of the following questions to get them thinking about improvements:

- Are there any unnecessary steps involved in the overall production process or in individual work procedures?

- Do quality problems occur more often in particular steps?

- Would the use of different materials increase productivity or decrease costs?

- Would a change in the layout of workstations improve efficiency?

- Is there a flaw in the flow of communication within the department that could cause mistakes or misunderstandings?

You should also promote participation by doing the following:

▶ **Discuss job problems with employees.** If you get stuck on a project, don't be afraid to ask your people for help. Many times, your workers can give you a fresh viewpoint, and the sense of participation they'll gain will help develop a climate in which they feel free to submit suggestions.

▶ **Explain your company's suggestion system.** If your company has a formal award-giving suggestion plan, make sure you understand it thoroughly, and then explain it to your workers. If you have questions, consult your boss or members of the personnel department.

Don't make the mistake of assuming that just because you have a veteran work group, they're all familiar with the procedure for submitting suggestions. They may not realize how the awards system works.

In order to be certain that everyone—old-timers and newcomers alike—fully understands the advantages of participating in the suggestion program, give in-depth explanations of the system at least twice a year. Any time someone in your group wins an award, use the occasion to dramatize the fact that suggestions do pay off.

▶ **Invite informal ideas.** If your company doesn't have a formal, award-giving suggestion program, you can still benefit from the good ideas lurking within your group. Encourage your people to think about their individual jobs and to look for ways to improve their own output.

Even without cash awards, you can assure them that any idea that proves helpful will win some sort of recognition. For instance, you can make a note on an employee's next merit rating, or you may be able to grant special privileges for a certain time.

▶ **Get them to address their own complaints.** When workers complain to you about their day-to-day problems, that's probably the best time for promoting constructive thinking on their part.

For instance, if Bob comes to you complaining that this is the third time his machine has jammed, ask him what he thinks is at the root of the foul-

35

up. This could start him thinking about a solution, and just may lead to a change that could solve a lot of people's problems, not just his.

▶ **Use regular encouragement.** If you have regularly scheduled departmental meetings, try to give a pep talk on the value of making suggestions at least every other meeting.

Refine, Define, and Present

Once a suggestion has been made, it's time to help the person refine the idea. You should check it over for practicality and set the idea down in writing, using a step-by-step procedure. Your company may have special forms for presenting a suggestion.

If possible, give estimates of the time, labor, and cost savings that are likely to be gained by the improvement. A suggestion that proves its own cost saving is one that's more likely to be embraced by top management. And the more often workers see their ideas implemented, the more motivated they will feel to come up with more cost-controlling recommendations.

Then process ideas *promptly*. Nothing can discourage an employee more from making suggestions than to see that their supervisor has done nothing about them. Don't let ideas get lost in paperwork or red tape, or sit on your desk for weeks or months.

And in submitting an employee's idea, be sure to give the person full credit for it. Again, doing so will not make you look inefficient for not thinking of it yourself; rather, it will make you look like a fair and effective supervisor who's making the best use of the talent in the department.

Also, you should *always* keep the suggester informed about the status of his or her idea. If it appears that it will take a long time for management to respond to the suggestion, tell the worker that the idea is under consideration, and you will let him or her know as soon as you have some managerial feedback on it.

Treat Rejections With Kid Gloves

Of course, not every suggestion issued by your people will be feasible, practical, and acceptable to upper management. And those ideas will inevitably be rejected. With some ideas, you'll be able to tell immediately that they are unworkable; with others, you'll have to wait for upper management to hand down a denial. But either way, you'll be the one to inform the worker of the rejection. And the way in which you handle the situation can mean the difference between the success and failure of your suggestion program.

When ideas are not accepted, workers are likely to become discouraged—and their dejection could lead them to feel that "it's no use bringing up any more ideas—they'll just be rejected and I'll feel like a fool." So handle all suggestion rejections tactfully and gingerly.

Start by thanking the worker for caring enough to submit an idea for improvement. Tell him or her that the idea shows a lot of ingenuity, and that you are impressed by his or her creativity.

Then explain why the idea is not feasible. Share management's criticisms of the idea with the worker—being careful not to hurt the person's feelings—so that he or she will understand that there are, in fact, concrete reasons why the idea will not be implemented.

If management has led you to believe that they would reconsider the idea, with improvements, at a later date, encourage the worker to "go back to the drawing board" and try to make the idea more practical. Offer your suggestions for improvements, and assure the worker that you'll be glad to help him or her work out the "bugs."

Your Involvement Is the Key

Your supervisory commitment to the suggestion program is crucial to its success. It ensures that a good idea is not lost when an employee is unable to fit an improvement idea into the bigger picture of operations that only you can see. And it allows you to help the suggester identify weaknesses or errors inherent in the suggestion, so that it can be made workable before it is passed on to higher management.

But what's in it for *you*? Plenty. Working with your people to generate suggestions:

• **Encourages communication** within your department. It keeps you in touch with your workers' problems and complaints.

• **Builds goodwill** when workers find that you are willing to discuss, help them define, and set in writing their ideas.

• **Builds a teamwork attitude** and reinforces workers' commitment to quality standards.

• **Gets employees thinking** about their jobs in

different, more productive ways. They become committed to doing the best job possible, rather than just getting by, because they've been encouraged to openly present their improvement ideas.

- **Draws workers into your company's overall concerns** by emphasizing their contributions to developing more efficient, cost-effective operations.

> **▶ WHAT YOU CAN DO →** *To make the suggestion program a resounding success in your department:*
>
> 1. Realize that you'll improve productivity—and be a more effective supervisor—if you invite ideas from everyone.
>
> 2. Provide workers with some ideas of the kinds of problems for which they may derive workable solutions. Don't be afraid to discuss *your own* problems with them to obtain the value of their feedback.
>
> 3. Make certain that everyone understands your company's suggestion program.
>
> 4. Offer to help employees develop their ideas and submit suggestions.
>
> 5. Process ideas *quickly*, and keep workers apprised of their suggestions' status.
>
> 6. Handle rejections with care. Always thank workers for their ideas, and explain why they aren't feasible. Then encourage workers to improve their ideas, and assist them in any way possible.
>
> *Supervisors who willingly tap their department's well of good ideas—namely, their employees—will enjoy the most success at creating a cost-effective operation.*
>
> **ACTION PLAN:**
> _____
> _____
> _____
> _____
> _____
> _____
> _____
> _____
> _____
> _____
> _____
> _____
> _____
> _____
> _____

MAKE HABITUAL TARDINESS A THING OF THE PAST

"Hey, what's a few minutes here and there? I still get all my work done, don't I?" That's a standard response when a supervisor questions an employee about chronic lateness. And upon reflection, the supervisor may even accept this defense. But chronic tardiness cheats the company as well as employees who make it a point to arrive on time. That's why you should do everything in your power to get habitual latecomers back on track—before their tardiness takes its toll.

37

Excuses, Excuses: Valid or Flimsy?

Basically, there are only two causes for lateness: Either a worker has run into an emergency that prevented a timely arrival, or the person didn't make enough of an effort to get to work on time.

When the cause of lateness is an unforeseeable emergency, there's not much you can do. But when a worker just didn't bother to make an effort, you'll have to find a way to motivate him or her so future tardinesses don't occur.

Plant the Seed

Of course, the best way to deal with lateness is to head it off before it becomes a real problem. The key is to explain the importance of promptness to new hires (and to existing employees who may not have already received the message). Here's a little story you could relate to make them realize the problems caused by tardiness:

"Suppose a worker making six dollars an hour fell into the habit of arriving ten minutes late every day. This employee is being paid a dollar a day which wasn't earned. Over the course of a normal work year, he or she will receive more than 200 dollars without putting in the commensurate time on the job.

"And the problem has a nasty tendency to snowball. When other employees see their co-worker getting away with being late every day, they'll probably begin to slack off, too. If ten employees ended up being as late as that first worker, it would cost the company over 2,000 dollars annually—a sobering figure indeed!

"In the long run, lateness might end up costing employees even more. How? The only way a department can get into the kind of state we just talked about is if the supervisor lets workers get away with it. I can tell you for a fact that I don't intend to let it happen here."

Having said all that, outline your company's policy regarding lateness and the penalties for unexcused tardiness. Ask employees to call you as soon as they know they might be late. That will allow you to plan your department's work better, if there is a crucial project to complete.

Nip It In the Bud

While it's an excellent place to start, talking with employees about lateness isn't a magic formula for completely eradicating the problem. You may still have to face the issue of tardy workers from time to time.

If you do see someone reporting for work late, the first step is to find out why. Should the person not have a reasonable excuse, or should the person have what seems to be a reasonable excuse—but on a steady basis—you'll have to find an effective way to motivate the worker to be here on time. This may include:

★ **A friendly—but firm—reminder.** Sometimes simply sitting down with workers and reminding them of their obligations to the company and co-workers will do the trick. Point out that their fellow employees may begin to resent the fact that they regularly come in late, since co-workers have to pick up the slack for the missing people.

★ **Disciplinary action.** "Repeat offenders" must be treated in accordance with your firm's method of discipline. Proceed with oral and written warnings, and if they don't have a measurable effect, consider suspending the employee for a period of time. The more serious the penalty, the more likely you are to see the worker start showing up on time.

★ **The threat of dismissal.** This would naturally be a last resort. It's not really that difficult to get to work on time, and an employee who reaches this point simply hasn't been trying very hard. However, this final option—"Get here on time or don't bother to come in at all"—could be the impetus they need to turn themselves around once and for all.

The Importance of Recordkeeping

The necessity of documenting instances of tardiness can't be overestimated. After all, you can't very well carry on a discussion about the problem with an employee if you have no tangible evidence of the extent of the problem. That's why, when a worker is chronically late, you need to write down the dates the person was late, and how much time was actually lost.

This documentation gives you a point of reference to discuss the problem. You can put your finger on specific instances rather than generalize about what seems to be the problem. If the worker says "Come on, I haven't been late all that much," you can get out your records to show him or her the error of that statement.

You can also use the records to figure out exactly how much the company has lost to a particular worker's lateness. Just multiply the time missed by the employee's rate of pay and tell him or her the result. Make it clear that "stealing" company time in this manner is really no different from walking off with company-owned tools or materials.

Your recordkeeping will assist you in another vital way: It can serve as necessary evidence in case you are driven to dismiss a habitually late employee. In presenting such concrete facts, you help ensure that a firing decision will hold up in a court of law.

The Exceptions to the Rule

There's a big difference between employees who are habitually late and those who are tardy only on rare occasions. Because there is a difference, you should take a different approach to each situation.

In fact, you should take a different approach to every episode of tardiness. This doesn't mean you should discipline offenders differently for the same offense; rather, you should consider each case on its own merits before imposing discipline.

For instance, let's say that one of your employees, Bob, hasn't been late to work in three years. Last Monday, however, he arrived 30 minutes late and was quite vague about his reasons for it.

And let's say you have another employee, Diane, who is ten minutes late a couple of times a week. She always seems to have an excuse that just barely falls within reason. Some are pretty farfetched, but it's possible that things happened as she explained.

How you handle each of these cases can make all the difference between having motivated employees and having a workforce whose morale is a shambles.

Okay, Bob didn't have a good excuse. But his past record should count for something. If you come down hard on him for his lateness, you're sure to upset him, and his resentment is likely to affect his productivity.

It's usually enough to mention to a conscientious worker like Bob that you did take notice of his tardiness. Chances are that he will return to his excellent pattern of promptness immediately, and that what you witnessed was a momentary aberration.

However, if Bob were to continue being late, you would have to make him subject to the same discipline process as everybody else. Sit down with him and ask if there is a problem you can help with. Let him know that you are pleased with his past record, and would like to see a return to it.

You may even want to appeal to Bob's sense of responsibility by saying that you are counting on him to set a good example for co-workers. This, in a way, constitutes an oral warning. If improvement is not made, follow through with the rest of your discipline plan (firmer verbal admonitions, written warnings, suspension, etc.).

Now let's address the other tardy worker, Diane—the one who always seems to have an excuse just good enough to get her off the hook. Employees like this are often simply playing games. They're taking advantage of your power to accept or reject excuses for lateness.

Remember, while there may be reasonable excuses for lateness from time to time, there is almost never a reasonable excuse for *habitual* lateness. Reasons like "My car wouldn't start again" or "My kid missed the bus and I had to drive him to school again" simply don't wash when repeated day after day. After all, if a worker has car trouble, he or she should repair the car or arrange for a ride to work. And if a child misses the bus several times, the parent should simply start waking him or her up earlier to prevent further problems.

In cases like Diane's, you will finally reach the point where the excuses no longer matter. The lateness itself must become the issue. When an employee provides a variety of excuses or repeats the same one all the time, sit the person down and tell him or her to get on the ball.

Come right out and say it: The excuses may be legitimate, but tardiness is occurring far too often. Insist that the person make the necessary changes to correct the problem, or you will continue to progress through the steps of the discipline process, leading ultimately to termination if necessary.

You're the Best Role Model

If you expect your people to take you seriously regarding promptness, you must take pains to be on time for work yourself. Your words will carry no weight if you don't back them up with your actions.

So always try to be the first one to arrive in your department at the start of the shift. When your employees see that you make a special effort to be on time, they'll probably try to do the same. And then you'll get the most you can from them every working day.

▶ **WHAT YOU CAN DO** → *To ensure that your employees get to work on time:*

1. Explain the importance of promptness their first day on the job. Let them know you take the subject seriously, and outline the penalties for failing to comply.

2. Discipline workers who make a practice of showing up late for work. Adhere to your company's policy regarding lateness, and apply it consistently and fairly.

3. Talk with workers who are late only on very rare occasions. Let them know you've noted the tardiness, and tell them you would like them to return to their past record of promptness.

4. Always be on time *yourself*. As the supervisor, you're expected to set the standards your employees must meet.

Keep in mind that there will always be occasions when tardiness is unavoidable. But don't hesitate to take a tough approach when chronic lateness becomes a problem among your employees.

ACTION PLAN:
_____
_____
_____
_____
_____
_____
_____
_____
_____
_____
_____
_____

TAKE A FIRM APPROACH TO END CHRONIC ABSENTEEISM

Most employees take their jobs seriously and make every effort to be where they are needed each day. They know that you—and the company—are counting on them, and they want to fulfill your expectations. But some workers are absent on a chronic basis, disrupting production schedules and, in the process, squandering company money. So you, the supervisor, must concentrate your attentions on reducing absenteeism and its ill effects.

Don't Ignore the Abusers

The majority of employees in your department are probably pretty conscientious regarding absenteeism. They fail to show up for work only when they are truly ill or bound by family emergencies. And even then, they apologize for inconveniencing you and the rest of the department, and return to work as soon as the fever has broken or the crisis has passed.

And yet, every supervisor has one or two employees who seem to miss *too many* days of work for a variety of reasons. A worker may call in sick with a cold one week, with the flu the next, with car trouble the following week, and with personal problems the week after that.

"It's a hassle—but I can't argue with the fact that they are solid producers when they're here," you may say. Perhaps they are. But, consider these

40

factors:

▶ **First,** an attendance record like this could decimate your department's productivity—and make you look ineffectual in the eyes of your superiors.

▶ **Second,** invalid absences cost the company money. Unproductive workers are being paid for an undeserved "day off."

▶ **Third,** unnecessary absences are unfair to your more dependable employees. When one worker is absent for illegitimate reasons, that person's work load may have to be dumped on your best employees to ensure that it's completed on schedule. Just imagine how this might affect the morale and productivity of your most valued employees!

For all these reasons, it's vital for you to pinpoint those workers who display a pattern of invalid absences—and do something about them.

Getting Down to Business

How can you tell if absenteeism is taking its toll in your department? Following these steps can help you get to the root of the problem and weed it out:

Record and monitor absences. Before you can target chronic abusers, you have to spot patterns of behavior. Careful recordkeeping can help you to do this. You might use daily time cards to collect the necessary information, then draw up monthly charts. These charts could then be used to detect absence patterns.

For instance, you might see that a certain employee is out every Friday or Monday, indicating that he or she is merely trying to extend the weekends. Or you might see that another worker is always absent before and after a paid holiday.

Recordkeeping has one other benefit: It will help you to judge all employees fairly and prevent accusations that you are playing favorites.

Approach the abusers. Once you have proof of a particular absence pattern, it's time to confront the guilty party. Your meeting, however, should not be to accuse and punish. You'll want to use this meeting as an opportunity for constructive discipline. Keep in mind that your ultimate goal is to get the employee back on the job and productive again.

You can do this in a nonthreatening manner by restating the company's attendance policy and by mentioning that you have noticed the worker's absence pattern.

At this point, most people will react in one of two ways. They may agree to improve their record, or they may deny the allegation. In the latter case, you should proceed by presenting them with your documented evidence.

Illustrate the high cost of absence. Show employees the costs of their absences in dollars and cents. Your object is to motivate people to want to be on the job by showing them how important their positions really are to overall company productivity. Use these convincers:

• It costs money to put extra people on the payroll to fill in for absentees. And it means there are more employees to share the wage pot.

• Overtime pay for people trying to do two jobs adds up fast.

• Machinery standing idle costs money. Show chronic absentees exactly how much it costs to have a lathe doing nothing for a whole day.

• Substitute workers produce more costly scrap and reduce quality.

• Disrupted schedules hurt the most important people of all—the company's customers. And everybody's job depends on satisfied customers.

Refer the employee to professional counseling. Often, chronic absenteeism is a symptom of more serious underlying problems, such as illness, alcohol and drug abuse or personal difficulties, either marital or financial. If you strongly suspect this is the case, or if the employee openly confirms your suspicions, do not attempt to diagnose or treat the problem—leave this up to a qualified professional.

If your company does not have an in-house physician or counseling service, refer the chronic absentee to Personnel. There, the worker may receive pertinent information about local assistance agencies.

Resort to discipline if necessary. If an employee absolutely refuses to amend his or her absent ways, you will have to turn to your company's policy of progressive discipline (which may consist of issuing written warnings, and finally, suspension or dismissal). By sticking to the policy and by enforcing it consistently for all workers, you will emphasize the importance of showing up for work every day.

Use a Prevention Policy

While it's vital for you to track down habitual absentees, get them to professional counseling, or discipline them if necessary, it's equally important to *prevent* absenteeism in the first place. Here are a few ways you can avoid absence in the future:

- **Emphasize the importance of attendance from the start.** As early as the hiring interview, tell employees that they are expected to be present for work every day, barring genuine illnesses and emergencies. Explain why their presence is important for production operations to proceed efficiently.

- **Avoid asking too much or too little.** When workers feel overburdened with job duties or feel that they are being asked to work at a superhuman speed, they may become exhausted or dread going to work. That's why you should regularly assess the demands you're placing on your people. Are you asking more of them than is reasonable?

Or, is the opposite occurring? Are you asking too *little* of your workers, allowing them to get by with a minimum of effort? If so, your employees may be getting bored and restless, causing them to "play hookey" rather than reporting to work.

- **Promote teamwork and group effort.** Employees who feel committed to their co-workers are less likely to let them down by being absent without due cause.

- **Catch first offenses.** Never ignore new employees' first absences—bad habits often develop early in workers' careers. Approach an absent worker the next morning when he or she returns and question the absence—without being accusatory—to determine if it was indeed valid. If the worker does not have a legitimate reason, stress the importance of coming to work and explain the liabilities generated by unnecessary absences.

- **Tie attendance to raises and promotions.** If possible, make attendance a factor in decisions concerning raises and promotions. Let workers know that you'll be taking a close look at their attendance records when it comes to these areas.

▶ **WHAT YOU CAN DO** → *To minimize absenteeism in your department:*

1. Commit yourself to pinpointing the chronic absentees. Spot these abusers through a recordkeeping system of daily time cards and monthly charts.

2. Confront an absentee about the problem. Use your documented evidence to back up your point. Illustrate the high costs of absenteeism.

3. Refer the worker to the proper professional assistance, if necessary.

4. Mete out discipline if the person refuses to toe the line.

5. Stress the importance of consistent attendance to all new hires.

6. Try to create a productive, pleasant work environment, so employees won't *want* to stay away.

When your employees exhibit good attendance, productivity will rise and your operation will become more cost-effective. With those results to be had, it pays handsomely to take the proper steps to reduce absenteeism.

ACTION PLAN:

_____
_____
_____
_____
_____
_____
_____
_____
_____
_____
_____
_____

HOW TO TURN THE TABLES ON TURNOVER

When a good employee suddenly quits, many supervisors naturally assume that the person found a better-paying job somewhere else. While money is an important consideration in a large number of turnover cases, it's by no means the root of all instances. Frequently, employees leave their jobs simply because they are fed up with the way the department is run, and decide that it's time to move on.

A Case in Point

When a well-trained, efficient worker leaves your department, what do you most often have to do? You must replace the person with an inexperienced new hire. And you know what that means—taking time out for a comprehensive training period and waiting for the new person to work up to speed, while losing a seasoned employee's contributions to overall productivity.

The bottom line is that turnover cuts deeply into company profits. The costs of training and lost productivity can be high. So turnover is one cost control issue that you should never overlook.

How can you reduce turnover and minimize its unprofitable side effects? First, you must strive to avoid scenarios like the following:

Mike Jekyll, production supervisor at an auto parts plant, was engrossed in studying the orders that papered his desktop when he was approached by Maria Rivera, one of his best employees. "May I have a word with you?" the worker queried.

"Sure, sure—just a second. Got to find an important form," muttered Jekyll, as he continued to riffle through his paperwork. Minutes later, he glanced up and almost seemed surprised to see Rivera still sitting patiently, waiting to speak to him.

"Oh—you're still here, eh? Well, you're going to have to make it snappy, whatever it is. I've got work to do," he said brusquely.

Rivera sighed. "Some things never change, do they?" she asked wryly.

"What are you talking about?" Jekyll demanded.

"You're always too busy to give us the time of day. Well, I guess that won't concern me any more—here's my resignation," she said, handing her boss a slip of paper. Jekyll snatched it, open-mouthed, and gave it a quick once-over.

"You're leaving us?" he asked incredulously. "What's the problem? I had no idea—"

"Maybe that's part of the problem," noted Rivera as she stood up and walked away.

Surprise, Surprise!

The fact that an employee wants to quit should rarely come as a surprise to you. If it happens all too frequently in your group, then you ought to seriously consider how effectively you are supervising your department.

Granted, there will always be isolated cases where an employee's two-week notice comes out of the blue. Perhaps Steve decides to join the military and announces that he's off to boot camp. Perhaps Laura receives a job offer from another company that's just too attractive to turn down. Or maybe Hope wins a million dollars in the lottery and decides to retire early.

These would be unusual occurrences, and no one's going to suggest that you were lax if any of them actually takes place. But when an employee quits because of displeasure with working conditions—and you are flabbergasted—there's a strong possibility that you haven't been paying attention and watching for the danger signs.

What are these signs? One clear indication that an employee is dissatisfied with his or her job is increasing tardiness or absenteeism. When a staff member starts to show up for work less frequently—and the absence cannot clearly be tied to illness or other legitimate cause—you can bet the person simply wants to stay away.

Every time an employee doesn't show up for work because he or she isn't happy on the job, you can think of it as a "mini-quit." And unless you take decisive steps to discover what is upsetting the person and then work to eliminate the cause, chances are those mini-quits will keep adding up until the employee quits once and for all.

Find Out Why

When you ask employees who are about to become *ex*-employees why they're leaving, you'll find they're usually evasive. Most workers prefer to avoid being brutally frank because they figure it doesn't really matter any more and they can't see any sense in stirring up ill feelings.

If workers say they're leaving for more money, dig a little deeper. Frequently this is given as a reason because it makes a handy excuse. Many times the real reason can be found in these five areas:

- **Poor communication.** Employees want to know exactly what is expected of them, they want to know about any rules or regulations that affect them, and they want to feel their supervisor will listen to them and answer their questions. But many supervisors insist on keeping important information about their department to themselves. They don't believe that their staff members have a need—or the right—to know details of impending changes or other happenings at the plant. But when employees are made to feel left out, they may begin to feel a lack of allegiance to the company.

- **Lack of opportunity for advancement.** Employees who feel they've reached a dead end are prime candidates to change jobs. This applies to both new and veteran employees. When an ambitious employee keeps running up against a brick wall when he or she wants to advance in the company, demoralization is sure to set in.

- **No chance to develop their talents.** When employees haven't received the training they need to do a first-rate job, or aren't allowed to tackle more complex jobs once they've attained a certain level of proficiency, they will begin to feel frustrated and stagnant.

- **Unpleasant or unproductive working conditions.** Frequent conflicts with co-workers, machinery that always seems to break down, feelings of being under constant pressure, uncomfortable workstations—any of these factors alone could drive an excellent employee to seek an atmosphere more conducive to high productivity.

Commit Yourself to Keeping Them Content

So how can you keep good workers from exiting your employ? Harold Carlson, a supervisor of highly skilled tool and die makers in a western machine-tool plant, has some helpful suggestions. Although local recruiting by defense-oriented plants is intense, turnover in Carlson's department has been gratifyingly low. This is how he explains his knack for hanging on to those highly prized experts:

★ **Provide well-earned recognition.** "Many supervisors I've seen figure that if workers are doing a satisfactory job, and show no signs of wanting to quit, they should be left alone," says Carlson. "But I think that the worst insult you can pay skilled employees is to ignore them.

"I don't mean that you should hang over their shoulders, but periodically talking about the job and their accomplishments will let them know you're interested in them personally. And it's a good idea to give workers a pat on the back once in a while. People know when they've done a superior job and like to be recognized. Used sparingly and sincerely, praise can do a lot to keep workers happy."

★ **Offer constructive criticism.** "I used to be afraid to criticize my workers because they're all experts and I feared that they might get mad and quit," Carlson explains. "But when I just had to a couple of times, I found out that they actually respected me for keeping close tabs on them. I never use ridicule or abuse when I criticize, and everybody seems to like the idea that in our department, standards are high. When employees take pride in their work, they're not going to be reading the want ads."

★ **Maintain smooth and efficient operations.** "Another thing that my department appreciates is orderly work procedures," says Carlson. "My staff knows exactly what they're doing and why they're doing it at all times. There's very little confusion or uncertainty, and that makes for a happy crew."

★ **Provide variety.** If workers are performing repetitive work all day, vary their jobs as much as possible. Move them to different positions on the line, and give them an opportunity to work with different people, so they can have a a little break from the monotony.

★ **Keep communication channels wide open.** "In our company, we've found that one of the biggest factors in turnover is lack of harmony and understanding between workers and their supervisor. That's why I listen whenever a worker has a gripe. More often than not, we can hash it out right then and there. Once workers realize that their supervisor will listen to them, gripes get aired before they build up into a burst of temper that could end with 'I quit.'"

★ **Make workers feel important.** "It means a lot to workers to know why their jobs are important, where they stand with management, and what the company's goals are. It's the supervisor's responsibility to help provide this information," notes Carlson.

"I wouldn't say that wages have no bearing on turnover. But a lot of defense plants pay a bit more an hour than we do. People aren't working here because they make a lot more money. Other things, like recognition on the job, a chance to learn and advance, fair treatment and a feeling of belonging to a good outfit are why our people stay with us."

Sometimes, despite your best efforts, an employee will quit anyway. You may see this as a failure of your attempts to fight turnover—and in some cases, you may be right. But even the loss of a good employee can produce positive results.

It tells you that, in general, you need to devote more attention to keeping workers satisfied. And it may reveal areas you need to improve right away.

So you should always conduct a thorough exit interview with employees who inform you they are leaving. Don't use the session to try to win back the worker—such efforts are almost always futile; a case of "too little, too late." Instead, try to find out exactly why the person was dissatisfied enough to leave. Then resolve that you'll never lose another valuable employee for that reason.

▶ WHAT YOU CAN DO → *To help prevent your workers from seeking greener pastures:*

1. Keep an eye out for the danger signs. Increased absenteeism without good cause is a frequent indicator that an employee is close to quitting.

2. Take an active interest in your employees and in the jobs that they are doing. Provide both praise and criticism to show that you appreciate good work and set high standards.

3. Strive for an open atmosphere. Share information that employees are likely to be interested in. Listen when workers have gripes, and take action to solve their problems.

4. Provide adequate training and opportunities for advancement, both in the department and in the company.

5. Find out the real reasons why a worker wants to leave. You may be able to correct the situation. If you can't persuade the person to stay, at least you can use the insight you've gained from the situation to help prevent turnover in the future.

The time you'll spend carrying out these steps will be negligible compared to the time you'll save in not having to train new hires to fill exiting employees' shoes.

ACTION PLAN:
_____
_____
_____
_____
_____
_____
_____
_____
_____
_____
_____
_____
_____

HOW TO AVOID UNNECESSARY OVERTIME

Avoidable overtime is a high-powered budget buster that can get completely out of hand unless you take steps to keep it in check. The most efficient use of humanpower and machinery is the first requirement. A thorough analysis of overtime that is not caused by mechanical failure, rush orders, or seasonal demands will give you a head start in trimming unnecessary costs.

The High Costs of Overtime

Overtime is costly for two fundamental reasons: The most obvious one is the higher pay rate for overtime hours. Then, there's the fact that people seldom, if ever, work as efficiently during overtime hours as they do during the regular workday.

Except for the short-term emergency when it is less costly to use available equipment a few hours a week on an overtime basis than to invest in new equipment or training new help, overtime is seldom justifiable.

It's a Cooperative Effort

Under normal working conditions, when everyone, including Production Control, Maintenance, Personnel, and the production supervisor, have their jobs under control and cooperate fully, production quotas should be realistic enough to avoid expensive overtime. As a supervisor, it's your responsibility to:

▶ Know your production requirements and the output capabilities of your group. When you anticipate the need for more help, give Management and Personnel enough notice so they can have time to do a thorough screening job.

▶ Allow yourself enough time in your own schedule for training your workers so they can keep up with production schedules. Train them to meet both quantity and quality standards.

▶ Make sure that you stick to preventive maintenance schedules on all equipment. When a major repair job is required, cooperate with Maintenance to help get the work done as soon as possible.

▶ Provide the kind of leadership and encouragement that discourages tardiness and absenteeism.

▶ Investigate the possibility of using workers from a temporary help service to fill in during a short-term emergency.

Analyze the Overtime

If a situation develops in your department in which the only way a project is going to be completed on time is putting your people on overtime—or if they've been on it for some time now—make a careful examination of this extra expense to see if it is really justified. Gather the facts and prepare a written analysis. Here are the things to examine:

● On a separate sheet, list each worker on overtime and the number of overtime hours worked in the past week.

● List the reasons for overtime and the tangible results, e.g., the number of parts turned out or assemblies completed in overtime hours.

● Consider the alternatives to working overtime. Use the analysis sheet to examine all possible ways of getting the required output without overtime. Ask for and consider the ideas of your workers as well as your own ideas.

Next, list the pros and cons of each solution. Here are some questions to guide you when considering alternatives:

    a. Could the work be done at a later date?
    b. Could someone else do the work during regular hours?
    c. Could overtime be avoided—without raising costs—if more people were put on the job?
    d. Could the work be done some other place—in or out of the department—at less cost?
    e. Could the job be done using another type of machinery to avoid overtime?

● Check the immediate and long-range costs of likely alternatives. Keep your suggestions simple so large cash investments for additional equipment, people, or space will not be required.

● Examine work loads and, where feasible, change some jobs around to eliminate the need for some workers to put in overtime.

● Try to make up your group's production schedules well in advance. And while laying out the schedules, don't forget to take factors such as normal absenteeism, holidays, seasonal peaks, vacations, availability of parts and materials, machine repairs and maintenance, and weather problems, if you live in an area prone to extremes in climate.

Keep Tabs on Timing

Making optimum use of time during the workday can greatly aid you in avoiding overtime. Here are a few ways in which you can improve the use of time in your department:

■ When making daily work assignments, check to be sure that all rush orders get an early priority. This will help you to avoid an end-of-the-day scramble that leads to those insidious and costly "few minutes" of overtime work to get the job out.

■ Set up your own schedule to enable you to check every workstation to be sure that all employees are functioning at full capacity during regular hours. If you can't possibly do this, delegate someone in each section to keep an eye on production and have that person report to you when new assignments are needed or material is in short supply. If you do assign someone to this duty, make sure you tell the rest of the crew. Otherwise, confusion and resentment could ensue.

■ Tour your department once or twice a day to determine if operations are running smoothly. Check to see if people are running out of work or materials. Ask if workers are having trouble, and help them solve the problem on the spot to prevent a slowdown that might result in the need for overtime.

Watch Out for Deliberate Slowdowns

One of the most serious situations that you might run into is a deliberate slowdown to create overtime. Alert yourself to practices such as spending too much time away from the job in rest areas, in idle chatter, and general fooling around.

If you strongly suspect that some workers are intentionally slacking off, put a stop to it immediately, resorting to progressive discipline (verbal and written warnings, suspension, etc.) if necessary.

Another type of slowdown that is more difficult to spot but that also produces avoidable overtime is a conscious effort to increase the time between finishing one job and beginning the next one. Closer supervision, strict adherence to time schedules, and realistic production schedules will help solve this sort of problem.

The most difficult slowdown to catch and correct is the unconscious type. Some workers adapt a leisurely pace because it fits their concept of what constitutes a fair day's work. They usually protest that it's just not humanly possible to turn out more on "this old clunker of a machine," or they manage to come up with a host of other excuses not to do a full day's work.

Dealing with this slowdown requires two steps from you. First, review your standards to be sure that they are realistic and fair. Then, try to find the particular spur that will make them want to produce more for you. Recognize high achievers with praise and small awards—it might make low producers sit up and take notice and strive to earn the same appreciation.

You Can Always Do Something

When the subject of overtime comes up, a frequently heard excuse is: "We operate like a job shop. There's nothing we can do about overtime. Every job is different and they're all rush jobs."

Actually, however, something can be done, even in a job shop. It's a matter of attitude and planning. The superintendent of a job shop in New England explains how the overtime problem was reduced in his plant:

"We know, of course, that some overtime is unavoidable in a job shop such as ours, but we think of it as an emergency measure only. By planning as carefully as possible, we've been able to reduce overtime steadily."

One measure taken in that shop was to increase supervision. By assigning foremen and group leaders to operations that had been unsupervised at the production level, output was increased all along the line. Another effective measure was to modify equipment to meet the special requirements of the work.

Stick to Your Schedule By Monitoring Production Progress

Whenever you find that work is falling behind, do something about it *right away*. Don't let it slide.

OVERTIME ANALYSIS FORM
(Sample)

Week Of _____

Employee name, job, clock number	Henry Johns Lathe Operator #1345
Overtime hours Number of hours of overtime by days	Mon. — 2 hrs. Tues. — 2 hrs. Wed. — 1½ hrs.
Reason for overtime What situation or event necessitated overtime work?	Shipment must be completed before end of month to avoid gov't penalty.
Results of overtime What was accomplished by working overtime? Give facts & figures.	75 more parts completed and sent to assembly.
Instead of overtime —what?	Change setup on another machine to make this part.
What else could you have done? List all alternatives.	Schedule these parts into next week, perhaps forcing entire assembly dept. into overtime. Schedule earlier delivery of stock to take advantage of any free time that might turn up for any lathe.
Planned future action What alternative have you chosen? (Perhaps overtime is best.)	Schedule earlier delivery of stock but, if unable to start on job any earlier, continue to use overtime.

Get the facts about your current overtime situation. On the form, list each worker subject to overtime, the overtime hours worked, and the results obtained.

Consider the alternatives to working overtime. Use the analysis form to examine all possible ways of getting output without overtime. Write down your own ideas and those of your associates. Study the pros and cons of each solution.

Here are some questions to ask when considering alternatives:

➥ Could work be done at later time?

➥ Who else could do the work during regular hours?

➥ Could overtime be avoided—without raising costs—if more people were put on the job?

➥ Is there some other place, in or outside the department, where the work could be done cheaper?

➥ Could the job be done on another machine to avoid overtime?

Check immediate and long-range costs. Make your alternatives simple so large cash investments for additional equipment or space will not be called for. (Don't forget that one alternative is to continue the overtime.)

Try to change work loads to eliminate overtime. But make sure you don't cause more overtime by forgetting such items as normal absenteeism, holidays, seasonal peaks, vacations, inventories, weather problems, and machine repairs.

Here are the four main types of overtime you run up against:

➥ *Emergency overtime*—caused by a customer's rush request, a breakdown, or a deadline.

➥ *Recurring overtime*—arising periodically, such as inventory work, end-of-the-month rush periods, or holidays. Since these situations are usually predictable, planning may eliminate them. For example: Taking inventory of different products at differently scheduled intervals will help reduce the high payroll costs normally associated with one-shot inventory taking.

➥ *Weekend overtime*—caused by the need for additional output beyond regularly scheduled work hours, or to perform maintenance tasks that cannot be done during the regular workday.

➥ *Daily overtime*—of one or two extra hours added regularly to the workday. When such overtime becomes a matter of course, it's a symptom of inefficient scheduling.

And don't hesitate to ask for advice or help from your boss or other supervisors. You're headed for trouble and expensive overtime if you have frequent breakdowns of equipment, delays in getting parts and materials, tardiness, absenteeism, or anything else that disrupts schedules.

Use this checklist as a planning guide:

At the start of the shift—

✔ Are all employees on line, with operations running smoothly?
✔ Are the materials on hand adequate?
✔ Is equipment in top working order?

During the shift—

✔ Are all jobs progressing according to schedule?
✔ Are special instructions being followed?
✔ Does anyone have a problem to be solved?

At the end of the shift—

✔ Was the day's production schedule met?
✔ Does everyone know the schedule for tomorrow?

▶ WHAT YOU CAN DO ➔ *You can effectively reduce avoidable overtime if you:*

1. Know your production schedules and the capabilities of your workers.

2. Train your people to meet production schedules while maintaining quality standards.

3. Cooperate with the maintenance department by having workers take care of tools and machines.

4. Analyze your overtime needs and seek less costly alternatives.

5. Plan your production schedules realistically and follow up periodically to keep workers on schedule.

6. Alert yourself to any work slowdowns, either deliberate or unconscious.

If you achieve the proper balance between production needs and available facilities, you will eliminate the high direct labor costs associated with excessive overtime.

ACTION PLAN:

MAINTAIN HIGH PRODUCTIVITY FOR EFFECTIVE COST CONTROL

Getting the most work done with the least waste of time, materials, and energy—that's optimum productivity. It means greatest output—both in quantity and quality—per labor and materials cost. And where does productivity occur? Right in your own department. That's why it's up to you to see that your department maintains a positive output-per-cost ratio.

Work Smarter, Not Harder

There's a lot of talk these days about productivity—or rather, the lack of it. "People just don't work as hard as they used to," grumble some individuals. And you may agree—but stop and ask yourself: Is getting people to work harder really the answer to increased productivity?

Working harder will not necessarily ensure effective, efficient production. But working *smarter* will. And that's what both you and your people must do to have a truly productive department. "But how can I effectively build a climate that produces the greatest amount of work with the fewest errors?" you may ask.

The fact is, there's no secret to getting the most from your employees and equipment. All it takes is some simple steps to make your department as productive as possible.

Personal Productivity

When looking at the productivity of your department, you have to start by looking at yourself. Just how much do you get done in a day's work? How much time and energy do you waste? Step back and take a hard look at the way you handle your responsibilities.

Is there a job description for your position? If so, dig it out to see how accurately it reflects your daily routine. Try keeping a journal of your day-to-day activities to see how closely your actual duties jibe with the job description. By evaluating what you do every day you can—

▶ Eliminate tasks that take up your time but contribute nothing toward your effectiveness as a supervisor.

▶ Reduce duplication of effort where your work unnecessarily overlaps that of others.

▶ Revise routine duties so that they better meet your department's needs and objectives.

Such an evaluation will tune up your own productivity rate by helping you better organize your time and efforts.

If you want your workers to work as productively as they can, you must first set a fine example for them to follow. If you slack off and fail to exhibit the attitude that productivity is important, the chances are your employees will do the same thing.

On the other hand, if you organize your duties and keep your nose to the grindstone, then it's highly likely you'll enjoy a workforce that's as productive as possible. It doesn't take a taskmaster to build a productive atmosphere; it takes a supervisor who has mastered the task of inspiring high output from his or her workers by giving the same.

Your Operation's Productivity

After you've examined your own productivity, you should look at the productivity of departmental operations. Week in and week out, you schedule work through your department to maintain a steady, productive work pace.

But there are many factors that can interrupt the work flow, make mincemeat of your schedules, and reduce the productivity of your people. Sometimes these problems cannot be anticipated or avoided.

Careful analysis may reveal many areas in which problems are predictable—and preventable—however. Check for these time or material wasters within your operation:

■ Lack of materials, tools, or supplies. How many times is work interrupted because an employee doesn't have the right tool to do the job? How often are substitute materials used incorrectly so that a job has to be done over?

See to it that your people have all the things they need in order to do the job properly. Keep an eye on your supply inventory and the use rate of materials. Have important tools replaced if they are damaged.

■ **Unclear work orders or insufficient instructions.** How often is the work flow delayed because an employee needs additional instructions on how to handle a particular job? How often are mistakes made because a job wasn't explained clearly? How much extra, unnecessary work occurs because employees are not sure which steps are important and which could be eliminated?

Make sure your work assignments are clearly delivered, and that your employees know exactly who is to do what, and by when. Also see that they have the proper training to handle the tasks they are given. Establish an atmosphere that will encourage your people to come to you with questions and uncertainties. Don't let poor communication sap your department's output.

■ **Equipment downtime.** How often is a job held up because of a machine breakdown? How often must work be rejected because of slipped adjustment settings? When you're working with older equipment, some breakdowns may be unavoidable—parts do wear out. However, more often equipment breaks down because it has been poorly maintained or used improperly.

For equipment to last, it must be used and maintained correctly. So be sure your people are trained in the proper use and care of their machines and equipment. See that cleaning and preventive maintenance are performed on a regular basis.

■ **Routing or scheduling errors.** How many times is a work stoppage or slowdown caused by routing mistakes? How often are deadlines missed because work is misplaced or just put aside because it was thought unimportant?

Watch the flow of work in your department to catch snags that might crop up. If mix-ups occur frequently, find out why. You may need to devise a system that will identify job lots or work assignments clearly with their deadline requirements, priority standing, routing schedules, and other standards. If problems stem from misunderstandings on the part of workers, you might want to review work procedures and priorities with them.

Your Employees' Productivity

In addition to organizing your operation to eliminate the factors that prevent you from having an efficiently run department, you must address your attention to ensuring that your employees are doing the best possible job. Worker performance is the key factor in improving overall productivity because that's where the work actually gets done.

What are the things you need from your workers to guarantee a productive department? Here are five basic factors that affect the contributions each employee makes to your operation:

Output: Just how much do individual workers produce? How closely do they meet production standards? Do they exceed or fall short of one another? If an individual's output is below average, is it because of lack of effort, trying too hard, insufficient knowledge of the work, or time wasted talking away from the workstation?

Quality: What's the frequency of worker errors, according to the job? How much rework is required? How much work results in waste? If the quality of work is poor, is it because of plain carelessness, hurried work, lack of experience or lack of training?

Dependability: How frequently are employees absent or late? Do certain workers waste time if left to work alone? Do workers follow instructions and follow through on work assignments?

Adaptability: How quickly do your people learn new jobs or methods? How readily do they accept change? Can they adjust to situations that are out of the ordinary?

Cooperation: Are employees willing to pitch in and help fellow workers? Can they be counted on to push harder in an emergency? Do they offer productivity improvement suggestions?

Remember, *attitude* is as important to high productivity as ability. And you play a pivotal role in fostering the positive attitude in your workers that will guarantee the most productive use of their abilities. You can achieve this by keeping daily tabs on the above factors for each employee on your staff, and taking corrective action where necessary.

Tell Them Why It's Important

Another crucial way you can motivate your people to work productively is to explain what "productivity" really means—to the company and, ultimately, to them.

Many workers fail to maintain a high performance level because they don't see how their individual jobs affect the economic well-being of the company—and, in turn, their own financial security.

How can you help workers understand what productivity is really all about? By sharing information.

Hold a "productivity-awareness" meeting with your staff. Explain the realities of market competition: that your company must achieve and maintain optimum output in order to vie successfully for a comfortable place in the market.

Tell workers that the company can't do it without the help and cooperation of each member of its staff. Discuss how their failure to work productively can jeopardize company status and ultimately place their jobs in a tenuous position. When workers are made to understand that their personal goals (job security)—and corporate goals (a profitable operation)—are interdependent, they'll be more willing to cooperate in your productivity-raising efforts.

You Get What You Ask For

One of the most vital points to keep in mind regarding employee productivity is this: You get what you ask for. Your employees will probably be only as productive as they think you want them to be. Granted, there may be one or two who outproduce their colleagues, but for the most part, you can expect no more than you ask for.

For that very reason, you should never stop communicating high expectations to your people. Tell them exactly how much productivity you want from them—use figures if necessary to illustrate your message. When you've made it clear that you expect great (and attainable) accomplishments from your people, they will work harder—and smarter—to live up to your expectations.

On the other hand, when you show by word or deed that you don't think they can meet high output goals, you may be setting the stage for a self-fulfilling prophecy!

So make sure you have a positive attitude about your staff—and display that attitude at all times. Your optimistic outlook will probably catch on and lead employees to believe that they can achieve high productivity goals on an ongoing basis.

And occasionally, set "stretching" goals that will allow your people to reach beyond the limits of what they think they can do. For example, you might challenge them to meet a production deadline a few days ahead of schedule. When a goal of this nature is reached, employees feel better about themselves and their abilities. And they're much more likely to rise to the challenge of meeting a new productivity goal that stretches them even further.

▶ **WHAT YOU CAN DO** → *You can increase your department's productivity rating if you:*

1. Reduce the amount of unproductive work you do by better organizing your time and energies.

2. Make sure that your department has all the supplies, materials, and tools it needs to do the job.

3. Give clear, complete instructions to avoid mix-ups and misunderstandings.

4. Keep production equipment in good working order to avoid downtime.

5. Monitor employee performance on a regular basis, and make corrections when problems crop up.

6. Explain how each individual's productivity benefits the company's financial picture—and helps to guarantee job security.

ACTION PLAN:

_____
_____
_____
_____
_____
_____
_____
_____

7. Let your people know that you expect the best from them. The more productivity you ask for, the more you will get.

Productivity improvements don't happen by themselves. You, the supervisor, must make them happen. By following the above strategy, you'll enjoy a highly productive department and rein in costs in the process.

TEACH YOUR PEOPLE THE IMPORTANCE OF QUALITY

You can have the best designed and the best engineered product in the world, but if it's put together poorly, it won't sell. True, inspection might catch flawed items before they get out the door, but you know how costly a high rate of rejects and rework can be. And you, the supervisor, are management's first line of defense against the high cost of poor quality.

Cutting Scrap to the Quick

One of your most crucial supervisory duties is imparting quality awareness to your employees. And that begins with *your own* attitude regarding quality. If you're not truly committed to putting out a top-notch product, you'll fail to effectively drum up that commitment in your people.

If, on the other hand, you make it a point to beef up employee quality consciousness by stressing the importance of doing it right the first time, your people will proudly fulfill your exacting expectations. Here's a case in point:

Keith Axelrod was a supervisor in the manufacturing department of an outboard engine maker. One day, he was thinking about the scrap problem in his department and what he might do to reduce it. Suddenly, something dawned on him: The amount of scrap his workers generated daily was virtually the same.

The scrap bin was filled to capacity every day—but it almost never overflowed. So, he decided to try a little experiment. He took out the big scrap bin and replaced it with a slightly smaller-capacity barrel. Guess what happened?

The barrel was filled every day—but it very seldom spilled over. So, Axelrod went one step further, and put in an even smaller barrel. He got the same results—*reduced scrap*.

What's the moral of the story? While some quarters may say that it's unreasonable to expect workers to produce zero scrap, you *can* reduce the quantity of scrap they do generate by simply letting them know—even subtly—that you expect higher quality work from them.

It'll Take a Concentrated Effort

Besides trying a simple tactic like the one employed by Keith Axelrod, what else can you do to enhance product quality in your department? Your first move should be to thoroughly analyze your workers' performance—and determine exactly what is keeping them from doing a first-rate job.

Here are some common quality roadblocks, which you can easily remedy with the proper care and attention:

• **Lack of knowledge**—workers lack the know-how or training necessary to create a high-quality product.

The Remedy: The obvious answer is to give uninformed workers the training and guidance they need. If it seems that inadequate training is a widespread problem in your group, you should reassess your training methods—perhaps you're not giving new hires the comprehensive instructions they require to do the job right.

- **Not understanding requirements** —workers lack a grasp of your department's quality standards.

The Remedy: You can't expect employees to work to specifications if you haven't told them what they are. It's often much easier to convince workers of the need for close tolerances when they understand why they're necessary.

So explain to your people how their work fits in with the work in other departments and why customer satisfaction depends on their quality-minded, conscientious performance.

- **Lack of ability**—workers do not have the "right stuff" to do the job correctly.

The Remedy: Choosing the right person to do each job is one of your most important functions. When you find that the wrong choice has been made, you have no alternative but to correct it immediately. If possible, you should transfer the worker to a less demanding position.

However, if you fear that discharge will ultimately be the only way to solve the problem, make sure you've documented each instance of poor performance, including dates, facts, and figures. Make sure, too, that you keep a written record of your efforts to help the poor performer to improve.

- **Carelessness**— workers are being lax in their attention to their work.

The Remedy: If you've determined that a worker does not require added instruction, and if the worker has demonstrated an ability to perform his or her job and still makes many mistakes, carelessness may be the problem. You may need to take a careless worker aside and explain that it's imperative for the person to exercise greater care, otherwise, his or her job may be in jeopardy.

- **Defective equipment** —the machinery and tools your people use are faulty, in need of repair, or incapable of holding tolerances.

The Remedy: Another of your major responsibilities is to ensure that the tools and equipment your workers use are in tip-top operating condition. That's why you must set up a schedule for inspection, lubrication, and minor repairs—and then try to stick to it.

- **Poor quality materials**—the raw materials your department is receiving from the supplier are just not up to par.

The Remedy: An excessive amount of defective materials coming into your department probably means that you had better tighten your incoming inspection procedures and get tough with your supplier. Reject any materials that are not up to your strict standards—if your vendor doesn't get the message pretty quickly, you would do well to research other suppliers and take your business elsewhere.

Check with your workers frequently to see if they're having any problems with materials.

Be Realistic About Quality

It's clear that you have a responsibility for seeing that quality standards are adhered to. But you also have a responsibility to see that money is not wasted to obtain a level of quality that is far in excess of your company's specifications.

Here's a checklist you can use to examine your personal performance in maintaining quality within budgeted costs:

✓ **Do you thoroughly understand the quality requirements?** Whenever you need information on tolerances, finishes, or other critical areas, be sure that you get it from reliable sources only—such as your company's quality control manager.

✓ **Do you thoroughly understand your company's inspection procedures?** Learn all you can about them, and cooperate fully with the inspectors and quality control department. It'll save you needless, time-wasting arguments.

✓ **Do your workers understand quality requirements and the role of inspectors?** Make sure that there is cooperation between operators and inspectors.

✓ **Do your workers realize that producing below standards makes more work for themselves** and employees in other departments, as well as making the ultimate inspector, the customer, very unhappy with the product?

✓ **Have your workers been convinced that producing within quality standards will mark them as superior workers**—and will improve their chances for advancement and pay raises?

One final question: In addition to making periodic checks on the quality of raw materials coming in, do you take precautions to assure that finished assemblies are properly handled and stored?

▶ WHAT YOU CAN DO → To keep product quality at top level:

1. Make certain that workers are properly trained and understand the required standards.

2. See that people and positions are well-matched. Transfer workers who can't handle difficult tasks to simpler duties.

3. Inspect equipment regularly, and adhere to maintenance schedules.

4. Carefully monitor the quality of incoming materials—your people can't manufacture a good product with poor raw materials.

5. Encourage your people to exercise care in everything they do.

6. Keep your production well within required specifications—but don't exceed standards without a go-ahead from higher-ups.

The cost of poor quality will never damage your company's financial picture as long as you and your crew are committed to excellence.

ACTION PLAN:

_____
_____
_____
_____
_____
_____
_____
_____
_____
_____
_____

USING PREVENTIVE MAINTENANCE TO CONTROL DOWNTIME COSTS

The costs associated with equipment maintenance and repair can be staggering, both in terms of parts and labor and in terms of lost productivity due to downtime. So your mission to keep costs under control should include doing all you can to reduce equipment maintenance costs in your department.

Your Maintenance Role

It's much more cost-effective to prevent problems than it is to correct them. That's especially true where the equipment and machinery in your department is concerned. A little attention can keep it in tip-top shape, thus preventing production delays. And when this attention takes the form of a preventive maintenance (PM) program, you'll be even more successful at putting the brakes on the high costs of breakdowns.

Properly conducted, a PM program can save your company a lot of dollars by cutting repair and operating costs. It can also save on the production delays that are likely to follow from machine downtime. Savings like these are always appreciated by top management, and they reflect well on you as a supervisor and on your department.

What constitutes an effective PM program? Ideally, it includes:

1 Periodic inspection of your department's equipment to uncover conditions that may ultimately cause it to malfunction or break down.

2 Necessary maintenance to alleviate the conditions that have been discovered—before they create major problems.

Maintenance Personnel: Your PM Partners

You may feel that your potential role in a PM program is minimal; that in fact, the maintenance department has sole responsibility for keeping equipment in good shape. But it's your job to see that your employees stay productive at all times, and keeping their machinery running is one way to ensure that they will stay productive. Granted, maintenance personnel do play a big part in the PM program—but not the only part.

Think of your colleagues in Maintenance as your partners for PM. While they carry out many of the functions that will keep your equipment in top running condition, you must work with them to get the most from your PM program.

For that reason, you must strive to keep pleasant, productive lines of communication open between your department and Maintenance. A common complaint by maintenance supervisors is that supervisors from other departments often fail to cooperate with them. Everybody wants things done at breakneck speed, but this is unreasonable and can undermine the effectiveness of the maintenance process. So don't treat maintenance people like minions on your personal staff by ordering them around.

Here are some other "Don'ts" regarding your healthy relationship with Maintenance:

★ **Don't wait until a machine breaks down before you call Maintenance.** If a piece of equipment is not running properly, alert Maintenance immediately. They might be able to make a minor adjustment that will prevent serious trouble.

★ **Don't try to prevail upon maintenance workers to do another "small job" while they're fixing something else in your department.** Preventive repair jobs should be scheduled according to procedure.

★ **Don't summon Maintenance with false alarms.** Some workers are inclined to blame their troubles on their machines when something else is really at fault. Make sure the problems don't stem from poor materials, inadequate training, or an improper tool before you send out an SOS.

★ **Don't impede Maintenance's efforts to conduct routine preventive maintenance.** In the interest of time, many supervisors push their equipment to the limit, refusing to shut down for PM. However, this can cause calamitous consequences in the form of downtime later when a major breakdown occurs.

Maintenance personnel can't be at your beck and call all the time, but they'll be more than willing to help you set up a PM program. That's because it will save them—as well as you—time and effort in the long run.

Start With a Survey

Before a preventive maintenance program is initiated, you or your company's maintenance department will probably have to take some corrective action. This is because a lack of preventive maintenance in the past may have led to some real problems in the present. For example, a machine that has been allowed to become run down will have to be reconditioned before it can be maintained in good condition.

A survey of equipment can be a big help here. Examine past maintenance records to see which machines have required the most attention in the past. If this information isn't available (and even if it is), it's a good idea to draw upon your knowledge of which machines seem to give the most trouble. You can also talk to your employees to learn any insights they've gained from working with the equipment daily.

Once you've found the machines that are in the worst shape now, talk to the people in the maintenance department. Ask them to include special attention to problem machines in their upcoming repair schedule, and let them know that you'd like to work with them from now on so that machines don't get into such a run-down state again.

Tune In To Frequencies

After you've identified the equipment that will be part of your PM program, you must decide how often to carry out the required inspections and repairs.

Keep in mind that you can't develop the program on your own—you're going to need the aid of Maintenance to carry out PM tasks, so you should make sure it plays a big role in the planning. Sit down with upkeep personnel and work out a schedule that will be convenient for both your department and the maintenance department.

Where can you find the data you'll need to determine how much attention each piece of equipment will require? The manuals and instruction booklets that accompanied the machines when they were new are good sources of information. But if these are no longer available, or don't meet your current needs, try to contact the manufacturer of the equipment directly to get some assistance.

Of course, experience is the best teacher when it come to establishing inspection and maintenance frequencies. The tendency in the early stages of a PM program is to overinspect. This is perfectly all right; it's better to start the inspection frequencies on the high side than on the low side.

But to adjust maintenance frequencies to a proper level, you'll have to keep an eye on the production downtime caused by machine failure. Here's an example of how to make those adjustments:

Let's say you have a machine that is being serviced once a month. If all goes well and it experiences no breakdowns, you wait six weeks between routine maintenance. If you still find that the equipment is running efficiently between service calls, you wait two months between maintenance.

But at this point, the machine may give you trouble. It could break down in the seventh or eighth week and contribute to production delays. If so, you have determined that the optimum period for performing preventive maintenance on this particular piece of equipment is about six weeks.

With this method, you can make the final adjustments on preventive maintenance schedules for the machines in your deparment. Just decrease the amount of maintenance little by little until you are getting maximum performance with a minimum of monitoring.

Prevent Equipment Abuse

In addition to cooperating with the Maintenance department and setting up a PM schedule, you have one more responsibility in the field of maintenance: Preventing improper use and rough treatment of the expensive equipment entrusted to your care. Here are the steps you can take toward that end:

■ **Be certain that all employees are properly instructed in the operation of their equipment and machinery.** When a new piece of equipment is brought into the department, have a copy of the manufacturer's directions on hand, and hold a comprehensive training session for all employees who will be operating the equipment.

■ **Make certain that all employees are properly instructed in the routine care of equipment for which they're responsible.** This care might include cleaning, oiling, greasing, replacing fuses, or checking gear drives. Also make sure they perform these chores regularly.

■ **Tell workers that they must never abuse their machinery by pounding on it or otherwise damaging it.** Take swift disciplinary action if you witness a worker taking his or her frustrations out on machinery. Also, prevent workers from overloading their equipment in a misguided attempt to increase production.

■ **Take precautions to safeguard any machinery that happens to be standing idle.** For example, don't allow workers to use a dormant piece of machinery for a snack or lunch table. A spilled cup of coffee could wreak havoc if it got into the workings of an expensive machine.

After a Repair

There are three measures you should always take after a piece of equipment has been repaired to ensure the effectiveness of your general maintenance program.

First, you should take a moment to run the machine and determine that the repair was indeed successful before you reintroduce it to production operations. That way, if it is still malfunctioning, you can alert the maintenance department immediately so they can rectify matters—and prevent the machine from producing defective items or otherwise impairing production.

Second, check all safety devices after a machine has undergone a repair (or even routine maintenance) to ensure that they have been properly replaced and to keep employees from becoming injured.

Third, make a written record of all repairs, along with dates and costs incurred. Then refer to it periodically to determine whether costs are getting out of hand, or your PM program is yielding the desired results, namely, a minimum of breakdowns and repair expenses.

> ▶ **WHAT YOU CAN DO** → *To reduce maintenance costs and diminish downtime:*

1. Establish a cooperative relationship with Maintenance personnel. They're going to play a major role in the program, so you'll want to have them on your side.

2. Survey your equipment to find out which machines are causing the most problems now. Then you'll know where to focus your initial maintenance efforts.

3. Work with Maintenance to develop a schedule of routine servicing and inspection for your department, and adhere to the schedule religiously.

4. Use the trial-and-error method to fine-tune your PM schedule. Decrease planned maintenance occasionally until each machine is being serviced as infrequently as possible but often enough to keep it operating smoothly.

5. Train workers to take proper care of their equipment. Do not permit employees to overload or abuse their machinery.

6. Take special steps after a repair to confirm proper machine function and safety and determine whether or not maintenance costs are staying under control.

By developing a pleasant and constructive working relationship with your colleagues in Maintenance and taking pains to ensure proper care of the equipment in your department, you will be doing your utmost to keep your machinery in optimum working order. And that means low repair costs for your company and high productivity for your group.

ACTION PLAN:
_____
_____
_____
_____
_____
_____
_____
_____
_____
_____
_____
_____
_____
_____
_____
_____
_____
_____

STRIVE FOR IMPROVED MATERIALS HANDLING

Do you have any idea how much it costs your firm to move and store production materials? Experts estimate that for most companies, the expense of handling materials—and the cost of mishandling them—runs between 25 and 40 percent of the total cost of manufacturing. That's a pretty hefty figure. But you can reduce it by protecting materials from damage and by streamlining operations.

Find a Better Way

In the average production process, a part may be handled 50 or 60 times before the job is completed. And each time a part is handled, there's a good chance it can become damaged, misused or lost.

So what am I supposed to do about it? you may ask. *The responsibility for proper distribution, storage, and use of parts is with the materials handling department—right?*

But as a supervisor, you are in an ideal position to help your company get its money's worth from the materials it has purchased. Your contribution may not look large to begin with, but even a few percentage points one way or the other can spell the difference between profit and loss.

Let's examine some of the ways in which you can save company dollars by improving your department's method of dealing with materials.

What You Can Do

Here are seven suggestions for upgrading your current materials handling techniques. If you already follow these steps, congratulations—you're doing your part to better your company's financial picture.

1 Ensure proper storage. Proper storage is one crucial element of efficient materials handling. You can prevent many losses simply by establishing a storage system that puts each part in a particular place until it is needed.

For example, you can place needed items in color-coded bins. This has a double advantage: Employees who need parts can find them more easily, and anyone who finds a part just lying around can return it to the proper bin with little confusion.

2 Provide adequate instructions to newcomers. If you teach new hires from day one that materials are to be handled with care, you'll help prevent damage due to human carelessness. Here's a case in point:

A supervisor in a metalworking plant was busy when a new employee reported for work. So, he claimed, he didn't have time to give detailed instructions to the worker. The newcomer was simply told to stack aluminum sheets "like the other employees were doing."

When the supervisor checked later, he found that 10 sheets had to be scrapped. Improper stacking had scratched some sheets and bent others. Each sheet cost the company about $8, exclusive of labor, for a total loss of $80—a loss which could have easily been avoided if the supervisor had taken a little more time to give instructions. Or, he could have asked an experienced worker to explain the procedure to the new employee. He would have saved himself a lot of explaining and the company some money. Instead, he neglected to heed the adage: "It costs money to train, but it costs more *not* to train."

3 Have workers sign for each part or batch of parts they use. This gives each person the responsibility for using items correctly, and you'll be able to follow any trends that point to a particular employee using an excessive number of parts.

If you do come across a situation where it appears materials are being wasted, you can go to the worker and find out what the problem is. Perhaps additional training is needed in order to get the employee to use parts correctly, or maybe you simply need to raise the person's consciousness about wasting parts.

4 Talk in dollars and cents. "There's so much of this stuff around—what difference does it make if I break a couple?" If this is the attitude in your department, you have a little educating to do. An effective method to get the message across is to show employees just how much scrap and waste can add up to in a month.

By putting the value of parts in concrete terms, you make it easier for employees to understand the

A Materials Handling Checklist

It's easy to assume that your present methods of handling materials are as efficient as they can be and to overlook possible improvements in the movement and storage of goods, parts, and tools. But it can be costly to be complacent. Any time you spend analyzing your materials handling techniques will be well worth it—and will be reflected in smoother work flow and lower costs.

Here are some questions to ask that will give you a clear picture of your present system's efficiency and the improvements you need to make:

✓ Do you know the number of times each type of material or part is handled in your department?

✓ Are materials and parts being damaged in transit? Would special racks, bins, or trays reduce these costly losses?

✓ Are skilled workers spending valuable time handling materials, heavy tools, or products? Could such jobs be done by other workers?

✓ Is it possible to reduce the number of workers handling materials?

✓ Is there a steady flow of work by the most direct route in the least possible time?

✓ Is the production area cluttered with parts and materials waiting to be used?

✓ Have you had any accidents that can be attributed to careless materials handling?

✓ Do all employees understand the importance of judicious materials handling?

✓ Have you investigated and suggested the use of mechanized equipment such as cranes, conveyors, hoists, and lift trucks?

If you find your department lacking in any of these areas, take whatever action is necessary to improve the situation. Make materials handling an *efficient* part of your group's operations.

---

importance of working conscientiously. Holding a short presentation for your crew should do the trick. Begin by showing your people examples of components used in your work process, and tell them how much each item costs.

Then, you can show them some parts that have been damaged, and explain how the damage took place. This combination of examples and figures should inspire your employees to handle materials more carefully.

5 Protect materials from damage during operations. Once materials are in the hands of employees, there are further steps you can take to protect the parts from damage. Especially sensitive items can be placed in special packaging to ward off the normal knocks and bumps a part is subjected to during production. Check on the advisability of using specially fitted containers, boxes, or protectors for parts in process. Here are two examples of how this might work:

When a Detroit automobile manufacturer began getting complaints from dealers about noisy transmissions, all supervisors were alerted to try to find the cause. A supervisor in a gear machining section noticed that after machining, the gears were tossed into open bins.

Suspecting that the machined surfaces might be getting damaged, she examined them under a magnifier. Sure enough, there was considerable scratching and denting which would affect their operation, even though it didn't prevent assembly. The solution? She had special racks built to hold the gears, and the complaints soon ended.

In another case, the supervisor in a fastener plant was concerned because cartons piled close to the end of aisles were being damaged by trucks continuously bumping against them. He solved the problem by placing metal corners on the end cartons in each aisle.

6 Examine the work area for environmental hazards. Leaks, condensation, excessive heat or cold, and other factors can contribute to materials damage. If you detect such a problem, do something about it immediately.

For instance, if an overhead pipe has a tendency to drip onto an employee's workstation, have the pipe repaired right away. If you don't, a whole batch of parts could be ruined by water damage—and you'll have no one to blame but yourself.

7 Stress good housekeeping. Impress upon your workers the importance of picking up and setting aside materials dropped on the floor. Much of this is salvageable but is wasted because, left on the floor, it gets damaged beyond repair. This is most significant where small parts are involved and in assembly operations. Few people will take the trouble to pick up small parts unless they are reminded to do so, so the parts get kicked aside, under a bench or into a corner.

A supervisor in an electronics parts plant salvaged much of what was formerly wasted by the simple maneuver of placing cans in various convenient locations throughout the department. Another way to prevent waste is to protect small parts from contamination by the use of tweezers, tongs, or other handling tools.

Streamline Work Processes

Tailoring work procedures is another step you can take to prevent damage to components. You'll recall that we said a part may be handled 50 to 60 times during a typical average production process.

Ask yourself if there is any point during production when a part is handled unnecessarily. For example, a circuit board may be taken from its point of assembly and placed on a centrally located table. Then another worker may be required to pick up the circuit board and bring it to his or her workstation to be inserted into a video game assembly.

Would there be any advantage in changing this method? Yes. It might be a better idea to take completed circuit boards directly to the workstation of the people who assemble the video games. This eliminates the step of picking up the board from the table, and means only one person will have to handle it between the points of circuit board assembly and game production.

Also, don't forget to ask your people to provide you with suggestions for streamlining procedures. They have the expertise needed to make valuable improvements.

▶ **WHAT YOU CAN DO** ➡ *To increase the effectiveness of materials handling in your work area:*

1. Protect parts and materials from damage by ensuring proper storage. Provide containers and other protective devices where possible.

2. See that workers are trained in the proper way to handle easily damaged materials. Stress good housekeeping.

3. Impart the cost picture to your employees. Explain how much materials cost, and how quickly unnecessary expenses due to damage can add up for your company.

4. Examine the work area for environmental conditions that might cause material damage.

5. Ensure careful handling during actual production. Use special packaging or implements to manipulate materials and keep them safe from damage.

6. Streamline production processes to eliminate any unnecessary handling of parts. Ask your workers for input on this subject, and try out some of their suggestions.

Remember: Improved handling means a more cost-effective production operation—and that's something every supervisor should strive for.

ACTION PLAN:

PREVENT THEFT FROM IMPAIRING COST-EFFECTIVENESS

Employee theft is one cost control issue you should never neglect. The cost of theft at the workplace totals tens of billions of dollars a year. That cuts directly into company profits, and means there's less money to go around for plant improvements and pay hikes. So it's up to you to thwart thievery in your department.

To Catch a Thief

When it comes to employee theft, your first response might be "It can't happen here. My workers are as honest as the day is long." But don't be so sure.

A recent study suggests that one out of every three people steals from his or her employer. The items stolen range from supplies such as pencils to expensive tools—all the way up to intangible but valuable items such as trade secrets.

It all adds up. Money spent replacing purloined equipment is a drain on all the people who work for your company. So it's imperative that theft be stopped before it cuts into the bottom line. As a supervisor, you have a major role to play: You have to keep an eye out for theft while instilling in all your employees the attitude that preventing losses is everyone's business.

Why Do They Steal?

What leads employees to steal from their companies in the first place? Understanding the following reasons can help you to be on the lookout for possible suspects when a pattern of theft arises:

1 They feel underpaid. Let's say that Roy feels his wages are too low. To make up the perceived difference, he may "take it out in trade," stealing and reselling company property.

2 They are in debt. Financial pressure can cause otherwise honest people to step over the boundaries of honesty at times.

For example, if a worker's wife has been unemployed for a while, he may be tempted to steal items from the department to make up for the temporary shortage in income.

3 They are supporting a drug habit. Feeding a drug habit takes a lot of money, more money than most people could hope to make working honestly. So they usually must find ways to supplement their income. Theft from an employer is often the route they choose to take. And if this is the situation in your department, you would do well to refer drug abusers to the appropriate professional agency for counseling.

Of course, these are only a few examples of what might induce an employee to take things from the department. There are as many reasons for theft as there are instances of theft. So you must remain on the lookout for anything that might tempt your workers to take what doesn't belong to them.

A Pound of Prevention

Whatever the reason for employee theft, it's up to you, the supervisor, to make the actual act more difficult to carry out. There are a number of ways to do this:

■ **Make company property easily identifiable.** Anything that can be stolen eventually might be stolen. That's why easily removed items should be clearly marked to discourage would-be pilferers. Items such as tools can be assigned an identification number to be engraved on the piece of equipment. Larger items can be painted a distinctive color or marked with a company logo.

■ **Pay special attention to temporary help.** People who come into your department to fill a temporary need may feel less loyalty to the company than your usual full-time workers. Consequently, they may feel little compunction in walking off with company property. So take extra security measures whenever your department is involved in such a situation. This could simply mean observing these workers frequently and taking stock of tools and supplies more often.

■ **Promote good housekeeping.** When there's a place for everything, but everything is not in its place, you can't even tell if you have a theft problem. So keep equipment and supplies in specific, designated areas. You'll know immediately if any items disappear simply by taking a quick look around.

■ **Follow up on equipment loans.** From time to time, you may allow trusted employees to borrow equipment (if you have permission from higher up). If this is a common practice in your department, always be sure to follow up each instance of a loan to ensure that the item was actually returned. Writing a short memo to yourself and tacking it over your desk is one good way to keep a loan in mind.

■ **Use adequate controls.** Controls over tools, supplies, and equipment need not be elaborate in order to work. For example, limiting the number of people who have a key to the tool crib is a simple but effective form of control. So is using sign-out sheets.

How do sign-out sheets work? Each time an employee uses a controlled piece of equipment, he or she signs a sheet which identifies the item used. The worker is then responsible for seeing that the item is returned.

This method brings to bear some subtle peer pressure: An employee is unlikely to steal something that a fellow worker is going to be held responsible for. And when people are being held responsible, they're more apt to do everything in their power to see that the item doesn't "disappear."

Keep Information Safe, Too

Information security is often overlooked when supervisors consider the issue of employee theft. But a leakage of vital company data can generate disastrous repercussions for your company's financial picture.

What types of information would do the most damage if they were to fall into the hands of an unscrupulous rival? The following are high on the list:

▸ Newly developed products and production processes
▸ Marketing plans and strategies
▸ Installation of new equipment
▸ Increases in production overtime and trouble making quotas and deadlines
▸ Budgetary information

An information leak in any one of these areas could be enough to allow the competition to beat your company to the punch in the marketplace. Since your competitors are basically familiar with your operation, they don't need to find out every detail.

In fact, there have been many situations where a few errant facts were sufficient for a competitor to piece together a fairly accurate picture of what's going on behind a company's closed doors.

That's why you must take special steps to safeguard information from theft, as you do physical materials:

✔ Keep all confidential reports, charts, graphs, and other documents under lock and key. Limit the number of people who have access to such data.

✔ Erase blackboards as soon as the information has been used. That will lessen the chance of the information being recorded and stolen by a dishonest person.

✔ Encourage employees to report instances of co-workers removing paperwork from company premises. They may be stealing classified data which they will attempt to sell to the highest-bidding competitor.

When the Unthinkable Happens

Sometimes, despite your best prevention efforts, an employee will steal. When that happens, it's best to tread carefully. And to ensure that you do, it's a good idea to have a policy already in place for dealing with employees who pilfer.

The policy can be a written part of the company manual, or it can be an informal agreement based on discussions with your superiors. What should such a policy outline? Here are some important factors:

▸ **The amount of evidence that must be collected before an employee is confronted.** You must be absolutely sure that you are holding the right person responsible for the theft. Are your suspicions the result of an anonymous tip or a report from a co-worker who may have a grudge against the reported filcher? Or has inventory shrunk inexplicably whenever a particular worker is left alone for any period of time?

Whatever the source of your suspicions, it's important that you collect enough evidence to back up any accusation you make.

What can happen if you don't? For one thing, you could mar an innocent person's work record for life. Also, you can subject yourself and your company to a lawsuit if you decide to fire an employee based upon unproven allegations.

▶ **The steps that should be taken to recover missing property.** How far is upper management willing to go to get back what was taken? That answer depends, in part, on the value of the stolen item. But you should know whether or not your boss thinks it's desirable for local police to be contacted when company property is discovered missing.

▶ **The extent of the punishment for the employee.** Again, you should know if upper management want police brought in to make an arrest when company property is stolen. If not, find out how far you should go. Is termination of employment to be applied in every case, or are you allowed to take mitigating circumstances into account?

Building a Case

If you're fortunate enough to have a security force where you work, you can simply go to them with your suspicions, turn over any evidence you have collected, and let them take it from there. This has the pleasant benefit of not placing you in a direct confrontation with one of your employees.

Of course, it's very possible that there is no security force at your company, which means you'll have to take on more responsibility when theft is a problem in your department. It will be primarily up to you to build a case against an employee who you suspect is pilfering company property.

This doesn't mean you have to don a trench coat and tail the worker throughout the plant. Rather, document what property you have on hand, and make a note when something disappears.

Then determine whether the person you suspect could have carried out the theft. For example, if you accuse Mark of walking out with an expensive piece of testing equpment, and he wasn't even at work on the day the theft took place, you're going to have a lot of explaining—and apologizing—to do.

Keep careful, accurate records. Recordkeeping is the key to building a fair, honest case against a suspected worker.

Make Everyone a Security Guard

One of the best ways to cut down on employee theft is to make everyone in your department aware of the problems that pilferage can cause, and to enlist their aid in preventing it.

This isn't to suggest that you turn your department into a police state where everyone is turning in co-workers on the slightest pretext. It simply means you have to raise each person's security consciousness and make everyone willing to report suspicious circumstances.

Of course, if you expect employees to come to you with information about thefts, you have to guarantee them that you will protect their anonymity and then make good on your promise. If you let an informant's identity slip just once, you can expect not to get any further help from the people you supervise.

To win employee support and increase the likelihood that they will report thefts to you, always maintain clear lines of communication with all your people. An open, honest relationship between a supervisor and employees is often all it takes to create a department that is productive, a pleasure to work in—and theft-free.

▶ **WHAT YOU CAN DO** → *To keep theft from taking its toll on effective cost control:*

1. Recognize what causes employees to steal. Workers who feel they are underpaid or have drug problems are likely candidates.

2. Stress prevention. Make sure company property is distinctively marked to discourage employees from pilfering it for later sale.

3. Use a control system, such as sign-out sheets, to keep careful track of who had possession of an item last.

ACTION PLAN:

_____
_____
_____
_____
_____
_____

4. Realize that information is a company asset just as physical equipment and supplies are—and do all you can to safeguard it as well.

5. Document cases of theft carefully to avoid charges of wrongful discharge if you decide to fire a worker suspected of theft.

6. Encourage your people to come to you with reports of any thefts they witness, and always ensure confidentiality.

Using these techniques will have the desired effect of cutting down on pilferage in your department—something that benefits the entire company in the long run.

ENERGY CONSERVATION HELPS KEEP COSTS IN CHECK

Choosing a plantwide energy management system may be beyond the scope of your authority, but simple conservation techniques are not. As a supervisor, there are numerous changes you can make to save energy in your department. And management is sure to appreciate your efforts when you save energy dollars.

Make Conservation a Top Priority

You probably make sure that your employees take good care of company property: Equipment is operated properly, supplies are used judiciously, and work areas are kept neat and clean. But there's another kind of property you should pay close attention to—*energy*.

Energy is company property? You bet. It must be purchased just like anything else your company uses to stay in business. Would you throw a box of new supplies in the wastebasket? Of course not! So why waste energy by leaving light bulbs burning unnecessarily or equipment running when it's not in use?

Some of the energy-saving tips we'll take a look at can be carried out by you or by your workers. Other strategies may require the assistance of Maintenance or other departments. Either way, the discovery of areas where you can save is up to *you*. If you can instill energy awareness in your employees, upper management is bound to sit up and take notice of your department—and the savings it's generating.

See the Light on Lighting Efficiency

One area in which you can have a definite positive impact on energy costs is the lighting used by your department. Improper lighting is an energy drain that can really add up to dollars and cents.

What can you do to save money while keeping the department bright enough for your employees to work productively? Here are some examples:

★ **Cut back on general overhead lighting.** If employees have sufficient lighting at their desks or workstations, your present number of overhead

65

fixtures may not be necessary. Consider reducing the wattage here and in other areas—such as aisles and hallways—where it has little impact on safety and worker performance.

★ **Suggest that Maintenance install fluorescent lights wherever possible.** These provide up to five times as much light per watt as incandescent bulbs and last almost 10 times as long. Also, when bright light is needed, see if you can use a single high-wattage bulb rather than three or four low-wattage bulbs. Four 25-watt bulbs produce about 50 percent less light than a single 100-watt bulb.

★ **Keep all bulbs and fixtures clean.** Dirt and dust absorb light and can cut illumination in half. A regular cleaning effort ensures that you get the most of every lighting unit.

★ **Group workers who must perform close work together.** This will enable you to make maximum use of a minimal number of point-of-operation lighting fixtures.

★ **Shut off lights that aren't needed.** Encourage workers to turn off incandescent fixtures not in use during lunch breaks, lights in storage areas, and general lighting at the end of the workday.

Pinch Heating Pennies

The best way to begin cutting your heating bill is to lower the thermostat setting a few degrees. If you can't do it yourself, ask Maintenance for assistance, explaining what you're trying to accomplish. (You should also consult your boss and obtain his or her approval for such a move.)

To keep your employees warm when the temperature is cool, encourage them to wear sweaters or layer their clothing. One sweater can add up to 4 degrees of warmth. And layers are beneficial because they trap body heat and help to insulate against the cold.

There are other positive steps you can take to conserve the heat being pumped into your work area:

■ **Keep heaters and duct openings free of obstructions.** Allow at least three feet of space in front of radiators to ensure the proper circulation of heated air. This may require some minor rearrangements of work tables or equipment, but the energy savings will make it worth your while.

■ **Increase the humidity to make lower temperatures seem more comfortable.** This can be done by filling shallow pans with water and leaving them near heating elements. The pans should be refilled regularly since water evaporates quickly during the dry winter months.

■ **Keep warm air in—and cold air out—** by making sure all entrance doors and windows are properly sealed. You can limit further heat loss through windows if your department has window shades. Tests show that when outside temperatures range from 20 to 50 degrees Fahrenheit, a drawn window shade with a quarter-inch clearance on each vertical side can reduce heat loss through the window by more than 30 percent.

Keeping Cool and Controlled

If you're reading this in San Antonio, Texas, or in Ft. Lauderdale, Florida, chances are you're not overly concerned about conserving the energy generated by heating. More likely, you're concerned about saving while *cooling* your department.

Cooling a building is as much of an energy drain as heating it. You can begin to keep cooling costs under control simply by not firing up the air conditioner until it's absolutely necessary, and then using it only on the warmest days.

Here are some other methods you can use to control cooling expenses:

● Shut off heat-generating lights or equipment when not in use. A single light left burning over a workstation for just a short while can raise the temperature in the immediate area by a few degrees. And a few degrees can mean the difference between worker comfort and discomfort.

● If lighting is adequate, you can reduce the heat gain from the sun's rays by keeping shades and drapes drawn to avoid the "greenhouse effect."

● Open doors, windows, and vents to facilitate the flow of air through the department. This can stave off the need to start up air conditioners.

When it *is* necessary to turn on the air conditioning, keep all outside doors and windows closed tightly to keep out the heat and humidity. Keep the temperature as high as possible without causing discomfort to workers. And shut off the air conditioner approximately one-half hour before quitting time. The work area isn't likely to become uncomfortably warm again in that period of time, and the savings can be appreciable.

ENERGY CONSERVATION CHECKLIST

ITEM	JAN	FEB	MAR	APR	MAY	JUN	JUL
Thermostat at improper setting							
Window left open							
Door closes improperly							
Air leakage around doors & windows							
Cracked weatherstripping							
Heater/air conditioner blocked							
Machines left idling							
Lights on in storage areas							
Dusty light bulbs							
Machines not maintained							
Light fixture blocked							
Dirty thermostat							
Leaky faucets							
Drapes left open at night							

(FIGURE 2-1)

What About Equipment?

If you think about it, your equipment provides you with one more opportunity for energy savings. Consider all the times you took a walk through your department and noticed machinery left running even though no one was using it.

These wasted dollars can be saved, and *you* can do the saving. How? By developing a tagging system that tells your employees which machines should be shut down when they are not in use.

To start, survey your department with the help of Maintenance personnel and your plant manager. Together, determine which machines can be shut off when they aren't needed and which should be kept running to avoid costly warm-up times. Then, tag this equipment with different color-coded labels, for example:

- **Green** for machines that can be turned off when not in use.
- **Yellow** for equipment that can only be shut down with approval
- **Red** for equipment that must run constantly

Finally, explain this system to your staff and ask for their cooperation. Tell them that you need their help to turn off the appropriate machines throughout the workday, and particularly at the end of it. It might be helpful to assign workers to your "switch-off" detail on a rotating basis. You might also consider sending out memos right before long weekends, holidays, and vacations to help jog everyone's memory. This program calls for initiative, but it has great potential for conserving energy. And, it's an ideal way to show your commitment to cutting energy costs.

Chart Your Savings Course

There are many other areas to consider when you're trying to discover ways to conserve energy. One good way to make sure you cover all the bases is to audit your department's "energy status" regularly. A simple checklist can help you keep track of the necessary factors.

Begin by drawing up a list of all possible energy-wasters in your department. Ask your employees for suggestions, and add their expert observations to your list. Then, once a month, take a look around to see if any of them are in fact contributing to waste. Check off the items that are an energy drain and take action to plug the leak—or contact Maintenance for help. The next month, check again to make sure the problem hasn't reoccurred.

Look at Figure 2-1 to get a general idea of how to draw up your own checklist.

Set a Shining Example

No matter how many of these energy-saving steps you ask your employees to carry out, they're not going to take you seriously unless they see that *you* are conservation conscious at all times. If you tell an employee to turn off an idle machine, and then leave your office light burning while you are in the cafeteria having lunch, you're conveying a message—but it may not be the one you intend. If you want your people to follow your lead, make sure your actions are sending the right message.

Make your message stronger by stressing that energy conservation is essential to the survival of your company in today's tough business climate. The more money your company can save on energy costs, the more secure your job and your employees' jobs are going to be. And the ability to ensure that security is well within your collective power.

> **WHAT YOU CAN DO** → *To enhance your group's conservation consciousness:*
>
> 1. Make conservation a top priority. Alert employees to the need to be careful with company energy resources.
>
> 2. Check the lighting in your department to locate areas where you can cut back on illumination.
>
> 3. Lower temperatures and have your employees wear warmer clothes to cut down on heating costs. Take proper measures to ensure maximum circulation of heated air.
>
> 4. Use an air conditioner only when absolutely necessary. Shut it off before the end of the workday to realize even more savings.
>
> 5. Start a program that encourages employees to shut off equipment when it's not in use.
>
> 6. Prepare a checklist of potential energy wasters and check them monthly.
>
> *Following these simple steps will help your company save big bucks, and will show top management that you're concerned about the use of its resources.*

ACTION PLAN:

CHAPTER THREE
THE SUPERVISOR'S TRAINING RESPONSIBILITY

TRAINING IS AN INVESTMENT

When new people become part of a department, the supervisor is presented with a golden opportunity: the chance to mold these new hires into productive, valuable members of the team. Sadly, these opportunities are often lost when the training a new worker receives is hurried, disorganized, or incomplete. Investing in effective training is the key to keeping such special occasions from passing you by.

Seize the Opportunity

Does each new employee who joins your crew fit in easily and work up to full performance capacity quickly? Or do recent hires frequently seem disoriented, confused about their duties, and unable to keep up with production and quality demands—even after they've been with the group for several months?

If the latter case strikes a more familiar chord, it might point to a lack of proper training when employees enter your department.

I know training is important, you may say. *I do the best I can with my tight schedule. Sometimes, new workers simply have to sink or swim.* You should realize, however, that when workers "sink," the overall effectiveness and productivity of your department go down with them.

"As a former supervisor, I understand the problem of having too little time to train new employees," says Bob Leber, Superintendent of Personnel Development at **Union Electric Co.** (St. Louis, MO). "All too often, other duties prevent you from giving people the benefit of your experience."

"But training is an integral part of your daily job as a supervisor. Even when your company has a formal, in-house training program like ours, it doesn't mean anything if the supervisor doesn't expect people to do their best work. Over 50 percent of our program is controlled by supervisors. We depend on them very much."

He stresses that training is an *investment*—one that you can't afford not to make. Ron Coleman, Plant Service Foreman for **Union Electric,** couldn't agree more.

"It's up to you to let new employees know you're going to help them successfully accomplish their new responsibilities," he says. "The 'sink or swim' method of training can actually waste precious time, when workers have to struggle with new skills. It's far better to *invest* in proper training."

How to Train Effectively

Leber and Coleman advocate a logical, methodical approach to training, one that consists of the following steps:

1 Identify specifically in your own mind what you want trainees to learn. You need to have a

> ## Two Training Preparation Tips
>
> Effective training always means plenty of advance preparation. You need to decide who needs to be trained, who will do the training (if you rely on training assistants), and what must be taught.
>
> But in order to make your training efforts as successful as possible, you should take preplanning a little further. With that in mind, here are two little tips for rounding out your training preparation:
>
> ◆ **Have training materials on hand and in good condition.** Make sure you have all the materials, supplies, and equipment you need. Use the highest-quality materials; don't scrimp by using flawed items. Also, don't make the mistake of using obsolete or malfunctioning machines for training.
>
> ◆ **Ready the workplace.** See to it that the workplace is properly arranged, just as you'd expect your trainees to keep it. Pay strict attention to housekeeping, and set a good example for impressionable trainees to follow.
>
> You want all of your trainees to learn under optimum working conditions. Taking the above steps will ensure that they do just that—and truly get started on the right foot.

clear idea of what your people need to know before you can properly convey such information. You might try writing a list of tasks that new hires absolutely must be able to execute to work in your department. Anything extraneous can be saved for a "training update" later on.

2 Explain and demonstrate tasks one step at a time. Give trainees time to master one skill before you add another to their work load. "Be careful not to give people too much information too quickly," warns Coleman. "Start workers out with a bare minimum of physical and mental stress."

"Don't try to do too much at one time," says Leber. "As a supervisor, you should realize that you can't create a 20-year experience level with a day or two of training."

3 Use technical terms carefully. New hires may not understand much of the technical terminology used in your department. "You might say to one of your trainees, 'Let's use that,' and mention the name of a tool that's unfamilar to the person," says Leber.

"With new employees, you should keep in mind that they may not know what some tools are. So, when you tell someone to use a certain tool, you may have to explain what it is and what it does—don't take it for granted that the person knows what everything is."

4 Invite questions. "Encourage people to ask questions openly," advises Coleman. "Effective follow-up to these queries helps workers to learn their jobs more quickly and feel comfortable in the new environment."

"You have to ask questions to get questions," states Leber. "And there's no such thing as a bad question. Every question is a good one. I feel that if people shy away from asking me about things, it may be that they don't have confidence in me."

5 Make regular progress checks. Once new employees have learned the fundamentals of their job, check their progress on a scheduled basis. If a newcomer is assigned to work with a seasoned member of the team, as many are, talk with *both* employees. This will help you to get a handle on the trainee's strengths and weaknesses, and you'll then know how best to help the worker improve his or her performance.

"Don't accept shoddy work," says Leber. "Work with trainees (or people you're retraining) until you have some assurance they can do the task. If you see someone making a mistake, redemonstrate the correct way immediately. You should always offer constructive suggestions when you call attention to a problem. It doesn't do any good simply to confront someone—point out what's wrong."

6 Give all your new people equal time. "You musn't concentrate all of your efforts on workers who are below average," says Coleman. "Pay attention to your above-average people as well. If you don't, they'll go downhill before you know it.

"You want *all* new employees to learn their jobs well. This way, whenever you assign them work, you know it will be done correctly and safely."

7 Encourage self-sufficiency, but be available

for assistance. "Keep in mind that the whole idea behind starting new hires off right is to get them to the point where they can stand on their own two feet," says Coleman. "However, you should always let trainees know that you'll be around to give them whatever guidance they need along the way."

"Keep your expectations high, but provide extra help when you see a need for improvement," says Leber.

8 Provide plenty of reassurance. Let employees know when they've done a good job," says Leber. "Sometimes we forget to show people that they've performed up to the expected level." He suggests that the importance of patience in training can't be overemphasized. "Have patience with trainees as you show them the job."

Dovetail Your Efforts With Those of Outside Trainers

As Leber stated earlier, you, the supervisor, are the key to making outside training efforts successful. If new workers are being trained outside the department, or established employees are being retrained, your attention is still sorely needed.

"We learned that you cannot hire professional trainers to come in and single-handedly solve productivity problems," he says. "If supervisors don't provide them with information about their department's needs and problems, the programs can be four times longer than necessary because they contain unnecessary information."

He cites an example that happened five years ago

Training Methods

No single training technique fills the bill all the time. Often, a combination of methods is required.

Here's a brief description of eight common training techniques and suggestions for applying them most effectively—either when used alone or in conjunction with other training methods:

Method One—Individual Instruction
Suggested use—To teach an important new or complicated skill
Example—How to operate a new or different machine
—How to use a new or redesigned form

Method Two—Group Instruction
Suggested use—To present basic facts that need not be explained at an individual's workstation
Example—Explaining the importance of an operation or the reasons for a new and different method

Method Three—Lecture
Suggested use—To provide basic information on a specific subject
Example—To provide technical information on such subjects as mathematics, electronics, and job evaluation

Method Four—Demonstration
Suggested use—To clarify the attainment of manual skills and highlight a key problem or principle
Example—To show the right way to use production machines
—To show, by using models, a solution to a work area layout problem

Method Five—Conference
Suggested use—To solve problems and direct or change attitudes
Example—How to improve attendance
—How to prevent waste

Method Six—Meeting
Suggested use—To exchange information and obtain group ideas; to solve immediate problems
Example—Department production or safety meetings

Method Seven—Written Instructions
Suggested use—To provide important information in permanent form for immediate or later use
Example—Procedure for reporting absence
—Company policy and rules

Method Eight—Oral Directions
Suggested use—To give in short form information needed immediately
Example—What job to do next
—Where to send a special order

when his company's training program was just getting off the ground: "When our apprentices were going to night school and the time came to take their certification test, 50 percent failed the test on the first try.

"Our welders must be certified because they do welds on high-pressure piping and tubing. As soon as line supervisors began participating in the formal training, the failure rate dropped to zero on the first test."

Give Them Goals to Shoot For

One common concern of new hires is the issue of advancement. Many wonder whether their new jobs will afford them the opportunity to move up in the company, or whether they will eventually become stagnant.

"Everyone's interested in personal advancement," says Coleman. "For example, one new worker told me that he'd like to become a pipe fitter. He said that on his last job he just moved turning valves. So I explained that he'd get a chance to learn pipe fitting.

"Let people know that you plan to help them develop their careers and sharpen their skills," continues Coleman.

"Then, keep records of every skill that newcomers learn, and help them to set new goals. We keep training and cross-training people as long as they are with us."

▶ WHAT YOU CAN DO → To start new hires off on the right foot . . .

1. Decide exactly what they need to know to carry out their jobs.

2. Explain and demonstrate tasks one step at a time. Also, explain technical terms—don't assume that trainees are familiar with them.

3. Invite questions by asking questions. Give trainees a chance to clear up any confusion that they may have.

4. Conduct regular progress checks, and make corrections when needed. Always let workers know you're available for help along the way.

5. Cooperate with outside training efforts. Your input is always needed to make such efforts effective.

6. Assure trainees that there's room for advancement, and give them goals to aim for.

A strong start means smooth sailing later on. Invest proper care and attention in training whenever new people come on board.

ACTION PLAN:
_____
_____
_____
_____
_____
_____
_____
_____
_____
_____
_____

INSTILL CONFIDENCE IN YOUR TRAINEES

Effective training is truly the cornerstone of good worker performance. But there's a lot more to training than simply drumming the mechanics of the job into new hires' heads. You must also dedicate your efforts to instilling in them a healthy dose of self-confidence.

Confidence Is the Key

Starting a new job can undermine the confidence of even the most self-assured person—with learning new skills, adjusting to a new schedule, and trying to fit into a new group of people. And a lack of confidence can prevent new employees from attaining the high morale and enthusiasm needed to do a job productively.

In spite of this fact, many supervisors fail to attend to new hires' need for confidence, concentrating instead on imparting the mechanics of the job. If you want your training efforts to be truly successful, however, you need to build both job skills *and* self-confidence in your trainees.

No one is more acutely aware of this than John Gray, Plant Superintendent at Skills, Inc. (Moline, IL). In fact, training for confidence is the primary focus at his firm, which operates as a nonprofit corporation specializing in rehabilitating disabled people. About 50 people constitute his staff, performing subcontracted manufacturing for area companies. Employees perform a variety of production jobs at the plant.

"We accept people in our program who show signs of physical or emotional problems in coping with a traditional work environment," Gray explains. "Most are referred from social or government agencies and from private individuals or insurance companies. But all participants have one thing in common. They must squarely face their individual handicaps and allow us to build their confidence and motivation while they learn good production skills.

"Our basic challenge is to train and follow through to make sure our staff does everything right so that we get a quality product, on time and at a good price. We know what it means to work effectively toward this goal."

Whether or not your staff is made up of handicapped workers, you can still apply Gray's principles to instill confidence in your trainees.

Evaluate First—Then Start Off Slowly

In order to reduce the stress that training can place on your new people, Gray recommends evaluating employees before you actually begin the training process. That way, you won't burden a worker right off the bat with tasks that are too difficult.

"We found out how important evaluation is to find a person's capabilities and frustration level," he says. "You can't afford a situation where the worker becomes very anxious or has a negative experience while trying to learn a complex task.

"If there's any doubt about someone's ability to perform a skill, testing is done to simulate the operation required. Then, floor supervisors carefully consider the test results and use the information to make their work assignments."

Gray strongly advises you to start new workers out on simple, repetitive tasks to increase their speed, stamina, and, most important, their confidence. "We've learned to apply this basic rule: *The simpler the task, the more confidence is built,*" he explains.

For example, in constructing box springs, many of his employees use an air-powered staple gun to fasten sections of wooden frame together. Then they place a coil and a flat spring on the frame. These procedures are fairly easy to grasp, so workers are assigned these tasks first and are allowed to practice them before receiving more complex assignments.

Make Quality Expectations Clear

Once a trainee has been taught a certain technique, it's crucial that the person soon enjoy success with the job. Otherwise, confidence is likely to flag—or fail to develop at all. In order to help new people successfully execute recently acquired skills, you need to provide them with the appropriate information during training.

"Monitoring quality is different in any operation, and maybe more so in ours," says Gray. "What it really gets down to is that for each job, both floor supervisors and workers must know all the requirements to produce a quality product. Then, a check must be made to ensure that they've been applied."

How To Deal With Training Stress

Trainees are bound to make frequent errors until a new process has been fully learned. You've come to expect this, and usually take it in stride.

However, there are times when a new worker just doesn't seem to be catching on, despite your painstaking efforts to teach a particular skill. And those times can tax even the most laid-back supervisor's patience.

When this happens, you can't afford to lose your cool. Not only would doing so make you look like an unkind, impatient supervisor but it would harm your confidence-building efforts.

"Our floor supervisors have learned how important it is to stay in control, even under stressful conditions," says John Gray. "Our workers already have problems and don't need any more."

How can *you* "stay in control" when dealing with a trainee who's having more than a fair share of problems with getting the hang of things? Here are four suggestions:

★ **Take a "time out."** If you find yourself becoming dangerously frustrated, remove yourself from the situation for a few moments. Take a quick walk around the plant, go outside for a breath of fresh air, or flip through some reading material at your desk. Just give yourself a change of scene. It will clear your head and enable you to face training tasks with renewed resolve.

★ **Ask a trusted worker to aid with training.** Many new hires may feel intimidated by "the big boss" (you) and consequently become so nervous that they botch even the simplest of tasks. And the more they mess up, the more uptight you can become; it's a vicious circle.

You might ease this situation by asking an experienced worker to take over the task of training a new person for an hour or so. The trainee may respond more readily to a peer on the crew. And you'll be able to take a much-needed "breather."

★ **Talk over training problems with your own boss.** Gray instructs his supervisors to come to him whenever they're frustrated with a new hire's progress. How can this help you?

It's a good way to get things off your chest. Plus, your boss may provide some valuable insight on how to deal effectively with the situation.

★ **Confer with fellow supervisors.** Discovering that your peers have faced similar frustrations can help to alleviate that "why me?" feeling many supervisors get when things are going awry. In addition, your colleagues may be able to offer you some sound advice.

A good time to discuss training problems with other supervisors is during regular department meetings. "Monthly meetings are an excellent time to share training tips with other supervisors," asserts Gray. "They also provide an opportunity to encourage one another when the training program becomes very demanding."

Suggestion: Post or hand out written specifications for each product your people manufacture so that they can see exactly what's expected of them. Sharing quality guidelines with workers gives them a point of reference for assessing their own progress, and helps to ensure that they'll meet the standards. And the more quickly workers master a job, the earlier they'll develop the self-assurance necessary to strive toward higher skill levels.

Follow-up Is Essential

Your ongoing support and guidance are of utmost importance in ensuring long-term training effectiveness. You can provide this support in three ways, suggests Gray:

■ **Double-check all tasks.** Don't just deliver directions and leave your people to fend for themselves. Observe workers on a regular, daily basis to make sure they're on the right track. And if they're not, don't come down hard and heavy.

You should always *temper criticism with tact.* When someone makes a mistake, first reassure the individual that you appreciate the effort, stresses Gray. Then, explain that you want to help the person to do a better job and that you'll work closely with him or her to make improvements.

■ **Maintain your composure at all times.** Sometimes it might be difficult for you to maintain your composure with a worker who's not catching on. But you need to keep a cool head, or your training efforts will be thwarted. Few things can cut a trainee's confidence to the quick like having a new supervisor blow up during training.

(See Box for some tips on how to stay serene in a trying training situation.)

■ **Solicit feedback.** Approach your new people directly, and ask if they are experiencing problems in any particular area. Even if a worker seems to have the hang of a job, he or she may still be having a tough time understanding certain aspects.

You can clear up these problems by opening the forum for candid, open, one-on-one discussions.

■ **Give plenty of encouragement.** Trainees need lots of positive reinforcement to work up to potential. So you should always tell trainees when they've done a good job—it's a proven way to build confidence as workers develop and improve skills.

Confidence-Building Pays Off

The training method developed by John Gray was designed primarily for disabled workers. That's why it is especially thorough and considerate.

But implementing a comprehensive strategy like Gray's can greatly benefit *any* training effort—because, when you think about it, everyone is "handicapped"—to one degree or another. All workers possess shortcomings in addition to their strengths, and it's up to you to address each one as you strive to impart both job skills and self-reliance to your new hires.

Gray reports that since he has adopted such an attentive training philosophy, productivity at Skills has increased severalfold.

"You must be genuinely interested in and concerned about your trainees to accomplish this," he emphasizes. "But it can be done—even under stressful conditions. Remember, your employees are the ones who will make you or break your production efforts."

▶ **WHAT YOU CAN DO** → *Building self-confidence in your trainees is pivotal to the success of any training effort. So when training new hires, make sure you . . .*

1. Evaluate new hires. That way, you'll pinpoint raw skill levels and avoid placing newcomers under undue stress.

2. Start trainees off on simple, repetitive tasks. Then move toward more complex operations.

3. Make quality expectations clear. It's one way to ensure that trainees make a minimum of mistakes.

4. Double-check all tasks for accuracy—don't leave trainees to flounder.

5. Maintain your composure during training—don't fly off the handle, no matter how much your patience is taxed.

6. Ask workers for feedback and address their questions promptly.

7. Give positive reinforcement whenever possible.

Remember: Confidence-building is part of the training process that should never be neglected. Do all you can to make certain that all employees who enter your department develop both skills and self-assurance.

ACTION PLAN:
_____
_____
_____
_____
_____
_____
_____
_____
_____
_____
_____
_____
_____

PROPER ORIENTATION IS IMPORTANT

When a new employee starts in your department, it takes him or her a while to get up to speed. There are new people to meet, a new layout to learn, and new procedures to become familiar with. It can take a worker six months to two years to become a fully productive member of your team. So just think how much better it would be to shorten the break-in period!

Make It As Effective— And Short—As Possible

Let's say your department has just added a new employee, whom we'll call Bill. Naturally, Bill will start receiving his salary the first day on the job. But will your company be getting the productivity that it's paying for on that first day? Probably not.

It's only natural for a worker to take some time to learn the ropes, but you should strive to make that time as short as possible. That way, your company gets a return on its "investment" in the least amount of time.

Begin Before the Beginning

Shortening the break-in period requires you to make some preparations before the new employee walks through the door of your plant. These preparations include getting your other workers ready to meet, accept, and work with the new hire.

Your first step is to alert the general workforce that an addition to the department is expected. Ideally, this announcement should be made at a group meeting, which means you won't have to inform each worker individually—and possibly neglect to inform someone.

The next step is to talk with the employees who will be working directly with or alongside the new person. Tell them what duties the rookie will have, and ask them to be available if the employee has work-related questions. They'll be pleased that you think enough of them to ask for their help, and will probably be more than happy to provide some aid.

Your final step before the new employee comes on board is to select a trusted veteran worker to "take charge" of the rookie. This person can show the new worker the ropes and can be available to answer questions if you're not around at the moment. Using this type of "buddy system" also helps the new employee to gain acceptance from the general workforce, because he or she will be seen as already accepted by someone whom the others have known for a long time.

On the First Day

Breaking in workers effectively means helping them learn the layout of the plant and the basic rules of the department, as well as the techniques that will make them productive workers. Especially if the new hire must interact with people in other departments, you (or a designated subordinate) should conduct a tour of the facility before putting the rookie to work. Show the employee where the cafeteria is, where the rest rooms are located, where the personnel office is, and where he or she can get first aid if necessary.

When the tour is over, give the employee a simple map of the workplace in case he or she forgets where an important room, item, or person can be found. This map need not be a layout of the entire plant. To make it effective—and useful—decide which departments and rooms new employees will have to be famliar with, and then sketch them out on a basic floor plan of your plant.

Remember, the more landmarks your map includes, the easier it will be for employees to use. Water fountains, fire extinguishers, windows, and bulletin boards are all good landmarks to use as points of reference on your map.

Taking the time to draw up the map has a double benefit: Not only will the employee develop confidence because he or she won't have to ask directions, but neither your time nor your subordinates' will be taken up in repeatedly giving those directions.

Tell Them the Rules

The next step in the breaking-in process is telling new employees the rules of the department as they relate to safety and acceptable behavior. At many companies, the personnel department supplies new employees with a sheet or booklet containing company rules and policies. If this is the case at your plant, only a supplementary list will be necessary.

This supplementary list should include the rules

that are specific to your department or operation. It should also highlight those particular rules you feel strongest about. Why is this so important?

Let's say that your new worker, Bill, wants some time off for a doctor's appointment. As a new employee, he doesn't have any vacation time yet. Furthermore, the appointment isn't a medical emergency and could easily be scheduled on a Saturday. But because he doesn't want to tie up a Saturday going to the doctor, Bill decides it would be convenient to take a "sick day" off during the week.

What Bill isn't aware of yet is that you feel very strongly that sick time should be taken only in the event of true illness. Bill could save himself the trouble of asking and you the trouble of answering no if you make it very clear on the list of rules that you feel this way about use of sick time.

The bottom line is that you must tell new workers not only the rules but also how you enforce the rules. Why waste time and energy letting each new employee stumble into the knowledge of how you interpret the rules when it would be so much easier to lay it out clearly for workers the first day on the job?

Basic Training —And Not So Basic

Of course, the major part of the break-in period is spent teaching a new employee the techniques and methods of the job. You can carry out this task yourself or assign the task to a veteran subordinate, but there's no way around it: You must give new employees a solid foundation in the skills they will need to perform effectively.

While you don't want to overburden new hires with details when training, you can shorten the break-in period considerably by including an explanation of certain contingency measures to be used in case of unusual situations. Drawing on your experiences, or those of your employees, tell your rookies about common problems inherent in the job and typical ways in which they are dealt with.

For example, if you have a policy of calling Maintenance immediately when a machine begins to leak oil, rather than having workers keep on going or try to fix the problem themselves, tell new hires.

Armed with this type of information, new employees will be better able to cope with problems themselves, without interrupting the work of others. Any potential "emergency" or unfamiliar situation will become just part of the routine the worker is expected to know. Naturally, you will still want to encourage employees to come to you if a problem develops that no one in your department has experienced before. The solution you devise can then become part of the regular training regimen for any employees you add to your group in the future.

A Special Case

There's a particular type of new employee to whom you should give special consideration during the break-in period. These are the people who have experience in the type of work done in your department, but who have never worked for your company.

A supervisor who hires a person with this kind of experience may think the person does not require the same comprehensive orientation. This is a dangerous misconception, however, and should be avoided.

These people may have experience, but they still don't know what the layout of the plant is, what rules your company has, and what steps to take when an emergency arises. No matter how technically proficient an employee is, these areas must be addressed if you want to properly initiate the person into your department and into your company.

Make It a Routine

Shortening the break-in period for new employees is fairly easy, as long as you devote some thought and work to it. To make it even easier, develop a set routine for breaking in recent arrivals to your department. This routine should become second nature to you, in the same way that other aspects of your job have become routine.

There are a lot of predictable snags that new workers will run into when trying to learn the ropes. Pinpointing those problem areas *for* these employees and explaining how to get around them will be a big help in getting these workers off to a smooth start.

Supervisors who spend a few minutes laying the groundwork for rookies will see the time pay off down the road, when the break-in period is shortened and the new worker quickly becomes a productive employee.

▶ **WHAT YOU CAN DO** → *Management is counting on you to make new workers productive as rapidly as possible. You'll accomplish this more successfully if you...*

1. Prepare veteran workers for the new arrival. Assign a "buddy" to show the rookie the ropes.

2. Give new hires a tour of the plant, pointing out important stops along the way.

3. Draw up a simple map of the sites a worker will need to be familar with, using landmarks for clarity. Make copies for future new hires to carry with them.

4. Explain the rules relating to safety and acceptable behavior. And be sure you explain what form your discipline takes so that there will be no misunderstandings.

5. Outline contingency measures. This is where you can make the greatest gains in shortening the overall break-in period. Give employees backup information they can use when faced with an unusual situation.

6. Give each new hire, regardless of past experience, the same comprehensive orientation. Don't take anything—or anyone—for granted.

By accelerating the process of breaking in new workers, you'll be able to meet the challenge of orienting and training them thoroughly, but in an economical period of time.

ACTION PLAN:
_____
_____
_____
_____
_____
_____
_____
_____
_____
_____
_____
_____
_____
_____
_____
_____
_____

ASSESSING TRAINING NEEDS

Training is not only something you do to develop the skills of new hires when they enter the department. In order to keep employees' skills sharp throughout their careers on your staff, you must make training a continuing process. And the first move toward preparing your ongoing training program is to determine what type of training would best suit the needs of each member of your team.

Take an Inventory

A first step in a continuing training program is to determine where employees now stand—in other words, who needs additional training and who is trainable. A practical way to do this is to list all the people in your department by job clas-

JOB BREAKDOWN	
IMPORTANT STEPS —*What the Employee Must DO*— Every separate part of an operation that advances the work toward completion. (Include setting of Speeds and Feeds; Number and Depth of Cuts; Dimensions and Tolerances.)	**KEY POINTS** —*What the Employee Must KNOW*— Anything in a Step that might: "Make" or "Break" the Job; save time, energy, or material; prevent trouble, accidents, or damage. Knacks or "Tricks of the Trade."

(FIGURE 3-1)

sification. Include their time with the company and length of time in their present positions.

A simple form can be prepared to show how employees fit into the following groups:

1 Those planning to retire in a few years who have indicated they're content in their present jobs and have no wish to upgrade their skills. If, however, it becomes evident that some retraining is necessary—say, if new technology is introduced into the department—you'll have to be ready to do a selling job with them.

2 Those who are fully qualified in their current positions and can be trained for advancement.

3 Those who are trainable and need training to improve on their present jobs. This group might be considered for promotion in the near future.

4 Those who still require training to come up to standard on their present jobs.

5 Those who have thus far demonstrated limited potential for improvement, but who might benefit from additional guidance.

A simple form can be prepared to show how employees break down into these groups. Remember, workers should be *carefully evaluated* prior to being classified. When you have finished, a complete summary should be included on the form used, showing graphically where employees now stand.

Pinpointing Job Requirements

In addition to determining *who* needs to be taught, you must look into *what* needs to be taught. This is where making a "Job Breakdown" card (Figure 3-1) can be useful.

It is easy to forget details and overlook things when you're teaching a job that's so obvious to you. The Job Breakdown is an effective memory jogger for you (or your assistant trainers), which also ensures uniform instruction on the same jobs and establishes a ready reference for the next time this training is needed. You should set up a separate card for each job in your department.

When breaking down a job, you must consider *all* the requirements of the job. On the left side of the card, for example, you should list, in careful order, the concrete steps needed to bring a task to completion. On the right side, you should list the *knowledge* a worker needs to acquire in order to carry out the job successfully. This includes safe-

JOB ANALYSIS CHART

Operations (Steps)	Operation Points (What to do)	Knowledge Factors (How to do it)
1 _____	(1) _____	(1) _____
	(2) _____	(2) _____

NOTE: Job title should be fully descriptive, enough to distinguish it from all others. An operation is a step within a job; steps may vary in size. In breaking down a job into operations, keep this in mind—each operation should include a group of activities that, taken together, will result in a definite step toward performance of the job. Operation points are small groups of activities necessary to job performance—they show what is to be done. Knowledge factors bring out how it is done.

To illustrate, here's a sample of a filled-out Job Analysis Chart with an assumed job title as an example:

JOB ANALYSIS CHART

Operations (Steps)	Operation Points (What to do)	Knowledge Factors (How to do it)
I Remove protective covering.	(1) Slit protective covering with braid-stripping tool provided by company.	(1) a) Remove all kinks from cable where covering is to be removed. b) Hold cable in left hand above point from which covering is to be removed. c) Hook cable stripper into covering at point from which covering is to be removed. d) Use forefinger of right hand to guide blade of stripper. e) When blade is firmly engaged in covering, shift right forefinger to lower guard of stripper. f) Encircle cable and handle of stripper with remainder of fingers. g) Place right thumb on top of stripper, clear of hole. h) Pull stripper firmly to end of cable, slitting covering.
	(2) Peel covering full length at slit	(2) a) Use long-nose or diagonal pliers to spread covering on each side of slit at end of cable for several inches. b) Grasp covering in left hand. c) Grasp core of cable in right hand. d) Peel covering from cable to end of slit by pulling covering and core in opposite directions.

(FIGURE 3-2)

JOB TRAINING PROGRESS RECORD

Trainee   Department   Unit

Position

INSTRUCTION ON THE JOB

NOTE: Record hours of training in black opposite work job and in column showing date of training.

No.	WORK JOBS	HOURS REQUIRED	DATES OF TRAINING	TOTAL HOURS COMPLETED
1.				
2.				
3.				
	TOTAL HOURS			

The job performance and knowledge on the above work jobs are satisfactory.

Date   Instructor   Date   Supervisor

(FIGURE 3-3)

ty and contingency measures, and any "tricks of the trade" that will help a trainee learn to do a job more efficiently.

The Job Analysis

Another way in which you may break down jobs in your department to facilitate training is to write out a Job Analysis of each task (see Figure 3-2). This involves dividing your department's overall operation into the major areas of work, then into smaller subdivisions.

Then, subdivision work can be further broken down into individual knowledge factors—"how to do" each task. This procedure of dividing a job into smaller operations—and each operation into knowledge factors—ensures a systematic and thorough analysis.

Once you've analyzed jobs in this manner, you will be better able to pinpoint the areas in which your employees need additional training.

The Progress Report

Whether you're training new hires or retraining experienced people, keeping records is a must. You need to know exactly how much training each worker has received in a given area so that you can better assess how well the person is doing and how much additional training might be necessary.

That's where maintaining Job Training Progress Records (see Figure 3-3) for each employee comes in. All that is needed is a simple daily notation of what each worker has been taught. On the front of the record, you insert the work job to be learned and the number of hours of training required.

After the instruction has been administered, you record when it was given and for how long. On the back of the record, you may make a notation of any special instruction that the worker received, either by you, an assistant trainer, or a companywide or outside training program. This rounds out your picture of an employee's training experiences and evolving skill level. Keeping progress reports is also beneficial because it gives your people proof of their accomplishments.

> ▶ **WHAT YOU CAN DO** → *To assess your training needs effectively:*
>
> 1. Perform a needs analysis for each worker on your staff. Determine which employees require additional training to develop into the most productive and highly skilled workers they can be.
>
> 2. Set up a Job Breakdown card for each job in your department. Sort out what workers need to do, and what they need to know, to perform each one efficiently.
>
> 3. Perform a Job Analysis of your operation, dividing the overall operation into smaller procedures and steps.
>
> 4. Compare employees' skills levels with your job analyses, to determine which workers require more instruction to learn new jobs or better perform the ones they're already responsible for.
>
> 5. Use Job Training Progress Records to keep track of the training each worker receives.
>
> *In order to make ongoing training effective, you need a systematic approach. That's why it's important to be analytical and thorough in determining training needs.*
>
> **ACTION PLAN:**
> _____
> _____
> _____
> _____
> _____
> _____
> _____
> _____
> _____
> _____
> _____
> _____
> _____

PUT TRAINING INSTRUCTIONS IN WRITING

Any supervisor faced with the task of training needs as many tools to assist with the process as possible. One such tool that is a boon to many companies' training programs is the instruction manual. Let's see how this aid can benefit your training efforts.

A Valuable Tool

When you and your assistants must train new hires or retrain long-term workers, you have a formidable task ahead. You must convey vital information about work procedures as effectively as possible if you want workers to put out a stellar performance.

At such times, you and your trainers need all the help you can get. After all, it can be difficult to meet your many work obligations in a timely manner and still address adequate attention to the needs of your trainees—especially when there's always so much a new worker should ideally learn.

That's where training manuals can be a big help.

When clearly and comprehensively written, these reference guides can give trainees easy access to the answers they need. And, because all trainees are given the same manual to study, you ensure that each worker receives identical information—something that can't always be guaranteed when each new hire is trained by a different training assistant.

Who Should Develop the Guidebook?

Your first step in developing a reference guide is to determine what type of information it should contain. Your best bet is to go right to your experienced people and ask for their input.

Why should you consult veteran employees? They know the job better than anyone else. They will be able to determine effectively what information a new hire needs to get the job done—and done well. And that's the main purpose of a training manual: It's a tool to help new people do their work. It should contain information that's easy to understand and to the point; it should *not* be an intimidating, overly technical manual that employees will find too confusing.

Setting It Up

To make the guidebook easy to use, compile job-related information by topic in a notebook or a ring binder. Use a tab system to make subjects convenient to locate.

The topics your experienced people include in your department's reference guide can run the gamut from the meaning of company jargon to ways of recognizing flawed materials or products. It might contain sections of technical, equipment-oriented manuals or employee handbooks that directly pertain to your work group.

The following is a rundown of some of the areas you may want to cover:

■ **Safety.** Even though your company's employee handbook may cover safety in detail, there are always special considerations for every department. Because it has been compiled by employees, your guidebook can explore these from the worker's point of view.

The value of safety will be more likely to hit home if employees can apply specific rules to their own work situations. Remember, the idea is to make sure a trainee knows how to respond to any safety problem that might be encountered in the course of the job.

■ **Department organization.** Spell out who employees can talk to about job problems if you are unavailable or absent. Make sure that workers know the responsibilities of each leadperson, supervisor, and manager. Then they will know where to go should they have specific difficulties.

■ **Equipment.** Give employees a complete description of all the equipment used in the department. Include information on function, start-up and shut-down, safety features, and routine maintenance. Mention the importance of proper handling of all equipment, and any special care particularly sensitive machines might need.

■ **Definitions.** Provide a specialized glossary in the guide so that newcomers can look up the meaning of unfamiliar words or phrases. New employees can become frustrated when they hear terms they can't understand. And a lack of understanding prohibits trainees from giving their all on the job.

■ **Scheduling.** Instruct employees in how to read work schedules and in methods for counting materials and production units. Your schedule might include the size and type of materials used, the customer it's going to, the date it's due to be shipped, and so on.

■ **Floor policies.** Explain the rules of the plant, such as those governing hours, overtime policies, work breaks, and other matters that affect day-to-day functioning of the department.

■ **Use of idle time.** List ways employees can be productive during slow or idle periods. For example, you might encourage people who finish ahead of schedule to pitch in and help others.

■ **Special product handling requirements.** Include the names of all customers whose products require special handling procedures.

■ **Materials handling.** List the materials used in the manufacturing process. Describe the proper procedures for handling each type.

■ **Materials procurement procedures.** If new employees are sent to get materials, they should know exactly where they are located and how they should remove those materials from their storage areas.

■ **Workstation setup.** Spell out how to set up

workstations and where to place working materials so that they are close at hand.

■ **Defect standards.** What constitutes a defect? How severe must a defect be before the material is unusable? To save money and time, make sure this information is clear-cut.

■ **Waste handling.** Set forth your waste-handling policy. You can save a lot of dollars in your department if workers are careful to reuse or recycle scrap instead of throwing it away.

■ **Production overview.** Show employees how what they produce fits into the entire production process. Giving trainees an idea of how their work fits into the big picture will drive home the importance of producing precise, high-quality material.

Once the manual has been completely compiled by your experienced people, make sure you include authorship credit. The book should state that a group of employees produced it. A worker-produced handbook means more to employees, both new and old, than one put together by people who have never even set foot on the production floor.

The Benefits of Putting It in Writing

What are the advantages of having training instructions set down in writing? You will have standardized material to guide instruction. And you'll also have set performance standards, which will be of great value when you conduct performance evaluations later on.

Another plus is that written training instructions are tangible. They remain the same until you need to update them. But when you rely on oral training communication backed only by your memory, you may not give exactly the same instruction each time. And you may end up saying something like this to a trainee: "I know you think you understand what I think I said. But I'm pretty sure you don't realize that what you heard is not what I meant."

That message, of course, is almost incomprehensible. But it does point out that some oral communication is difficult to understand. You *need* written guidelines to back up your oral instruction. With written directions in hand, you and your trainees will have less room for misunderstanding.

▶ **WHAT YOU CAN DO** → *To put training instructions on paper effectively . . .*

1. Ask veteran workers to asist you in composing a training manual. Their experience will be invaluable to this effort.

2. Set up the manual topic by topic in a notebook or binder, using tabs to make information easier to locate.

3. Include all relevant subjects in the manual. Cover such topics as safety, work procedures, job behavior, and quality considerations.

4. Give authorship credit to the employees who've helped you develop the manual.

Using training reference guides can be a great way to help new employees find their way in your department. Because the guides give trainees a source for handy reference, they will free up a substantial amount of the time you and your assistants formerly spent in answering questions.

ACTION PLAN:

_____
_____
_____
_____
_____
_____
_____
_____
_____
_____

BUILD WORKER SKILLS WITH COACHING AND COUNSELING

Your initial goal in training employees is to help them develop the high skill level they require to work productively in your department. But after you've finished training new hires, you have a new objective: ensuring that their skills remain sharp. How can you achieve this aim? By exercising two of your own supervisory skills: namely, coaching and counseling.

It's a Continuing Challenge

Whenever new hires join the ranks, you have a challenge: turning them into productive members of your staff. This means devoting a great deal of attention to your novices when they first enter the department.

But once an employee is working up to par, your training duties are only half over. Why? Because your workers will still need your attention—on an ongoing basis—to maintain the high skill levels you strove to impart at the start.

All too often, performance takes a definite downswing soon after many employees have completed their initial training period and have been left to work on their own. This can happen for a variety of reasons: personal pressures, lack of confidence, job tensions, or just plain boredom. But whatever the reason, you can't afford to stand idly by and watch recently trained, enthusiastic novices devolve into poor producers.

You need to continue your skill-building efforts by engaging in daily coaching and counseling.

Coach to Strengthen Abilities

When you coach your employees, you follow the example of a typical athletic coach—instructing and training your team members. If you do it well, your people will want to make high performance their personal goal.

To reach this point, you'll have to train your staff to be analytical. They have to learn both from their mistakes and from positive experiences. It takes patience and perseverance, but if you're willing to put forth the effort, coaching will allow you to create a workforce composed of highly skilled achievers.

In exactly what ways can you use coaching to help your ongoing training efforts? Consider applying it in the following areas:
- To help an employee recognize the need to improve in a specific area
- To offer information, guidance, and additional training when needed
- To provide an opportunity to master a brand-new skill
- To secure a commitment toward a common performance or productivity goal

As you can see, coaching is designed to build capabilities. As such, it involves helping your people to learn new skills and maintain or improve current ones. But isn't it a waste of time to dwell on skills that have already been learned?

Not at all. Following up to make sure employees' skills haven't eroded is just as crucial as preparing them for the future.

Four Steps to Effective Coaching

You've learned that coaching is geared toward teaching and polishing worker skills. These four steps will help you get your message across more clearly as you coach an employee:

★ **Demonstrate the specific skill you want the employee to master.** Showing the person precisely what you would like him or her to do will clear up any potential confusion. It will also give the person a tangible goal to shoot for.

★ **Ask the worker to perform the task** before you leave him or her to carry it out alone. That way, the person will be able to ask questions, and you'll be able to determine whether further instruction is necessary.

★ **Give feedback on employee performance.** This should be in the form of positive reinforcement (such as praise) if the job was done properly, or constructive criticism if the worker did the task incorrectly.

★ **Make adjustments until the skill has been learned.** It might take time, but give the worker whatever guidance is needed to get the job done right. Your rewards will come when the employee finally gets the hang of the job and you have a more productive worker in the department.

The Basics of Counseling

Whereas coaching builds capabilities, counseling is aimed at ensuring competence. It allows you to help employee attitudes by dealing with problems—both job-related and personal—that can cause poor performance.

Counseling involves face-to-face discussions with your people, in which you talk over impediments to career development. These impediments may include feelings of boredom and stagnancy, plus the belief by some workers that they've been placed in a job for which they are poorly suited.

Off-the-job problems that are having a detrimental effect on productivity—for example, marital or financial difficulties or substance abuse—are more difficult issues for you to deal with. After all, you aren't a trained doctor or psychological counselor, and you therefore lack the expertise necessary to adequately address these types of problems. When counseling workers, then, you must broach only job-related issues. (If you have strong reason to suspect that the root of a poor performance is a deeply personal difficulty, or if an employee openly admits to such a problem, refer the person to professional assistance.)

In addition to the problems mentioned above, a variety of performance killers can be corrected by counseling. Here are just a few examples:

- Unsatisfactory job performance
- Poor relationship with you or peers
- Frequent bouts of temper or lack of cooperation
- Chronic tardiness or absenteeism
- Poor attitude toward the company

Keep in mind that counseling is not something you do to an employee, it's something you do *with* an employee. You must remember that an individual's actions are based on personal perceptions about the situation. No one will change behavior without having a good reason to do so.

Therefore, when counseling, you need to help the employee to change the perceptions and attitudes that will—in turn—change the behavior that's affecting job performance.

The approach you use when counseling employees will depend upon your personality, the employee's temperament, and the problem at hand. Here are three good approaches to take:

◆ **The Directive Approach.** This involves asking specific questions designed to pinpoint the reasons for the performance problems you have observed. This approach usually prevents the employee from sidestepping the issue or passing the buck. It's the quickest way to get to the bottom of the difficulty.

◆ **The Nondirective Approach.** When using this technique, you introduce the subject to be discussed—say, a worker's sudden difficulty with carrying out a certain task. Then you let the employee guide and direct the conversation. The benefit of this approach is that it gives workers a chance to unburden themselves and disclose the real reason behind their apparent inability to do a job—for example, a dispute with a co-worker.

◆ **The Joint Approach.** This is a mutual discussion of the issue at hand, and can usually only take place when there is an open, trusting relationship between you and the worker. It allows both of you to get to the heart of the matter quickly.

To Coach or Counsel?

Now that you know the basics of coaching and counseling, how can you tell which of your employees require which type of attention? Each of your people falls into one or another of four groups, and there are different courses of action to follow for each circumstance:

■ **Case #1: Low-competence, incompletely trained workers.** Although you may believe you've adequately trained each and every worker on your staff, think carefully. Have there ever been instances when a new hire has joined the team on a day when you were particularly busy with attending to other tasks? Perhaps the person really didn't receive as much comprehensive training as he or she needs to do an outstanding job.

If this is the case, the person is not ready for either coaching or counseling. Instead, you need to put the person through a general training program and get him or her working up to par. Later on, you can concentrate on coaching to maintain a basic skill level and on troubleshooting performance problems.

■ **Case #2: High-competence, incompletely trained employees.** If you have workers who are bright and enthusiastic, yet they haven't been trained in as many skills as possible, their talents are being wasted.

A Guide to Effective Cross-Training

One way in which many supervisors enrich their employees' skills is to *cross-train* them, or teach them how to perform the jobs of other workers in the group. The benefits of cross-training are severalfold: First, learning new skills provides employees with a challenge. It gives them new goals to strive for and injects variety into their jobs; this, in turn, boosts morale and enthusiasm.

Second, cross-training makes workers more valuable to the department and to the company; the more tasks they are qualified to carry out, the more responsibility you can give them. And the better they can fill in when co-workers are out sick or on vacation, and lend a hand in other areas when there's a big production push or a major change in operations.

One group of supervisors used cross-training effectively when new, automated equipment was installed in their production department. They realized that it would be necessary for employees to assist one another on the line while the new system was being implemented, in order to keep production moving swiftly. How did these supervisors go about cross-training their people? Here's the course of action they followed:

▶ **Train two other employees for each worker's job.** The supervisors decided that although the cross-trained workers would be familar with the absent employee's job, they wouldn't be quite as adept as the employee who was experienced in the position. So when fill-ins were needed, two heads would ultimately be better than one.

▶ **Switch workers around during the course of the shift.** That way, employees would enjoy some variety while gaining practical experience in the jobs they were cross-trained in.

▶ **Let workers decide when to switch from one job to the next.** Once workers gain a reasonable amount of experience in each position, give them the authority to decide when they should switch jobs or move to another area to provide assistance. This helps to finely sharpen their newly acquired skills. (Of course, you should monitor their activities to be sure they're working and switching in an efficient manner.)

Three Things to Keep in Mind

Whenever you are cross-training employees, there are three factors you should remember: employee comprehension, goal-setting, and employee consideration. Here's why attention to these three areas can make your cross-training efforts a success:

● **Comprehension.** The first component of effective cross-training is making sure that each of the employees to be involved has a thorough understanding of the purpose and the need for cross-training. Why is this important?

Because employees often become anxious when they find themselves being trained for a different position and they don't know *why* they are being so trained. They may be afraid they are losing their old positions, or they may be concerned about their ability to handle the additional duties.

So, it is essential that you explain why cross-training is occurring; that is, to enhance employee skills, offer variety, and make a more productive department.

● **Goal-setting.** You need goals to keep the cross-training activity in your department on schedule. If you don't set a target and develop a review process to check progress periodically, your program will not be successful.

Setting realistic goals will be easier if you get input from several different sources. You'll need input—and commitment, of course—from higher management. You'll require you own ideas, as well, and those of the workers to be cross-trained.

Also, someone from the training and development department should be consulted. Such a person has an overall picture of the company and a knowledge of the progress being made in cross-training throughout the organization.

Then, *set a schedule* for the attainment of your cross-training goals—and stick to it. Arrange to have the employees who are involved receive training in a certain area for a specific amount of time, and then move on to the next area, also for an allotted amount of time.

● **Consideration.** Overloading employees during cross-training is a big mistake. In most cases, they will still have responsibilities for their regular functions as they are learning new tasks. So, arrange to have someone else take some of the burden for their usual jobs, or set up the training schedule so that workers are not rushed into learning.

In this case, you should coach the employee one-on-one, demonstrating and imparting more advanced skills and procedures so that the person may work up to higher levels of technical expertise.

■ **Case #3: Low-competence, completely trained employees.** If you have a worker who has been thoroughly trained in general procedures but remains unproductive, counseling is in order.

Your goal should be to unearth the causes of low productivity—for example, any of the problems we discussed above. If an employee has been properly trained and still seems unable to handle the job, it's highly likely that an underlying problem is impeding good performance.

■ **Case #4: High-competence, completely trained employees.** Here, the worker is focusing energy where it should be, on getting the job done, and is highly productive and quality-conscious. With this type of excellent employee, you may be inclined to train the worker in progressively more advanced skills and duties and then sit back and watch the person produce. But don't get too comfortable!

It's possible to give a good worker too much too soon, and that could lead to burnout (in which case, you'd have to counsel the person). The most sensible way to deal with a #4 worker is simply to coach the person in new skills gradually, always setting new, but attainable goals. That way, you'll prevent the problems that can occur when a fine employee feels overburdened.

Daily Improvement

Whether you use coaching, counseling, or a combination of the two, you're providing workers with a necessary supplement to your general training program. You're giving them the special attention they need to maintain—and surpass—the level of performance they attained after their initial training period.

Coaching and counseling on a daily basis also eliminates the need for exhaustive retraining efforts. It's easier to work with employees every day than it is to allow their skills to become obsolete and have to start all over again.

It's better for the employees, too, because they'll find it far easier to learn a little each day than to learn everything all at once.

▶ **WHAT YOU CAN DO** → *You can make training a continuing process if you . . .*

1. Commit yourself to learning the skills of coaching and counseling to help workers to produce at full potential.

2. Use one-on-one coaching to help workers polish old skills and acquire new ones.

3. Ask employees to demonstrate a particular skill you want them to master, or to show you work they've completed so that you can offer constructive feedback.

4. Counsel your people face-to-face to get at the root of job-related and personal problems that are causing skills to slip.

5. Act on career impediments that you have the power to do something about—such as feelings of job frustration. Refer difficult personal problems to company or outside experts.

6. Learn to distinguish the four main types of workers, and categorize your people accordingly. Then ad-

ACTION PLAN:

dress each employee's individual training needs.

As a supervisor, you're in the ideal position to help your people to develop and maintain the skills they need to be truly productive. Individualized coaching and counseling are two tools that can help you to accomplish this challenging goal.

DEVELOPING EMPLOYEE TRAINERS

If you're like most supervisors, you'll agree that training is one of your most crucial supervisory tasks. Proper training is one of the paramount factors in helping new workers achieve maximum performance and productivity. However, it can be difficult for busy supervisors to find enough time to devote to training efforts. That's just one reason why you should develop mentors among your staff.

Train Some Trainers

You'll probably agree that training employees is one of the key jobs you carry out. It's absolutely essential that new workers learn how to use equipment properly, which work methods and techniques will lead to top productivity, and what the rules of the department are.

Naturally, you probably believe that, of all the people in your department, you're best qualified to teach new employees their jobs.

You're correct in that belief. Chances are that no one else has the knowledge, experience, and judgment you possess; otherwise, you wouldn't be the supervisor. But just because you're the *best* trainer, that doesn't mean you're the *only* person in your department who's capable of doing an adequate training job.

Finding and developing trainers among the people you supervise can save you valuable time in the long run, increase your own productivity on the job, and provide a morale boost to those employees who act as training assistants.

Who's Right for the Job?

Before you can begin training trainers, you have to locate some likely candidates. It's possible that you already know of one or two members of your staff who could be trusted to carry out training duties. However, you could be overlooking some equally qualified instructors.

Here are many of the qualities that make a person an effective teacher of fellow employees. Consider whether any members of your workforce fill the bill:

★ **Expertise.** You'll want your trainers to be proficient in the tasks that they are assigned to teach. And you'll want them to teach newcomers the most efficient ways of doing things without compromising quality standards. (Still, you should make it clear that you'll be available to answer any questions the trainers might have about a particular job they are teaching. You wouldn't want them to pass along inaccurate information to their trainees.)

★ **Patience.** A good trainer must be patient with the learning employee in order to get the best results. Flying off the handle when a mistake is made and trying to push the initiate too hard are common mistakes made by inexperienced trainers—and can completely undermine a new hire's self-confidence.

★ **Honesty.** The trainer must be honest enough to tell the new employee how easy or difficult a particular task will be. That way, the worker will never be surprised—and thus discouraged—when a task turns out to be harder than expected.

Also, the trainer must be able to address openly a trainee's weaknesses as well as strengths. It doesn't do a new hire any good to be told that he or she is excelling in a certain task when, in reality, the person is fouling up. New workers must be

BEST-QUALIFIED TRAINER CHECKLIST

Rate your candidates on a comparative basis on each of the following qualifications. Whomever you consider as excellent gets a double check (✓ ✓); single check (✓) for acceptable; X for inadequate or unacceptable. Whoever gets the most check marks and the fewest X's is your logical choice for your "stand-in" trainer.

Qualifications	A B C Candidates
Works accurately	
Knows the job thoroughly	
Is cost conscious	
Puts over ideas effectively	
Accepts responsibility	
Is a stickler for accuracy	
Knows how to handle people	
Is safety conscious	
Has pleasant personality	
Is liked by most workers	
Has patience	
Is considerate	
Knows how to criticize	
Is helpful	
Makes friends easily	
Plays no favorites	
Doesn't jump to conclusions	
Is not selfish	
Knows how to listen	
Expresses opinions well	
Sets a good example	
Knows how to analyze problems	
Makes accurate decisions	
Has initiative	
Is always willing to cooperate	
Knows how to follow orders	
Generally looks ahead	
Is energetic	
Is neat and tidy	
TOTALS Double checks: Single checks: X's:	

(FIGURE 3-4)

INSTRUCTOR'S CHECKLIST

Instructor's name _____ **Date** _____
Name of new employee _____

- ☐ Determine how much skill you expect the new employee to have, and by what date.
- ☐ Break down the job, list the important steps, pick out the key points.
- ☐ Make sure that the work area is in order and that the newcomer has all necessary supplies.
- ☐ Be sure that the workplace is properly arranged, just as the employee is expected to keep it.
- ☐ Try to put the individual at ease. Show an interest in any ideas and ambitions the worker may offer.
- ☐ Explain the job. Find out what the employee already knows about it.
- ☐ Show the newcomer how to do the job, but illustrate one important step at a time.
- ☐ Be patient as you instruct—stress each key point.
- ☐ Instruct clearly, completely, but no more than can be mastered at a time.
- ☐ Let the person do the job. Have each key step explained to you. Make sure the worker understands what is going on.
- ☐ Continue until you know that the individual knows.
- ☐ Show the person around the entire department. Introduce each person the newcomer will be working with and all the people within the immediate vicinity of the working area.
- ☐ Carefully review all the rules every one of us should know (safety procedures, first aid, when and where smoking is permitted).
- ☐ Have the worker fitted for safety shoes, glasses, goggles, uniforms.
- ☐ Explain cleaning requirements and services, replacements.
- ☐ Arrange to have lunch together on the first day. If possible, join some of the others in your department.
- ☐ Make sure the employee has a locker and key.
- ☐ Explain the limitations of company responsibility for lost articles.
- ☐ During the first week, talk to the worker at least once a day about the new job. Show your interest; let the worker know you care.
- ☐ Check occasionally to see whether you can be of any assistance.
- ☐ Notes and comments: _____

_____
_____
_____
_____

(FIGURE 3-5)

made cognizant of their shortcomings so that they can work to overcome them.

Finally, trainers must be honest in relation to *their own* limitations. If they don't know a job well enough to teach it, they should be willing to come to you for added instruction so that the training assignment can be carried out effectively.

★ **Empathy.** Workers who are capable of putting themselves in the position of others are very valuable as trainers. They're more likely to put the learning employee at ease by telling trainees not to worry about the small, common mistakes that all new people tend to make. Empathy is a quality often possessed by people who remember the trials of their own training periods.

★ **Strong communication skills.** Trainers should feel comfortable delivering instructions and explanations to others, and should be able to do so clearly and precisely.

They should also feel at ease about initiating conversations. Many new hires are shy about speaking up when they are confused or anxious. For this reason, your trainers may often have to draw them out by starting a discussion.

★ **The ability to follow through.** If a trainer tells someone how to do a particular job and then simply walks away, there's no guarantee that the trainee knows how to do the job.

To be effective, a trainer must give a trainee the opportunity to ask questions, and must *listen* to those questions. Then the trainer should provide helpful answers to get—or keep—the person on track. Ignoring this aspect of training prevents the teacher from finding out if the instruction has been accurate, adequate, and understood.

★ **Commitment.** Being a mentor means that a worker has to sacrifice some personal time in order to meet with the pupil. Make sure your prospective trainers are aware of this; then gain their assurance that they're willing to make the sacrifice.

★ **Goal-orientation.** Good trainers are goal-oriented. But that means they do more than meet the goal at hand: training a fellow worker.

Those who are truly goal-oriented also have the ability to teach others the importance of moving efficiently toward a larger production goal while maintaining quality standards.

★ **Team spirit.** There's a tendency among some people to treat new employees as something less than equals. They boost their own egos by criticizing recent additions to the department. Obviously, these people are not suited for training duties.

Keep an eye out for employees who consider themselves part of a team of workers who are equal in all respects. They'll provide a training atmosphere that's cooperative, and reduce the tension often felt by new employees.

★ **Respectability.** The person you choose to carry out training of new employees should be respected by other members of the department. This increases the likelihood that the new worker will be accepted readily, because he or she will have been trained by someone whom other employees already accept as an authority.

To better determine which of your employees qualifies as a trainer, see the "Best Qualified Trainer Checklist" (Figure 1).

What Should You Teach Your Teachers?

The qualities we've just looked at, for the most part, can't be taught; a person either possesses these characteristics or does not. However, there are some things you *can* teach the people who *do* have these characteristics in order to make them effective trainers. For example, tell them to:

◆ **Teach just enough and no more.** The fundamentals of any task are most important. A trainee needs to be well grounded in basic techniques before trying to move on to more involved aspects of the job or any "tricks of the trade." Also, a glut of training material can lead to confusion. So, ask your trainers to present new material in a step-by-step fashion rather than all in one torrent.

You should also instruct your trainers to phrase their instructions in a positive manner rather than a negative one. For example, it's much more effective to say "This is how to do this procedure" than to say "This is how you *shouldn't* do this." Why? Because frequently it's the *negative* that sticks in the mind, and when the time comes to actually carry out a procedure, a worker may mistakenly use the wrong method because that's the first one that he or she remembers.

◆ **Give the trainee hands-on experience.** It's much better to learn by doing than to learn by watching. For that reason, ask your new trainers to give initiates as much hands-on experience as possible. The instructor can then follow up on the spot, point out errors, and give the worker an opportunity to correct any mistakes on his or her own.

♦ **Be supportive.** Explain to your trainers the need for not coming down hard on new workers who make mistakes. Tell them to correct in a positive fashion, and to compliment for any successes, no matter how small they may seem. Criticism certainly has its place, but it should be mixed with a measure of praise.

♦ **Provide a positive role model.** In a very real sense, your trainers will create new employees in their own image. That's why they must be careful to be punctual, cooperative, and productive themselves. Remember, a trainee is not simply learning how to carry out the mechanics of the job; he or she is also learning how to be a conscientious employee.

♦ **Know when to let go.** While trainers may take great pleasure in teaching and overseeing their pupils' work, there will come a time when the trainee must be "pushed out of the nest" and try to go it alone.

Once a trainee has demonstrated that he or she can correctly carry out a task, tell the trainer to pull back and see if the employee can perform the job without close supervision. Of course, the trainer should still be available to answer any questions that come up and to monitor the trainee's performance. But the sooner a trainee is allowed to apply his or her recently acquired skills, the sooner the person can build the independence and confidence needed to function as a fully productive member of your staff.

These are the basics of training that you'll want to teach to the people being developed as trainers. But chances are, there are some techniques and methods unique to your business, company, or department. How can you decide which of these are most important and must be learned by trainees?

One good way to identify some less than obvious aspects of training is to talk to employees whom you trained yourself. Ask them which components of their initial training have been most valuable to them in performing their jobs, and which components they would stress if they were training a fellow employee.

The answers you receive to these questions will help you to train your own trainers. You can pass along what you learn, which means their instruction will be more complete and more likely to result in success.

You may also provide your trainers with an Instructor's Checklist (Figure 3-5, page 88).

Luring Your Trainers

Training can be a time-consuming and sometimes frustrating effort on the part of the trainer. Or, it can be an opportunity to share job skills and tricks of the trade with others. How potential trainers view training assignments will depend on how you present them.

For example, experienced workers will be more likely to accept training assignments with enthusiasm if you tell them that they were chosen because of the characteristics they possess—great patience, for instance—or because of their proficiency in a particular job task. You needn't use false praise here. Simply tell the person why you think he or she would make a good instructor.

You could also tell prospective trainers that you intend to build training time into their schedules by lightening their work load in some way. You might accomplish this by shifting a few of their tasks to other employees (without overburdening them, of course). After all, you'll want to give them enough time to educate new employees thoroughly.

Finally, appeal to their pride in their job or profession. Point out that a training assignment will give them a chance to share their knowledge with others. It will also give them satisfaction to see their students' performance and productivity improve during the training period. In addition, you should share with prospective trainers the fact that training experience can greatly benefit an employee who wishes to move up in the company.

▶ **WHAT YOU CAN DO** ➡ *Turning trusted employees into trainers can enhance your overall training efforts. You can do it by . . .*

1. Identifying the potential trainers on your staff. Look for people who possess the characteristics that will allow them to work with new hires successfully.

ACTION PLAN:

_____

_____

_____

2. Teaching them how to teach. Explain how they should train employees for maximum effectiveness.

3. Asking veteran workers which aspects of training they found most helpful. Then pass this information on to your trainers.

4. Generating enthusiasm in potential trainers by building training time into their schedules and by appealing to their pride in their work.

5. Thanking your trainers for their help and cooperation. The much-deserved recognition you provide will spur them to persevere in future training efforts.

By using employee trainers, you do more than relieve your busy schedule. You also ensure that new hires receive the thorough instruction they need to reach maximum productivity and performance potential. Also, you bolster the pride and enthusiasm of the employees you've chosen to be trainers.

MAKE THE MOST OF YOUR TRAINING DOLLAR

Training employees in key skills can mean reduced waste and increased overall efficiency. But will the results of all your training efforts justify the expense? Many supervisors would reply: "You can't know until you've spent the money." But you can *know beforehand, just by performing a simple analysis. And when it is completed, it will help you to make training pay for itself.*

Is It Really Worth the Cost?

More and more companies are taking a hard look at their training programs and asking themselves: "Are the programs doing what they're supposed to be doing? Are they worth what we're paying?"

The answers they're getting are sometimes surprising. The fact is, many supervisors request or start training programs without comparing the value of the potential results to the programs' costs. The result is that the *cost* of training frequently overshadows any *benefit* to be gained from training.

A Case in Point

A little over a year ago, Sally Lorenzo, supervisor of 20 employees in her company's production department, ran into a problem. Her people were taking too long to complete routine projects and were spending too much of the company's money on materials. No matter how much she pushed them to be a little quicker and less sloppy, they still contended that they were already doing their best.

What they need is some sort of refresher course that'll put them back on the right track, Lorenzo told herself. *I know they've got the skills and the know-how. They've just let them slide to the point where their mistakes are stretching deadlines out and putting a strain on our budget.*

Her first move was to get some hard figures on

the delays in the department. When she got the results—an astonishing average of a week's overrun on a four- or five-week project—she was convinced that improvement was a *must*. That much delay has to be costing the company money. And if it wasn't, the materials were.

While mulling over her problem a few days later, Lorenzo happened to remember a training program that the company had used a few years earlier to train new employees. She didn't consider herself an expert on training, but she was sure that with just a little updating and adapting, the old training program could be just the answer.

As she investigated, she kept finding other sources that she thought she might fit into the course. By the time she finished, her refresher course covered a variety of topics and had an estimated cost of $1,200 per worker. *Not bad,* she thought, *when you consider all we'll save in the long run.*

Did the End Justify the Means?

From all outward appearances, Lorenzo's training program did get the job done. When the final results were in, the delays had shrunk to an acceptable two or three days, and there was half as much waste of supplies as before.

But in fact, should Lorenzo have been happy with the program's outcome? Not really. What she didn't realize was that the program had brought about a *real* savings of only $500 per worker per year.

While the program was a success in terms of getting her people to reduce waste and meet, or come close to meeting, their production deadlines, it was a costly victory for the company—to the tune of $14,000! If Lorenzo had understood this, would she still have considered her program a successful one?

A Training Value Analysis

If you had been in Lorenzo's shoes—and you may very well be some day—how could you have prevented this waste of the company's training dollars?

One excellent method would have been to make an analysis of your proposed training programs *before* actually putting them into operation.

Here is how an analysis might have been made in the case of Lorenzo's program:

1 Performance Problem—This is the deficiency that needs correction. This should be stated briefly, yet clearly enough to ensure no difficulty in identifying the problem. Lorenzo's problem: too much delay and too much waste on employee projects.

2 Training Objective—This is the positive goal of your training program. For example, Lorenzo may have set her objective at cutting overruns one or two days beyond deadlines and reducing waste by one third.

3 Saving Unit—A measurable unit by which you can account for savings brought about through training. Of course, in Lorenzo's case, she is dealing with an abstract commodity (time), but she can use output per worker per week as her basic unit.

4 Unit Value—An approximate evaluation of what each unit is worth in dollars and cents.

5 Units in a Given Period—The number of units that would have been completed had workers met deadlines. In Lorenzo's case, each worker "lost" an average of two or three hours a week over a 50-week year (100 to 150 lost hours per year).

6 Workers Involved—In this case, 20.

7 Cost of No Training—If the performance problem is allowed to continue—and no training is given—what will be the cost to the company? This is determined by multiplying the values of items 4, 5, and 6.

8 Expected Savings Through Training—Realistically speaking, no training program may ever eliminate a performance problem entirely. In Lorenzo's case, the objective is to reduce overruns by 33 percent, with a total savings of $400 per year per worker.

9 Training Expense—Many times we underestimate this amount. Program materials (books, charts, films, etc.) make up obvious cost items. But you must also include the time employees and trainers (if the program is conducted by in-house personnel) are away from their jobs. The cost of Lorenzo's overextended program was approximately $24,000.

If Lorenzo had made an analysis of this sort, she would have seen in black and white that her proposed training program was impractical. A glance at the bottom line would have shown that the value of the program (in terms of actual savings for the company over the period of one year) was $10,000 more than Lorenzo had expected, but still far less than the actual cost of the program. In fact, the company lost $14,000 on Lorenzo's program that year.

Some Advantages

A Training Value Analysis, adapted to your own particular needs, offers some very tangible advantages in solving a performance problem through training.

First, it tells you whether the program you have in mind is economically sound. It does this by establishing a break-even point above which a training program is not sound. Lorenzo's break-even point was $10,000. A training program that cost less than that figure and promised to get the job done as well not only would have been sound, but would have been *profitable*. As it happened, the program that Lorenzo had in mind came nowhere near the problem's break-even point. By implementing it, she may have won the battle, but she lost the war.

Such an analysis is also a valuable tool for evaluating alternative training programs. Few performance problems are so specialized that there is only one way to go about solving them. By performing an analysis of each, you can readily tell which one offers the best return on your training dollar.

The real value of a Training Value Analysis lies in the fact that it gives you a fair indication of the economic value of a given training program—not in the terms of an accountant, perhaps, but in real, practical terms, nonetheless. In cases where the shift of a few dollars and cents will influence your decision, you'd be wise to look for an alternative anyway.

▶ **WHAT YOU CAN DO** → *You can get full value from your training dollar if you analyze the need for training by . . .*

1. Clearly identifying the problem and setting a realistic objective.

2. Establishing measurable units to be saved through training, and giving each unit a definite value.

3. Figuring out the costs of no training at all for a particular problem, to provide a comparison.

4. Determining what percentage of the problem can be eliminated by training and what the actual savings will be.

5. Realistically figuring out all expenses involved, including time away from the job for both trainer and trainees.

A well-trained workforce is the objective of every supervisor. But overtraining can be expensive. That's why successful supervisors prove the value of a training program before beginning it.

ACTION PLAN:

PROMOTE CONTINUING EDUCATION

As a supervisor, you already understand the importance of proper training. When new employees come on board, you do everything in your power to make sure they know the job before you "turn them loose." But just as important as initial training is continuing training—having workers learn new techniques to help them brush up and to make them well-rounded.

It's Too Important to Overlook

Training is important to business and industry; that's why more than $4 billion is spent on training annually in the United States. What does business get in return for all those dollars? It gets a competent, skilled workforce. But after a while, skills erode, and new technologies are introduced that make current methods seem prehistoric. That's why *continuing* education is so important.

And it all begins with *you*. Whenever possible, you have to work with your employees in-house to help them to improve. But when specialized instruction is needed and you can't supply it, a training program outside the company may be the answer.

Let's take a look at in-house education and how you can make it a valuable experience for your employees.

Doing It On Your Own

What kind of in-house education should you use to refresh your employees' skills? In one approach you can review or update their original training, taking care to add any improved methods that may have been developed since initial training took place.

There are three potential trainers within your own department:

▸ **You.** The most desirable person to conduct training is you. You know exactly what you want your employees to learn, and you know how you want it taught to them. By carrying out the training yourself, you can be sure that workers will get the instruction they need.

▸ **Your assistant.** When you can't find the time to conduct training on your own, the next best choice is your assistant. This person is most likely to know departmental goals and is likely to take them into consideration during training.

▸ **A veteran worker.** If you don't have a designated assistant, a veteran worker is a good alternative trainer. This person will know all the ins and outs of the job, and should be able to pass them on to other employees.

Once you've decided who will do the training, you may have to locate some materials to help with the instruction. Government publications, professional and industrial bulletins, and other supervisors are all good sources of training information.

Maintaining Your Control

To get the results you want, it's best to conduct employee education on your own. But many companies have training departments, and workers are taught their jobs by professional trainers—not their supervisors. Other firms bring in specialists to upgrade employee skills from time to time. And some rely on supplier training programs conducted by companies that provide their equipment and services.

On the surface, this seems to have the pleasant side effect of freeing the supervisor (you) from training duties so that you can devote time to other matters. But the danger here is that you have relinquished full control over the training process. Here's what you can do to ensure that your employees will get the most out of the training they receive from:

■ **The training department.** Provide input to the trainers before the program begins. Let them know your needs and concerns, and identify any aspects of the job they may not be familiar with, since they aren't necessarily specialists in your specific area.

■ **Consultants.** Ask to review a detailed course outline and any course materials. This can help you to decide whether the program is right for your workers. Then, report to management on whether it will suit your needs.

■ **Suppliers.** Since the ultimate purpose of supplier training programs is to sell something, you may have a tendency to shy away from them. But because they are often prepared by advertising specialists, most of the information in them is well presented. There will be exceptions, however, so once a supplier program has taken place, help your employees to separate product hype from concrete information they can use on the job.

Careful Selection Is the Ticket

Sometimes, information is so specialized, or time is at such a premium, that it becomes necessary to send employees to another location to increase their job skills and knowledge. Nearby colleges and universities are good places to locate training pro-

Tips on Sending Employees for Training

Why do you send your employees for training or to update their skills? Just because it's somebody's turn, or because it's on your schedule? "That's not a very good reason," says Connie Colussy, a midwestern Training and Development Administrator. "Training should have a specific objective.

"Try to look into the available training and find something that's exactly what a particular employee needs," she advises. "Then discuss your thoughts with that person and tell him or her why you think the training will be helpful on the job."

It could be any of several reasons—perhaps the person isn't handling the job very well, or is ready for advancement. Or, maybe the worker came to the department at a time before certain specialized training became available.

Colussy says that before any employee attends a training session or program, it's a good idea to discuss these two points:

▶ **What you expect the employee to get out of the training.** Inform the worker that he or she will learn new skills that should make the work easier and more meaningful. Point out how this, in turn, should increase the worker's performance and productivity.

▶ **What the employee should look for in the training.** What particular points should be most helpful and interesting? You can facilitate this as you review the course content and have a clear idea of what the employee needs.

The Reasons Behind Unwillingness to Train

If you've supervised one group for any length of time, you may have come to the conclusion that certain workers lack certain abilities, and that's that. One employee may be all thumbs when it comes to a particular task, and another may look puzzled every time he's supposed to interpret written instructions.

One Chicago supervisor relates, "I had one employee who had needed additional training for ages, but he'd always managed to wiggle out of going. Everyone on my team had received extra training once or even twice, but not this guy!

"He wasn't keeping up, because he was in the dark about too many aspects of his job. One afternoon he messed up again, and I informed him that I was scheduling him for training—whether he liked it or not. Actually, I didn't think he'd like the idea—I thought he was avoiding training because he was lazy. But he surprised me by admitting that he was afraid he'd fail and that I'd get a bad report on his training."

This is why you should make it a point to put employees at ease and explain how training will benefit them. Explain, too, that you're behind them 100 percent and are anxious to help them succeed.

The Other Side of the Coin

While some workers hold back, others will grab at any training that's available—whether they need it or not—because they think it will enhance their image, warns Colussy.

What should you do if you have such an employee? "Make it clear that the person is not just taking the course so that it will look impressive on his or her personnel record, but for some definite reasons," she advises. "Then tell the employee you'll be looking forward to dicussing results of the training as soon as he or she gets back."

And, of course, when the employee does return, flush with new skills and new ideas, sit down for a debriefing session. Talk over ways in which the worker may put some of those ideas into action. "In this way, you make it clear that the training is important to the person, to you as a supervisor, and to the company," says Colussy.

grams or seminars.

In some cases, your company may even be able to set up a course designed specifically for your employees—if you can assure the college of sufficient enrollment.

What should you look for in any outside training program? Here are some points to keep in mind:

- **Choose courses that will give employees practical experience** they can use on their jobs. Avoid courses that are more "philosophical" in their approach.

- **Review course materials in advance** to decide whether they will be suitable for your employees. Make sure they are neither significantly above nor below the level of your workers.

- **Be mindful of expense.** If a program's cost seems out of line, compare it with that of other programs in the area to see if you can find a better value.

One word of warning about outside training courses is in order: Don't let your employees apply anything they've learned in such a program until you've made sure it's compatible with the way your company operates. *All* the information they glean may not be applicable to your operations, so encourage them to talk to you about what they've learned, and then show them the best way to utilize it in their jobs.

Persuading the Reluctant

Once you've located a suitable outside training program, the next step is to point out its advantages to those employees who you feel would benefit by participating. Many of your people will be enthusiastic about increasing their knowledge, but others may not see the value of further education. Let's take a look at how one supervisor dealt with the objections her employees raised:

Supervisor Carla Thompson had just finished delivering a presentation to her employees about a training program sponsored by a local community college. After outlining what the course was all about, she opened the floor for questions.

Brian Hill was the first to raise his hand. "What about people who have been out of school for a long time?" he asked. "All the students are going to be a lot younger than I. Even the instructor may be younger than I. And I haven't been to school in so long I've forgotten what it's like to be a student."

"I can understand your feelings," said Thompson. "But more and more people are returning to school later in life, and their successes haven't been hampered by their age. In this case, a lot of your fellow employees will be right alongside you, so you shouldn't feel out of place."

Marge Corbin spoke up next. "My husband works nights, and we only have one car. I'd have no way to get to and from class."

"We may be able to set up a car pool," Thompson pointed out. "That should save everybody a little money. Anyone else who might be interested in joining a car pool for the course, let me know at the end of the meeting. Are there any other questions?" Since there were none, Thompson dismissed her employees.

What can you learn from this example? You see that employees' anxieties often manifest themselves in objections that can easily be overcome by a supervisor who exhibits a caring and helpful attitude. So be prepared to make an effort to find a solution for your workers' problems, and demonstrate your enthusiasm for continuing education at all times.

Reaping the Rewards

What are the benefits for employees—and the company—when they further their education? Training courses and programs, whether inside or outside the company, can increase employees' efficiency and provide them with some insight into problem-solving techniques. Perhaps best of all, they develop personal satisfaction because they have a greater understanding of their jobs and can make a greater contribution to the company.

But how can you tell if employees are reaping the rewards of continuing education? One way to decide whether a program has been worthwhile is to compare the performance of a group of your people both before and after they have completed the course. Another way is to ask workers if they thought the training was a valuable experience. They'll probably give you an honest appraisal of the merits and the drawbacks of the program they participated in.

And, by asking employees that simple question, you'll show them that you care about them, you're interested in what they have learned, and you're truly committed to helping them apply it to better themselves as well as the company.

▶ **WHAT YOU CAN DO** → *Continuing education is important to keep your workers up-to-date about new methods for doing their jobs. You can encourage them if you ...*

1. Recognize the role you play in getting them to take advantage of training programs. Always be enthusiastic about continuing education and its benefits.

2. Select training materials that are suitable for your people. Other supervisors, professional bulletins, suppliers, and government agencies are all good sources of information.

3. Locate outside training courses that are consistent with what you would teach employees yourself. Then make sure workers apply their newfound knowledge properly.

4. Evaluate the training programs your employees participate in to determine whether you should continue to use them.

Keeping employees motivated, challenged, and skilled is your responsibility. By providing opportunities for continuing education, you'll be better able to meet that obligation.

ACTION PLAN:
_____
_____
_____
_____
_____
_____
_____
_____
_____
_____

CHAPTER FOUR
SAFETY AND THE SUPERVISOR

A SAFE WORKPLACE BEGINS WITH YOU

Have you ever looked across your department's floor and wondered what guardian angel has been protecting your workers? When you think about it, staying safe in any factory environment is something you have to work at. There are a number of hazards to be wary of—even in a company that is strongly committed to a safe and healthful workplace for its employees.

Job Safety Begins With a Committed Management

Few people know this better than Tennan Barnard of the Parma Company (Parma, ID). "When our management team took over, we quickly realized that the plant contained a number of accidents just waiting to happen," he recalls.

Parma employs 35 to 50 people in the manufacture of farm equipment—potato, onion and sugar beet planters and harvesters. The very nature of the work makes safety an important issue. "Our workers handle cast iron and steel parts that can weigh hundreds of pounds. Just fasten one on the hoist wrong, swing it too fast or miss your mark, and you've got somebody hurt bad," says Barnard.

Other common accidents that they were seeing involved injuries like cut fingers, slag in an eye, and bruised toes. "Almost all could have been prevented," he concluded, "so we made up our minds that we were going to cut down on them—even if they were minor. If we didn't make that commitment, some of those safety problems we saw might have grown from minor to major. We realized that it wasn't going to be easy to change things so that we could keep people from getting hurt. But that had to be our goal."

Guidelines Must Be Clear and Practical

Barnard says that when you are creating a safety program—or simply expanding safety guidelines as they were doing at Parma Company—you have to study the situation carefully and tailor your efforts to the needs of your plant and your workers.

"Too many company safety manuals are too theoretical," maintains Barnard. "People don't want a lot of theory. They need to have a practical reason why you insist on certain safety rules. But most of all they need to know what it is that you want done and how you expect them to do it. They need the guidelines in print, they need you to go over the rules with them, and they need to be shown the *right* way to do the jobs. It takes all three to really make a workplace like ours safe."

Capitalize on Employee Judgment

Barnard feels that the supervisor's basic function comes into play when workers have been trained and know how to do the job. "Most of our people have been with our company for years," he explains. "This experience is invaluable to us because these people know how and what to do. The problem was that they'd never thought much about safety before. They were just instinctively careful.

"But when we came, they had to put safety awareness into a more tangible form—safety shoes and safety glasses, respirators with or without masks (depending on the job in the paint shop). Sure, these things had been used before, but now they had to be used every time.

"Any time you get into manufacturing," he adds, "the worker is the one who has to get into the habit of always applying the proper safety precautions. He has to learn when it is beyond his capacity to lift a heavy iron casting—and he has to put that knowledge to use by going for a hoist."

Capitalizing on that instinctive desire to be safe can pay off, however. "At Parma, we've had only two serious back injuries in seven years. In neither case were the injuries critical," notes Barnard, "but they were costly in terms of absenteeism and retraining and replacing the workers." And these are just the sorts of things that the company's safety program is designed to prevent.

Keep Safety Meetings Lively and on Target

Most supervisors will readily agree with the argument that motivation is critical to maintaining a safe department. Barnard was no exception. "You read all the theories, so you've got to try," he observes. And they did.

Unfortunately, the results were not what had been expected. "There was nothing wrong with these approaches," he says. "As you might expect, these motivational approaches created quite a bit of interest among the workers. But they didn't make any difference. We kept on having the same number of annoying little incidents happening."

And when they tried modifying their motivational attack? It was more of the same, says Barnard. "Our accidents didn't change for better or worse. They stayed just about the same."

So, what does Barnard suggest to get your safety message across to workers? For a start, you can make the most of your safety meetings, he says.

"We still have some minor accidents," he admits, "but we're convinced that you may be able to prevent serious problems from developing by talking to people rather than trying to pull psychology on them.

"We try to have safety meetings at least once a month. And we use that time to go over the accidents and near-misses that have taken place since the last meeting.

"You have to be careful," he warns, "not to point fingers at people, humiliating them in public for their mistakes. You concentrate on the mistake that was made, *not the person who was to blame for it*. You talk about how it could have been done better—and you let the employees suggest their ideas. This is important: You don't tell people; you let them tell you."

Use Outside Resources

You don't have to carry all of the burden for safety meetings on your shoulders. Barnard is quick to suggest taking advantage of the resources that your insurance company can offer. "We contacted ours, and they sent a representative to show our people films about back injuries and lifting. It produced quite a lot of discussion for a week or two, and I think that it helped people to understand that in most instances, back injuries can be prevented."

Show That You Care

Barnard thinks that a key reason for the Parma Company's good safety record is that management makes a conscious effort to show its concern about safety to workers.

"Say, for instance, that a new worker coming on the crew doesn't have the right safety shoes—or the money to buy them. Or maybe he's never heard of the need for wearing safety glasses. You have to take the time to explain why these things are necessary—and then you have to make it practical for that person to comply.

"At Parma Company, we have a policy which states that if a person can't afford these things, the company pays—and the employee can repay us a little at a time from his or her paycheck.

"This shows the employee two things," he says. "First, that you are serious enough about job safety to believe that the worker will stay around long enough to pay you back. And second, that you don't let anybody work—even for a single day—without the proper safety equipment."

The company's concern is also demonstrated in other ways. "We try to show people by tangible means that we appreciate their good work. We try to praise them for being safe workers—and to show them that appreciation both personally and publicly.

"We also try to give our people as much job security as we can," comments Barnard. This isn't easy, because Parma's business is somewhat seasonal. "It's not always possible to keep everyone all the time," he admits. "But when we lay someone off, we call that person back if we can. In fact, we have a backlog of people who have worked for this company for years—and they know how to do the work the right way to keep from getting hurt and hurting others." And these people get first call when it's necessary to staff up again.

> ▶ **WHAT YOU CAN DO** ➔ *You can make safety work in your department if you...*
>
> **1.** Demonstrate that you honestly care about your people and their safety on—and off—the job.
>
> **2.** Construct and enforce simple but firm safety guidelines. They need to know what you want done and how you want it done. They also need to know that you won't put up with any nonsense where safety is concerned.
>
> **3.** Hold regular safety meetings to get your message across. Stress the proper how-tos but be careful not to point fingers or place blame in public. Your goal is improved safety, not bad feelings.
>
> **4.** Use outside resources to keep your meetings lively and interesting.
>
> **5.** Make regular checks to ensure that people are following safe work procedures at all times.
>
> *When you follow these guidelines, you'll demonstrate to employees that safety is a primary concern for you— and that you expect them to share that concern.*

ACTION PLAN:

_____
_____
_____
_____
_____
_____
_____
_____
_____
_____

MAKE SAFETY COME ALIVE

How do you convince people to work safely? Do you tell them to work safely "because I say so"? Or do you rely on the sort of statistics that are available to most supervisors and trust that your workers will have enough sense to see the wisdom of working safely?

Make It Real

If you are really interested in creating a safer department, you probably won't have much success with the "because I say so" approach. When you get right down to it, people are more likely to work safely if they *want* to work safely—if they recognize that it's to their own benefit to do so.

As for showering workers with safety statistics, Wiley Barnes suggests there are better ways to win workers over. As safety manager of the Construction Division of Tanner Industries, Barnes avoids statistics when discussing safety with workers.

"In most cases, it's a matter of changing the state of mind of a person," he observes. "Some people are very receptive, but others think safety is unimportant—and that the supervisor is just there to badger them.

"Tanner companies have never had that attitude. We prefer to train people in the proper way of doing the job. That way, you have more valuable employees and a safer jobsite. Besides, statistically speaking, a workplace that's accident-free is more productive. The job gets done quicker and cheaper."

Friendly—But Firm—Persuasion

"You've got to talk to people about *how it actually is* on the job—about what they face on a day-to-day basis," says Barnes. That takes some blunt words, but he's convinced that that's "the best approach."

"I like to point out that we're in one of the most dangerous jobs in the world. We have to keep our eyes and ears open every minute of the day, and concentrate on what we're doing. Otherwise, someone's going to get hurt.

"Of course, no one *wants* to get hurt, so you have that in your favor right off the bat. But some of your workers may think that safety regulations are a lot of bunk, depending on how the subject has been presented in the past. If that is the case, you've got to convince them otherwise.

"You want to appeal to common sense, but at the same time you have to remember that you're dealing with adults," he cautions. "Some supervisors assume a professor/student attitude—and get nowhere.

"A much more effective approach is to strive for a one-on-one relationship. You can *and should* be 'one of the guys' while lending a hand with problems. Then, if the job involves something that's unfamiliar, you can both stand back and take a look at it from the safety standpoint."

But when you see someone working unsafely, you should deal with the offender promptly, firmly—and tactfully. "A good approach is: 'Hey, you're doing something that sooner or later will get you hurt.' Then, show the worker what's being done wrong—and why. Don't just jump down his throat," Barnes advises.

"Remember that everybody needs some recognition for jobs well done—as well as to feel secure in the job. But job security is more than having a job tomorrow. It's also being able to do the job tomorrow without getting killed."

Five Steps That Improve Safety

In Barnes's estimation, most accidents are not a failure of machines or systems *or* an act of God. When you get right down to it, he says, they're generally the person's own fault.

What can you do to improve safety awareness—and safety performance—in your department? You can start by following these guidelines:

■ **Take note of near-misses.** If someone trips over some stripped decking that still has some nails in it that should have been bent (and the decking cleared away), take it as a warning.

"Maybe this time no one was hurt, but it's a mistake to let the incident go unnoticed," Barnes stresses. "Take steps to correct the problem and tell your people about it. Like anything else in safety, you get all kinds of inklings of what may happen down the road. When you learn about a near-miss, this is a good indication that something is dead wrong somewhere—and someone should look into it before that near-miss becomes a serious injury or a fatality."

■ **Keep an eye on the big picture.** This is particularly important in high-hazard jobs, Barnes believes. Notice the way that machines are being operated—how alert people are on the job. Are they doing their jobs in a professional manner, or is there a lot of "horsing around"?

■ **Take immediate action.** If you see someone doing something that might cause an injury—to that worker or to his or her co-worker—talk to the worker then and there. Don't put it off.

You may be tempted to put off that talk, figuring that the unsafe act was a one-time thing that won't be repeated. Or you may think that the talk is something that can be put off until a more convenient time.

In either case, putting off that talk is a mistake. The unsafe act may be repeated—and it may cause a serious injury before that "more convenient time" happens along.

■ **Emphasize the right way.** "At this company, we call it 'the Tanner way,' " says Barnes. "That means doing things right the first time, so that the task doesn't have to be done over again—*and* so that it's done safely. In the long run, if you weigh the cost of accidents, jobs done correctly are done safely." When you think about it, Barnes is right: The safe way is the *only* way!

■ **Finally, think like a salesman.** Barnes says, "Believe in your product. If you believe in safety, that message is easy to pass on to other people."

> ▶ **WHAT YOU CAN DO** → *You can build safety awareness—and performance—if you...*
>
> 1. Make safety real to your employees. Instead of abstract concepts, stress real hazards that people see every day and show workers how to avoid them.
>
> 2. Use "near-misses" to drive your points home. Even the most jaded employees will be able to appreciate the impact of a well-aimed "one fraction of a second more and it might've been you!"
>
> 3. Stress the positive whenever possible. The safe way should be the *only* way. So, avoid muddying the issue with too many don'ts; all your people need to know is the right way to get the job done.
>
> *Follow these rules, and you will have an effective action plan for achieving improved safety performance in your department.*
>
> **ACTION PLAN:**
> _____
> _____
> _____
> _____
> _____
> _____
> _____
> _____
> _____

WHAT OSHA EXPECTS

Some supervisors look on the prospect of a visit by an OSHA inspector with even less relish than they do the proverbial confrontation with the "in-laws." In most cases such fear is not only unfortunate—it's unnecessary. OSHA wasn't set up to be something for supervisors to fear; its only purpose is to ensure the safety and well-being of your workers. There's nothing to fear as long as you...

Follow the Rules

The main responsibility of line supervisors is to see that ALL safety rules are enforced at ALL times and that ALL required safety devices or wearing apparel are used at ALL times. It's not enough that your company recognizes the need for safety equipment and makes it available for workers. There must also be a firm commitment to making sure that the equipment is used by everyone who needs it. What it boils down to is a matter of attitude.

A Case in Point

The Safety Committee of Plaza Food Products, a food processing firm, did a study of noise levels in its main plant and discovered that there were several areas in which the noise levels were quite high. The supervisors in those areas were called in and asked if they had any ideas on how the high noise factor in their particular departments might be reduced. After a fair amount of discussion, it was decided that, short of a major program of installing sound-absorbing panels, protective earmuffs would be the best approach to take.

The committee reviewed the requirements with the representatives of several manufacturers and selected one type of ear protector that could be used in all of the affected areas.

"You Mean We Gotta?"

As soon as the shipment of earmuffs was delivered to the Plaza plant, all of the supervisors in the noisy departments were given their quota of them and told that they must be worn at all times. Worker reaction was predictable—they said that the earmuffs were uncomfortable, and protested the order that they had to be worn at all times. The crew in Larry Thorne's department was no exception. "We never had to wear these things before," one worker objected. "Why now?"

"Because the company says so, that's why," Thorne replied. "There's this law that says the company is responsible for giving you a safe place to work, and that's why we've gone to the expense of buying these things—to protect your hearing."

"What's hearing got to do with safety?" the worker asked.

"If you work too long in a noisy place, you can go deaf," Thorne answered, his voice tinged with exasperation. "Look, they're for your own good. If you want to go deaf, do it on your own time. But while you're around here, I want to see these earmuffs on. No exceptions."

The worker gave him a you-can't-fight-city-hall shrug, and the meeting was closed. At first, everyone seemed to follow the edict and the muffs were worn at all times. As the weeks went by, however, observance of the rule became more and more lax. Whenever Thorne found workers without muffs on, he told them to put them on; but no action was ever taken against workers who broke the rule.

The Backslide

The company became aware of this lax attitude, and a campaign was begun to get better employee cooperation. The subject of noise pollution was discussed at department safety meetings, and large red signs were posted in high noise areas stating that the protective earmuffs were to be worn at all times. There was some improvement in employee cooperation, but it proved to be temporary. In a short time, most employees were back to their old habits. Management knew this, but it figured that it had done all it could. If the employees weren't willing to go along with the program, management felt that the employees would have to bear the consequences.

The Inspector Disagrees

Unfortunately, the compliance inspector who visited their plant later that month didn't agree with that line of reasoning. One of her first comments on entering Larry Thorne's department area was, "Shouldn't these people be wearing some sort of ear protection?"

The plant manager winced and asked Thorne why the workers didn't have their earmuffs on.

"We've done what we could about it," Thorne replied. "Some wear them, others refuse. We've tried talking to them, and we've got signs up all over the place. They just ignore them. No cooperation at all. I figure if they want to go deaf, let 'em."

The inspector shook her head. "That's a violation," she told them.

"How can that be?" the plant manager blurted out. "We bought them all protective earmuffs. We even spent more than we had to—just to be sure we had the best. I don't see why the company should be held responsible if they refuse to wear them."

"I don't make the rules," the inspector said calmly. "Let's get on with the tour."

"We'll contest it," the plant manager told her.

The inspector merely shrugged and headed off down the aisle.

The Company's Response

Plaza Food Products based its defense (a) on parts of the law which said that protection will be provided when noise levels exceed those permissible under Section 1910.95 of the OSHAct, and (b) the section of the law which stipulates that employees are required to comply with standards. The company felt it had complied with the law insofar as it was able to, by providing equipment that would abate the noise hazard to acceptable levels, by publicizing the need for such equipment to be worn, and by reminding employees who did not wear earmuffs that they should be wearing them for their own protection.

A judge, in reviewing this case, upheld the complaint and the amount of the fine. The employer, said the judge, was aware that employees had not been wearing earmuffs and had failed to take "affirmative action" to correct the situation.

Attitude Is the Key

The thing that makes this case different from some others, in which serious injuries have occurred but no citation was issued for a violation, is the actions of supervisors and higher management. When definite disciplinary action has been taken against workers who violate safety rules, a company is usually considered to be making a genuine effort to enforce the regulations and therefore is not considered to be in violation of the Act.

The issuance of a citation in this case, and the finding of the judge, point up the significant fact that the safety law strikes not merely at hazards, or violations of existing rules—it strikes at the very attitudes of employers. What it boils down to is this: If you are not prepared to exert yourself to see that workers work safely, you're going to get into trouble with OSHA. Going through the motions, the way Plaza did, is not enough.

▶ **WHAT YOU CAN DO** → *You have nothing to fear from an OSHA inspection if you...*

1. Follow all the rules all the time.

2. Provide all necessary equipment to protect workers from hazards, including those that may not produce visible injuries.

3. Explain to workers in detail the reasons for specific safety rules and the need for protective equipment.

4. Once safety equipment is provided, be certain to police the situation continuously to prevent backsliding.

5. Take firm disciplinary action against workers who refuse to comply with safety and health rules.

The attitude of management, including the department supervisor, concerning the enforcement of safety rules is a key factor in determining whether its safety effort is effective.

ACTION PLAN:
_____
_____
_____
_____
_____
_____
_____
_____
_____
_____

SAFETY, WORKERS, AND YOU

Some people consider it the single most important obligation of the supervisor: protecting employees from injury-causing hazards in the workplace. There's no doubt that it is one of your most crucial duties—so how well are you doing it? Here's a chance for you to review some important facts and improve your . . .

Safety Sense

Every year, about 8 percent of American workers suffer an injury on the job. These injuries range from minor cuts and burns all the way up to permanent impairments. While it's true that there are some injuries that just can't be prevented, the vast majority of accidents in the workplace should never take place—and wouldn't, if supervisors and workers were on the ball.

Accidents are the result of a three-link chain: habit, attitude, and unsafe acts or conditions. If an employee is in the habit of ignoring safety rules in order to work as quickly as possible, you've already got a problem. The problem can be compounded if your attitude conveys that working fast is more important than working safe. Add an unsafe act or condition to this formula, and you might as well call an ambulance right now.

The key to a safe workplace is to break this chain, destroying all its links: Break employees of the habit of working unsafely, look at your own attitude toward safety, and strive to remove unsafe acts and conditions from your plant.

Safety Starts on The Very First Day

Far better than breaking employees of the habit of working unsafely is preventing them from developing such habits in the first place. Any time a new worker joins your department, stress to him or her how important it is to follow safety rules. Let the person know that there's no room for compromise where the well-being of employees is concerned.

And go beyond explaining the rules by pointing out why the rules are in place. Describe the types of injuries that are common in work settings like yours and how following the rules can prevent them. When employees understand that safety regulations are for their protection, they're much more likely to obey them at all times.

Old Habits Die Hard

If you've only recently raised your own safety-consciousness, it's possible that your employees have fallen into unsafe work habits. Naturally, you'll want to indoctrinate new workers with a safety attitude, but what can you do for veteran workers who have to be brought around to a safe way of thinking?

A series of safety meetings is a good way to start. But rather than lecture employees about the proper habits and techniques, pinpoint specific hazards. Also, describe accidents and injuries that have taken place in your department in the past and outline how they could have been prevented.

In addition, you can put employees on notice that you intend to take safety attitudes and habits into account when conducting performance appraisals. When future raises and promotions are tied to safety-mindedness, you can be sure that workers will take the subject seriously.

Say Good-bye to Unsafe Conditions

Sound training, safety meetings, and safety as part of the performance appraisal should cut down—or eliminate—unsafe acts by employees. To further ensure the well-being of your workers, however, you'll have to eliminate any unsafe conditions in your department.

Unfortunately, most hazardous conditions only come to light when they have already resulted in injury to an employee. Then management must patch up the problem while productivity lags because of the person's absence.

Think how much better it would be to survey conditions in advance and eliminate any that could contribute to injury. Then you wouldn't have to wait for a worker to go "down for repairs" before taking action.

Begin by making a list of all the equipment used by the people you supervise. Then examine each item to ensure that it conforms with safety standards. From there, take a look at the physical condition of the floors in your department. Are they free from cracks, grease, or anything else that could cause workers to slip or fall?

If you do discover anything during your survey, take care of it immediately. Have cracks repaired, and make sure that any grease or oil spills are cleaned up. If equipment must be upgraded to ensure safety, bring this fact to the attention of your superiors. Let them know what must be done to eliminate hazards in your department, and ask for their help in that regard. Management is sure to appreciate your efforts to protect employee safety.

Learning the Hard Way

Of course, there may be times when you learn about hazardous conditions the hard way: when an employee is injured on the job. No amount of diligence on your part will guarantee that you can eliminate 100 percent of the hazards in your workplace, and this fact is likely to come home to you at some point in your supervisory career.

The first step to take when an employee is injured at work is to make sure that he or she receives any medical attention required. This may be as simple as giving on-the-spot first aid, or as involved as getting the person to a nearby hospital. If you have any doubt about the extent of a worker's injuries, don't take a chance by underestimating them. Get professional medical help immediately, and let the professionals determine what kind of treatment is needed.

Once the emergency is taken care of, don't think your obligations are at an end. Your next step should be to find out exactly what caused the injury in the first place. When you've investigated the incident and assigned the blame somewhere, consider the following:

If the person committed an unsafe act, you haven't met your obligations to fully train employees and inform them about the potential dangers they may face as a result of working hazardously.

If an unsafe condition existed, you haven't met your obligations to investigate equipment and work areas and eliminate any hazards.

If the accident was the result of a new unsafe condition, you now have the obligation to remove it from the work process.

Remember, the ultimate responsibility for employee safety falls on you. Any time a worker is injured on the job, you have failed to meet that responsibility. Even if an employee willfully violates a safety rule, you're still responsible: After all, the person might not have broken the rule if you had been more forceful about enforcing it.

The point here is that once an accident has happened, it's your duty to make sure that it doesn't happen again. If you've been remiss about training employees for safety in the past, resolve to place more emphasis on the subject in the future. If a new hazard develops, take steps to eliminate it once and for all. You don't have to feel guilty when an injury occurs, but you should feel an obligation to prevent future occurrences.

The Cost of Working Unsafely

By now you should be convinced that it's important to insist on safe work habits by your employees. But there is likely to be a small minority of supervisors who believe that workers are responsible for their own safety, and that if they get hurt on the job, it's their problem alone. If you count yourself in that minority, pay close attention to the information that follows.

Between 10 and 15 percent of a company's payroll goes to pay the cost of workers' compensation insurance. In industries that are especially hazardous, these rates can run as high as 40 percent.

Like any other form of insurance, workers' compensation premiums are based on the past accident and injury rates of the individual company purchasing the insurance. Premiums are also determined according to job descriptions and the accident rates for each position. For that reason, the premium for a particular job in a safety-minded department may be far less than that for a department in a company with a poor safety record.

The point is this: If the continued well-being of your workers isn't enough to inspire you to keep safety uppermost in everyone's mind, there's a reason that may convince you to do it anyway. Every extra dollar the company pays for workers' compensation is one less dollar that can go into employee paychecks—maybe even yours.

▶ WHAT YOU CAN DO → *The safety of your workers is one of your biggest responsibilities. To eliminate hazardous acts, conditions, and attitudes...*

1. Explain safety rules to employees their first day on the job. Let them know that you take the rules seriously and expect them to do the same.

2. Break veteran employees of bad safety habits by having them attend a series of safety meetings and by letting them know that you will consider safety records when conducting performance appraisals.

3. Conduct a survey of your department to see if you can find any machines, equipment, or work areas that ap-

ACTION PLAN:

_____

_____

_____

_____

_____

_____

pear hazardous. Then correct the problems.

4. Learn from your mistakes. If an injury occurs despite your safety efforts, determine the cause of the injury and resolve that it won't happen again.

You can't raise the safety consciousness of employees until you've convinced yourself of the importance of working hazard-free. Hopefully, the information presented here will help you do that.

HOW TO PREVENT ACCIDENTS AND INJURIES

Accidents and injuries on the job don't just happen. They're the result of unsafe acts or conditions. Yet the experience of hundreds of supervisors and thousands of employees in plants all over the United States proves that competent supervisors can eliminate—in a reasonable and practical way—at least 50 percent of all unsafe acts and conditions. In other words, they are able to prevent one half of all accidents and injuries on the job. How? By knowing how to recognize and check the danger points.

How to Check Danger Points

"Unsafe acts" refers to employees' actions. They fall into the category of human failure. On the other hand, "unsafe conditions" refers to the condition of tools, machinery, clothing, or other inanimate objects. These are mechanical failures.

Failure to act safely will often lead to an unsafe condition. For example, an employee may forget to replace the cap on a drum of gasoline. This is an unsafe act. If the drum is allowed to remain uncovered, it sets up an unsafe condition. If fire breaks out as a result of this situation, it's a product of human and mechanical failure. It's caused by both an unsafe act and an unsafe condition.

Most accidents and injuries are caused by unsafe acts rather than by unsafe conditions. In accidents on the job, roughly four are caused by unsafe acts for every one caused by unsafe conditions. Here's the total breakdown:

Cause of Accident
Human failure (unsafe acts) 78%
Mechanical failure (unsafe conditions) . . . 20%
Acts of nature (floods, storms) 2%

Unsafe Acts—Human Failure

How can you recognize an unsafe act? Study the following list. It describes the possible categories of human failure that can result in an accident.

Operating Without Authority This includes any unauthorized action such as jumping on a moving vehicle, operating someone else's equipment without permission, and using tools or machinery for which the employee has not been trained.

Failure to Secure This refers to failure to tie down materials on a loaded vehicle; failure to lock or shut down switches, valves, doors; failure to shut off equipment when not in use.

Failure to Warn This includes failure of the employee to signal properly; failure to place warning signs or tags; failure to take any action necessary to let others know that they are doing something that may put them in danger.

Operating at Unsafe Speed This includes actions such as running instead of walking; driving an automobile, truck, bus, or other vehicle above or below safe speeds; feeding or supplying production

110

machines or assembly lines too slowly or too rapidly; throwing material instead of carrying or passing it; using shortcuts that are unsafe.

Bypassing Safety Devices Disconnecting, removing, plugging, or blocking safety devices; failure to inspect signals, fuses, valves, and other safety devices; failure to keep them in good repair; ignoring signals, warning signs, tags, or other safety instructions.

Using Unsafe Equipment Using tools, machines, or materials that have become defective through wear and tear or abuse, or otherwise made unsafe. This category also refers to the use of hands, feet, or other parts of the body in place of tools or machinery. It includes using safe equipment in an unsafe manner, such as gripping tools or other objects improperly or insecurely, or using the wrong equipment for a particular job.

Unsafe Loading Unsafe loading on a vehicle, platform, conveyor belt, or other apparatus means loading over the safe load limit, loading too high, or loading in such a way as to create a top-heavy load.

Unsafe Placing Unsafe placing refers to the placing of tools, equipment, or other materials in such a position as to be in danger of rolling or falling, or where they become an obstruction in work areas, aisles, or other normal travel routes. It also refers to the placing of hands in, on or between equipment, or at dangerous points of operation.

Taking Unsafe Position or Posture Lifting or carrying loads improperly; lifting with the body in a twisted or awkward position; walking or working on unguarded beams, girders, scaffolds; riding on tailboards, on running boards of trucks, or riding in precarious positions; passing on grades and curves; entering enclosures that are unsafe because of gases, temperature, or exposed power lines; failure to use proper methods of ascending or descending when working in high places; standing in the line of travel of falling or moving objects; taking a position that obstructs the free movement of others.

Working on Dangerous or Moving Equipment Oiling, cleaning or adjusting equipment while it is in motion; working on electrically charged equipment without cutting power; getting on or off vehicles while they are in motion; welding or repairing equipment containing flammable or explosive substances without first cleaning and venting; unnecessary handling of materials while they are being processed on moving machines or conveyor belts.

What to Do When an Unsafe Act Occurs

1. **Stop** the act immediately, consistently.
2. **Study** the job. If employees commit unsafe acts because they think there is no other way to do the job, investigate their work methods.
3. **Instruct.** Once you decide how a job operation can be done more safely, instruct employees in the correct method. Explain how the job should be done, and show them by demonstrating. Let them try it.
4. **Train** employees in safe procedures. Check up on them from time to time; make certain they understand the procedure and will not go back to unsafe methods.
5. **Discipline** employees only as a last resort, after they have repeatedly shown that they willfully refuse to follow safety rules.

Unsafe Conditions—Mechanical Failure

Here are types of unsafe conditions that can lead to occupational accidents and injuries. Keep in mind that unsafe conditions often come about as a result of unsafe acts.

Lack of Guards This applies to hazardous places such as platforms, catwalks, or scaffolds where no guardrails are provided; power lines or explosive materials that are not fenced off or enclosed in some way; machines or other equipment having moving parts or other danger points that are not safeguarded.

Inadequate Guards Often, a hazard that is partially guarded is more dangerous than one not guarded at all. Employees seeing some sort of guard may feel secure and fail to take precautions they would ordinarily take if there were no guards at all.

Defective Items Equipment or materials that are worn, torn, cracked, broken, rusty, bent or splintered; buildings, machines, or tools that have been condemned or have fallen into disrepair.

Hazardous Arrangement Cluttered floors and work areas; improper layout of machines and other production facilities; blocked aisle space or fire exits; unsafely stored or piled tools and material;

overloaded platforms and vehicles; inadequate drainage and disposal facilities for waste products.

Improper Illumination Insufficient light; too much light; lights of the wrong color; glare; arrangement of lighting systems that result in shadows and too much contrast.

Unsafe Ventilation Concentration of vapors, dusts, gases, fumes; unsuitable capacity, location or arrangement of ventilation system; insufficient air changes, impure air source used for air changes; abnormal temperatures and humidity.

What to Do About Unsafe Conditions

1. **Remove hazard** if possible.
2. **Guard.** If danger point (e.g., high-tension wires) can't be removed, see to it that hazard is shielded by screens, enclosures, or other guarding devices.
3. **Warn.** If guarding is impossible or impractical, warn of the unsafe condition. Let's say a truck must back up across a sidewalk to a loading platform. You cannot remove the sidewalk or build a fence around the truck. All you can do is to warn that an unsafe condition exists. Do this by posting a danger sign or device (bell, horn, whistle, signal light, striped paint, red flag, etc.).
4. **Recommend.** If you cannot remove or guard an unsafe condition on your own, notify the proper authorities about it. Make specific recommendations as to how the unsafe condition can be eliminated.
5. **Follow up** your recommendation. After a reasonable length of time, check to see whether the unsafe condition has been corrected. If it remains, it's your responsibility to notify the person or persons to whom you made the recommendations.

How to Develop A Winning Safety Attitude

The Emca Company was in the middle of a contest to boost production. The departments of supervisors Dan Miller and Al Scotti had been running nip and tuck, with Miller's in the lead. However, last week Miller had some machine downtime and it looked as if his department might finish behind schedule and be pushed out of first place. There was some good-natured heckling about it between departments, supervisors included, and the machine operators in Miller's department were not going to give up without a struggle.

That was obvious when Miller arrived at the plant in the morning. He was about 15 minutes early, but most of his crew were already at their machines, waiting for the starting bell.

That's the way it went all week. The staff worked at peak performance and by Thursday it looked as if they had a good chance of being on top again.

Then, Thursday afternoon, one of the machines jammed. The operator, Tom Hurley, one of Miller's best workers, tried to save time by fixing it himself. He reached in to free the jammed part and one of his fingers was severely gashed.

One of the crew got the first-aid kit and fixed a temporary bandage and Miller rushed him to the infirmary. "How is he?" the staff asked when Miller got back.

"The nurse did what she could and sent him to the hospital," he answered.

"He really meant it when he said we'd lose over his dead body," one of the employees said admiringly. Several others made similar comments and Miller realized that they thought the injured worker was some kind of hero.

"What he did was stupid," Miller snapped, "and a violation of a basic safety rule."

But he knew that the real crisis would come when Hurley came back to work. What action should Miller take and how should he explain it to the department? Think about it and then compare your answer with what actually happened.

A Positive Approach

Miller knew that Hurley had taken the chance of reaching into the machine out of loyalty to him and the department. And, of course, the other workers realized this, too. *But you can't let workers risk their hands to get the work done,* Miller reasoned. *If I don't take some action, the staff might feel that I approve of someone taking a chance now and then.*

When Hurley came back to work, his hand still bandaged, Miller waited until the other machinists had gathered around to welcome him back. Miller then walked over and said, "Glad to see you up and around."

"This is nothing," Hurley said, obviously proud of his wound. "It won't keep me from doing my job."

"It's more serious than you think," said Miller. "And I'm afraid it is going to keep you from doing your job because I'm suspending you for two days for violating safety rules."

The employees were stunned for a second, then

began to protest loudly.

"Knock it off," Miller ordered. "You'd all better get one thing straight. No one in this department can violate safety rules and get away with it, no matter what the reason. Everybody knows it's against the rules to reach into a jammed machine while the power is on."

Then, he turned to Hurley. "Maybe you thought you could save some time so we could keep producing and get ahead again. But look what really happened. I lost you and the use of your machine for several days. As a result, we not only failed to get back on schedule, we'll probably end up behind for a second month. So, you see, you could have lost your entire hand for nothing."

Miller knows that his reprimand caused a lot of talk, but he also knows that it increased the safety awareness in his department and there was not much actual resentment after the crew understood the need for observing the rules.

It's Your Job

The incident at Emca Company might not have happened if each worker had had the proper "safety attitude." Obviously, Supervisor Dan Miller has the right attitude himself and is unwilling to permit injuries in order to have a good production record. But, somehow, he had failed to transmit this attitude to the people working for him.

Communicate Your Attitude

The first day new employees are on the job is the time to begin developing the proper attitude. Even if they are experienced, they should be given the company rules and any special instructions pertaining to your particular department. But it is after the introduction that maintaining a high interest in safety becomes difficult. After workers become familiar with their jobs and the department routine, they can easily get careless. Most plants have either a full-time safety director or someone designated to run a safety program on a part-time basis. In either case, without the full cooperation of every supervisor, the safety program will not be successful. Naturally, if all workers understand that management—from the very top to department heads and group leaders—has a great interest in safety, it is easier to convince them of its importance.

The main task of the supervisor is to convince the few people in each department who have the attitude that safety rules are foolish, or "kid stuff," that taking time to be safe is not wasting time. Here is a series of rules for supervisors that can help foster the proper attitude:

• Always be on the alert for unsafe practices, unsafe tools, and unsafe conditions. The attitude of all employees in this respect is of greatest importance, and by never ignoring an obvious hazard yourself, you help to keep everyone alert.

• Bring several persons in on the investigation of serious or potentially serious accidents. Frequently, investigating an occurrence where an employee barely misses serious injury can be of great value in forming the proper attitudes, especially for someone who has disdained safety.

• Be on the alert for indifferent employees. Bring them in on accident investigations and be sure they understand the rules.

• Analyze the need for appropriate training and see that it is carried out.

• In the appraisal of employees, make safety attitude a factor equal in importance to leadership, production, and cost consciousness. This makes you, as supervisor, as well as the employees more aware that their attitudes toward safety are indicative of their feeling of responsibility.

• Make safety a daily concern. By having a safety talk with at least one member of your group every day, you help to make safety a personal matter.

• Maintain firm safety discipline. Be consistent in enforcing all safety rules and be fair in applying discipline.

• Insist on prompt reporting of all accidents no matter how small they may seem. This will get trouble spots cleared up in a hurry and point up the importance you and higher management place on safety.

Perhaps your most important contribution to accident prevention can be communicating your own desire for working safely to the entire department. Lack of, or faulty, communication between two people—you and each of your workers individually—can wreck a safety record or program. People don't get hurt because they want to, but they sometimes do unsafe things for these reasons:

❶ They don't know that what they are doing is wrong.

❷ They misunderstand instructions.
❸ They don't consider the instructions important.
❹ They are not given specific instructions.
❺ They deliberately disregard instructions.
❻ They haven't been properly trained.

To improve communication, be certain that you issue instructions in clear, simple language and ask enough questions to know that the instructions are understood. Then make periodic checks with all employees to remind them of the basic company rules.

The best viewpoint for a supervisor to take is one of "professional pessimism." As one safety director put it: "You can have all the safety equipment you need—goggles, hard hats, fire hoses strategically located, safety belts—but you've still got to check up to see that these things are used as a matter of course. People get what I call 'safety lazy.' They know what to do but don't do it. Ninety percent of the problem is people, so you just can't let up."

Carelessness and Willfulness— Enemies of a Safe Attitude

Asked about the so-called accident-prone worker, another industrial safety director said: "I don't believe in that theory. People get hurt because they are careless or willfully violate safety rules."

Seeing that workers form safe work patterns and actually acquire the safety habit is a continuous job. Our work habits are built around the easy and natural ways of doing things. Psychologists tell us that it takes about seven years to firmly establish a new habit or break ourselves of an old one. That is why you must be repetitious and why you must find new and interesting ways to tell the same old story. At times your people may complain of boredom with the subject of safety, but it's worth the effort to have them develop the safe habits they need to prevent injuries.

It is not enough for you to tell your staff about safety or that they should work safely. Supervisors must communicate to their people the attitude they should follow. That's why you must have a good safety attitude and, by your actions, demonstrate that safe procedures are truly important.

Build Individual Responsibility

If you hear excuses from your workers such as "The switch was hard to throw and it strained my back" or "The lathe was running and it threw my hand into the chuck" or "The air hose flew around and hit my leg," you can be quite certain that they feel that they are innocent victims and that they can do nothing to eliminate the cause of injuries. But they're wrong, and you must prove it.

This is when individual responsibility must be developed. Workers who think like this must be made to realize that a lathe chuck does not reach out to hold hands with them and that an air hose is not a snake that hisses and bites. This sort of idea can often be put across in a department meeting by using a humorous approach.

Safety has been called a state of mind. Learn to recognize the following tip-offs to unhealthy safety attitudes so you can guard against their developing into bad habits:

▶ I forgot to flip the switch.
▶ I thought it was too much trouble to wear a hard hat.
▶ Nobody told me not to cross the wires.
▶ I didn't tell them not to do it that way because I'm not the boss.
▶ I didn't listen to them because I thought they were full of hot air.
▶ I didn't pick up the carton because I was tired and I didn't think anyone would trip over it anyway.
▶ I'd done the job so many times I thought I could do it blindfolded.

These rationalizations could easily be excuses for accidents that could have been avoided. Here are the wrong attitudes underlying those excuses:

- Absentmindedness
- Hostility
- Tiredness
- Overconfidence
- Laziness
- Ignorance
- Indifference

Once you convince your people that safety trouble is people trouble and it's people's own thoughtlessness and carelessness that cause injuries, you have made real progress in developing the proper safety attitudes. Personal responsibility properly directed can accomplish extraordinary things. Use it to develop safety consciousness in each individual in your department.

Take Action When Needed

One of the quickest ways to undermine a safety program is to neglect reported unsafe conditions. Suppose, for example, one of your workers notices a crack in his machine guard and reports it to you on Monday morning. Nothing happens. He sees the safety director on Tuesday and mentions it to her. Nothing happens. On Wednesday he tells his union representative. Nothing happens. Then, on Friday, you call him into the office for the weekly talk about safety.

How is this talk going to be received? How can the attitude that the safety program is all talk and no action be avoided? When action is called for, never hesitate, whether it's making necessary repairs or correcting a worker's unsafe procedure. Sell Safety Positively—When an accident occurs, avoid criticizing the individual; criticize the situation and point out how the same type of accident can be prevented in the future. If ignorance produced the accident, be sure to correct the ignorance through positive and intensive training.

Accidents are frequently caused by emotional tensions and anxieties that distract workers so they are not giving their full attention to their jobs. Many times, if supervisors will simply give their employees an opportunity to talk about their problems, they will partially reduce the tensions that tend to cause trouble.

Model Injury Report

A worker in your department has just been injured. You find him sprawled on the floor, groggy and unable to move.

Your first concern is the victim. You summon a doctor or a nurse immediately. Once you've done this, your next job is gathering all the available information about the accident.

If the victim regains his senses, you might question him. But if the injury is serious, he may be too upset to be of much help. In this case, any questioning should be at the discretion of trained medical personnel.

Probably there were bystanders who witnessed the accident. Talk to them, as many as possible, to ensure that you have a complete picture of exactly what happened. Some witnesses may give a slanted and incomplete version of the accident—because they weren't in a position to see just what happened, or because they, too, are upset.

Be exhaustive. The report you prepare on the basis of your questioning must be as complete as you can make it. It will be important for three reasons:

1. It will help you to locate the cause of the accident and help you to prevent similar occurrences in the future.

2. It will help you and the personnel department in determining quickly how long the employee is likely to be out of work and how his injury will affect his future performance.

3. It will provide information to protect the interests of both the employee and the company in case of compensation and other claims.

Every accident report must cover *who* was injured and *what* injuries were sustained . . . *where* the accident took place and *when* . . . *what* caused the accident . . . and *what* steps are needed to prevent the accident from reoccurring.

It's important to keep in mind that the idea behind an effective accident investigation is not to place blame for what happened. Rather, the idea is to find the real cause of what happened and to learn from it. Then, you and your people will be in a good position to take concrete steps to prevent such an accident from happening again.

▶ **WHAT YOU CAN DO** → *If you want to make real progress toward eliminating accidents and injuries in your department, make it a practice to . . .*

1. Look for unsafe conditions. Physical hazards account for about 20 percent of all accidents.

2. Look for unsafe acts. Human failure (carelessness and blatant disregard for safe operating procedures) accounts for almost 80 percent of all accidents.

3. Learn from your mistakes. Investigate every accident and near-miss to find out why they happened and how they can be prevented—then follow through by imple-

ACTION PLAN:

_____

_____

_____

_____

_____

_____

menting those steps.

No accident has to happen. When you and your people are committed to eliminating hazards and the human failures that lead to accidents, the result is a safety effort worth crowing about.

MACHINE OR MAN-EATER?

In a plant, there are all kinds of machines, many of which can contribute to a serious injury. And when the operation of a machine or incidental contact with it can injure employees, the hazard must be either controlled or eliminated. Failure to watch out for the safety of your workers can result in tragedy, and that's something you don't want . . .

On Your Conscience

Many workplace hazards related to machines are avoidable. And as the supervisor, it's your obligation to do everything possible to ensure that your people have a safe environment to work in.

When it comes to machines, one of the chief safety methods involves the use of guards. These devices can make all the difference in the world between worker safety and serious worker injury. Perhaps your company uses guards now, and injuries are still occurring. If so, the information contained in this issue can help you determine why this is happening.

Where Are the Hazards?

There are three areas of any machine that may require you to use some form of safeguarding. The first is the point of operation. This is where the worker actually performs his or her tasks, such as cutting, shaping, boring, or forming.

The second area is the power transmission apparatus. This includes all components of the mechanical system that transmits energy to the part of the machine performing the work. These components can be flywheels, pulleys, belts, connecting rods, couplings, cams, spindles, chains, cranks, gears, and so on.

Finally, every other moving part of the machine poses a hazard, including reciprocating, rotating, and transverse moving parts as well as feed mechanisms and auxiliary parts of the machine.

Take the time to look over each machine in your department. Examine each area we've mentioned and determine whether your equipment is properly guarded at present. In the next section, you'll learn what is considered a proper and effective guard.

Some Safeguarding Basics

To protect workers against machine hazards effectively, any safeguards you use must meet certain general requirements. For example, they must prevent contact. That is, the worker's hands, arms—or any other part of the body—must not be able to come in contact with moving parts. Furthermore, the guard must be secure; workers should not be able to remove or tamper with it easily. All safety devices should be made of a durable material that will withstand normal use, and should be firmly secured to the machine they are intended to make safer.

By the same token, the guard should not inspire workers to tamper with it by virtue of interfering with the work that must be done. Any safeguard that impedes an employee from performing the job quickly and comfortably might soon be overridden or disregarded. And that's when injuries occur.

Injuries can also occur when an object falls or is dropped into an operating machine, so your safeguard must be capable of eliminating this possibility. A small tool or fastener dropped into a cycling machine could become a deadly projectile that may strike and injure the operator of the equipment or a fellow employee working nearby.

To avoid injury to maintenance personnel, the guard should allow safe repair and lubrication without removal of the device. For example, oil reservoirs can be located outside the guard with a line leading to the lubrication point. This reduces the possibility that an operator or maintenance worker will come in contact with a hazardous area.

Finally—and ironically—some safeguards are hazardous themselves, and you should take care not to use those that are. A safeguard defeats its own purpose if it has a sharp point, jagged edge, or an unfinished surface that could cause lacerations. The edges of guards should be rolled in such a way that these problems are eliminated.

On Guard

Now that you know what problems guards should prevent, you'd probably like to know what types of machine guards are available. There are four common types, and each has its relative advantages and disadvantages. You'll have to decide which characteristics are desirable for the equipment in your department.

The first type is fixed. As its name implies, a fixed guard is a permanent part of the machine. It isn't dependent on moving parts to perform its intended function. It may be constructed of sheet metal, screen, wire cloth, bars, plastic, or any material substantial enough to withstand impact and endure prolonged use. The fixed guard is usually preferable to all other types because of its relative simplicity and permanence.

A second type of guard is known as interlocked. When it is opened or removed, the tripping mechanism and/or power automatically shuts off or disengages, and the operator cannot start the machine up again until he or she has put the guard back in place on the equipment. This type of safety device works well in departments where employees are prone to modify—that is, tamper with—guards in order to make the job easier.

Finally, there are two types of adjustable guards. The first allows the operator to change the device when various sizes of stock must be accommodated. The change is carried out manually, which contrasts with the self-adjusting guard. The openings of these barriers are determined by the movement of the stock. As the operator moves the stock into the dangerous area, the guard is pushed away, providing an opening that is only large enough to admit the material. After the stock is removed, the guard returns to the rest position.

To a large extent, the type of machines your department uses will determine which type of guard you use. Talk to your employees to see if the guards currently used are doing the job and are comfortable to work with. Their experience with the equipment has probably given them a measure of expertise in this area.

Training: The Best Guard of All

The best, most expensive safeguarding system in the world won't be good enough if your employees don't know how to use it—and why they should use it. For that reason, you should make safety one of the watchwords of your department. Go beyond machine guards to talk about the overall need for safety; how unsafe work habits can contribute to worker injuries and thus lowered productivity.

And when a new employee does come on board, make sure he or she is given a thorough foundation in the proper use of machine guarding techniques. This training should involve instruction and hands-on sessions related to the following:
- A description and identification of the hazards associated with each particular machine.
- The safeguards themselves, how they provide protection, and the hazards they are supposed to mitigate.
- How to use the safeguards, and why they should be used as a matter of course.
- How and under what circumstances safeguards can be removed, and who is authorized to do it (in most cases, repair and maintenance personnel only).
- What to do if a safeguard is damaged, missing, or unable to provide adequate protection. In virtually every case, the employee should report the situation to you immediately—and not use the machine under any circumstances.

When the Unthinkable Happens

If you follow all these steps, learn about guards, select them carefully, and train employees in their proper use, then chances are you won't have to face a worker injury caused because a machine wasn't guarded properly. But there is a small chance, and it's one you should be alert for.

How can a guarded machine contribute to injury? Perhaps the injured employee removed the guard because he or she found it easier to work without it. Perhaps the guard had not been replaced correctly the last time there was repair work or preventive maintenance done to the equipment. Perhaps the guard really wasn't compatible with the machine it had been placed on.

Whatever the reason, you must reconcile yourself to the fact that either your message hasn't gotten through or that your duty to provide your workers with a safe environment hasn't been fulfilled.

If the problem lies with you, conduct an investigation after an injury has taken place. Determine what you could have done to prevent the situation. It's possible that you didn't choose the right type of guard or didn't provide training that was extensive enough for workers to understand the dangers.

On the other hand, if employee tampering caused the injury, the situation will carry its own message: There's nothing like seeing a colleague rushed off to receive first aid to inspire workers to use machine guards properly in the future.

▶ **WHAT YOU CAN DO** → *Machine hazards can lead to serious employee injury, up to and including loss of limbs or life. To protect your workers...*

1. Learn about the potential hazards posed by machines in your department. Analyze them to determine which should be guarded.

2. Decide which type of guard is suited to each piece of equipment. Choose from fixed, interlocked, adjustable, or self-adjusting devices.

3. Provide thorough training to employees. Stress the dangers inherent in tampering with machine guards and explain the right way to use them.

4. Use vivid, real-life examples to reinforce your points. If you know of an incident when tampering with guards led to an injury, don't hesitate to share it with employees.

It's your responsibility to help protect workers from being injured on the job. Taking these steps will help ensure that you meet your obligations to the people you supervise.

ACTION PLAN:

_____
_____
_____
_____
_____
_____
_____
_____
_____
_____
_____

CORRALLING HORSEPLAY

"Horseplay"—the word itself sounds innocuous, almost fun. But it's serious business. An estimated 25,000 workers are injured "fooling around" on the job each year. That can add up to productivity problems, because an injured employee won't be available to perform his or her job. Therefore, you have to let workers know that it's time to...

Quit Fooling Around

There are several good reasons why horseplay should not be allowed in the workplace. The obvious one is that employees who engage in such behavior compromise their own safety as well as the safety of their co-workers. Horseplay-related injuries can lead to workers' compensation claims or even lawsuits, something no company wants to face.

Injuries caused by horseplay have other detrimental effects: They seriously impair the productivity of your department. When an employee can't come to work because of an injury, others have to take up the slack. Therefore, it's imperative that the supervisor eliminate horseplay from the department and see to it that it doesn't start up again.

A Little Game of Catch

Supervisor Chris Teague walked out to the plant floor just in time to see the plastic lid of a coffee can go sailing past her nose. Fifteen feet away, Jerry Rusk made a leaping catch of the lid.

Looking in the other direction, Teague saw that the "pitcher" was another one of her employees, Hal Sposato. "What's going on here?" demanded the angry supervisor.

"We were just playing a little game of catch," replied the startled Rusk.

"Around all this machinery?" asked Teague. "Are you guys crazy? You could get seriously hurt, or hurt one of your co-workers. Not only that, but I would like to think you could find something more productive to do than flinging a coffee can lid around. Get back to work."

"But we don't have anything to do," protested Sposato. "Both of our machines are down, and we're waiting for Maintenance to fix them."

"Well, find something to do," ordered Teague. "I've told both of you at least a dozen times that horseplay is off-limits in this department, so you should understand that I mean it."

Dual Responsibility

Who's responsible for this potentially dangerous episode of horseplay? The two employees certainly are; their actions are both childish and inexcusable. But the supervisor is just as responsible for what has taken place.

How can this be so? Didn't Teague order the employees to stop what they were doing and get back to work? Of course she did, But to put it bluntly, so what? By her own admission, she had told the workers the same thing numerous times in the past. It obviously didn't do any good then, so it's not likely to do much good now.

Also, if Rusk and Sposato have time to play catch during working hours, there's probably something wrong with Teague's supervision. Employees should not look at slack time as an opportunity to goof off and fool around, but as an opening to turn their attention to other tasks, such as general housekeeping chores.

Cutting down on—or, hopefully, eliminating—horseplay is a matter of responsibility, both yours and your employees'. It's your responsibility as a supervisor to get your employees to act responsibly. Education and consistent discipline are the best ways to accomplish that—a course of action that Chris Teague would do well to adopt.

Tell Them Why

When employees understand the dangers that can arise from horseplay, they're more likely to obey your rules regarding it. And there's no sense in waiting for something to go wrong—for a worker to be injured—before you take action and tell employees that horseplay isn't allowed. Their education should begin the first day on the job.

On a new employee's first day in your department, make it a point to outline the dangers and penalties attendant to fooling around on the plant floor. Don't hold back—if you can provide them with a graphic example of how someone you know was injured because of horseplay, by all means tell them about it. It will reinforce the message you're trying to get across, and better illustrate your remarks.

"Too Much Time on My Hands"

It's easy for employees working at repetitive jobs to turn their attention to horseplay in order to relieve the monotony. And it's usually easier for workers to fool around in a slack period than to ask the supervisor for another assignment. Both of these areas call for education.

First, you can solve the problem of the bored employee in most cases by providing all your workers with cross-training. Then you can rotate them from task to task, which should help in keeping them active and occupied.

Second, impress upon your employees that when they find themselves with nothing to do, they should come to you and find out if there are any other tasks they can perform. Cross-training pays off here, too: You can place an idle worker at any spot in the process if he or she already knows how to perform all the functions of the department.

Also, idle time is a good time to clean equipment, to do some preventive maintenance, or to sweep up around the workstation. In other words, you can always find something for a worker to do in order to forestall horseplay.

Paying the Price

If the only price employees have to pay for engaging in horseplay is getting a half-hearted rebuke from you, chances are they won't take you too seriously. That's why you must consistently discipline offenders and not allow a single instance of horseplay to pass unchallenged.

Let's look back at the example we considered at the beginning of this discussion. Supervisor Teague handled the situation incorrectly, mostly because she hadn't backed up what she had said in the past about horseplay being off-limits. What's the right approach for her to take?

First, Teague should have informed every employee that there are serious penalties for being involved in horseplay, and she should have spelled out what those penalties were. Then, the first time she caught anyone in the act, she should have warned the person not to do it again.

Of course, Teague did give a verbal warning—but that's all she did. The next time an instance of horseplay occurred, she just issued the same empty warning again. What Teague should have done was issue a written warning, or take the next step in her predetermined discipline plan. From there, suspension and even dismissal would have been appropriate if the employee persisted in the forbidden behavior. That action would have removed an insubordinate, dangerous worker, and would have shown other employees that Teague was serious when she said that horseplay would be punished.

This point can't be stressed enough: You must take action every time you witness horseplay. If you allow it once, employees may think they can get away with it another time. You must be consistent if you expect employees to heed your warnings when it comes to horseplay.

Here's the Bottom Line

All of this may seem a little severe to you. Sure, people have been hurt because of horseplay. But if the gang wants to toss a paper airplane around on their break, or bounce a little rubber ball to each other, what's the harm? You may think you'll just alienate your people if you come down hard on them.

Well, what if that paper airplane stays on the floor at the end of the break and someone slips on it? What if that little rubber ball hits Jack while he's working at his machine, startling him and causing him to lose a finger?

Here's the bottom line: There is never, never, never a reasonable excuse for engaging in horseplay or allowing your workers to do so. The risks just aren't worth it. And what justification could there possibly be for playing games on company time?

In the final analysis, you should never "lighten up" where horseplay is concerned. Be adamant when telling your employees that it is forbidden, warn them of the consequences of it in terms of both safety and discipline, and follow through on that discipline when an episode of horseplay does take place. That's the best way to corral horseplay in your department once and for all.

▶ **WHAT YOU CAN DO** → *Horseplay is one of the leading causes of productivity-killing injuries in the workplace. Keep things serious in your department by...*

1. Educating employees about the dangers inherent in horseplay. Explain some of the common injuries that such behavior can lead to.

2. Warn them about the department's disciplinary policies concerning horseplay. And let them know that you'll make full use of the discipline available to you.

3. Keep your word. When any horseplay takes place, no matter how innocent it seems, discipline the offenders promptly and appropriately.

ACTION PLAN:
_____
_____
_____
_____
_____
_____
_____

4. Be consistent. If you ignore some fooling around just once, you are undermining the message that horseplay is unacceptable.

There's never a good reason for horseplay in the workplace. Impress this message upon your employees and you'll stand a better chance of keeping their productivity high.

_____
_____
_____
_____
_____

HOW TO BE PREPARED FOR DISASTERS

When supervisors think about safety, they usually limit their observations to their immediate surroundings—the workplace. But there is a gray area of safety that many companies forget to include in their programs—preparing for the disasters that Mother Nature dishes out. And if she rears her head during work hours, you'll be responsible for your employees' safety. So you should know what to do...

When Disaster Strikes

You can't schedule natural emergencies. Hazards like earthquakes, floods, and tornados can strike at any time with lethal swiftness. Would you know what to do if a hazard struck while you were in charge?

Sad to say, most supervisors and managers aren't prepared for natural disasters. Many companies' safety programs simply don't stress this aspect of safety. Yet there should be a plan for any natural emergency that has some possibility of striking your workplace.

You're Responsible

While it is ultimately up to the company to establish safety guidelines, it is you who is responsible for carrying out management's policy. Being a supervisor puts you in the best position to run a safe department. But if your company has no policy for coping with natural disasters, it is your responsibility to bring unsafe conditions and ideas for change to the attention of your superiors at once.

Here are some suggestions on how to set up an emergency preparedness program.

Step One: Catalog Your Risks

You don't prepare to meet a snow emergency in Albuquerque. You find out which disasters are likely to occur in your area of the country. How do you discover this information? You can turn to a variety of sources:

Start with your local library. There are books on all types of natural disasters, and many have excellent national maps that pinpoint your chances of getting hit by an earthquake, a flood, or a tornado.

Contact your local police, fire department, or sheriff's office. These officials can tell you who has responsibility for emergency preparedness or disaster action in your community.

Check with your local office of the National Weather Service, which can give you the latest information about the occurrence of natural disasters in your section of the country.

Don't skip this first step. You may think you know of all the possible natural hazards in your area, but your memory may be short. Just because you don't remember an earthquake or a tornado doesn't mean one can't occur.

You should also get accurate information on the weather patterns if you work in a newly developed industrial park. Why? Because the area might have

Evacuating Disabled Workers: How to Do It Safely and Easily

Imagine this: Your department is on the top floor of a building and a fire suddenly breaks out. Power is interrupted. The elevators are jammed, and employees must get out by taking the stairs. As the supervisor, you're responsible for getting everyone out—including several disabled staffers. Are you prepared to handle such a situation?

While this scenario is hypothetical, the situation is not farfetched. Casualties happen under similar conditions every day. That's why you should have emergency evacuation procedures in place that can be relied upon to get all employees, including the disabled, to safety.

Bettering the Buddy System

Many companies use buddy systems that require able-bodied staffers to help disabled employees get out in case of an emergency. But this system has loopholes. In some locations, wheelchairs and stretchers aren't easily maneuvered down a stairwell, explains one Midwestern safety expert.

However, there are ways to improve this type of buddy system. How? By using specialized evacuation chairs for disabled employees. Two able-bodied workers may still be assigned to a disabled person, but these chairs can take some of the burden off the able-bodied employees. One company who adopted this new evacuation aid reports that wheelchair-bound workers now feel more confident about their prospect of weathering an emergency, and employees who aren't disabled no longer feel uncomfortable about helping others out.

Training for Smooth Operation

In any evacuation plan, whether you use specialized equipment or not, training is the key to a safe departure from a building in a crisis. You should train all staff members to operate special safety devices. Here are the steps to follow in such training:

- **Provide visuals.** Visual aids are always a plus when showing workers how to operate new equipment. Show a videotape or slides that explain how an evacuation chair works and present general guidelines for using it during an emergency.

- **Prepare written guidelines.** The video should be supplemented with written instructions developed in-house to show how the chair is used in an evacuation. These guidelines reinforce the video and are retained at the workplace for reference.

- **Give employees hands-on experience.** Watching how a product works and reading about it are good ways to learn how to use it. However, people will never be fully confident unless they actually work with the product. During your training program, you should be sure that workers are given a live demonstration of how to use the chairs and are allowed to practice using them.

- **Hold evacuation drills.** Once employees are familiar with how to use the chair, practice evacuation procedures. In order to minimize interruption to production, stagger the drills so that part of your crew is working at all times. Your company may have already set up standard drill procedures, according to floor, department, or some other way that is convenient in your facility. Whatever the case, it's essential to practice under "real" conditions. Then, in the event that an emergency *does* occur, workers are not likely to panic.

Prepare for the Worst, Hope for the Best

You may think that elevators and a simple buddy system are enough to suit the evacuation needs of your disabled workers. But keep in mind that elevators aren't always readily available and they are susceptible to power failures. Plus, your able-bodied employees will feel more comfortable—and able—knowing they can easily help handicapped employees down the stairs to safety.

It's up to you to make sure your department is prepared for every potential crisis. If you have doubts about your current evacuation procedures, then make a change for the better.

been forest or open fields at one time. Conditions such as flooding would not have been noticed. So get all the facts before you develop your emergency plans.

Step Two: Set Up Guidelines

You've done your research. You know that tornados, floods, hurricanes, or blizzards can be a threat in your area. Now you're in a position to formulate some plans. Here are some guidelines you can follow to deal with specific emergencies:

■ **Floods.** If you live in an area where flooding can be expected during heavy rains, the local authorities have probably mapped out evacuation routes. Find out what they are and make sure all your employees know them. These routes have been set up as the fastest and safest.

Warn your people to travel with care. They should leave the workplace early enough to avoid being trapped by rapidly rising waters. What looks like a few inches of water might be a 3-foot-deep pond covering a washed-out section of the road.

■ **Hurricanes.** Chances are you'll have enough advance warning so that you probably won't be at work when a hurricane hits. But here are some precautions to follow regardless of where you are during the storm:

- Have plenty of batteries on hand for flashlights and radios.
- Stay tuned to the radio or television for updates. Pay special attention to hurricane watches, because tornados sometimes accompany hurricanes.
- Board up or tape windows to prevent glass from shattering in the high winds.
- Keep vehicle gas tanks full in case of evacuation.
- Know the evacuation routes.

■ **Tornados.** In areas where tornados are prevalent, the local authorities may set up systems to alert the public. There are three specific stages in these procedures that you should be aware of:

Stage one is called a tornado alert. If tornado weather conditions exist, a city or town would alert residents with a siren.

Stage two is a tornado watch. This means conditions exist such that the formation of a tornado seems imminent, or a tornado has been sighted in the area. A siren alert is also used in this case. The siren pattern for a tornado watch would differ from the tornado alert pattern.

Stage three is a tornado warning and means take cover. Again, a siren is used to alert the public.

Your company can duplicate this method by using the public address system to keep employees informed of tornado danger. If your company doesn't use a P.A. system, then suggest using the fire alarm to warn everyone.

If a tornado is headed your way and the safety of personnel is endangered, do not let anyone leave the building. Instead, all personnel should go to preassigned locations for cover. The basement is usually the safest area of a building.

If you happen to be driving to work when a tornado forms, leave your car. Find shelter in a nearby building or lie flat in a ditch until the storm passes.

■ **Blizzards.** If a storm takes place during the night and continues on into the morning, many companies broadcast closings on the local radio station. If the storm occurs during working hours, some facilities give their employees the option of going home.

If there are deep drifts and icy roads, however, no one may be able to leave. Then what? It could be a long time before anyone goes home. You should be prepared with some disaster necessities.

Use this checklist to stock your department not just in the event of a blizzard, but for all potential disasters:

- **Flashlights**
- **Blankets**
- **Fire extinguishers**
- **First-aid kit.** In addition, ask employees who take special medication to keep an emergency supply on hand.
- **Food.** Keep 72 hours' worth of food on hand for as many people as you might have to put up. Canned juices, powdered or canned milk, cereals and unsalted nuts store the best.
- **Water.** Figure three gallons per person for a 72-hour stay.
- **Tools.** If you don't have access to a machine shop or have a fully stocked toolbox around, obtain at least the following: a variety of wrenches, including pipe and crescent in case you have to turn off both the gas and the water main; an assortment of screwdrivers; pliers; shovels.

Keep in mind that these are general guidelines. They will enable you and your people to weather most natural emergencies but should be expanded to suit the specific needs of your situation.

Natural disasters account for over $17 million worth of damage and thousands of deaths each year. But you can reduce losses and save lives if you are prepared. Don't wait for the alarm to go off; if you do, you've waited too long.

> ▶ **WHAT YOU CAN DO** → *There's nothing you can do to redirect a tornado, stop a hurricane, or tame a blizzard. But you can stave off some of the worst that nature has to offer if you...*
>
> 1. Recognize the need for disaster preparedness and understand your role in bringing this to the attention of your superiors.
>
> 2. Investigate the kinds of natural disasters that occur in your area of the country.
>
> 3. Draw up plans for each possible natural disaster, and then make sure all your employees understand them.
>
> *Keep these plans updated as necessary and keep your fingers crossed that you'll never have to use them!*
>
> **ACTION PLAN:**
> _____
> _____
> _____
> _____
> _____
> _____
> _____

TRAIN WORKERS TO BE SAFETY EXPERTS

There's no doubt that accidents have no place in your department. But it's often difficult to find effective ways to keep them at a minimum—or to eliminate them altogether. It can be done, however, relying on resources you already have at hand—your employees.

It's an Ongoing Need

No matter what your department's safety record may be, there's *always* room for improvement. Even a minimal number of accidents each year can cost plenty—in terms of employee disability, lost productivity, and higher insurance rates for your company.

Therefore, you have an *ongoing need* to reduce the number of accidents in your department. And you can fulfill this need by giving your employees the responsibility for preventing accidents and injuries.

You Need a New View

Experts say that the problem with many supervisors' safety efforts is that they attempt to *control* employees. They tell workers, "do this" and "don't do that—or else!" This approach often fails because—let's face it—few people like to be told what to do and what not to do. They like to feel that they're taking a particular action because it's *their* idea, because *they* believe it's necessary—not because they are being coerced into it.

With this in mind, you must allow employees to assume responsibility for solving their own safety problems. And providing them with this task is going to require a certain style of thinking on your part. For example, you must:

Believe that individuals make a difference

Think in a cause-and-effect fashion

Concede that employees are capable of setting their own goals

Be willing to provide feedback that will tell employees how they're doing

Accidents aren't a result of fate, luck, chance, or magic. If employees don't believe their efforts will make a difference, that is the time when accidents will occur. So, *you* have to believe that employees can think for themselves and make valuable contributions to your quest for a safe department—and then impart that faith and confidence to your people.

When workers are made to trust their own judgment and allowed to put their gray matter to work, the search for safety solutions becomes a discovery process—a learning experience that helps workers understand how accidents occur and how they can be forestalled—and thus increases their commitment to hazard elimination.

Promote Team Problem-Solving

Your first step in involving workers in safety efforts is to put them through a series of exercises that build decision-making skills, team problem-solving, and group interpersonal relationships.

For example, a typical team-building exercise might include "creating" a tough problem and then asking employees to work it out individually first, then as a group.

For instance, you might create an imaginary scenario in which your people are involved in a plane crash in the sub-Arctic with a short store of supplies. You should instruct them to solve this problem alone by coming up with a way to use those supplies in order to survive.

Then, after they have solved the problem on their own, you should instruct them to work together as a team to solve it. Based on the experience of one company, the team did a better job of solving the problem than any of the individuals *90 to 95 percent of the time*. It was an effective synergy.

For instance, in the subarctic survival exercise, one of the "tools" workers are given is a compass. While many individuals might rank this high in importance, it is hoped that at least one individual in the group would be sharp enough to remind everyone that since magnetic north is *in* the sub-Arctic, a compass is basically useless.

The eventual goal, after a number of such exercises, is to improve workers' ability to solve problems as a group. At first, it may be hard for them to believe that the games they're playing are safety related, but they eventually see the connection: namely, that several heads are far better than one in solving difficult issues.

Strengthening the Safety Connection

When employees get to the point where they are comfortable with and skilled in group problem-solving, you can begin to relate these skills to solving actual safety problems in your department.

You can do this by taking the following steps:

1 Present employees with a real safety problem. For instance, you may have too many back injuries in your group. Ask employees, "What can be done to correct this problem?"

Your action will tell workers two things: First, you're telling them that you feel they are smart enough to solve their own problems. Second, you're letting them know that they can come up with their own solution instead of having one dictated to them.

In this way, you're sending employees a message that says: *You're* the ones getting hurt. Your own solutions to your problems are likely to be more effective than anyone else's solutions. In addition, you should be eager to buy into the solutions because you came up with them on your own.

2 Ask them to set reduction goals. Let employees set their own goals in terms of accident reduction. If you ask employees, "How many injuries are you willing to accept?" their answer will probably be "None"—no worker wants to get hurt or see a co-worker get hurt. And because that's the case, employees will come up with ways to meet the tough goal of total injury reduction.

3 Offer guidance and positive feedback. Although you want employees to solve safety problems on their own, keep in mind that they'll still need the benefit of your experience and advice to keep them on track. So ensure them that you're ready to listen to any possible solutions they may have and advise them of their feasibility.

You may also need to facilitate their problem-solving efforts. How? For example, if your people are tackling the problem of reducing back injuries, they may come to the conclusion that such injuries would be reduced if worktables were raised (or lowered). And in such an instance, they might depend on you to contact the Maintenance supervisor to make the appropriate adjustments.

And after an employee problem-solving effort has resulted in success, be sure to praise the workers involved for a job well done. Even if a safety team idea is not practical or workable, you should always offer a pat on the back for the effort and encourage them to go "back to the drawing board." This will help them to see that their contributions are appreciated, and that they *can* and *do* make a difference.

▶ WHAT YOU CAN DO → *You can turn your people into safety experts if you...*

1. Adopt the philosophy that workers can develop solutions to their own safety problems.

2. Instruct your people in problem-solving techniques, first as individuals, and then as a team.

3. Present workers with a real safety problem and ask them how they would go about solving it.

4. Ask them to set their own accident and injury reduction goals.

5. Be available for guidance and assistance at all times.

6. Praise your people for a job well done when they come up with a workable solution, and provide encouragement when their solutions are less than feasible.

In a nutshell, what you really need to run an accident-free department is a concern for people and a belief that they can solve their own problems. Don't be a dictator of safety rules—become a "facilitator of safety solutions."

ACTION PLAN:

_____
_____
_____
_____
_____
_____
_____
_____
_____
_____
_____
_____

CHAPTER FIVE
YOUR ROLE IN HUMAN RELATIONS

DEVELOPING HUMAN RELATIONS SKILLS

You're a real pro when it comes to the technical side of your job. In fact, your high level of expertise is one quality that led management to promote you to supervisor in the first place. But how would you rate your skill at handling the "people side" of your work? In order to be truly effective in your supervisory role, you need to hone your human relations skills as well as your technical abilities.

Creating Healthy Relations

"No matter how broad your technical knowledge is, you still need to know how to fit human relations into your supervisory skills," says Leon B. Kleinheider, construction superintendent for Hensley Construction Co. (St. Louis, MO). "This means making an ongoing effort to address employee needs and foster a climate of harmony and cooperation."

Kendred L. Bryant, Jr., PE, CPE, CEM, a Division Engineer Manager for Burlington Industries (Burlington, NC), concurs. "The secret to successful supervision is this: You should remember at all times that you are responsible for a certain number of employees, and you should never let anything take precedence over that responsibility," he asserts. "Your first obligation is to the people who report to you. After all, they are the ones who allow you to accomplish your job goals."

How can you fulfill your professional and personal obligation to your employees, and thereby develop the human relations skills you need to be the best supervisor possible?

According to these experts, it takes a dedicated approach that combines building mutual respect, solving problems, and consulting employees about departmental changes.

Developing Mutual Regard

"Mutual respect is the cornerstone of a productive workplace," says Bryant. A good way to develop this understanding with workers is to demonstrate your thorough knowledge of the job. If your awareness of the job is complete and up-to-date, workers will feel more able to come to you with their questions, confident that you'll supply the right answers. Bryant relates an example of how job expertise helped him win his subordinates' respect:

A Case in Point: "In my first supervisory position, I was five years younger than my youngest employee," he recalls. To test the new and youthful supervisor's know-how and mettle, the unofficial "leader" of the employees created a bogus problem for Bryant to solve.

Fortunately, he saw right through the scheme. Instead of chewing out the employee, however, Bryant explained to him the need to perform his work carefully so that the "mistake" wouldn't occur again. The result? By displaying his knowledge of the job, and by handling the situation calmly instead of getting angry, Bryant instantly won the respect of his employees.

On the other side of the coin, showing subordinates that you respect *them* is just as important as having them respect you.

Before Bryant took over his duties as a new supervisor, he was warned by the outgoing supervisor about a certain employee who constantly complained about anything and everything. Bryant reserved judgment, however, and eight months later he filed his first evaluation of the employee, rating his attitude as "excellent."

Why was his assessment of the worker so different from that of the previous supervisor? Because he discovered that although the employee did complain quite often, he was also one of the best and most knowledgable workers in the department. On a number of occasions, Bryant called the employee in the middle of the night for help with troubleshooting. Once he even had him paged at a local basketball game to come to the plant and help him solve a problem. The worker's reply was always "I'll be there in fifteen minutes."

Although Bryant didn't particularly care for the employee's disposition, he respected him for his positive attitude toward keeping the plant running.

The bottom line is this: Respect and appreciate employees for the things they do well. Don't dwell on personality flaws that ultimately haven't much effect on performance. Instead, build on them, stresses Leon Kleinheider.

"Make the use of individual differences," he advises. "If you try to understand workers' personalities, you may find that you'll also get the cooperation you need to make use of their technical expertise." *All* your workers—even the ones who seem to cause more than their share of disagreements—bring something unique and special to their jobs.

For instance, you might have a worker whose "gift of gab" often gets in the way of his or her productivity. But, as Kleinheider suggests, you can make the most of this trait by involving the worker in some phase of your job that will channel the person's verbal energy. Allow your "chatterbox" to read safety updates to the rest of the team, relay reports to other supervisors, or handle any telephone calls that you're able to delegate.

Get to the Root of Performance Problems

While it's perfectly natural for you to expect—and demand—excellence and consistency from your workers, you need to understand that your employees are only human. Occasionally, a person's performance will decline or behavior will become inappropriate—often without warning. When this happens, it can be difficult for a busy supervisor to deal patiently with the situation. However, it's crucial for you to be patient, cool-headed and considerate when such problems erupt.

"For example, when an employee suddenly jumps down a co-worker's throat, you should try to understand the cause of the outburst," says Kleinheider. "Don't immediately jump to the conclusion that the person has a bad job attitude and berate him or her. Instead, take time to sit down and find the underlying reason behind the problem.

"You might discover that the flare-up wasn't triggered by the job," he continues. "It's possible that the person who is upset has trouble at home." He recommends that you arrange a short meeting with the employee who had the outburst. Although it's not your job to hand out personal advice, you should give the person a little of your attention and a chance to talk things out.

Bryant knows the value of listening firsthand. It helped him save a worker's job, in fact. On one occasion, one of his veteran employees came to work intoxicated. Bryant had the option of firing the man on the spot, according to his company's policy; but instead he decided to drive him home and think about whether termnation would be the best course to follow. On the way, the employee explained that he had been under terrible stress from a number of personal problems.

Realizing that the man's inappropriate behavior was caused by this extraordinary stress, Bryant decided to keep the worker on. He explained to the employee how valuable he was to the department, and asked him never to come to work in that condition again. The worker thanked Bryant and returned the next day—sober—and never came to work "under the influence" again.

"For every action, there is an underlying explanation," claims Bryant. "And if an employee doesn't volunteer the information you need, ask questions. Never assume—*ask*."

Consult With Subordinates

Another way to ensure that you're paying adequate attention to the "human side" of supervision is to keep employees informed of any changes that are about to take place in the department.

By sharing this information with them in advance, you prepare them for any inconveniences that may arise as a result of the changes. After all, workers may have some valuable suggestions about how to make a transition to a new production system or scheduling plan more effective.

A few years back, Bryant was faced with a major renovation effort that he knew would cause inconveniences for his employees. Instead of simply going ahead and handling the project himself, he decided to open a dialogue with his workers.

First, he explained what needed to be done and asked each of his employees if they would be able to keep production going despite the upcoming disruptions. "Not a person in the entire group said No," Bryant asserts.

Next, he showed employees the renovation plans and asked, "Is there anything you would suggest that we do differently?" The workers did indeed have some suggestions, one of which saved the company thousands of dollars.

What was the result of including his people in the changeover in this manner? During the seven months it took to complete the renovation, Bryant didn't hear a single worker complaint. If he had not forewarned his people and asked for their cooperation, however, chances are they wouldn't have been so enthusiastic about working under the strain of the renovation. By consulting with them, Bryant showed that he valued their feelings and he kept morale high in the process.

When the renovation was completed, Bryant thanked his subordinates for their cooperation and had the company photographer take a group photo of all those involved in the effort. He framed the prints and gave each person one to take home. "Before beginning work on your ideas, always discuss them with your people," he stresses. "And when the job's finished, give them full credit for everything they did!"

You, Too, Can Be a Human Relations Pro

The job of a production supervisor consists of considerably more than just keeping production machinery running. You must also keep your people "running smoothly"—and that means addressing the needs of your employees daily.

"Always be willing to listen to your subordinates and help them in any way you can," says Bryant.

"Just as you use technical facts to solve production problems, you should develop—and depend on—the human relations skills you need to help you deal with people's problems," concludes Kleinheider.

▶ WHAT YOU CAN DO ➡ *To become a "human relations pro"* . . .

1. Realize that you have an obligation to deal with your workers as human beings, rather than production machines.

2. Make an effort to develop mutual respect with your people.

3. Appreciate—and utilize—individual differences.

4. Remain patient and considerate when an employee displays a performance or behavioral problem. Take the time to talk to workers and listen to them when they're having difficulties.

5. Consult your workers when changes are in the wind, rather than springing a major alteration in operations on them.

6. Give your people credit and recognition for a job well done.

ACTION PLAN:

> When you show workers that you recognize and respect their needs and feelings, you develop the human relations skills you need to be an effective, well-rounded supervisor.

GET ACQUAINTED WITH YOUR PEOPLE

A large part of your effectiveness as a supervisor depends on how well you get along with your subordinates. If the relationship is positive, employees will be more productive. Also, a friendly, congenial atmosphere makes for a more enjoyable work experience—for you, the supervisor and for your workers. Let's learn how you can reap these benefits in your department.

Getting to Know Them

As a supervisor, you have many duties—hiring, scheduling, motivating, disciplining, and appraising performance. With all the tasks on your agenda, why should you take the time to get to know your workers? After all, time is a premium, and making idle conversation is just a waste of it, right?

Actually, getting to know your staff is *never* a waste of time. Understanding and appreciating them as people pays off in both the long and the short run.

For instance, if you devote a little time every day to getting acquainted with your workers, you'll see two specific improvements:

★ **A more cooperative work force.** It makes perfect sense: When you like someone, you want to work hard to please the person. This simple fact of human nature applies to your people, too. If your employees respect your position and like you as a person, they'll tackle their work with greater purpose. Difficult tasks will be a little easier to perform. And overall performance will show a dramatic improvement, too.

★ **A more comfortable work environment.** Job satisfaction often depends on the quality of our work relationships. For example, if employees like their co-workers and their immediate supervisor, they are more likely to stick with a job than jump ship to another company for a slightly larger paycheck. At the same time, a good work relationship with your employees can be beneficial to *you*, too. Wouldn't you prefer to supervise employees that you know and like?

If you agree that creating friendly relations with your people could result in higher productivity and a more pleasant work environment, there is one tried-and-true method that you can use—and that is simply conversing with your employees each and every day.

Making Conversation: Don't Be Intimidated

That dreaded time is nearing—it's 8:30 a.m. You walk into the plant through the employee entrance, heading for your office. Your employees are at their workstations, preparing for the day's tasks. As you hurry past, you feel as if all eyes are upon you—with good reason. Your workers are watching you go by, wondering why you never stop to say a simple "good morning."

You wonder what's on their minds, as you nod hesitatingly to a person or two and manage to work up a weak smile. They return your acknowledgment. You quicken your pace as you draw closer to the haven of your office. You've made it! Safe at last!

Does this scene sound painfully familiar? Do you become uncomfortable at the prospect of dealing with your employees in any context but the strictest work-related situation? It's to be hoped that you do not.

But if you're like many supervisors, you have difficulty making small talk with your workers. Essentially, there are two reasons why many supervisors find it tough to get friendly with workers. These are:

● **Difficulty in walking the employee/management line.** Supervisors who have been promoted from the ranks often find themselves in the middle between enforcing management policies and communicating workers' needs. And because they are technically part of the management team, they find themselves distanced from their employees.

● **A lack of the "gift of gab."** Not all supervisors have the outgoing personalities that some management experts claim you must possess if you're going to be an effective supervisor. The truth is that most of us have average personalities and don't have a natural talent for making conversation. We stand in awe of the rare few who converse with great ease, holding everyone's undivided attention.

Breaking the Ice

Fortunately, there's hope for those of us who have a hard time conversing with ease. And it doesn't involve undergoing a "personality transplant." Rather, it entails altering your everyday behavior.

To relate to your employees in a more positive manner, make an effort to initiate at least one informal conversation with a different worker each day. If you can get your employees to open up to you, they'll eventually begin to feel you're interested in their concerns and that you care about them.

What types of subjects should you broach with your people? You can look for specific ideas in one of these two areas:

▸ **Job concerns.** An excellent way to launch into conversations with your employees is to let them know you're interested in their opinions of their jobs. How do they feel about their work? Do they have any ideas on how to improve operations? You might also mention a problem that you're having and ask for their assistance in solving it. Departmental issues are something that you and your employees have in common, and it's always easier to break the ice with a topic about which you both share knowledge.

Don't get discouraged if your first few attempts at eliciting a response are met with little more than a monosyllable or two. If you make a habit of asking for worker input, your people will eventually begin to feel more comfortable about telling you what's on their minds.

▸ **Personal interests.** This area can provide a wealth of discussion topics: Sports, children, hobbies, movies, travel—the list is a mile long.

How can you open up such discussions? One good way is to bring up a subject that you know a worker is familiar with. For example, if you know an employee is an avid tennis player, start a conversation by expressing interest in learning more about tennis.

How's That?

Once you get employees talking about themselves, their interests, or their families, it's important that you remember the details of what you've discussed.

There's nothing more disheartening for someone than to think that you're showing a genuine interest, when in reality, you're not really listening to them.

Of course, you don't have to recall every minute detail of a conversation with a worker, but committing the important points to memory or to paper will help ensure that you don't draw a blank the next time a discussion topic comes up. You'll prove to your people that you have a genuine interest in them as people—not just as workers. Plus, you'll cement good relations and encourage high performance in the process.

▸ **WHAT YOU CAN DO** → *If you want to cultivate better relationships with your employees . . .*

1. Realize that getting to know your workers could increase your effectiveness as a supervisor.

2. Make conversation with each worker on a regular basis.

ACTION PLAN:

_____

_____

_____

3. Prepare topics of conversation—selecting from job concerns or personal interests—to help the talks go smoothly.

4. Listen carefully to your people, and make sure you retain pertinent details of your conversations. That way, if a subject arises in the future, you'll be equipped to pick up where you left off.

Create friendly relationships with your people—and watch productivity flourish in your department!

HOW TO GET ALONG WITH YOUR PEERS

Nobody would deny it: There's a great deal of responsibility involved in being a supervisor. You have to maintain the productivity of your employees, while keeping your superiors informed about what's going on in your department and implementing their directives. With all the attention you pay to your subordinates and superiors, it's easy to overlook the fact that you also have to devote attention to developing constructive relationships with your peers.

What Causes a Lack of Cooperation?

It's the big championship game. There are only a few seconds left, and the home team is losing by five points. The quarterback takes the snap, fades back, and lets fly a picture-perfect spiral in the direction of the wide receiver—who suddenly decides he's thirsty and goes to the sidelines to get a drink of water. The ball lands 50 yards upfield, and the home team loses the game.

Such a thing would never happen in real life, of course. But it's amazing how often something very similar happens in the working world. Supervisors looking out for their own needs often fail to give their colleagues the help required to ensure that work is performed properly.

Why? There are a number of factors that contribute to an uncooperative atmosphere among supervisors:

★ **Misunderstanding.** A supervisor might say something that a colleague misinterprets as unwarranted criticism. Or a supervisor may not understand why a counterpart carries out his or her job in a certain way. In any case, when misunderstanding occurs, interdepartmental help can become nonexistent.

★ **Jealousy.** Supervisors sometimes don't work together because they're afraid of helping someone else make it up the company ladder instead of themselves. That makes them reluctant to share valuable ideas—or to lend a hand when another department runs into a snag that hampers productivity.

★ **A difference in management styles.** In any company, there are going to be people in the same ranking position who do their jobs differently. But a difference in supervisory techniques doesn't make one person wrong. Often, though, one supervisor can show a lack of respect for a colleague because he or she disagrees with the way another department is run.

★ **The "loner" syndrome.** Sometimes, you'll run into supervisors who just want to be left on their own. They believe that they're managing their departments quite well, thank you, and certainly don't need to interact with other supervisors. But problems can arise when this lack of communication causes personality clashes or productivity problems in a department.

★ **A perceived lack of time.** Many supervisors are just too busy to come to the aid of their peers—or they *think* they are. They're completely wrapped up in their daily duties and regard relating to fellow supervisors as a frivolous waste of valuable time.

Whatever the reason for one supervisor not cooperating with the other, the result is the same: damaged productivity. That alone is reason for you to strive for strong, helpful relations with your colleagues in your own department, and in the other departments that make up your company.

Practice What You Preach: Be a Team Player

No doubt, you make a point of building a sense of team spirit among your workers. You've found that it's the best way to keep the work moving smoothly, and that it provides a basis for solving any problems that might crop up. But you may not think of your fellow supervisors as members of a team that you belong to—and that's a big mistake.

Because in fact, you and your peers *are* part of a very special team that provides a link between management and employees. And if you fail to become a team player, you rob yourself of your colleagues' valuable assistance and other supervisors of your own aid and insight.

In the sections that follow, you'll meet some supervisors who don't believe that it's necessary to cooperate with their peers, or who don't know how to get along. Then we'll find out why they're wrong and what they should be doing to be effective team members.

Case #1: Mind Your Own Business!

Supervisor Luke Casey was pretty easygoing. He always spoke to his people in dulcet tones, because he believed patience was the key to motivating workers. Jim Gant, the supervisor of a neighboring work group, was a supervisor of a slightly different color. He felt that sometimes a hard-line approach was more effective for turning worker problems around.

One day, while passing Gant's work area, Casey overheard him chiding his people for a production error they had committed. It wasn't the first time Casey had overheard such a thing. *This guy's got to ease up a little,* he thought. He strolled over to Gant later that day and put his two cents in. "You know, pal, you should really lighten up on your people," he suggested. "I know from experience—you'll get a lot more flies with honey than you will with vinegar!"

"For crying out loud, mind your own business!" sputtered Gant. "That was the third time I had to talk to them about that problem, and I figured it was time to get tough! What I do in my group is my own affair!"

Comment: Casey broke two unwritten rules of supervisory cooperation. First, he took it upon himself to criticize a fellow supervisor. Second, he criticized before he had all the facts. The only time you should bring up a colleague's perceived shortcomings is when serious consequences could result if you don't speak up right away.

Case #2: A Private Affair

Ginny Lyman knew better than to jump to conclusions and then criticize another supervisor on the basis of premature observations. So she waited more than two weeks while she observed employees in Will Hughes's group carrying out an important production step incorrectly.

When it became apparent that Hughes was going to do nothing about the situation—and this after several jobs had fallen behind due to delays caused by rework—Lyman decided to approach the other supervisor.

Hughes was talking to one of his employees when Lyman walked up to him and matter-of-factly told him his people were creating problems for other departments. Hughes reddened as he listened in stony-faced silence. Then he turned his back to Lyman. *Well!* she thought as she walked away. *You'd think he'd be happy that I straightened him out.*

Comment: Lyman was right to wait until her suspicions were proved correct, but she was wrong to criticize her fellow supervisor in front of someone else, especially an employee. If you have something to say to a colleague about his or her performance, *find a private setting* in which to say it.

Case #3: A Helping Hand

June Jacobs' department had finally gotten caught up on its work, and she was proud of the extra effort her people had put forth. Because she wanted to let her employees relax for a couple of days, she wasn't in a receptive mood when Mary Morris, a supervisor from a nearby group, asked for some assistance.

"I'm sorry you've fallen behind, Mary, but I'm going to give my workers a break for a while," she said. "This is the first slack period they've had in a long time, and I'm not going to take it away from them."

Comment: If she wouldn't help out during a slack period, then when would she do it? Supervisor Jacobs was in a perfect position to help out her fellow supervisor and win the goodwill she may need to rely on in the future.

Because of her shortsightedness, though, it's pretty certain that she won't be able to go to Morris if she ever finds herself in the position of needing help.

You don't always have to drop everything you're doing every time a colleague asks for help. But when you can provide much-needed aid, you should—it's as simple as that.

Case #4: Work Out Problems Together

"I say we do the Acme order first," said Supervisor Bob Jackson.

"And I say we process the Wilson order first," countered Supervisor Bill Heckler. "Look, this arguing is getting us nowhere. Let's mull this over during lunch, and we'll make a final decision this afternoon."

But rather than wait, Jackson took the dispute to the plant manager. He made a case for giving the Acme order precedence, without mentioning any of the valid arguments Heckler had made in their previous conversation.

The manager sided with Jackson, and even dashed off a memo that stated his decision. When Jackson and Heckler got together later that afternoon, Jackson smugly presented him with the memo.

"What did you do that for?" demanded Heckler. "There was no reason for you to go over my head on this. It would have been just a matter of minutes before we reached a compromise. Now you've made us both look like we can't handle a simple decision."

Comment: Heckler is absolutely right. Solving minor disagreements together provides both parties with the opportunity to learn more about a fellow supervisor, and usually means that the two people involved will work in tandem to ensure that the solution agreed upon is carried out properly.

Going to someone else to get your own way will only spark resentment and alienation on the part of your peer.

Case #5: "Out Here on My Own"

"Say, Mike, why don't you come to lunch with me and some of the other supervisors today?" asked Martha Van Dyke. "We're going to discuss that memo about the new tardiness policy."

Van Dyke didn't really expect Mike Engels to accept her invitation. After all, he had always made a practice of keeping to himself in the past. However, he always declined politely, offering a logical excuse. And there was no question that he was a hard worker.

For those reasons, his fellow supervisors liked him in spite of his lack of sociability.

"Sorry," said Engels, true to form. "I'd like to, but I've got to get caught up on some paperwork. I'll take a rain check, okay?"

Comment: Engels isn't hurting anyone but himself. His reluctance to join other supervisors socially on occasion denies him the golden opportunity to keep up on the latest trends at his company.

Worse, it robs him of a friendly foundation that he could fall back on if he ever needs assistance or advice on the job. In the end, Engels is the one who suffers as a result of his attitude.

Supervisory Cooperation: A Common Goal

In the cases we've looked at, the offending supervisor has forgotten that he or she is a member of a team working toward a common goal. That goal is simply this: providing a good product or service to the customers who patronize the company.

Only when supervisors realize that dissension in their ranks can affect the company's bottom line and make their jobs far less pleasant than they have the potential to be, will they put aside their differences and behave like members of a winning team.

Now that you know the consequences, aren't you willing to make "cooperation" your motto when dealing with other supervisors?

▶ **WHAT YOU CAN DO** ➡ *To create cooperative, peaceful relations with your peers . . .*

1. Keep your thoughts to yourself when you see another supervisor doing things differently, unless serious consequences could result. Don't forget that "different" doesn't necessarily mean "better."

2. Criticize in private when you must do it at all. You'll only embarrass and alienate other supervisors if you point out their shortcomings in front of others.

3. Help your peers whenever possible. You'll build goodwill that you can rely on when you need assistance yourself.

4. Solve problems together instead of going over someone's head. A compromise is better than a win-lose situation.

5. Don't pass up chances to socialize with your peers, if your schedule will allow it. Such activities can develop and strengthen bonds between supervisors and pave the way to enhanced problem-solving efforts and improved overall productivity.

One last note: When it comes to getting along with your colleagues, the Golden Rule is a good one to follow: Do unto other supervisors as you would have them do unto you!

ACTION PLAN:
_____
_____
_____
_____
_____
_____
_____
_____
_____
_____
_____
_____
_____

BUILD PRODUCTIVE RELATIONSHIPS WITH YOUR SUPERIORS

Just about every supervisor has a direct superior to whom he or she must answer. But not every supervisor enjoys an open, pleasant relationship with the boss. While it's true that personality plays a large role in determining how well two individuals will get along, there are other, more controllable factors involved as well. How can you improve and maintain healthy relations with your superior? Let's find out.

In Over His Head

Here's a story about one supervisor who committed a major gaffe regarding relations with his superior. As you read it, ponder the person's blunder. Why was his action such a big mistake?

Dave Chrysler supervised the production department of a small machine parts manufacturer. One day, while considering the high level of rework that his group had been forced to do, he hit upon a great idea for reducing it. Why not place inspectors at various points along the line, rather than have the parts scrutinized at the very end of the production process? That way, errors could be caught and remedied early on, instead of piling up.

Chrysler was sure his plan had time and cost-saving merit, and he wanted to make sure he received full credit for it. So rather than tell his manager, Carol James, about his brainstorm, he went straight to the company president. He was afraid that if he passed his suggestion up the chain of command, his superior might get the kudos he felt were rightfully his.

When Chrysler ran the idea by the president, he agreed that it had potential. "So, what did Carol James have to say about it?" he queried.

"Actually, I haven't mentioned it to her," Chrysler stammered. "I wanted to come straight to you. I-I just thought that the sooner we tried the new idea, the more time and money we would save."

"Perhaps," said the president. "But I really think you should ask Carol for her opinion on the matter. She has a lot of experience here, and she could give me the information I need to make a final decision."

Disappointed, Chrysler sought out James and told her about his idea and his conference with the president. She was understandably miffed that Chrysler had gone over her head. "Why didn't you come to me with this?" she asked, "I would have been happy to discuss the idea with you."

"I was really proud of my idea and wanted to make sure the big chief knew it came from me," he conceded. "I was afraid I'd get lost in the shuffle if I went through the chain of command."

"Well, if you'd only come to me in the first place, I would have been glad to give credit where it was due," James said stiffly. From the look on her face, Chrysler knew he'd seriously—perhaps permanently—injured their relationship.

Rule #1: Always Follow the Chain of Command

Chrysler violated one of the unwritten rules of conduct regarding superiors: *Never break the chain of command.* This only serves to strain your relationship with your boss.

Similarly, you shouldn't allow members of management to bypass your superior if they want special help from you. Say a manager from another department asks for your help in getting a project out on time. Stifle the desire to assist the other person, and instead, refer him or her to your boss for an answer. That way, you won't run the risk of committing yourself to something your superior doesn't want you to do.

The chain of command isn't the only thing you have to consider to win the continuing trust and respect of your boss. Let's examine some other aspects of your relationship that you must take into account.

Rule #2: Be Dependable

One of the best ways to maintain a good relationship with your boss is to always be conscientious about your job performance. This means coming to work on time, handling daily duties efficiently, and completing reports by the date your boss desires them.

If you receive a special assignment or request, give it top priority. Don't work on it to the exclusion of all of your other tasks, but pay as much attention to it as you can.

Furthermore, you should keep the boss apprised of your progress with all jobs, and especially special assignments. This will help you to finish the project on time, because your superior will be able to monitor you each step of the way. Also, this gives your boss a chance to steer you in the right direction should it appear that you're missing the mark.

And, most important, it will give your boss some concrete data to provide *his or her* boss with, when asked for a progress report. (Don't forget that just as you must answer to your superior, that person is in turn held accountable by a higher-up.)

Dependability also means being consistent in your opinions and decisions. If you're one of those people who change their views more often than their shirts, your boss isn't very likely to rely on you for your insight. Your goal should be to build a reputation as a person who is capable of making intelligent, thoughtful decisions—and one who stands by them once they've been made.

Rule #3: Take Responsibility

If you make a mistake on the job, how do you deal with it? Do you try to cover it up in the vain hope that it will go away? Do you pass the buck, blaming the error on another party, say, an employee? Taking either of these approaches will take you down several pegs in the eyes of your boss.

You'll gain far more esteem if you own up to your

mistakes and take full responsibility for them.

Go to your superior and tell him or her that you erred—rather than denying it and waiting for the boss to hear of your error from other sources. He or she will be more prone to trust you if you can honestly fess up. Elaborate apologies aren't in order, simply a statement of fact.

Then offer to make amends for the mistake. Offer several solutions to the problems that have arisen as a result of your faulty judgment. Your boss will appreciate your willingness to make restitution and the fact that you've thought up some solutions on your own, rather than burdening him or her with the responsibility of dreaming up remedies.

Rule #4: Know Thy Boss

A crucial aspect of getting along with your boss is learning his or her likes and dislikes. This goes beyond work-related matters and includes any facets of his or her personality that could be cause for disagreement.

For instance, if your superior is a big fan of a certain baseball team, you won't score any points on the likability scale if you openly root for the opposing team.

More important is the way your boss views work matters. Is he or she a stickler for accuracy, even at the expense of time? If so, you'd do well to encourage your people to take great pains in their work rather than rushing through it.

Conversely, does he or she insist on promptness, at the occasional expense of quality? Then you'd better make sure all production deadlines are met, and avoid laboring unduly over minor details.

Knowing these types of things helps you to please your boss, and prevents misunderstandings.

Rule #5: Make Suggestions For Improvements

A good way to get on the good side of your boss and stay there is to provide him or her with suggestions for departmental improvements. Every manager enjoys having subordinates who make work life easier, rather than more burdensome.

If you're lucky, your boss will deem your ideas fit for implementation, and will make it clear to top management that you were the one who came up with those ideas.

But even if you don't always get full credit for your suggestions, you can feel confident that your manager will appreciate your contributions. This rapport will enhance your relationship and make life at the plant more pleasant for both of you.

Do Unto Your Boss As Your Best Employees Do Unto You

The final key to a constructive relationship with your immediate superior is to behave for him or her the way your star employees behave for you. Ask yourself which people are your most valuable staff members, and then consider what makes them so special. Are they dependable, respectful, hardworking, or all of the above?

Whatever the characteristics that you admire, chances are that your boss would like to have you exhibit the same qualities. When you do, you'll have cemented a positive relationship—one you can fall back on when you need direction or can't solve a problem on your own.

▶ WHAT YOU CAN DO → *You'll build better relations with the boss if you . . .*

1. Follow the chain of command. Suggestions and questions should be presented to your immediate superior first. He or she can decide on a course of action from there.

2. Demonstrate dependability. Perform your job conscientiously and consistently. Don't change your views from day to day.

3. Assume responsibility. If you commit an error, admit it, and then go on to rectify it. Never try to pass the buck.

ACTION PLAN:

_____
_____
_____
_____
_____
_____

4. Know your boss's likes and dislikes. You'll avoid inadvertently crossing your superior if you know his or her sore points.

5. Make helpful suggestions whenever possible. Your boss will appreciate the extra assistance.

6. Model yourself after your best employees. The same qualities that make them valuable to you will make you valuable to your own boss.

In considering ways to improve your human relations skills, don't neglect one very important human: your boss. It pays to invest the effort in building the best relationship possible. The better you get along with the person, the easier it will be for you to approach him or her with job-related problems and requests.

THE IMPORTANCE OF RECOGNITION

Do you have a department full of conscientious, hardworking employees? Are you proud of their high-volume output and the quality of their work? If so, when was the last time you told them how proud and pleased you are? After all, you can't expect them to feel like turning out an excellent performance forever if you fail to provide them with the motivating praise they so justly deserve.

Why Bother?

Sam Diamond's production crew had been going full tilt for three weeks, trying to complete a major parts order for an important customer. Due to their superhuman efforts, the order was completed four days ahead of schedule.

When the last item had been processed on the line, the group let out a great cheer, which brought Diamond charging out of his office. "What's all the commotion?" he demanded.

"You'll be glad to hear that we just finished the Jackson order—and the deadline's not until Thursday," exclaimed one worker, Jackie Jones. "And you said we'd never do it! Isn't it great?"

"Well, let's not hold up production with a party now," said Diamond. "Get started on the Apex job. That's next on the agenda." And with that, he headed back to his desk.

"Boy, how do you like that? He could have offered us a crumb of recognition," muttered Joe Baumann, a recent hire.

"Let's not hope for *too* much," piped in Martha Dey, a longtime employee of Diamond's. "I've worked in this department for three years, and I've never heard an encouraging word from Sam. Sometimes, I wonder why I stay here."

"I'll tell you one thing, I'm never going to break my back for him again. I mean, he doesn't have to constantly shower me with praise, but I don't enjoy feeling that I'm not appreciated in the least," said Baumann.

Completely deflated, the group reluctantly initiated their next project. They plodded along at a snail's pace, devoid of drive and enthusiasm. While walking past the production floor later that day, Diamond noticed his people's lack of verve. "What's the matter with you people? Haven't you

138

been taking your vitamins? Come on, let's pick it up!" he shouted.

He didn't notice at all when we were really pumping it out, but he sure notices when we've slowed down a bit, the crew thought en masse.

Give Them a Tangible Reward

Diamond's consistent failure to show recognition for his crew's efforts produced several negative results. First, it made them feel unappreciated, which lowered their morale and enthusiasm for the job. This in turn diminished their productivity, and that meant reduced output for the department.

To keep your employees' energy and productivity at their peak, you need to positively reinforce their accomplishments. Recognition not only gives workers a much-needed morale boost, but it can also provide a challenge for improvement.

How? If George is a borderline worker and sees Sally being rewarded for her high performance, he may strive to increase his own productivity in an attempt to reap the same benefits.

Recognizing achievement also gives you a chance to gear down a little from the "boss-worker" mentality for a few minutes and exchange some pleasantries with the people you supervise. This can go a long way towards building an atmosphere of cooperation.

The Casual Approach

The best rewards of all are those that allow you to reinforce achievement on a regular—even daily—basis. These rewards are given without a lot of fanfare, but they will get the message across to employees that you would like to see more of the same. For example:

★ **Verbal praise.** This is one of the most effective methods for letting a worker know that you appreciate a special effort. You can simply walk up to an employee and, within hearing of other workers, tell him or her that the achievement has not gone unnoticed.

★ **A cutback in close supervision.** Once an employee performs well enough to be rewarded for it, it's probably no longer necessary for you to supervise the person as closely as you have in the past. You can create a feeling of worth and independence in such workers by allowing them to carry out their jobs with little direction from you, and by assigning them to special tasks, such as training new employees.

★ **Asking their advice.** It's a good feeling when someone comes to you to seek your opinion on a particular subject. That's why you shouldn't overlook the value of seeking your employees' advice as a method of recognition. Whenever possible, talk to high achievers to get their opinions about a change of techniques in the department, ways to improve output or quality of work, or about any other subject. By doing so, you'll be demonstrating that you consider them intelligent, capable, and important to the success of the department.

★ **Preparing them for advancement.** One of the most constructive things you can do for an outstanding performer (not to mention the company) is to prepare an excellent worker for advancement.

You can spend more time with the person to upgrade his or her skills, make the employee aware of promotional opportunities, and alert upper management to the fact that you have an employee who is a prime candidate for promotion. Then, if a slot for a team leader should open up in your department, you would have the time to give a fine worker an upgraded position.

A More Formal Affair

When you have the means at your disposal to recognize achievement in a more formal manner, you can supplement your day-to-day recognition efforts with more formal types of rewards. Talk to your superiors to find out what type of program they might find appropriate. Here are some suggestions:

● **Appreciation certificates.** This is just what it sounds like: a piece of paper that spells out the achievements of the individual or team and thanks them for the effort put forth. These can be printed in advance and the employee's (or group's) name can be filled in when it comes time to present the certificate. You might hold a brief "ceremony" during a break at which the certificate may be presented.

● **Gift certificates.** Some supervisors obtain these from local stores and restaurants and present them to those who meet or exceed their expectations. Remember, approval (and funding) must come from top management first, and it's vital that the certificate be for something the employee has a use for. If the reward is inappropriate, few people are going to make an effort to strive for it.

- **Banquets, picnics, and other get-togethers.** If upper management can supply sufficient funds, you may want to consider a get-together with employees to show them how much you appreciate what they've done. Banquets, luncheons, picnics, softball games, and the like, are all fun and effective ways to let your people know the pride you take in their accomplishments. And *they'll* feel proud, too.

- **Bonuses and raises.** This method of recognition will definitely require management approval. But it's one of the most powerful ways to acknowledge good performance. Needless to say, it's also one of the methods most appreciated by the recipients.

Make It Public

Whether you implement a formal or an informal recognition program, one of the most important things to keep in mind about praising employees is that it should almost always be done in public. After all, if other workers don't know about the accomplishments of your high achievers, how can they be expected to emulate them?

Public recognition is something most people enjoy, and it's another chance for you to take a moment from the usual boss-worker relationship for a few relaxed minutes with your employees. Again, this is an ideal opportunity to build better relations with your people.

There could be some exceptions to this rule, however. For instance, if you know for a fact that a certain employee would be embarrassed if he or she were singled out for praise, it would be a good idea to choose a recognition alternative that won't put the worker in the spotlight—for example, simply call the employee into your office for a few words of thanks.

Honor the Individual, But Don't Neglect the Group

In some cases, the success of your group may be dependent on the performance of a few key individuals. Or, one worker may show a dramatic improvement in his or her performance, while others fall below past productivity levels or remain static. Therefore, it's crucial to recognize individual achievement. You'll boost the morale of top performers while setting a standard for other workers to shoot for.

However, some employees are simply average—no more, no less—but that doesn't mean they should be neglected when it comes to recognition. You should always try to find *something* you can praise each of your people about.

Constantly being second best to a top achiever can have a negative effect on some employees. If they see others winning accolades all the time, and can't ever hope to measure up to the best performers no matter how hard they try, their morale is almost sure to suffer. And that can make it even harder for these workers to perform well.

Remember, even your "worst" employee can be praised for something: a slight improvement in productivity, an impeccable attendance record over a period of a few months, or making a money-saving suggestion. Just be sure the reward fits the accomplishment.

In a similar vein, don't praise every single little thing a consistently excellent worker does. That may make the person seem like a "supervisor's pet" in the eyes of your other people, which can have a dangerous effect on team spirit in your group.

Rewards in the workplace should be a challenge for further improvement on the part of other workers, and reinforcing small accomplishments may only encourage employees to think small. If you think big, your employees may do so, too, and they'll give you those big productivity and quality improvements you're looking for.

▶ **WHAT YOU CAN DO** → *You can implement a good recognition program by following these steps...*

1. Talk to your superiors and find out how extensive your recognition program may be. Learn what kind of support and funds are at your disposal before you launch into a formal appreciation program.

2. Use a casual, everyday approach to providing rewards

ACTION PLAN:

_____

_____

_____

_____

such as verbal praise and asking for their input.

3. Reward individual achievement. You should always give credit where it is due.

4. Praise in public whenever possible so that employees will realize that recognition for outstanding work will be forthcoming if they improve their performance, too.

5. Look for something good about each worker that you can praise so that no one feels left out in the cold.

Using these techniques will almost assuredly improve the morale of those who already perform well, while providing an incentive for those whose performance may be lacking.

PM FOR PEOPLE: HOW TO PREVENT PEOPLE PROBLEMS

Every supervisor understands the importance of keeping equipment in top condition with preventive maintenance. But many supervisors do not realize that the techniques used to keep machines in tip-top shape will work for people, *too. If you think of your workforce as a finely tuned piece of equipment, you'll understand the importance of preventing "people problems."*

Watch for the Symptoms

You can tell when a piece of equipment will be a candidate for repair in the near future. Perhaps it begins to make strange noises or doesn't warm up as quickly as it used to. In any case, there is most likely a symptom or two that alerts you to a problem.

The same is true of your workers. Where there is an increase in tardiness, a drop in productivity, or friction between co-workers, there is most likely an underlying problem causing the symptoms you see on the surface.

It's your job to get to the root of the problem and eliminate the cause. Thus, the conscientious supervisor knows that it's important to keep an eye out and should always

1. Be alert for the symptoms of marked changes in behavior and output.

2. Know what to expect if any of these symptoms occur. For example, co-workers who suddenly don't get along—and don't cooperate with one another—are apt to experience a slump in their productivity. If you're aware of what can happen when employees don't cooperate, you'll move more swiftly to solve the problem when it appears.

3. Take immediate action to prevent the problem from continuing. Very few problems can be solved simply by being ignored.

Productivity on the Downswing

Supervisor Dack Taylor was puzzled: Gina Connors, one of his best employees, had fallen into a rut lately. Her recent low productivity was a far cry from her usual output, so the supervisor's concern was quite justified. When Connors had started the job, she took pride in her work, and was always the first one to speak up when productivity and quality improvement ideas were needed.

But now she appeared to have lost interest in doing her job well. She was often late, seldom met the work goals Taylor set for her, and no longer seemed to care about improving operations.

Oh, well, Taylor thought. *Maybe she'll just snap out of it.*

But the sad truth is, she may not be able to do so without some concerned supervisory intervention on Taylor's part.

The Similarities Between People and Machines

Maybe Connors *will* snap out of it—and maybe she *won't*. If she does, it won't be because Supervisor Taylor helped her to do so. It will just be a lucky happenstance. If she doesn't come around, her productivity will no doubt continue to slide, and she could become even more discouraged. Eventually, that discouragement could cause her to quit her job.

The irony in this case is that if Taylor had a machine in his department that was dragging down productivity as much as Connors is, he would probably take corrective action immediately.

He would investigate the problem, pinpoint the cause, and take steps to repair any damage. In fact, Taylor probably doesn't wait for machines to create problems. Chances are, he takes steps to keep them from happening with a preventive maintenance program.

Of course, people aren't machines. But some of the methods Taylor employs to keep equipment productive can be successfully applied to workers as well. Let's take a closer look at how he—and you—can do that.

Know Thy Employees

When a new piece of equipment is introduced to your department, you don't just throw the "on" switch and let an employee get started on it. More likely, you study the manual, look over the machine, and determine how it works.

Preventive maintenance of people requires that you acquire the same thorough knowledge of your employees. Get to know your workers; learn the limits of their abilities and what kinds of attitudes they generally display.

For instance, if John usually produces one-third more work than your other employees but is now producing half as much, that's a sure sign that a problem has developed.

Keep in Touch

Once you've learned what each of your people is like so that you can be aware of deviations from the norm, you can't simply sit back and hope that nothing goes wrong. It's crucial to problem prevention that you keep lines of communication with employees open.

To do that, spend a few minutes each day talking to your workers. Come right out and ask them what's on their minds. Find out if they're experiencing any work-related problems, and if there's anything you can do to help them. Your openness should encourage them to voice their concerns before they grow into big problems that can damage departmental productivity.

In the case we looked at earlier, Supervisor Taylor was only halfway home. He saw the symptoms, and knew Connors had a problem of some sort, but he was content to sit back and wait for it to solve itself. He didn't take the important step of initiating a conversation with his employee to find out what was on her mind. That was one of Taylor's biggest mistakes. Machines don't repair themselves, and supervisors can't always expect their employees to cure their own work-related problems. So what should you do when troublesome symptoms become apparent?

Have a Pointed Discussion

When an employee exhibits the symptoms of a work-related problem, *you should sit down with the person and have an in-depth conversation.* This discussion should differ from the talks we mentioned earlier in that you're no longer trying to find out if something is wrong. Rather, you already know something is wrong, and you are looking for a solution to the problem.

The conversation should take place in private, where the employee will feel free to speak openly. To encourage an even more open discussion, be sure you display:

- **Empathy.** Empathy is understanding the other person's feelings; putting yourself in his or her shoes so that you can get a better grip on the problem and what it means to the employee who is experiencing it.

- **An open-minded attitude.** An employee who

feels that you won't acknowledge the validity of any complaints won't bother to make any. Then you'll never get to the bottom of the situation. Make it clear that you are interested in the problem and are more than willing to listen to the employee's side of it.

• **An ability to read between the lines.** The troubled employee may tell you one thing but really mean something else. For example, let's say that Dack Taylor does sit down to have a conversation with Gina Connors about her productivity problem. Connors may say something like, "All the changes being made around here are happening too fast."

That's not enough for Taylor to go on, so he questions her more closely. Then he learns what the real problem is: When new equipment was added to the department, Connors didn't receive enough training on it to keep her productivity at her usual high rate. And this has not only caused a decrease in unit output, but it has led to her frustration and lack of enthusiasm as well.

The message here is that you must keep digging until you are sure you've found out what's *really* bothering your worker.

When you do find out what is causing a people problem, you must take immediate action to find a solution. Why? Again, you must think of the worker involved as a very vital cog in the human "machinery" that makes up your department. You'll then begin to recognize the importance of moving swiftly to keep problems under control.

A minor machine part that is not functioning correctly can have an effect on the parts surrounding it. The other parts will have to work harder to take up the slack created by the damaged item.

The same is true of the employees in your department. If one worker isn't pulling his or her weight, the other employees will have to work harder, and that can spark resentment and even bigger productivity problems.

So do whatever you can to solve people problems—pronto! If a worker needs more training, provide it as soon as possible. If an employee has an ill child at home who is causing concern (and thus distraction), empathize with the person while pointing out the need for improved performance. Your demonstration of concern for work-related problems can be the catalyst that helps workers turn around and become top producers once more.

▶ **WHAT YOU CAN DO** → *To prevent people problems from affecting productivity . . .*

1. Get to know your workers. Learn what they are usually capable of so that you'll know when something is wrong.

2. Keep in close contact with them. To learn about the problems they may be facing, talk to employees often and ask them what's on their minds.

3. Have a private, in-depth discussion with employees who are showing the symptoms of a problem. Without prying into personal matters, try to find out what's at the root of their difficulties.

4. Implement a solution immediately to resolve the situation. Waiting will only make the problem fester.

Your ongoing concern and swift attention to existing problems are all that are needed to make up an effective "PM for People" program.

ACTION PLAN:

_____
_____
_____
_____
_____
_____
_____
_____
_____

HOW TO HANDLE EMPLOYEE COMPLAINTS

The employees you supervise are probably content most of the time. They do their jobs well and willingly without constant pressure from you. But even the most contented worker is displeased with some aspect of work life from time to time, and when that happens, productivity can take a downturn. By fielding complaints quickly and effectively, you can successfully maintain high output and morale.

Who's Griping the Most?

If you made an informal survey among supervisors, asking what type of worker registers the most complaints on the job, you'd probably get a near unanimous vote for the poor worker. But this opinion reflects the fact that supervisors most often remember the petty, irritating dissatisfactions they hear from poor workers.

However, a closer look at a large electronics company turned up some interesting facts about who actually does the complaining.

In an attempt to determine which employees griped about what, 50 top producers and 50 low producers were asked to fill out a question sheet asking how they felt about their jobs and the company. They were also asked to state any major complaints in their own words.

The results may surprise you: It was found that the first rate workers actually made the most critical comments about their jobs. The company's personnel manager explains:

"Our best people are our worst critics. Twice as many good workers complain about something or other as do poor workers. And here's another discovery—the two groups complain about entirely different things.

"For example, the better workers will say that the machines aren't repaired fast enough; that their assistants are never around when needed; that there's no chance for advancement; that missing parts delay the work. Mostly, their complaints seem to be about the things that prevent them from being more productive.

"On the other hand, the low producers have different worries: They don't get enough recognition; the work is too dirty; there should be more time for lunch; we should have a better ventilating system, and so on."

What Does It All Mean?

The first thing this study suggests is that you need to consider *who's* doing the bulk of the griping—and *what* they're complaining about.

If the complainers are your high producers, their complaining may be motivated by a desire for smoother operations and, therefore, greater job success. These employees are probably ambitious and set higher goals for themselves than those who are content to just plod along. They probably suffer more disappointments and take their complaints very seriously.

And you should, too.

But no matter who complains or how insignificant the gripe, it's your duty to deal with it—and the complainer—and try to satisfy the person to the best of your ability.

A Step-by-Step Strategy

Handling worker complaints is best done in five steps:

- Listening
- Investigating
- Acting
- Reporting
- Following up

And *listening* may the most important step of all. That's because you need to have all the facts straight before you can do anything about the problems weighing on your employees' minds.

For that reason, you should always maintain an open-door policy regarding complaints. Let your people know that you are willing to hear them out whenever they are troubled about an aspect of work life.

In addition, you can seek employees out on an individual basis to find out what's on their minds before they come to you with a complaint. Or, you can call the department together periodically for a gripe session to let them air their grievances.

Why go around stirring things up? Why not just wait until a problem occurs and your people come to you to complain? Because employees may let a problem fester before they work up the courage to approach you—and during that time, productivity can drop, since their minds are liable to be more on the problem than on their work.

Once you've encouraged employees to come to you with complaints, *listen carefully* to what they have to say. Ask questions to clarify any points that are cloudy in your mind.

Sometimes, employees may simply want to get things off their chests, so just being allowed to talk about it will be enough to satisfy them. But make it a point to ask complaining workers what actions, if any, they might suggest to remedy the problem. They may present a workable solution and save you a lot of thinking time.

Whatever the case, make it clear to complainers that you will investigate the matter thoroughly and get back to them as soon as possible.

Be an Investigator

Having said you will carry out an extensive investigation, you then have to go ahead and do just that. Speak to some of your other workers (without revealing that there has been a specific complaint) to see if they share the same concern that was presented to you. Again, demonstrating a willingness to listen is a good way to gather such valuable information.

Once you have a firm grasp of how extensive the problem is, discuss the matter with your superior and your fellow supervisors. They may have handled a similar situation in the past and will be able to give you some pointers on how to deal with the complaint.

At this time, you should make an effort to put the complaining worker at ease. For example, if an employee has problems with the sick-leave policy of your company, you won't be able to change the policy on your own. Finding out what your limits are—usually by talking to your superiors—means that you won't make promises to your people that you can't keep.

If your investigation becomes a lengthy process, make it a point to check back with the complainer from time to time to let him or her know that you haven't forgotten the complaint and are still on the trail of a solution.

Choose a Course of Action

Once you've gathered all the information you need to make a decision, you have to settle on a course of action. There are three basic options:

★ **Correct the problem immediately.** If the worker's complaint is valid, and if it's within your power to satisfy it, you should do everything you can to clear up the problem right away. For instance, if Susan complains of back pains because her workstation is too high, call Maintenance and ask them to make some quick adjustments.

★ **Investigate further.** Deciding not to pursue a course of action is a course of action in itself. If you're not completely sure that you're ready to choose a method for addressing the grievance, the best thing to do is wait until new information comes to light that might alleviate the problem.

★ **Refuse tactfully.** Sometimes an employee's gripe will have no basis in fact. Then—without adversely affecting the person's productivity—you must break the news that you can't do anything to correct the situation.

Report the Good News and the Bad

As we said earlier, employees often complain just to get problems off their chests, not really expecting anything to be done about their grievances. So those people will be pleasantly surprised when you get back in touch with them to tell them to plan to remedy their difficulty.

But no matter what course of action you choose to take—even if it is to take no action at all—you must *report back to your people* and let them know how and why you came to that decision.

The best way to do this is to call the complaining employee into your office to describe what approach you've chosen to take. You might explain it in one of the following ways:

◆ **The problem will soon be solved.** This is the best news you can give to an employee who has complained. What you're saying is that there is merit in the complaint, and that corrective action will soon be taken, if it hasn't been taken already. This can boost an employee's sense of self-worth, since he or she has played an important role in bringing about a needed change.

◆ **The matter is up in the air.** On the surface, telling employees that their complaints aren't resolved yet seems like a poor move. After all, what you're saying in effect is that their complaint has not led to any positive results. But you should take the time to let them know that you and other members of management are still investigating the situation to see what should—or could—be done. That way, workers will know that you haven't forgotten the problem and that you may yet come up with a solution that pleases them, but you just can't tell them how long it will take.

▶ **The problem doesn't merit action.** Denying a request is a tough chore for a supervisor: It means telling an employee that the complaint isn't a valid one and that you can't help them in that area. However, you should express appreciation for the fact that he or she took the time to bring the problem to your attention. Also, make it clear that you have considered it carefully before denying a remedy.

At this point, a complaining employee is going to feel a great deal of disappointment. But you can keep disappointment from turning into resentment and low morale if you fully explain *why* you're leaving things the way they are. Conclude the conversation by assuring the worker that even though nothing was done this time, you still welcome their complaints and will devote the same thorough examination to their problems in the future.

Don't Forget to Follow Up!

If one of your people came to you with a complaint that you investigated, resolved, and reported on as quickly as possible, you'd probably feel your job was over. But your work's not finished yet! Whenever you make a decision about an employee complaint, you should *follow up* to ensure that the correct decision has indeed been made.

What does such follow-up involve? Basically, you need to check back with the worker after a period of time (say, a month or two) to find out if things are now going along well. If they aren't, you can try to work on another solution. Following up your efforts to deal with a complaint proves that you genuinely care about workers' concerns and are willing to help them remove the roadblocks that affect their happiness and productivity.

▶ **WHAT YOU CAN DO** → You'll be able to deal with worker complaints more effectively if you . . .

1. Consider the source and realize that some of your best people are your worst critics—and frequently have legitimate complaints.

2. Listen carefully to all employee complaints. Ask questions if you're not sure you fully understand the problem.

3. Investigate the problem thoroughly. Talk to other workers, fellow supervisors, or members of upper management to get their feedback on the matter.

4. Decide on a course of action based on the information you've gathered.

5. Promptly let the employee know what you've chosen to do about his or her complaint.

6. Follow up after a period of time to find out if your decision was the right one. If not, look for a better solution.

Complaints are often the symptoms of an "illness" in your workforce, an illness that can weaken productivity. But if you follow these steps, you'll have the cure right at your fingertips.

ACTION PLAN:

_____
_____
_____
_____
_____
_____
_____
_____
_____
_____
_____
_____
_____
_____

COPING WITH CONFLICTS

Conflicts between employees are usually the result of a misunderstanding, a difference of opinion, or a personality clash. Such situations are inevitable when people work together. But you can keep these minor conflicts from snowballing into major battles that disrupt the harmony—and productivity—of your department.

Spot Conflicts ASAP

Employee arguments have an extremely detrimental effect on your people's productivity. Because of this, you should learn to recognize disputes in the early stages so that you can resolve them as soon as possible.

Since subordinates will try to hide personal conflicts in the hope that they will win the battle before you get involved, you may have to watch carefully for the signs of discord between employees. Have you noticed any of these telltale signs in your department?

- Discussions that flare into arguments
- Open, backbiting remarks made by one person about another
- A refusal by one worker to speak to another
- A request by a worker to move his or her workstation to another area
- A request for a transfer
- Other employees talking about a feud
- Increased absenteeism or tardiness

Any one of these signs might not indicate a full-blown conflict between employees. But if you notice several of them, the odds are high that there is a serious dispute brewing.

Of course, the most obvious way to find out about a conflict is for someone to walk up to you and tell you straight out that he or she is having a problem getting along with a co-worker. The following story illustrates the way a worker might approach you about a problem. If this should happen in your department, you'll know it's time for quick action!

Prevent Open Warfare

Supervisor James Alberti was walking along the production floor when one of his employees, Vic Arthur, came up behind him. "May I have a word with you?" the worker asked, visibly upset.

"Sure, Vic," answered Alberti. "Let's go to my office and you can tell me your troubles."

Once there, the two sat down. "It's like this," began Arthur. "That new worker, Chuck Morris, is really getting on my nerves. If he's not bragging about his latest feats on the ball field, he's telling me some stupid joke that I'd rather not hear. You've got to do something about this guy."

"Have you tried asking him to leave you alone?" asked Alberti.

"Countless times," said Arthur. "I'm telling you, if he bugs me one more time, I'll be sorely tempted to punch his lights out!"

Alberti has just been served notice that he's got a real problem on his hands. A heavy-duty conflict is brewing between two of his employees, and something has to be done fast to prevent a full-scale war from erupting on the production floor.

A conflict between workers is one of the most delicate situations you'll ever have to face. It takes skill and tact to cope with it effectively. You don't want to handle it badly and arouse resentment from the opposing parties, nor do you want to lose your credibility among the other employees who have probably taken sides.

On the other hand, you can't let conflicts rage on until they become full-scale attacks. You want your people to concentrate on their work, not on personal vendettas. So to keep disputes from leading to bad feelings and lowered productivity, you have to address conflicts as soon as they are called to your attention. Don't ignore them or try to wish them away, because they're not going to go anywhere on their own. They'll simply simmer until you take the appropriate action.

Remedying the Problem

Let's say that you have a problem similar to Alberti's—how are you going to handle it? Here is a series of steps to guide you to a solution:

★ **Take control of the situation.** Make it clear to the conflicting parties that you are now aware of their problem and that you are going to resolve it, with their cooperation.

Meet with each individual separately and tell them that you'd like to know what words or actions led up to the conflict. Hold the meetings in a private place to encourage the involved workers to say exactly what's on their minds.

★ **Use good listening techniques.** In order to gather all the pertinent facts to make an informed decision, you have to listen to all sides of the story. Is their conflict based on specific events, or do they just have bad feelings about one another? Dig to get to the root of the conflict. Ask open-ended questions that cannot be answered with a simple Yes or No. Then restate the facts to make sure there's no misunderstanding.

★ **Remain impartial.** Remember, your goal is to find a solution, not to fix blame on any individual. Fixing blame, even when it's justified, will only make people defensive and less willing to cooperate. So you have to be objective.

Maintain an interested, receptive, yet neutral tone in confronting the involved workers. Don't project an image of suspicion, disgust, or disagreement.

Conversely, don't nod in agreement as an employee explains his or her side of the conflict. You don't want either person to feel that you agree and are on his or her side. You want both people to believe in your impartiality.

★ **Help the parties to put the disagreement into perspective.** You may gain a lot more cooperation than you anticipated if you point out that both workers have one thing in common: They are integral to the success of the department and of the company as a whole.

Therefore, any conflict between them is detrimental to the company—in terms of departmental distraction and lost productivity. By showing them how their conflict can affect the big picture, you may help them to put their dispute into proper perspective.

★ **Form an action plan.** After listening to both sides and maintaining your objectivity, it's time to make a judgment and formulate an action plan. You might ask the people involved to offer a solution to the conflict, along with specific ideas on what both of them can do to resolve the situation.

Whatever your final decision, work with both sides to help them put their dispute to rest. Get their assurance that they will carry out the terms of their action plan. Then, write these agreements on paper and have each worker sign them. Let both sides know that failure to comply with their plans will result in further, more severe action.

Don't Forget to Follow Up

The meeting you hold with the disputing parties should bring the causes of the conflict out into the open and offer a course for change. But you can't assume the problem is solved when the meeting is over and the action plans have been spelled out.

Back in their work environment, the individuals may try to work the problem out for a short time but may soon fall back into old, destructive patterns.

So monitoring their progress may be something you'll have to do for weeks or months to ensure that the conflict doesn't resurface.

How should you go about monitoring their attitudes? First, simply have an informal chat with each party once a week just to check on the situation.

If the conflict isn't being resolved, you may be forced to observe their behavior without their knowledge in order to get ideas for a more workable solution.

Solutions that require cooperation from both parties, however, may prove impossible. Angry workers may agree to compromise with no real intention of holding up their end of the bargain. In such a case, you will be forced to take a more severe approach.

It might be time to physically separate the feuding employees by moving their workstations away from each other or by transferring one worker to another department.

Although these measures may seem drastic, they're preferable to having an ongoing conflict that results in lowered productivity and disrupting the rest of your staff.

The Disciplinary Route

If separating the employees or moving one to another department is unfeasible, you should turn instead to progressive discipline. After all, open personal conflicts are highly inappropriate behavior that can interfere with the effective functioning of the department. And in these instances, you have every right to stress the severity of the situation by exercising your authority to discipline workers.

In the end, you, the supervisor, are responsible for resolving conflicts, but employees must play along. You can't expect all of your people to like one another, but you *can* expect them to do their jobs.

> **WHAT YOU CAN DO** → *To keep disputes between workers from reaching the boiling point . . .*

1. Realize that some conflict is inevitable, but that you have to referee when disputes begin to take a violent turn or interfere with productivity.

2. Learn the telltale signs of employee conflicts so that you can resolve them before they become unmanageable.

3. Meet with the disputing workers separately to point out how their conflict is disrupting the department.

4. Allow each employee to tell his or her side of the story, and remain totally objective until you have all the facts.

5. Get workers to agree to an action plan that requires each of them to follow specific steps to help dissolve the dispute.

Handling employee conflicts takes a lot of investigation and negotiation. But your reward will be a more harmonious, more productive workforce.

ACTION PLAN:
_____
_____
_____
_____
_____
_____
_____
_____
_____
_____
_____

HOW TO HELP YOUR PEOPLE ADJUST TO CHANGE

Any supervisor who's had to shepherd his or her work group through a major change—either in location, in equipment, or in work procedures—knows how traumatic the transition period can be. And if employees are frightened or wary of the change, the transition can be even longer and more difficult. That's why, as a supervisor, you must do everything in your power to help your people shift gears and cope with the change.

Making Changes Go Smoothly

It's human nature: Most people become set in their ways regarding work habits and want things to stay just the way they are. Familiar old machinery and operational techniques can become just as comfortable as a pair of well-worn shoes. And the thought of a major upheaval can send many workers into a panic.

For example, when word comes down that your department is going to get some fancy automated equipment, getting your employees to accept the new technology can seem like an uphill struggle. Here's a typical worker reaction to the news:

"Did you hear we're getting one of those computerized 1031's down here?" one employee asks the other. "You're kidding," comes the reply. "What do we need one of those things for? We're getting along just fine without it!" "That's right. So now we'll have to waste a lot of time learning how to run the darn thing. I don't like it—not one bit!"

What's really taking place here? Do these people actually believe that introducing a computer or other form of automation will be a waste of time? If pressed, they'd probably admit that that's not what's bothering them. Then what is?

Fear. Many workers worry about whether they'll be able to learn to operate a "complicated" new machine. Others fear the more efficient machinery will mean a cutback in personnel—and they'll be among the ones to get the boot. As a result, they begin to fight the change before it even takes place. But with the right strategy, you can overcome most resistance to change. It begins long before the change is actually taking place.

Preparation Is the Key

The most important rule in introducing any kind of change is to discuss it with those affected *as soon as possible.* By announcing a change *before* it's made, you give everybody time to get used to the idea. They won't be suddenly hit with a surprise, or hear all kinds of exaggerated stories from the rumor mill.

So keep your people informed—the earlier, the better. Here are five things you should be prepared to tell your employees:

- **What** the change is
- **Why** it is being made
- **Who** will be affected by it
- **When** it will go into effect
- **How** it will be implemented

In short, tell them as much as you know. If you merely confirm that new equipment is coming, you'll do nothing to reduce the anxiety and confusion. So explain the facts carefully, and then give your people plenty of time to ask questions.

Accentuate the Silver Lining

Aside from sharing basic facts about a workplace change, you should also stress the positive aspects of the change to your people. That way, you'll help to vanquish some of the "disaster fantasies" workers are wont to dream up when a change is in the wind.

For example, you should provide the following information before new equipment is installed:

★ Why the new machines were selected and why you feel they're a good investment.
★ How the new machines will eliminate heavy or tedious work.
★ How they will reduce department costs and increase company profits.
★ How lower costs and greater efficiency can eventually have a positive impact on employees' paychecks.
★ That the purchase of new equipment is a sign that the company is healthy and profitable—not that jobs are in danger.
★ That you have every confidence workers will be able to learn the new machines quickly, and that you stand ready to help them do just that.

With a few modifications, you can adapt most of these explanations to any imminent change in the workplace. When you do, you'll find that your people are much more willing to keep an open mind about the matter.

Don't Downgrade the Tried and True

In attempting to convey the pluses of a prospective change, don't be so enthusiastic that you completely downgrade the methods currently in use. Be careful in the way you refer to whatever is being replaced, whether it's a process or a machine. Why?

If you imply that the old method is totally inadequate, you might hear comments like these:

"What's the matter? The human way isn't good enough anymore?" Or, "I've been doing this job for five years and nobody ever told me I wasn't cutting the mustard!"

The people who have been turning out what they considered good work will resent any implications that it was marginal. So whenever you introduce a change, say something like this: "You people have been doing a great job for me. And this change will help you to do an even *better* job!"

The Honesty Policy

Another important thing to keep in mind when a change is nigh is to be honest with workers about any difficulties or temporary inconveniences the change might present. Don't promise your people the moon by telling them all the department's problems will be solved by these machines. Let them know what they can and can't expect when implementation occurs.

For example, explain what effect the change might have on the arrangement of the work area. If tables, benches, and the like have to be dramatically rearranged, forewarn your people so that they won't be shocked when they arrive at work and find everything out of its usual place.

If, for some reason, crews have to be split up or rearranged, tell your workers as far in advance as possible. People often become friendly and familiar with their immediate partners or teammates, and can become upset if they show up for work and discover, out of the blue, that they're no longer going to be working with their old buddies.

Provide Adequate Training

Your people will never be able to adapt effectively to new machinery or a new operation if you haven't given them adequate training. What should be included as part of your training program? It will vary, depending on the type of technology you are introducing. But a good general program should include instruction from the vendor, featuring intensive, hands-on training for you and your employees.

As your people learn their new skills:

♦ **Allow them the opportunity to ask lots of questions,** and provide clear, specific answers.

♦ **Ask them if they have any suggestions** as to how their training might be made more effective. They're the ones who have to do the work and have the most intimate understanding of their own needs regarding instruction.

♦ **Give them plenty of time to practice.** This will build their confidence and help ensure that they'll work more efficiently with the new system.

♦ **Watch them in action and make corrections when necessary.** Your people need your guidance more than ever when there has been a major change in operations.

♦ **Ease up on the pressure.** It's unreasonable to expect your employees to produce as much as before when they are just getting the hang of running a new machine or production process. Therefore, it's important that you let them know you're going to relax your demands a bit until they've gotten the hang of it.

It's far better to let your workers learn to do a new task well than to rush through it without really understanding it. The time you devote to a break-in period will be short, compared to the time that could be lost to rework and retraining somewhere down the line because employees never really learned in the first place.

Special Cases

During a period of transition, you may notice that certain employees are reacting to the change with more alarm than their colleagues. This group frequently includes:

● **Employees who lack self-confidence** in their work abilities.
● **Veteran workers** who have spent years perfecting their existing skills.
● **Recently hired workers** who have just gotten accustomed to the current routine.

How can you help to reduce their anxieties? First, spend extra time with them in training. Let them know you're ready, willing, and able to assist them whenever they need a hand.

Also, make it a point to express your confidence in their ability to learn the new information and use it effectively on the job. Also, check back with them frequently to make sure they're on the right track and to see if they have any questions.

Maintain Your Flexibility

As your department progresses through the transition period, unexpected factors may come to light. A flexible attitude on your part can pay off in a big way.

If you lay down the law about how the change is to be carried out, your employees may follow orders blindly—even when it's become apparent to them that the change isn't working out as planned.

This is a time when the insight of your people is extremely valuable, because they're the agents that are driving the change in the first place. *Solicit your employees' suggestions frequently during the entire transition.* They'll be less intimidated by a change if they feel they have a part in its implementation. And you'll benefit from the wealth of their job knowledge.

What should you do if it becomes painfully apparent that your employees are right—that the transition is meeting with a dangerous stumbling block? You should make any needed adjustments to the change, after discussing the situation with your higher-up.

Sometimes even the most minor adjustment—such as shifting someone's workstation or having two people switch tasks—can make all the difference to the change's long-range success. But unless you've been open and flexible in implementing the change, there'll be no room for you to make any needed fine-tuning later on in the process.

One Last Word

Helping employees to accept new equipment or production processes is a major undertaking. An overall strategy of understanding, support, and guidance is needed to achieve success.

This means that you will have to examine *your own* resistance to change, as well as theirs. By performing a thorough analysis of how you perceive change, you will be in a better position to understand how your people feel, and guide them through to a successful transition.

▶ WHAT YOU CAN DO → *To implement change with the greatest ease and efficiency . . .*

1. Understand the reasons why your employees may be reluctant to accept a change. This reluctance could stem from fear of failure or fear of losing their jobs.

2. Discuss the change with your people as early as possible. Be sure you have enough information to answer the what, why, who, when, and how.

3. Accentuate the positive aspects of the change, but don't downgrade current methods. Also, don't fail to mention the potential difficulties the change may present. You owe your people an honest rundown of the situation.

4. Provide proper training. Your people will better adapt to the change if they are well versed in the new methods. Give them a gentle break-in period, and pay special attention to those workers who appear especially intimidated by the change.

5. Remain flexible and open to worker suggestions. It might be necessary to make some adjustments along the way to make the change work. Asking your workers for their ideas, opinions, and recommendations for improvement is essential to implementing a change with success.

6. Examine your own feelings about change. It will give you some insight as to your employees' feelings, and help you to better address their concerns.

Following these steps will help you make workplace transitions as smoothly and painlessly as possible.

ACTION PLAN:

_____
_____
_____
_____
_____
_____
_____
_____
_____
_____
_____
_____
_____
_____
_____
_____
_____
_____

OLDER WORKERS: MAKE THE MOST OF THEIR EXPERIENCE

As the general population grows older, the work population naturally follows suit. In the years to come, the percentage of older employees in the workplace will continue to increase. Some supervisors may think that certain workplace problems will increase, too—like lowered productivity, decreased quality levels, more accidents. However, these supervisors have succumbed to the "myths of aging." Here's why you shouldn't follow their example.

Separating Fact From Fiction

There's no doubt about it: Certain physical changes that go along with the aging process do affect our ability to perform our jobs to some degree. But that doesn't necessarily disqualify us from performing those same jobs.

A bigger problem faced by older employees is the perception by others that they are no longer capable of handling their jobs. If you're guilty of holding this attitude, you're doing a disservice to your employees, your department, and yourself.

Let's examine some of the physical limitations brought on by aging, and then look at the limitations mistakenly placed on older workers by well-meaning supervisors and co-workers:

♦ Diminished speed

Physical endurance does tend to decline with age. In fact, the maximum work rate drops off about 60 percent between 35 and 80 years of age. However, the ability to work consistently can remain with an employee right up to the day he or she retires.

So while your older workers may not be able to exert themselves for the same period of time they always have, chances are they will adjust their pace on their own to ensure that their productivity rate stays the same.

For example, a worker who used to put forth a burst of energy at the end of the day to get all of her work done may begin spreading the work out over the course of the day to meet her production goals.

To help older workers who are slowing down as they near retirement, assign them tasks that they can pace themselves at—ones that don't provide a great deal of stress or variation in the work load.

♦ Vision problems

Older workers are more likely to experience vision problems than their younger counterparts. While only 23 percent of those under 20 years of age have a visual disability, 94 percent of those past 60 do. These declines occur in certain specific areas that will require special measures:

- **Glare.** Older adults are less able to see subtle visual contrasts. Too much light is just as great a problem as too little.

- **Peripheral vision.** Older adults are less apt to notice movement out of the corner of their eyes.

- **Color vision.** Adults over 55 are progressively less able to match blues and greens.

- **Depth perception** declines to a limited extent.

- **Diseases of the eye,** such as glaucoma, cataracts, and tumors are an increasing tendency.

Of course, not all of your senior workers will suffer from these problems. But in the event that one of them does, you can greatly help the situation by taking these steps:

★ Suggest corrective glasses or prescription changes to workers who seem to be experiencing vision problems on the job.
★ Provide proper illumination at all workstations.
★ Present job-related information verbally as well as visually.
★ Allow older workers more time to read job instructions and other materials.

♦ Hearing loss

Declining ability to hear is a common, natural part of aging—everybody knows that. But few people realize that hearing actually begins to lessen around age 14! Later in life, there is a general, more progressive decline.

One special problem you may have to deal with is a worker's increasing difficulty with screening out interfering noise. This may make some positions—where noise is at a consistently high level—

unsuited for older workers.

To compensate for the hearing loss that some employees may experience, always give instructions in a clear, deliberate, and carefully modulated voice. And remember not to turn your face away when talking with them. Many workers—of all ages—will rely on facial and lip cues to help them understand what is being said.

One thing to avoid: In your attempts to make your words understood by older workers, don't shout at the top of your lungs or make exaggerated facial expressions. This is almost always unnecessary, and will only serve to embarrass your seniors!

Also remember that just as medical technology provides us with visual aids (like glasses and contact lenses), there are also hearing aids available to assist those with varying degrees of hearing loss. Many of today's hearing aids are practically invisible when worn properly.

So if you notice a worker having difficulty hearing sounds at a normal decibel level, gently suggest that the person go for a hearing test. Many company infirmaries or similar medical facilities are equipped to administer hearing tests to workers in need of them.

If the person is already wearing a hearing aid, a simple adjustment in the prescription may be all that's needed to return him or her to normal, healthy hearing capacity.

▸ Reduced manual dexterity

Manual dexterity is another physical characteristic that tends to gradually decline over a period of years, due to natural stiffening of the joints and medical conditions such as arthritis. But this can be a blessing in disguise for the quality of the work done in your department.

Studies have shown that when decreased manual dexterity causes a worker to slow down, he or she works with greater care, accuracy, and attentiveness. Praising the careful work can minimize the lowered self-esteem that often accompanies having to work slower.

Age Doesn't Equal Inability

The physical limitations that older workers experience are often negligible compared to the limitations imposed on them by the misconceptions of others. Those "others" can include co-workers and supervisors.

People tend to lower their expectations of co-workers who are close to retirement age. They don't think the older employee can handle the job as well as he or she could in the past. But lowered expectations can often lead to lowered performance, as the misconceptions of others become self-fulfilling prophecies.

Senior workers themselves can foster the wrong impression of their own abilities in a couple of ways. For one thing, they may resist learning new techniques that could make the job easier, such as changes in operations and the changeover to automation.

To aid those who experience this problem, emphasize to older workers that they've been able to learn new things in the past, and should have little or no difficulty learning new methods now. Point out their past and current successes to reinforce your message.

Your older employees are also more likely to question the reasons for a change. They will want to know what they have to gain from doing a task differently, when the old way worked just fine. This can make others perceive them as stubborn or unreasonable. But more often than not, their questioning attitude is a result of a lack of confidence rather than mere bullheadedness.

In a case like this the key is to take more time explaining the definite reasons for the change, stressing the benefits to the entire operation in general, and to the older worker in particular. For example, the introduction of automated equipment may intimidate a senior. But in reality, that modern equipment will most likely make your senior's job easier and less taxing physically. Tell the person this, as you explain why the company has decided to implement automation.

Also, don't set strict time restraints or put pressure on a seasoned worker to change his or her ways. This only tends to generate anxiety, which undermines the learning process. Instead, let the worker move at a comfortable pace until he or she feels ready to make the change to a new technique or method.

Older Minds Can Be Gold Mines

So far, we've looked at some of the problems that reduction of physical abilities and misconceptions about older workers can cause in the workplace. But there are real benefits to having older, experienced employees on your staff!

● **Assistance with your training efforts.** These people can make ideal trainers for new employees. The years they've invested on the job have imbued them with a wealth of information about how the work can be performed for maximum effectiveness.

- **Role models for greenhorns.** Senior workers can also provide leadership for younger members of your staff. They can be a stabilizing influence, people others can look to for advice and role models. Longtime employees are usually more punctual than their younger counterparts and tend to be absent less often. If those younger employees choose to emulate them, that can only be good news for your department's productivity.

- **Advice on departmental improvements.** Because older workers have presumably "seen it all," they're uniquely qualified to make judgments about proposed changes in work methods. For instance, you may think that a certain untried technique might improve operations. But if you ask one of your veteran workers for his or her views, you may learn that one of your predecessors tried the same technique without success.

Or, because your senior worker knows the job "inside and out," he or she may see a problem with your idea, and suggest a minor adjustment that could make the difference between abject failure and resounding success. That can save you a lot of time, trouble, and expense.

Their Present Is Your Future

Barring the discovery of the elusive Fountain of Youth, *you* are going to be an older employee yourself some day. That realization can help you to improve your own attitude toward aging employees. It should also spur you to foster a positive attitude toward them on the part of your other employees.

The best way to change your outlook is to put yourself in their well-worn shoes. When you reach their age, do you want your peers and superiors to think of you as a liability to the department? Of course not! So don't think of your older workers in that way. Your positive attitude toward them will help them to build a positive mental attitude of their own.

If you show respect for their years of wisdom and experience, help minimize the problems caused by minor physical limitations, and utilize the knowledge they've picked up on the job, you will keep their productivity high until the day they walk out the door to begin their well-earned retirement.

▶ **WHAT YOU CAN DO** ➡ *To make the most of your older people's experience . . .*

1. Recognize the physical limitations that may be brought on by aging. Make reasonable adaptations in their jobs to keep these limitations from hampering their productivity.

2. Don't lower your expectations. By asking older workers to maintain consistent productivity levels, you encourage them to continue meeting their job goals.

3. Make full use of their experience. Ask them to perform such special tasks as training new hires or use them as a sounding board when you are considering trying a new work method.

4. Put yourself in their place. Ask yourself how you would like to be treated if you were in their shoes, and then treat them in that considerate fashion.

Throw away your misconceptions and help your subordinates to do the same, and you'll see why having older employees on your crew can be a positive, productive experience.

ACTION PLAN:

HOW TO INTEGRATE DISABLED WORKERS

"Hire the handicapped" is a slogan we've all heard. And it's a practice many companies have adopted. But once a disabled person is on the payroll, who's responsible for turning him or her into a productive worker? In most cases, it's you, the immediate supervisor. Here's a look at how you can create the best environment possible when there's a disabled employee in your workforce.

Who Are They?

When is a person considered handicapped? The U.S. Government defines a handicapped individual as one having an impairment that substantially limits one or more major life activities. These impairments can range from blindness and deafness to paralysis, multiple sclerosis, muscular dystrophy, cerebral palsy, and other disorders.

There are more than 20 million people in the United States with some form of physical handicap. And many of them are perfectly able to hold jobs that are traditionally thought of as being reserved for nonhandicapped employees. In fact, there are some jobs that disabled people can do better than people with complete physical capacity.

One example of this is the hearing-impaired distribution clerks who work for the United States Postal Service. Their inability to hear keeps them from being distracted by the consistently high noise levels where they work.

Unfortunately, supervisors often make the mistake of assigning disabled employees to the "safe" jobs, the ones that are generally monotonous and routine. Also, supervisors may make a careful point of not placing any pressure on handicapped workers, which can make other employees upset over the "special treatment" they think they are observing.

The keys to making disabled people a productive part of your staff are to topple the physical barriers in the workplace, to break down the psychological barriers you and your staff may have, and to build up departmental morale by treating everyone who works for you equally.

It Starts With the Interview

You may have no qualms about hiring a handicapped job applicant. But let's face it: There's always a moment of surprise to find that one of the people you've decided to interview is in a wheelchair or is disabled in some other way.

This can be a problem if applicants mistakenly perceive your obvious surprise and concern over etiquette as a signal that the door has already been closed to them. You'll get the best results if you simply relax and honestly express your feelings. Try saying something like "I hope you can bear with me. I haven't had much experience interviewing people in wheelchairs, but I really want to understand you and your qualifications."

What questions are considered proper in interviewing a disabled person? Again, honesty is essential. If you have genuine concerns as to the individual's ability to perform the work in your department, it's important to get those issues out into the open. The key is to keep your interview questions job related.

For example, a correctly drafted job application form will say *Do you have a disability that will limit your capacity to do this job?* However, it is not proper to ask *Do you have a disability? Please explain* or *Do you have a history of workers' compensation? Please explain.* Similarly, in an interview you can't ask "What exactly is your disability?" That doesn't specifically address the question of whether the person can perform the job.

To fully ensure that you're complying with laws protecting the handicapped—as well as displaying good manners—*focus on the job's requirements* and whether the individual is able to meet those requirements.

Integrating the Handicapped Worker

Supervising a handicapped worker for the first time can be an unsettling experience—for the employee, for co-workers, and for you. You may be unsure of how to handle the situation, and your lack of assurance could make it hard for the disabled employee to fit into your group.

But you should make a concerted effort to make handicapped employees an integral part of your team. Why? Because the results will be well worth the effort expended. The disabled often feel they must work twice as hard as other employees to get where they want to go in the working world. And their industriousness and their skills are usually just as good as other employees'.

So how can you effectively integrate disabled workers into your department? First of all, relax. The most important thing to remember is that disabled workers are *workers* first, and disabled second. In most cases it will just take some minor adjustments to make them valuable members of your work crew.

Toppling the Physical Barriers

The problem of building accessibility is a relatively minor one for supervisors to contend with. Most companies these days have willingly made modifications aimed at accommodating the disabled. Those companies that haven't made changes willingly have been required to make them by federal, state, and local laws.

So, your biggest problem with physical barriers will likely be rearranging your work area to make it most comfortable. These alterations will usually involve something simple: for instance, lowering the height of a workstation to make it easier for a wheelchair-bound employee to carry out the job.

Here are some other points to keep in mind:

- Reserve parking spaces close to the building for disabled workers, to minimize the dangers involved in negotiating a busy parking lot.

- Allow handicapped workers to arrange their own work areas. They understand their own needs better than anyone else, and will therefore come up with the best setup for maximum efficiency and comfort.

- Equip water fountains with gooseneck faucets and paper cups to eliminate the need to lower drinking facilities.

Guidelines for Blind Employees

There are some special points to keep in mind when you have blind workers in your department. For example, all your training materials may be in written form. If so, record the material on a cassette tape for them to listen to. Of course, the best training technique of all is demonstration, so don't hesitate to use that method—just as you would for other workers.

If the blind employee has a guide dog, several of your other employees may be allergic to or afraid of the animal. In that case, it may be best to move workers who have such concerns to workstations as far away as possible from the dog.

On the other hand, some of your employees may be inclined to treat the dog as a pet. You have to make it clear to them that the animal is there to work, just as they are, and should be left alone to do its job.

Hiring the Hearing-Impaired

If an employee who joins your department happens to be hearing-impaired, there are several steps you can take to help orient and train the person more effectively. The first consideration you must make is in regard to communication. An interpreter from a state agency may be obtained to help during the initial training process. But what about communication over the long haul?

One way in which you could greatly benefit your working relationship with a deaf worker would be to learn the American Sign Language. If you don't have time to do this, however, you might try writing notes to get particularly complicated messages across.

Fortunately, many hearing-impaired people are adept at lip-reading. Keep these factors in mind whenever you speak to a deaf employee:

- **Address the worker directly.** Look at the person head-on to facilitate lip-reading.

- **Speak slowly and distinctly.** But avoid exaggerating your lip movements. This will only make it harder for a hearing-impaired worker to understand you.

- **Use appropriate body language.** Gestures that emphasize your words can make your messages clearer.

Once you've bridged the communication gap, training should proceed smoothly, but avoid the temptation to slow down or overexplain because a worker has a hearing problem. While you want to ensure that the person adequately learns the job, you need to understand that people learn jobs at different speeds, whether they have perfect hearing or not. So, rather than overcompensate, simply use the same judgment you'd use with anyone else.

The Buddy Syste n

One matter you'll want to pay close attention to concerning handicapped workers is emergency

The Handicapped and Discrimination

Do you discriminate against the handicapped when making hiring decisions? The first step in dealing with state and federal laws banning handicap bias is to recognize who is protected by these laws. The Rehabilitation Act of 1973, which has served as a model for most of the states that have developed their own laws, covers:

- Anyone with physical or mental impairments that substantially limit one or more of life's major functions.
- Anyone who has a history of such an illness or disability.
- Anyone who is perceived as having such a disability.

The first group is the most easily recognized. Down's syndrome, hearing disabilities, and visual impairments can be readily identified. The second and third groups, however, are often less perceptible.

Anyone with a history of a disability is covered by the Act, especially when the employer regards that history as an indication of high risk. The courts do not consider high insurance rates and low life expectancy as contrary to business necessity. Therefore, the job opportunities for recovered cancer patients, diabetics, heart attack victims, and recovering alcoholics can't be limited for reasons of risk.

One company claimed increased business costs and the possibility of decreased efficiency justified its refusal to hire a man suffering from leukemia. A medical consultant had advised the company not to hire the man because he ran a high risk of infection from even minor injuries. But the Wisconsin circuit court noted that the company never claimed the man wasn't qualified for the job. He *was* qualified, ruled the court, so the refusal to hire him solely because of his cancer constituted discrimination.

The third category protects people who have no disability but are perceived as having one. In other words, an employer's misconception could bring an individual with no disability under the Act's protection. For example, the Washington Court of Appeals has ruled that such a worker was covered by the Act. The court awarded him two years' back pay and ordered the company to reinstate him. He had been discharged because his employer erroneously believed that he suffered from epilepsy.

■ **Putting Policy to Work**

Affirmative action policies are usually written by high-level executives and their legal counsel, but personnel directors, managers, and supervisors make them work. As a supervisor, you make decisions that affect hiring. You often develop job qualifications and evaluate job performance, so you must be sure your decisions aren't discriminatory. Your firm's policies will work best when you follow these rules:

- Use tests that are solely job-related. For instance, someone with a speech disability should not be given an oral test if the job entails little oral communication.
- See that physical requirements are job related. Physical exams, when used, should be given to all job candidates, and standards should be applied uniformly.
- Form job-related qualifications. Describe only the skills needed to perform the job.
- Reshape the job. Wherever possible, fit the job to the worker. If a disabled person can't do one minor task, give it to someone else and assign the disabled worker some other task. Slight modifications to equipment or work areas might be all that's needed to help a disabled worker fit into a job.
- Consider and reconsider disabled workers—for training programs, promotions, etc. Don't give them the easiest tasks for fear they wouldn't be able to handle the challenging ones. This would be discrimination, since it would keep them from gaining the experience necessary for advancement.

■ **Reaching Out**

Do you have an effective strategy for seeking out and accommodating the disabled? First, you must know where to look for disabled workers. Vocational rehabilitation agencies, sheltered workshops, and colleges will find you disabled workers who can do the job.

If your efforts to employ the disabled are to succeed, you can't sit back and wait for the handicapped to apply for jobs at your company. You must:

> - Review your hiring procedures to see if these individuals are being recruited.
> - Examine the physical and mental requirements of the work you have available and make sure these qualifications are directly related to the job and aren't obstructing employment opportunities.
> - Analyze your screening process and interviewing techniques to be certain they aren't discouraging disabled applicants.
> - Check your promotion policies for similar snags.
>
> Above all else, you must remove any attitudinal barriers that stand in the way of the disabled. Improve employee awareness of the special problems and needs of disabled workers. If you can eliminate stereotyped thinking concerning their abilities and potentials, the disabled will be able to get what they need: the same chance as anyone else to prove themselves.

preparedness—the need to evacuate disabled employees from the building in the event of an emergency. Blind workers and those who can't walk may find it difficult to get off the premises quickly enough, and deaf employees naturally wouldn't hear the bells, sirens, or PA announcements that normally warn workers of a fire, a chemical spill, or a natural disaster.

By working out an evacuation plan for your disabled workers their first day on the job, you can be sure that no tragedy befalls them. Give them an extensive tour of the building, pointing out emergency exits.

The best safeguard, however, is implementing a "buddy system." Assign trusted employees to "buddy up" with your handicapped people in case of an actual emergency or emergency drill. The buddies can be responsible for notifying handicapped workers that a problem exists and safely leading them out of harm's way.

Handling the Rest of the Crew

While you may be perfectly willing to accept a handicapped employee as just another member of your crew, there could be problems getting your other workers to do the same. At least at the beginning, you're likely to devote a lot of attention to your disabled workers and to try to make special accommodations wherever possible. But that could make your other employees resentful.

For example, let's say that Bill has to be moved to another workstation because the one he has been working at is the most convenient place to locate Jane, who is in a wheelchair. Bill's been with the company a long time, and he felt comfortable where he was. So he could become upset over the situation, and his morale—and performance—could plummet.

Bill's reaction may seem childish to you, but it's "only human" for him to react this way. So don't ignore his feelings. Have a talk with him, and let him know the reasons for the change before you make it. Taking a few minutes to provide him with an explanation can make the difference between resentment and understanding.

In fact, show concern for the feelings of *all* your workers during the integration of a handicapped worker. As soon as you've hired the person, set up a discussion session for the people who will be working with him or her.

Prepare your people so they will have time to emotionally ready themselves for a disabled co-worker, and react with a minimum of shock, surprise, or discomfort when the new hire arrives for the first day on the job. Also, provide background information about the handicap so that people won't be tempted to make unfounded assumptions about their new co-worker's limitations.

Give your people plenty of opportunities to ask questions during your discussion period, to make sure doubts and confusion have been cleared up.

Exercise Equality

The most important thing you can do to keep your department running smoothly when there is a disabled person on your staff is to treat workers equally, regardless of the presence or absence of a handicap.

The disabled don't want to be treated any differently from other workers. They want to be subject to the same rewards, the same discipline, and the same responsibilities as everyone else who works for you.

So when a disabled worker creates a discipline problem, or isn't meeting your performance standards, what should you do? The answer is simple: Handle the situation the same as you would for a worker who is not disabled.

Remember, hiring—and working with—the handicapped is not something to fear. The disabled are people with strong abilities, and a desire to work hard and be rewarded for it, just like everyone else. If you treat them as such, they'll fit comfortably and productively into your work environment.

> **WHAT YOU CAN DO** → *You can successfully make a handicapped person an integral part of your workforce if you . . .*

1. Make the work area as comfortable as possible for the disabled person. Ask for ideas about the setup; he or she will probably know what layout would be most efficient.

2. Assign a trusted worker to be a "buddy" to the handicapped employee. Such an arrangement can be very helpful in an emergency.

3. Treat the disabled person as you do your other workers. Fair treatment is all that the vast majority of handicapped workers desire—and it can prevent resentment from brewing among the rest of your staff.

4. Help your other workers to understand the situation. When you must make accommodations for the disabled person, explain the changes to your other employees, and express your appreciation for their cooperation.

Following these steps can make the addition of a disabled worker a positive experience for all involved—including you.

ACTION PLAN:

_____
_____
_____
_____
_____
_____
_____
_____
_____
_____
_____
_____

THINK BEFORE YOU DISCIPLINE

It's part of your job to dole out discipline when employees behave in an unacceptable manner. And part of making the disciplinary process effective is knowing just which course of action is appropriate for a specific offense. If you overreact and render excessive punishment, employees may become resentful and lose respect for company regulations. On the other hand, if you let rule-breaking go uncorrected, you may be setting a dangerous precedent. That's why, before you discipline an employee, you should take time to think things through.

Don't Take It to Extremes

Let's examine this scenario, in which a supervisor fails to think before he disciplines:

After fighting unusually heavy traffic on his way to work, Supervisor Chet Hartley grabbed a cup of coffee, flopped into his chair, and began tearing through the stack of orders on his desk. A half hour later, he looked up from his work and saw Jean

Hahn, one of his employees, come through the door and quietly head toward her workstation.

"Hold it right there, Jean," Hartley called out. "Do you have any idea what time it is?"

Hahn stopped in her tracks. "Yes, I—I know I'm late, but—" she stammered.

"No but's," Hartley said angrily. "You're half an hour late. And you've been late every day this week. I'm not going to put up with this any longer. You're suspended for one week!"

"Isn't that a little harsh?" Hahn asked the supervisor, on the verge of tears. Work on the production line ground to a standstill as employees listened to the confrontation.

I guess it is, Hartley thought to himself. *But I'll look like a fool if I back down now.* "I'm not changing my mind," he announced. "Consider yourself suspended!"

Questions to Ask Yourself

Disciplining your people may be the most unpleasant and difficult task you'll ever have to perform as a supervisor. Yet workers must be corrected when they fail to obey company rules—particularly because those rules have been designed to promote productivity and safety.

Still, there are certainly better ways to handle disciplinary situations than the way Supervisor Hartley went about it. What mistakes did he make?

First of all, he failed to speak to Hahn about her tardiness on the very first day. Instead, he ignored the situation until he couldn't stand it anymore; then he exploded in anger and overreacted, giving her an extremely harsh punishment.

If Hartley had stopped to think first—*before* he issued his decree—he would have realized that his initial reaction was inappropriate. If he had really considered Hahn's tardiness to be a problem, he would have come up with a more suitable reprimand—one that would have been fairer to Hahn and would have motivated her to get to work on time.

Disciplining may not be easy, but it can be made a little less painful if you make a commitment to *think* before you *act.* When you're faced with a discipline problem, exactly what should you think about? Be sure to ask yourself the following questions:

- Is this the employee's first offense?
- What is the employee's explanation for the unacceptable behavior?
- How have I dealt with similar offenses in the past?
- What punishment would I expect to receive if I were in the worker's shoes?

By applying these questions you'll arrive at the fairest possible decision. And you won't have any regrets—as Supervisor Hartley did. Let's take a closer look at each of the factors that you should ponder before you make a disciplinary decision.

Check Their Records

The first thing you should consider before disciplining is the work record of the employee involved. Has the person received reprimands in the past? Were any of them for similar offenses? Or is this episode the first time you've felt it necessary to discipline this employee?

Checking the record can help you uncover any outside problems that may be contributing to the employee's behavior. For instance, you may come across a case where an employee who has consistently performed well is suddenly violating the rules. This often points to a problem outside the workplace, and you may want to give the person a little time to come around before taking serious disciplinary steps—such as verbal and written warnings, suspension, or dismissal.

At the very least, checking a worker's record will help put the person's inappropriate behavior into perspective. It will show you where he or she now stands in the discipline process, and what the proper step to take might be.

Give Them a Hearing

The second thing to keep in mind is that it's very important to listen to the employee's side of a story before determining disciplinary action. All too often, a supervisor will have made up his or her mind on the spur of the moment, without letting the employee have a say in the matter. This is a mistake. The worker may have information that you didn't know about—facts that could change your mind about the discipline you'd intended to carry out.

For example, if Supervisor Hartley had allowed Jean Hahn to finish her explanation, he would have learned that she'd had to wait for a sitter to stay with her ailing son. That's what had made her late for work.

If Hartley had known this, he might have asked Hahn to make up the lost time by working late at the end of the day. Or he might have suggested that she come in early or stay late the following week when she didn't have to rush home to a sick child.

So, unless you listen closely to an employee's version of an incident and then carefully weigh what you've heard, there's no way you can be sure that you are making the best possible decision.

Be Consistent

A key to winning employee respect both for the rules and for yourself is always to demonstrate consistency when disciplining. If workers perceive that some are getting lenient treatment while others are having the boom lowered on them, they will naturally start to resent your approach to supervision.

Therefore, it's best to make a considerable effort to strive for consistency. That's easier said than done, of course, because it's natural to like certain employees and have negative feelings about others. Still, you should never let this affect the manner in which you apply discipline.

To avoid the charge of favoritism, ask yourself, "What did I do the last time a worker broke this particular rule?" You'll find that it's best not to deviate from past decisions; if you do, you may set yourself up for future problems with employees who can rightfully say, "You gave Joe a break when he did the same thing—how come I'm not entitled to the same break?"

Always handle a particular offense in the same way for all employees—unless, of course, there are extenuating circumstances, as in the case of Jean Hahn. If you approach certain problems in the same way every time, you'll be on firm ground and will always be able to justify your actions.

Consult With Others

As you try to make up your mind about how to discipline an employee, the many considerations may just leave you confused. It's helpful to talk to fellow supervisors who may have dealt with similar problems in the past. Not only will this allow you to draw on the experience of others, but it will give you an objective viewpoint, which you may lack because you are too close to the situation.

You might also develop a recommendation and then check it with your boss. This will prevent any overreaction on your part and, once again, will involve an outside party.

Make It a Learning Experience

The most important thing to keep in mind as you discipline is that you should treat workers as you would want to be treated yourself. That means using the rules not as a curb, but as a tool for motivating workers to keep productivity and quality high.

Poor performance can be corrected by counseling, assistance, training, and proper job placement. Disciplinary action should be taken only when it becomes apparent that the employee is not trying to improve, or will not improve no matter what you do.

Discipline should also be used to weed out those workers who commit deliberate acts against company policy, whether to draw attention to themselves or simply because they are troublemakers. But no matter what the reason for disciplining, it should always be done in a manner that preserves the pride and feelings of the employee.

You won't achieve positive results by berating a worker in front of others, or by using the discipline process to badger workers into obeying the rules.

Instead, you should demonstrate consistency and fairness, and combine those traits with a desire to use discipline only when absolutely necessary. In this way, you can be sure that you're choosing a path that is suited to the offense—and the circumstances.

▶ **WHAT YOU CAN DO** ➡ *Applying discipline is never pleasant. But when a problem arises and you feel discipline is necessary . . .*

1. Stop and think—then decide on a specific course of action.

2. Check the problem employee's record to see if this is a first offense or a chronic problem.

ACTION PLAN:

_____

_____

_____

_____

3. Give the employee a chance to explain his or her behavior.

4. Settle on a course of action that is consistent for all employees.

5. Consult with fellow supervisors and your boss to see if your recommendation for discipline seems reasonable.

6. Put yourself in the worker's shoes and ask yourself whether your choice is consistent and fair.

You can make the discipline process more impartial and effective by taking time to carefully consider your move before you make it.

EVALUATING EMPLOYEE PERFORMANCE

One of your greatest—and potentially most difficult—responsibilities is evaluating the people who work for you. The judgments you make can have a long-lasting effect on an employee's career. But performance appraisals aren't just a tool for deciding if a person deserves a raise or a promotion. You can also use them to set meaningful goals for improved performance.

The Rating Game

You probably have an opinion about each of the workers you supervise. Joe is an "excellent" worker. Nancy is "good." Fred ranks "average." And if your department is typical, a couple of your people might even fall into the "poor" category.

But what are your opinions based on? Are they just "feelings" you have—or are your views the result of a carefully planned, objective evaluation process?

Objective evaluation is preferable by far. A well-planned performance appraisal is the only true barometer you can use to make well-justified decisions regarding raises, promotions, demotions, and other employment determinations.

More important, you can use the results of a performance appraisal to locate aspects of an employee's performance that need to be improved. Once you've zeroed in on these "trouble spots," you and the employee can work together to bring the person's performance level up to par before the next appraisal.

With those benefits in mind, let's take a look at what you should—and should not—do to make your performance evaluations a positive experience for all concerned.

Decide on a Time Frame

One of the first questions to decide is how often you will carry out your employee appraisals. Generally speaking, you should evaluate every worker at least once a year—but *twice* is better.

If you do it less often than that, your memory may not serve you too well as you rate a worker, and performance problems may rage out of control until it's almost too late to amend them. If you do it much more often than every six months, you may find that you are judging single occurrences rather than overall performance.

There's another sound reason for not having your evaluations too close together: Employees will

163

have time to make the improvements you discussed in the previous evaluation. And that helps ensure that their next appraisal will include recognition of the great strides they've made.

Choose a Rating Method

Once you've determined how often you're going to evaluate employees, you need to decide what technique of rating you're going to use. There are several to choose from:

▶ **Completely written.** With this method, the supervisor writes down his or her impressions of each employee. No attempt is made to rate the worker—the evaluation is simply a record of how the supervisor feels the worker is performing.

▶ **Rating scale.** Here, the supervisor assigns a certain number of points to each aspect of the worker's performance based on a previously determined scale. This method allows you to judge an employee against a standard (say, on a scale of one to ten) and against his or her co-workers.

▶ **Employee ranking.** This technique carries employee comparison much further. Each employee is judged against peers, and assigned to either the top third, the middle third, or the lower third. You can then determine which workers are most in need of attention in order to bring their work up to snuff.

Your company may provide a standard appraisal form for you to use, upon which you may add extra comments at the end. Or, you may be free to develop your own approach to evaluation. Whatever the case, *the important thing is that you do conduct evaluations, and that you do so regularly and fairly.*

What Should You Evaluate?

We've taken a look at when you should evaluate, and which methods you may use to carry out an appraisal. Now let's look at *what* you should be appraising. There are many facets to each position you supervise, and it's possible that no two jobs are exactly the same.

Even so, there are certain elements common to all jobs that you can base an evaluation on:

★ **Quality.** How well is the work being done? Sheer volume is not the only measure of good performance. The output must also meet quality standards.

★ **Productivity.** Does the employee make good use of his or her time? Compare the quantity of work put out with the standards you expect for the job.

★ **Flexibility.** How well does the employee adapt to changing conditions on the assigned job? Consider how quickly the person grasps new work and adjusts to change, and the ease with which varied tasks are handled.

★ **Dependability.** Can you rely on the worker? Consider the employee's sense of responsibility as it relates to attendance and successful completion of the work assigned.

★ **Cooperation.** Does the employee help further the objectives of your work group and the company? Does the person contribute to harmony and teamwork within the department?

★ **Safety.** How is the employee's safety record? Base your judgment on things the worker does which are potential causes of accidents, and on actual mishaps the worker has experienced. Consider whether the person readily complies with regulations concerning safety gear and hazard awareness.

Depending on the specific types of jobs you supervise, there may be other factors to take into consideration. For example, if your people perform work that necessitates a great deal of innovation or creativity, you might want to evaluate these qualities as well.

However, the characteristics outlined above can provide the basis for a very thorough appraisal.

Beware These Evaluation Pitfalls

You now have a clear idea of what factors you should base your employee evaluations on. But it's just as important to know what factors to avoid as you appraise worker performance. For example:

● **The "Halo Effect."** This happens when a supervisor allows his or her opinion of one aspect of the employee's work to influence the opinion of other aspects. Guard against this by breaking the job down into its components and then judging each of them separately.

- **Conscious Bias.** You're only human, and you probably like some employees more than others. That's normal and understandable. But your personal feelings about a worker should never show up on that worker's evaluation unless they have a direct bearing on the job. Take care to put your personal likes and dislikes aside when evaluating.

- **Unconscious Bias.** Everyone has certain prejudices which are difficult to overcome. You may not even realize you're taking them into account when appraising, so try to become aware of your own prejudices and keep them in check as best you can.

- **Overemphasizing Isolated Instances.** Sometimes, an outstanding employee can go through a period when he or she performs poorly. Or a borderline worker can exhibit flashes of brilliance. Be careful not to be swayed by these aberrations when making your appraisal. Rather, look at the whole picture of what the employee has done during the latest rating period.

The Deskside Chat

Once you've properly completed your evaluation of an employee's performance, you may think your task is over. In reality, it's only half done. Now you must inform the employee of the results of your assessment and work to improve any areas where performance is lacking.

One of the best ways to get this information across to the worker is through a counseling interview. What happens here is that you and the employee sit down together and discuss strengths and weaknesses. You praise the worker for those things that are being done well, and point out where performance has been below par.

Here are some points to keep in mind as you conduct a counseling interview:

■ **Hold the session in private.** If you discuss an employee's appraisal within earshot of other employees or in a noisy area, you won't get much accomplished. Find an area where you can speak freely without distractions. Never allow other workers to hear a peer's appraisal. This information must be kept confidential at all times.

■ **Listen carefully.** Remember, a counseling interview should be a give-and-take affair aimed at improving performance. So don't do all the talking. Give the worker a chance to ask questions and to respond to your comments. By listening to what the other person has to say, you may learn what is standing in the way of good performance, and that will help you to better solve such problems.

■ **Avoid arguments.** Sometimes an employee may disagree with your assessment, even to the point of losing his or her temper. Don't follow suit. By getting heated up yourself, you'll only make a bad situation worse. Stay calm and explain your evaluation in rational, businesslike terms.

■ **Arrive at an agreement.** At the close of the interview, you and the employee should establish some goals and develop a plan that will assure that the goals are met. That gives you a basis for discussion during your next interview.

■ **Follow up to cement your efforts.** You don't have to set up a formal review session—you can simply call the worker into your office for a brief conference about his or her progress. If the problem you discussed during the counseling interview has continued or become worse, you want to call it to the person's attention and find out why things haven't improved. Maybe he or she requires additional coaching or training, which only you can provide.

Conversely, if the problem has cleared up and the person has shown a dramatic improvement, you must be sure to acknowledge that improvement face-to-face. Giving a bit of well-earned praise is one of the best ways to ensure continued high performance.

What's In It for You?

What is the advantage of conducting performance evaluations and counseling interviews in the manner we've discussed? Aside from the obvious benefits of identifying both good and poor workers, these techniques can help you:

- **Maintain a permanent record of employee progress.** Documenting the evaluation process gives you easy access to valuable information regarding the status of your people. By referring to your files, you'll be able to tell at a glance who should be rewarded with raises, promotions, and praise, and who is a likely candidate for dismissal or demotion. And you'll have written evidence to back up any employment decisions you may make.

- **Identify where an employee best fits into your department.** A good performance review can point out that you haven't been utilizing a worker in the area most suited to his or her skills. For instance, after scrutinizing a worker's strengths, you may learn that while he's not much on speed, he has a keen eye for detail and is a stickler for good workmanship. You may opt to put such a person in an inspector's position, where his quality sense can be put to best use.

• **Learn how** *you* are performing. Workers are often only as good as the person who leads them. When you evaluate employee performance, you're also evaluating how well you are helping them to become better workers.

▶ **WHAT YOU CAN DO** → *To make evaluations effective, just be sure to . . .*

1. Conduct appraisals at proper, regular intervals. Give employees time to make necessary improvements before conducting the subsequent appraisal. However, don't allow too much time to elapse between evaluations. Time has a way of making once-crucial matters seem to lose some of their urgency.

2. Select a rating method that best suits your department. If your company doesn't already have a standard format for conducting appraisals, you may choose from a variety of alternative methods, including rating scales, comparison rankings, or strictly written evaluations.

3. Beware of biases, which can color the overall appraisal of an employee. Put personal feelings and prejudices on a back burner (if you can't completely overcome them) when evaluating your people.

4. Conduct a counseling interview to let the worker know which areas need to be upgraded, and which are just fine. An appraisal program is fruitless unless you communicate it to employees and use it to upgrade performance.

5. Follow up. Allow a reasonable amount of time to pass after the counseling interview (say three months). If the problems persist or have taken a downswing, talk to the worker and try to determine what adjustments might improve the situation. And if the worker has made great strides, offer congratulatory recognition.

Applying each of these points when you appraise performance will show your people that you are a fair and conscientious supervisor. And this will encourage them to make more of an effort to improve for you.

ACTION PLAN:

HOW TO HANDLE EMPLOYEE SUBSTANCE ABUSE

The abuse of drugs and alcohol in business and industry is widely publicized. Yet there are still many supervisors who deny that any of their employees could be involved in such activities. Whatever your attitude concerning your people and substance abuse, you need to face the fact that the problem is prevalent—and learn how to deal with it when it crops up in your department.

The Problem Is Far-reaching

Some experts say that substance abuse is leveling off in the United States. Others insist that it's still on the rise. But both sides agree that the misuse of alcohol and drugs is a major problem to which you, as a supervisor, need to address your attention.

How bad is it? Estimates of annual cost to industry of employee substance abuse vary from $50 billion to $100 billion *annually*—in decreased productivity, and increased absenteeism, tardiness, health and welfare services, property damage, and medical expenses. That's no small sum.

Okay, so substance abuse by workers is a big issue, you may say. *But what can I do about it?* There's a great deal you can do. As management's representative, you're in the best position to notice a drug or alcohol problem. Should you fail to detect such a problem, or ignore it in the hope that it will go away, or try to hide it out of a misguided sense of loyalty to an employee, the situation will simply fester.

But just how do you detect such a problem and stem its growth? What do you do about suspicions you may have about a particular employee? Should you fire an employee caught with drugs? What are the odds that firing a worker for use or possession of drugs will lead to a grievance or lawsuit?

Having the answers to all these questions and more will enable you to limit the harm substance abuse among employees can do to your department's operations.

It Starts With Recognition

Before you can attack this problem, you must be able to determine if indeed it exists in your department. The following general signs should alert you to the possibility that substance abuse is taking place in your work area:

- Employee theft seems to be on the rise.
- Strangers are frequently seen hanging around the parking lot.
- Some workers visit their cars at odd times during a work shift.
- Accidents are becoming more commonplace.
- Absenteeism and tardiness are increasing.
- Defect and rework rates are skyrocketing.
- Drastic mood swings and changes in personality are occurring among some workers.

If you are experiencing even a few of these problems, you have good reason to suspect that substance abuse is taking its toll. This is especially so if various complaints always seem to lead to the same few workers. If they do, you should observe these workers for specific signs of drug or alcohol problems. Here are some danger signals that could point to abuse:

- Deteriorating job performance
- Inappropriate work or personal behavior
- Recurrent tardiness from lunch or breaks
- Frequent visits to the rest room
- Increase in injuries or errors
- Slurred speech or unsteady gait
- Bloodshot or watery eyes; very large or small pupils; runny noses or sores around nostrils

Of course, you must keep in mind that these signals don't *always* mean a substance abuse problem. That's why, if you suspect a drug or alcohol problem, you must always. . .

Rule Out Other Causes First

Production Supervisor Craig Frink was perplexed about the uncharacteristic behavior of one of his assemblers, Mary Lou Burdick.

For a couple of days, Burdick had been working at a snail's pace—which was highly unlike her, as she was normally one of his speediest employees. She'd acted like she hadn't even heard the supervisor when he'd confronted her the day before about forgetting to sign her time card. When she *did* sign it, her hand trembled, and her signature was an almost illegible scrawl, not her usual tidy John Hancock. And Frink had noticed her eyes were red and tearing.

He shook his head and went back to his desk to look over his group's defect figures for the previous two days. When he took a look at Burdick's, he just about choked. She had produced more rejects than the rest of the crew combined. *I wonder what her problem is,* Frink mused to himself.

The next morning, Burdick still seemed to be in a funk. She spent the first few minutes of the shift sitting on her stool rubbing her eyes. And when Frink watched her work, he noticed that she frequently looked up and stared into space.

This woman has got to be on drugs, thought Frink. *I can't think of any other reason she would be acting so spaced out.* He decided to spend the rest of the day engaging in some surveillance to see if he could catch Burdick in the act.

At eleven o'clock, she left her station and headed toward the water cooler. And when Frink peered around the corner to see what she was doing, his suspicions were confirmed. Burdick pulled a small plastic bag filled with white pills out of her purse and downed a couple of them. When she looked up, Frink was standing over her with a self-satisfied grin.

"Aren't I allowed to get a drink?" Burdick asked.

"Sure—how else would you take those drugs? I thought you had to be on something—" Frink was quickly cut off.

"These pills are a prescription from my doctor. If I've seemed out of it, it's because I've had a bad cold—and this medication makes me a little drowsy."

"If it's a prescription, why isn't it in a bottle with a label on it? And why didn't you tell me you were sick in the first place?" queried Frink.

"They're in the bag because they're easier to carry around that way. And I didn't tell you I was sick because I don't like to complain," said Burdick.

But Frink was so sure she was making excuses to cover a drug abuse problem, he suspended the worker for three days. He was stunned, however, when he received a phone call from Burdick's doctor affirming her condition. And he was further chagrined when Burdick took a complaint to court—and won.

What does this story tell you? Namely, that you should never jump to conclusions regarding employee substance abuse. Before you take any action to remedy the problem, you must be sure— without a shadow of a doubt—that an employee is indeed abusing drugs or alcohol.

As you've seen, a worker may manifest external symptoms of substance abuse because he or she is ill and is taking legitimate prescription medication. Other causes of strange behavior or poor performance may be:

- **Personal problems.** For example, if an employee is having marital trouble, he or she may act depressed. Or, if there's a new baby in the house that's keeping an employee up at night, he or she may seem drowsy or may even doze off on the job.
- **Personality conflicts.** When employees don't get along with co-workers, they may become hostile or antisocial. And because they are distracted, defects may begin to crop up more frequently.
- **Burnout.** If a worker has been doing the same type of work over and over again for a long period of time, boredom may set in. And that could cause a lack of attention, which might induce quality problems.
- **Inadequate training.** Sometimes an employee's productivity or quality can fall off when he or she must take on a new assignment but hasn't been thoroughly trained in how to carry it out.

Make sure you rule out these possibilities before acting on your suspicions that a worker is abusing alcohol or drugs. "Innocent until proven guilty" should be your motto.

How Do You Proceed?

Once you're convinced a particular employee or group of employees has a substance abuse problem, you've got to tread carefully. Unless you've been trained as a drug and alcohol abuse counselor, you lack the expertise necessary to properly aid your troubled worker. Therefore, if you try to diagnose and treat the problem yourself, you're likely to exacerbate it, rather than alleviate it.

Here's the best course of action to take:

★ **Document all performance problems.** While addressing and treating a substance abuse problem is out of your jurisdiction, it's part of your job to point out job-related performance problems. In fact, it's the best way at your disposal to begin chipping away at a substance abuse problem.

Begin by keeping exact records of each instance of inappropriate behavior or poor performance. Never jot down a suspicion ("Al came back from lunch drunk today"), even if you have reason to believe it's true. Instead, write "Al came back late from lunch, dozed off at his worktable, and then produced a high number of defects in the afternoon."

You need specific, tangible evidence of substance abuse before you can bring the problem to a worker's attention. (You also need such evidence—and records of your efforts to correct the performance problem—in case a decision to terminate is challenged in a court of law.)

★ **Confront the worker.** Using the evidence you've assembled to back up your claim, arrange a private meeting with the employee.

Sit the person down and inform him or her that performance has been substandard; cite dates, times, and specific instances. Don't offer any personal speculation as to the cause—just stick to the facts.

★ **Outline specific ways in which performance might be improved.** For example, if the worker has been generating a lot of rework, offer to provide additional training or guidance. If the person has been dozing off, suggest that he or she try to get more sleep.

Again, never say anything like "Cut out the noontime tippling, and I'm sure your performance will pick up." Also, mention that disciplinary action may be necessary if the person does not show desired improvement.

★ **Refer the person to your company's Employee Assistance Program,** to Personnel, to the company health office, or to a counseling service if the person admits to a substance abuse problem. You should always urge the person to seek professional help, rather than offering amateur advice.

But remember that this action must be voluntary on the part of the worker. You may not force an employee to seek such assistance, even if the person concedes to alcoholism or drug addiction. You may only take action concerning a refusal to improve job-related behavior.

★ **Consult your superiors.** Another important thing you can do in your efforts to handle a potential substance abuse problem is to discuss the issue with your higher-ups.

They may have dealt with a similar problem in the past, and perhaps can share valuable advice on how you might best cope with the situation.

Going to your superiors is particularly important when you catch an employee using or possessing illegal drugs at the workplace. This is no time to act alone. Go to your superior's office immediately with all the details.

If You Have to Resort to Dismissal

Chances are your company has outlined strict policies and procedures for dismissing employees. There may even be a policy that explicitly states that substance abuse on the job is grounds for immediate termination. But be careful of this course of action. If you don't handle the dismissal properly, you could get into trouble with the law, the union (if your workforce is organized), or both.

If a substance abuser volunteers to seek treatment, you might be required by state or federal law to let that person take a disability leave. Discharge would probably be justified if a known drug user refused treatment, or if you caught someone in possession of or selling drugs—provided that company policy is clear on this matter.

Remember, each case must be weighed individually, and you and your company must seek the advice of medical, security, and legal experts to make an informed decision.

A Final Word

Drug and alcohol use in the workplace is a serious problem that should not be approached haphazardly. Therefore, it is up to you to get the facts about such abuse.

Know how to recognize the danger signs of substance abuse, and take the appropriate action when you suspect such a problem. Hiding your head in the sand and hoping the difficulty will clear up by itself is no answer—and will only serve to imperil the safety and productivity of your department.

Make sure you're acquainted with company policy for dealing with drug and alcohol use, policies for screening and testing employees, assistance referrals, and disciplinary procedures.

Introduce these policies to your staff in a meeting, explaining the rationale for the policy, specific behaviors that will warrant discipline, exceptions to the rule, and methods for proving abuse. Once you have given your workers this information, circulate it to them periodically. A one-shot deal won't be as effective as regular reminders.

If you show employees that you—and your company—take substance abuse seriously, you may effectively deter such behavior and prevent accidents, performance problems, and the need for disciplinary action.

▶ **WHAT YOU CAN DO** ➡ *To prevent the detrimental effects substance abuse can have on your department ...*

1. Acknowledge the fact that it's a serious problem—one that must be faced and dealt with.

2. Learn how to recognize the danger signs—such as diminished productivity, quality problems, and strange or inappropriate behavior.

3. Rule out other causes for poor performance before taking action.

4. Document all performance problems carefully—taking care not to make diagnoses.

5. Confront the employee about the unacceptable performance. Mention ways in which his or her work may be improved—again, without mentioning substance abuse.

6. Refer the worker to professional assistance if he or she openly admits a substance abuse problem. Consult Personnel to determine the appropriate course of action.

7. If you must resort to dismissal, do it carefully, always abiding by company policies.

8. Make sure you're well acquainted with all company procedures concerning substance abuse; then share the information with your people.

Substance abuse is one of the most sensitive issues you'll encounter as a supervisor. By learning to deal with it properly and effectively, you'll help to maintain a productive and safe environment for the employees whom you oversee.

ACTION PLAN:

THE ISSUE OF SEXUAL HARASSMENT

One human relations issue that more and more supervisors are forced to confront is that of sexual harassment. Think it'll never happen in your department? Think again. It's been estimated that between 50 and 80 percent of all working women have been sexually harassed on the job. And since these oc-

currences often lead to productivity problems and costly lawsuits, it's your responsibility to watch for such behavior and promptly nip it in the bud.

What Is Sexual Harassment?

There are many answers to that question—and that's what can make the problem so difficult to detect and to deal with. What might seem, on the surface, to be merely harmless fun between co-workers can really constitute dangerous abuse, according to the courts.

Here are three examples of sexual harassment, as defined by various courts around the country. As you can see, they range from the subtle to the blatant:

- The telling of lewd jokes and stories
- Unwanted physical contact
- Requests for sexual favors

How can you determine when such behavior can in fact be interpreted by a worker—and a court of law—as sexual harassment? The Equal Employment Opportunity Commission (EEOC) offers these criteria:

- The employee must submit to the offensive conduct as an explicit or implicit condition of employment (strictly prohibited by Title VII of the Civil Rights Act of 1964).
- The employee who rejects the advances risks losing a job, promotion, privileges, or benefits, whereas the employee who submits gains favors and advantages.
- The employee's job performance is affected by the sexually-oriented behavior, or the person views the work environment as hostile or intimidating.

The Consequences Are Far-reaching

One seemingly minor incident of sexual harassment can cause major problems, not only for the victim but for the harasser, the area supervisor, and their employer. What kind of problems? Here are two examples:

Diminished productivity. The most immediate problem for the supervisor is that sexual harassment can affect the morale—and in turn, the productivity—of the workers in his or her department. When members of the workforce are being tormented and embarrassed, they're going to have trouble keeping their minds on their work. (It's obvious that the offenders' thoughts are elsewhere, too.)

Victims of such harassment often become stressed, nervous, or depressed. They may begin to show up for work late or call in sick to avoid a confrontation with an offender. In many cases, such workers eventually quit or are fired, leaving the department with a vacancy to fill—one that would have never been formed if the person had obtained relief from an attentive, effective supervisor.

Expensive legal battles. Sexual harassment can also hit your company—and you—squarely in the pocketbook. For example, one employer was recently ordered by the courts to pay close to $200,000 in damages to a worker who filed a sexual harassment charge. Another company was forced to pay a record $7 million to settle a sexual harassment case out of court!

In addition, many supervisors have been held personally liable when it was determined that they didn't take every step in their power to prevent a worker from being sexually harassed.

Fortunately, forestalling the above difficulties isn't as tough as you might think.

The Wrong Approach

Before we examine the methods you may use to effectively deal with sexual harassment on the job, let's consider this fact-based tale of one supervisor who did *not* handle such a situation in the best possible manner. As you read this case, consider the ways in which the supervisor handled the problem, and what he might have done differently.

Supervisor Jack Pratt checked the big clock in his office, and wasn't too pleased when he saw the time: 8:45. One of his new employees, Flora Brown, was late again.

When the worker first joined the department, she proved to be a competent and conscientious employee. Tardiness had never been a problem with her—not until about two weeks ago. Pratt had caught her sneaking in fifteen minutes late six times already. And she'd called in sick a few times, too. *Obviously, she's not the top performer I thought she was,* Pratt sighed to himself.

When Brown finally straggled in at ten past nine, Pratt called her into his office. "I had high hopes for you," the supervisor began. "But between your latenesses and absences, you've hardly done any work. What seems to be the problem?"

Brown turned beet-red and tried to avoid her supervisor's gaze. "You might think this is silly, but I'm so upset I can barely sleep nights! Ever since my first day here, Ben and Eugene have been hassling me. They're constantly telling dirty jokes and making rude comments about my body. I've begged them to stop, but they just laugh and keep on bugging me.

"I've tried to avoid them but they hang around my workstation every morning. So, if I come in a little late, sometimes I miss them. I certainly don't want to lose my job, but I dread coming to work. And if they don't put a lid on it, I—I don't know what I'm going to do!"

Well, now I know why her performance has taken such a turn for the worse, mused Pratt. *She's just overly sensitive—she's got to learn to laugh these things off.* "I'm sure Gene and Ben don't mean any harm—that's just their way of being friendly," Pratt said. "Why don't you just ignore them and let this thing run its course? They'll probably ease up once you show them they're not getting your goat."

Brown wasn't convinced. "I've tried ignoring them, and it doesn't do any good! Can't you say something to them to get them off my back?"

"Believe me, you're making a mountain out of a molehill. Just ride it out. They'll get the message," said Pratt.

However, the two offenders *didn't* get the message. They continued to make Brown's worklife a living misery, and she continued showing up for work late and calling in sick. Finally, she couldn't endure the situation another second. She marched into Pratt's office, and tearfully expressed her exasperation. "They haven't given me a moment's peace, and I'm not going to tolerate their nasty remarks any longer. I'm sure I have a case for sexual harassment here, and I'm taking it all the way to court!"

What Can You Do?

Did Brown indeed have a sturdy sexual harassment case? You bet. Her supervisor chose to make light of her problem and take no action, rather than taking the situation in hand and implementing the appropriate solution.

What should he have done about it—and what should you do to prevent a similar situation? The first step to take is simply to make a firm, personal commitment to stamping out sexual harassment in your department. Then prove your commitment to your people by following this course of action:

- **Circulate or post a written policy statement** clearly informing employees that sexual harassment, in any form, will not be tolerated. Make sure that every current employee and every new hire sees and understands the statement.

Outline the specific types of behavior that may be considered sexual harassment. Encourage workers to ask questions if they seem confused about certain points. There's no room for lack of clarity when dealing with such a serious issue.

- **Make legal and financial consequences clear.** Just as you and your employer can be held liable for sexual harassment, so can your employees. For instance, one court made a supervisor and several employees each pay $1,500 in damages to the victim of their sexual harassment. The money was paid out of their own pockets.

- **Welcome any and all complaints.** Let employees know that they can come to you with a complaint of sexual harassment. In fact, take this one step further and tell workers that you expect them to come to you, at the first incident of abuse by a fellow employee.

- **Guarantee victims' anonymity.** Many people hesitate to report instances of sexual harassment because they fear reprisal by their offenders. That's why you need to assure employees that their complaints will remain confidential.

- **Investigate complaints promptly and thoroughly.** Neglecting to act on a complaint implies that you condone sexual harassment, and that makes you and your company liable. Therefore, it's not enough to ask workers to come to you with their problems. You must be prepared to deal with them once they've been brought to your attention.

Talk to all the parties involved, seek out witnesses, and *fully document each step* as you go. In the end, the accusation may prove invalid, but it's still your duty to check into every complaint, however insignificant it may seem.

- **Discipline offenders swiftly, appropriately, and consistently.** Don't wait the problem out in hopes it will go away by itself. The odds are good that it won't.

The Supreme Court of Minnesota has pointed out that the failure to act could contribute substantially to a victim's already intolerable working conditions. And other courts have noted from litigants' experience that holding group policy meetings isn't sufficient action to squelch sexual harassment. Implementing progressive discipline is required to put a stop to the problem.

But Nobody's Complaining!

What if you haven't received any complaints of sexual abuse or witnessed any such incidents? Does this mean your department is trouble-free, and you are free to sit back and breathe a big sigh of relief? Maybe. But if you're wise, you'll still keep a sharp eye out for the danger signs. Some of these might be:

◗ A sudden decline in a worker's morale or productivity, or an increase in absences or tardiness.

◗ A worker who consistently tries to avoid a fellow employee.

◗ Personalized, derogatory or suggestive graffiti in halls, rest rooms, or workstations.

◗ Cartoons or jokes about a particular employee circulating among your workforce.

When you notice any of these danger signals, it's time to do some digging to find out if you have a bona fide sexual harassment problem. If your investigation indeed yields such a problem, take the appropriate disciplinary action immediately.

Unfortunately, no workplace is immune to sexual harassment. But you can strive to restrict its occurrence—and its ill effects.

▶ WHAT YOU CAN DO ➝ *Follow this course of action for handling sexual harassment in your department . . .*

1. Take the issue seriously. Before you can wage an effective campaign against sexual harassment, you need to make a solid, personal commitment to eradicating it.

2. Circulate and explain your company's policy against sexual harassment. If no such statement exists, make it a point to let your employees know that you won't tolerate such abuse in your department.

3. Maintain an open-door policy in regard to complaints of sexual harassment. Let employees know that they should not feel uncomfortable coming to you with a problem. Guarantee the anonymity of all who register a complaint.

4. Investigate complaints immediately and thoroughly. Get to the bottom of the problem as quickly as possible so that you can begin to work on a solution.

5. Discipline offenders promptly and be consistent in your treatment. Otherwise, you could be charged with discrimination.

6. Keep an eye out for signs of sexual harassment. Even if you're receiving no complaints, watch out for instances of sexual harassment, however subtle.

By keeping these points in mind, you'll greatly diminish the chances that you'll be faced with the difficult legal and human relations problems that sexual harassment can cause.

ACTION PLAN:

AVOID WORKPLACE DISCRIMINATION

As a supervisor, it's of paramount importance that you avoid discrimination in all of your employment practices—in the interest both of fairness and of legal considerations. However, some forms of inequity are far more subtle than others. How can you tell if you're discriminating against women, minorities, or other "protected groups"? You can start by asking yourself several pointed questions.

Ponder These Posers

Are your employment practices perfectly fair and within legal bounds? Asking yourself the right questions can help you to determine whether you are discriminating on the job. For example:

- Do you require applicants to have job-related experience?
- Must all applicants have a minimum amount of education?
- Do you give special consideration to relatives and friends of your reliable employees?
- Is the percentage of women and minorities in your workforce in proportion to the percentage of qualified women and minorities in your area?

The practices mentioned above may seem innocent enough, but each could be grounds for a costly lawsuit charging that you and your company maintain a pattern and practice of discrimination—a type of discrimination defined in the *Congressional Record* (14270, June 18, 1964) as a denial of rights that is "repeated, routine, or of a generalized nature."

Because these suits can cover a wide range of practices affecting large numbers of job applicants or employees, the damages awarded are often devastating. What can you do to detect and eliminate any seemingly innocuous practices that are quietly forming patterns of discrimination?

Look for Patterns

With a discerning eye and some simple arithmetic, you can detect patterns formed by your employment practices. First, take a long, hard look at your workforce. Do any protected groups such as women or minorities appear to be underrepresented? If so, find out what the percentage of women or minorities is in the pool of potential job applicants in your area. How does that figure relate to the percentage of women or minorities you actually employ?

Even if you hire a percentage of women and minorities greater than that in your pool of potential applicants, you're not necessarily home free. Where those people are placed—and where they go from there—is just as important.

Are these groups adequately represented at the skilled level, or are they largely relegated to unskilled, dead-end jobs? If any protected group *is* underrepresented at any level, you have a pattern of discrimination. And sooner or later someone—most likely EEOC or a state or local equal employment agency—is going to want to know what's causing the pattern.

Like Fire and Smoke

Even an employment practice that's applied uniformly can be unlawful if it has an adverse impact on members of protected groups. Consider the many employment practices that have been ruled discriminatory by one court or another:

■ **Testing.** This is a seemingly neutral practice that sometimes tends to discriminate against minorities, women, and older workers. What causes testing to have such tendencies? Consider the historical difference in the cultural and educational experiences of different minorities and women. If a test eliminates a disproportionate number of minorities or women because of those differences, and the test isn't really a valid predictor of job performance, you are discriminating.

Even if you can prove the test is closely job related, you must still consider alternative ways to find suitable employees. So, unless your test is the only way you can accurately predict a job candidate's ability to perform the job, and you can prove this to be true, you'd better consider the risk of using the test at all.

■ **Nepotism and word-of-mouth recruiting.** These practices can perpetuate the existing racial, ethnic, or religious composition of your workforce. That's fine if your workforce is balanced—if all groups are evenly represented.

If, on the other hand, a workforce lacks balance, an all-in-the-family approach to recruiting isn't likely to survive court scrutiny. In one case, for example, a company landed in legal hot water when it failed to hire Blacks referred by a union hiring hall.

Relying instead on referrals by incumbent employees, almost all of whom were white, the company hired only white employees. When EEOC charged race discrimination, the US District Court ruled the employer's exclusive use of in-house referrals discriminatory.

■ **Height and weight requirements.** These can have an adverse impact on many women and certain racial and ethnic groups. For example, women are, on the average, of smaller stature than men. But that doesn't necessarily mean they are incapable of handling a physically demanding job.

■ **Arbitrary experience or educational requirements.** Requirements of this sort can make it difficult for women and minorities to get hired and win promotions. A group of women applying for a boilermaker apprenticeship program, for instance, discovered that their lack of related work experience and military service was putting them at a distinct disadvantage in this traditionally male-dominated field.

When they charged sex discrimination, the US District Court found that giving special consideration to applicants who had related work experience or had served in the military eliminated a disproportionate number of female applicants. The employer could not show that these requirements were accurate indicators of future job performance, so it held the employer liable for sex discrimination.

Good Intentions: What Are They Worth?

On the subject of discrimination—whether age, race, or sex—do good intentions count for anything? If you can show that you made a real effort not to discriminate, can you escape liability for any discrimination that might have occurred, or at least reduce its liability?

The answer to both these questions is qualified by the circumstances, of course, and the perception of the court hearing the case. A fuller understanding of how discrimination cases are legally scrutinized can help you prepare your employment procedures so that your good intentions, for what they are worth, are clear to both judge and jury.

If you were found guilty of discrimination under the Equal Pay Act or the Age Discrimination in Employment Act (ADEA), you and your company could be assessed not only the back pay due the victims of discrimination but also "liquidated damages," which are equal to the amount of back pay. Why?

Liquidated damages hinge entirely on intent. If EEOC or an individual were to prove in court that you willfully violated the law (knew the law but broke it anyway), it would be almost a certainty in age bias and equal pay suits that you would have to pay liquidated damages. This is part of EEOC's "big stick" approach to conciliating complaints between employers and complainants.

Knew or Should Have Known

What does it take for a court to find an employer guilty of willfully violating ADEA or the Equal Pay Act? Most courts take the view that a violation of these laws is willful if the supervisor or employer "knew or should have known" that its actions were covered by law and that those actions might be in violation of the law.

An employer's claim that it acted in "good faith" usually isn't enough to escape liability for liquidated damages just because it "probably did not act in bad faith."

Thus, it is clear that the mere claim that you and your company acted in good faith is not enough to escape liquidated damages—you must be able to show that you had a reasonable basis for believing that you were in compliance with the law. The U.S. Supreme Court, for example, ruled that liquidated damages were not appropriate in an age-discrimination case in which the employer had sought legal advice and had consulted with union officials in an effort to comply with the ADEA.

When the record shows that you made such affirmative, good-faith attempts to ascertain the requirements of the law and to ensure that you were in compliance with the law, then you and your firm should at least be able to escape double damages for willful violations.

All-Important Records

The best proof of your good intentions is real evidence that you have taken affirmative action to comply with the law. Under Title VII, this means taking affirmative action to recruit and maintain a balanced workforce. Of course, good recordkeeping is an essential part of this effort.

175

If, for example, you have lowered the educational requirements for work in your department, or changed the physical requirements, or altered other demands on applicants that might weigh more heavily against a protected group but are not necessary to perform a job, keep accurate records of these changes.

Your sincere and well-documented efforts to follow the laws will go a long way toward proving your good intentions. Those good intentions won't necessarily help you escape liability, but they certainly won't hurt. Discrimination has no place in your employment practices. So make absolutely certain that you're supervising fairly.

> **WHAT YOU CAN DO →** *Take this six-step strategy . . .*

1. Make a commitment to eradicating discrimination from your employment practices.

2. Analyze your employment practices for indications of discrimination. Ask yourself the right questions as you do so.

3. Use simple arithmetic to find patterns of bias against women and minorities.

4. Understand that good intentions can't always render you and your company innocent of discrimination charges.

5. Do all you can to change the current practices that could be considered unjust.

6. Document all efforts to reverse unfair employment practices so you can later prove you acted in good faith.

Don't wait for a discrimination charge to be filed against you and your company. Take time out—now—to review your employment procedures, and then take steps to change the ones that are, even subtly, discriminatory.

ACTION PLAN:
_____
_____
_____
_____
_____
_____
_____
_____
_____
_____
_____
_____
_____
_____

EMPLOYMENT-AT-WILL: HERE'S WHAT YOU NEED TO KNOW

Firing an employee is without question one of the most unpleasant chores you have to face as a supervisor. And to make a tough situation even tougher, a greater number of discharged workers are suing their employers for "wrongful discharge"—and winning. Here's what you need to know in order to pre-

vent a sticky legal mess due to a firing decision you've made.

That Was Then—This Is Now

Until recently, American employers were free to dismiss an employee "at will"—that is, at any time and for any reason they chose. Without a written employment contract, a supervisor could "axe" an employee simply because the worker grated on the supervisor's nerves. It didn't matter how many years the employee had worked at the company, or how competent he or she had proved to be.

This arrangement worked both ways. If the employee was offered a better job elsewhere, or had an argument with a supervisor, there was nothing to prevent the worker from clearing out his or her locker or work area and leaving on the spot, with no notice—regardless of how much it might disrupt operations.

In short, the employment-at-will setup left both parties in the employer/worker relationship vulnerable to each other's whims. But the employee probably suffered more because the sudden loss of a job can be a devastating blow, both economically and emotionally.

These days, however, an employee who may be a victim of the at-will relationship can sue the employer for wrongful discharge—and have a good chance of winning. Employees who have brought suit successfully in the past few years have won not only back pay and reinstatement to their old jobs, but in some cases compensatory damages—money awarded by the court for "mental suffering," or "emotional distress."

How You Fit In

It's no wonder, then, that employers are concerned. And you should be, too. Why? Because your company could be held accountable for your mistakes. More often than not, it's the supervisor who makes the decision to discharge a worker. So, the more you know about what constitutes a legitimate reason for filing a wrongful discharge suit, the better prepared you'll be to make sure it doesn't happen in your department.

Does this mean that whenever you fire a troublesome worker, you'll end up in hot water? Of course not. There are still many legitimate grounds for discharge—the primary one being incompetence. Rule violations are another.

Your company's policy manual should be your guide here. It should detail exactly what violations will be considered grounds for immediate discharge, and which ones would merit lesser forms of discipline. Share this information with your employees to help prevent problems from arising in the first place.

In many companies, the kinds of behavior that often justify an immediate discharge include:

★ Possession, carrying, or being under the influence of alcohol or drugs during working hours
★ Stealing or attempting to steal company property
★ Possession of firearms or explosives on company premises
★ Bodily assault or fighting
★ Sabotaging or defacing company property

Your company's policy manual probably includes the above rule violations as well as many other forms of misconduct. This list simply serves to show you that you do have some authority in firing an employee for just cause.

Watch What You Say

Still, since it's within your power to discharge workers, and since wrongful discharge suits can leave you at the mercy of the court, you should be aware of how to avoid trouble. The best way is to devise a strategy for handling discipline and discharges. And this strategy should begin from the start—with the hiring process.

For instance, when you're interviewing a job applicant, never make promises you don't have the authority or intention of keeping. Don't, for example, portray your department as one big happy family where job security is practically guaranteed.

Even though it may be true that employees who come into the department tend to stay there for a number of years, you could be sued for "implied contract" if you indicate that employment is in any way "permanent."

If your company feels strongly that at-will employees should be informed of their status, consult the personnel department staff for advice on when and how this message ought to be conveyed. Sometimes it's better to relegate this statement to the job application form than to beat employees over the head with it during the preemployment interview.

You certainly don't want to mislead a new worker, but at the same time, you don't want to portray yourself or your company's management as tyrants.

Follow Company Disciplinary Procedures

Another important way to protect yourself is to know exactly what your company requires regarding disciplining and discharging employees. Always follow such procedures to a "T".

If your policy manual states that discipline must include a verbal reprimand, a written warning, a disciplinary conference, and suspension before you can fire someone, beware of taking shortcuts. This progressive discipline provides excellent protection against a wrongful discharge suit.

How? Let's say an employee was disciplined on more than one occasion, yet persisted in his unacceptable behavior. He would have a hard time succeeding in court. On the other hand, if an employee was fired "out of the blue," she would be more likely to win a lawsuit. It is the latter type of discharge that you want to avoid. Unless, of course, the violation involved is a clear-cut case for immediate discharge.

Counsel Problem Employees

Within the progressive discipline process there is often a step between the written warning and a disciplinary suspension, designed to solve a problem before the employee's job is in serious jeopardy.

Sometimes known as the "disciplinary conference," this is a face-to-face meeting of the employee and the supervisor, during which the problem is brought out into the open, and goals are set for improvements in behavior or performance.

The following is a brief illustration of how you should handle these meetings to correct a problem before it leads to dismissal and potential lawsuits:

Supervisor: John, have a seat. I want to talk to you about that incident yesterday—when I found you sleeping on the job.

Employee: But I wasn't really asleep. I was just resting my eyes. These new contacts are really giving me trouble.

Supervisor: The fact remains that you had your head down on your worktable and you didn't respond when I called your name. When I asked around, I found out that you often put your head down for twenty minutes or so after lunch. Several other people have seen you that way on quite a few occasions.

Employee: Well, maybe I've been working too hard. I'm taking an adult education course in the evenings, which doesn't leave me much time for sleep.

Supervisor: Have you thought about shifting your work hours? That's the whole point of our flextime plan. Why not sleep a half hour later in the morning and stay half hour later in the afternoon?

Employee: That wouldn't leave me much time to spend with my family before I leave for my class. But I suppose I could try it for a week or two and see if it helps.

Supervisor: That sounds like a good idea. Why don't we get together again in two weeks and see how the new schedule is working out? I'm going to jot down here in your file that we've discussed this problem and that you're working on a solution.

Important: Document All Infractions!

Keeping written records of all instances of employee misconduct and your disciplinary efforts is essential to preventing the legal and financial problems you and your company could suffer in coming out on the losing end of a wrongful discharge suit.

You need to have thorough written records to prove that the employee was properly notified of infractions, was given a chance to change his or her ways, yet persisted in misconduct. Proper, thorough documentation has won many a case for employers.

Get a Second, Authoritative Opinion

Whenever you've been driven to consider firing a worker, always consult your immediate superior to get a second opinion on your decision. Ask that person to review the file you've kept on the person—this should include dates and times of infractions and your attempts at disciplining the worker. This will not only give you the benefit of your boss's feedback, but it will also allow you to step back from the situation and reconsider the wisdom of your actions.

This doesn't mean your hands are tied when an immediate discharge suit is clearly warranted. But it's very important to have somebody else review the decision you've made, when the circumstances surrounding it may be questionable or open to interpretation.

Finally, if your superior upholds the firing decision, *handle the actual termination process with utmost care.* Sometimes all it takes is a poorly handled exit interview to give the departing employee a reason to want to get even. So give the worker ample time to clear out his or her desk or locker and to discuss the status of benefits with Personnel.

And never humiliate the employee, especially in front of co-workers. All disciplining—and firing—should be done in the privacy of your office or some other location.

Make the Exit Interview As Painless as Possible

When you call the employee to your office, you need to make the exit interview as painless as possible for the worker. You can do it by following these guidelines:

- **Get to the point.** Don't drag the interview out with meaningless small talk. Nine times out of ten, the worker who's called in to be discharged knows why you've called him or her to your office. And frequently, the individual is actually relieved to have the situation clarified once and for all. So don't keep the worker in suspense; it's too easy for the person to become emotional if you don't get to the point at once.

- **Forget clichés of regret.** If you tell an employee, "This hurts me as much as it hurts you," for example, the person's reaction will probably be "That's a lot of baloney!" The phrases that might seem as if they'd smooth the way really only serve to cloud the issue, so keep them out of the exit interview.

- **Stick to performance facts and skip the personality analysis.** An exit interview is no time to tell an employee that you don't like his or her attitude or personality. This type of "true confession" will do nothing but cause hard feelings. Discuss only the job-related behavior that warranted the dismissal.

- **Be discreet with good advice.** When an employee is being dismissed, he or she probably isn't overly receptive to taking advice from you, so avoid "preaching" to the person about what he or she should do to self-improve. There's one exception you might make. If you're completely convinced

A Lesson in Legalities

One of the most important things you can do to make yourself—and your company—as "suit-proof" as possible is to be aware of the many labor laws currently in existence.

So it would greatly benefit you to study—and learn—the special regulations that concern employer-employee relations and the right to due process. Here are just a few of the laws that you need to be familiar with:

■ The National Labor Relations Act. This act introduced the concept of due process in a termination proceeding at the workplace.

■ The Equal Employment Opportunity Act. A section of Title VII of the Civil Rights Act of 1964, this law deals with discrimination on the basis of color, religion, sex, or national origin.

■ Miscellaneous other laws, such as the:

▸ Fair Labor Standards Act

▸ Occupational Safety and Health Act

▸ Age Discrimination in Employment Act

▸ Employee Retirement Income Security Act

Although "legalese" is a language difficult for most of us to grasp, and you can't possibly memorize *every* aspect of these laws, you should take the time to learn the basics of each act and how they affect you as a supervisor.

One thing you'll learn is that even the statements you make during *hiring* can have an impact on a wrongful discharge suit filed *years later.* This can come about when a court holds that statements made during an employment interview are, in effect, contractual promises. Since it may require a court of law to sort matters out in the event of a wrongful discharge claim, it is best not to make shaky promises in the first place.

Another important point to keep in mind is that these laws don't prevent you from discharging an employee who has committed a serious breach of discipline, such as striking a supervisor. You can feel secure that a court will back you up in firing a worker for this type of action.

that the person will never make it in a similar position and you have copious facts to back you up, you can do him or her a service by being honest. And if you have a clear idea of where the worker might redirect his or her talents, you should make some suggestions.

- **Show some consideration.** If an employee becomes upset at the dismissal and begins to blow off some steam, try to be patient and let the person talk. Listen without interrupting and without losing your temper. You can afford to show some courtesy under the circumstances.

- **Strive for positivism.** Do your best to convince the worker that losing this job isn't the end of the world. Be sure to tell the person that you're sure he or she can work out in a different atmosphere with a different company. If you know of another company in the vicinity that has openings you think the worker can fill or if you know of private employment agencies that handle this type of skill, share that information with the employee.

The subject of employment-at-will is a complex and confusing one. By knowing how to handle disciplinary problems and dismissals, you can keep yourself and your company out of legal hot water.

▶ **WHAT YOU CAN DO** → *You can reduce your vulnerability to unjust discharge suits if you ...*

1. Realize that employees who may be victims of the "employment-at-will" relationship have a greater chance of winning lawsuits against their employers.

2. Acknowledge that it is the immediate supervisor (you) whose behavior and actions usually land the company in court.

3. Devise a strategy for handling discipline and discharges. Start with the hiring process by taking care not to suggest that a noncontract employee is "permanent" in any way.

4. Follow company disciplinary procedures to the letter. Use progressive discipline to avoid charges that a firing came "out of the blue."

5. Talk with problem employees and give them a chance to improve their performance or behavior.

6. Consult your superior for advice on how you should handle the problem. An authoritative second opinion could shed light on an aspect of the problem—or your handling of it—that you haven't considered.

7. Document all instances of employee misconduct and your attempts to turn the worker around. Tangible, written evidence will serve as valuable ammunition if you and your company are served with a wrongful discharge suit.

By following these steps, you'll be less vulnerable to the financial, legal, and human relations problems employment-at-will can cause.

ACTION PLAN:

CHAPTER SIX
HOW TO BE AN EFFECTIVE COMMUNICATOR

MAKE IT YOUR BUSINESS TO BE UNDERSTOOD

In today's high-tech business environment, more industries than ever use computers, electronic mail, robotics, and widespread data processing networks. But despite the wonders of modern technology, communication problems continue to exist. It takes a special effort to communicate exactly what you mean. Supervisors, in particular, have become ...

The Ones in the Middle

Supervisors are the most important part of a company's communication network: they deal directly with workers, with management, *and* with fellow supervisors. As both senders and receivers of information, it's up to them to develop techniques for getting through to employees.

You'll be able to get better cooperation and have a smoother running department if you learn to recognize the pitfalls that make the transmission of ideas and policies difficult.

Barriers to Communication

There are many reasons why communication between individuals breaks down, states Dr. Jeannine Sandstrom, a human resources specialist with Rhodes & Associates (Dallas, Texas). Different internal and external roadblocks can keep you from speaking the same language as the person you're talking to. Sandstrom points to a number of these barriers, any of which can cause communication interference:

- **Background noise.** "This can cause the listener to have a hard time hearing what's being said or to miss the message altogether. If noise is a problem, consider having the conversation in a different location, perhaps in an office where you can shut the door and eliminate the distraction."

- **Internal noise.** "We can think much faster than we can talk. So, while you're talking, your listener might be taking a vacation from the conversation and thinking about lunch or a meeting scheduled for later in the day," she says. Stray thoughts keep people from paying attention and focusing on what you're saying.

- **Language.** "It's important to remember that words can mean different things to different people and can cause misunderstandings in and of

Talk the Same Language

Communication between individuals can also break down simply because people don't always say what they *think* they're saying. Each person has individual speech habits and patterns, which can interfere with communication. When communications are misinterpreted, we typically repeat ourselves—more loudly, usually.

But when people don't understand you, they can't be expected to know what you want them to do. And that usually means either that no action is taken or that the wrong action is taken.

Here is an example of what can happen when a supervisor fails to get a message across:

Chief Inspector Jim Caldwell knew that some out-of-tolerance work was being passed by his inspection crew because they were shorthanded and everything was rush-rush. He didn't realize how bad it was, however, until one day the production manager called him and told him customers were returning material as unacceptable. Jim was told, "You've got to do something about your crew's sloppy procedures and do it fast."

Caldwell's first act was to send a memo to all inspectors, calling attention to their poor work. The next week he called a meeting to get across the message—improve or else. The next month he had another meeting.

"There's been some improvement," he told the group, "but not enough. If this keeps up, some of you will be looking for another job."

A few days later the production manager called Caldwell into her office. "A customer just returned a hundred Mark 3's," she said. "One of your people is responsible for our losing a good account—look into it."

Caldwell investigated and found that the items had been passed by inspector Don Burbank. "I've told you about this before," Caldwell told Burbank. "We'll have to let you go."

"Why are you firing me?" Burbank asked. "This is the first time you've said anything to me personally about my work. If I was doing something wrong, you should have told me so that I could correct it. I deserve some warning."

"It wasn't necessary," Caldwell said. "I warned all of you three times that the work of some people would have to improve."

What Went Wrong?

Why did Jim Caldwell fail to get his message across? In the first place, he was much too general. He couldn't expect people to take his warnings seriously when he merely intimated that "some people had to improve."

Also, he was too vague about what should be done. To get his point across, he should have used simple, direct language and given specific instructions. As it was, he permitted his employees to interpret his meaning in their own ways.

---

themselves. The word 'directive,' for example, might mean simply a memo to one supervisor. To another, it could mean a set of instructions. Realize this and choose your words carefully."

● **Our own perceptions.** People do not always react to the situation that's at hand, but rather to his or her perception of reality. We all have our own perceptions—perceptions that are colored by everything that has ever happened to us. Our perceptions influence every area of our lives.

"For instance, if your employees feel as though you don't appreciate the work they do, it's going to affect the way that they work for you and cooperate with you," says Sandstrom. "You might, in fact, place a very high value on their work. But as long as they perceive it to be true, you've got a problem."

To communicate well, we must remember that none of us experience the world in exactly the same way. Certain events or details tend to become ingrained in each person's memory—rather than a whole, objective picture.

Say What You Mean

Thinking of all the things that can go wrong with your communications can make you wonder how anything ever gets accomplished. Is it just luck when instructions are followed correctly? That may be the case at times

But there are certain positive steps you can take to ensure that your communications are as effective as they can possibly be. According to Sandstrom, these steps are:

■ **Think** through what you want to say—before

you actually say it. "Don't be afraid that people will think you're a weak supervisor just because you hesitate before you speak. It's much better to take the time you need and formulate your thoughts as clearly as you can."

■ **Simplify** your message. Be explicit. If you absolutely have to use jargon or technical terms, make sure that the person you're talking to understands the meaning.

■ **Slow down.** Don't rush your words, Sandstrom advises. "Take all the time you need to speak carefully and clearly. You know what you're about to say, but your listener doesn't. Think of yourself as anchoring a television newscast, where people can't go back and reread a page or ask questions. They have to be able to understand you the first time around."

■ **Review** important points. "It's usually a good idea to conclude your conversation with a summary of the action you expect and the agreed-upon completion date."

Make Use of Many Methods

Ordinary daily conversation is the most important type of communication between you and your workers. But as a supervisor, you also communicate in other mediums—in written materials and in meetings. How do you measure up in these areas?

Unfortunately, many people who speak clearly and express themselves effectively in conversation have a tendency to become flowery in their written communications. Try to write simply and in the language of the readers. Confine each memo or notice to a single subject. If, for some special purpose, you think a letter should be sent to an employee, make it personal and brief.

When you hold a meeting with workers, try to make it as free and informal as possible. Encourage discussion and answer all questions as completely and frankly as you can. If you don't know the answer, promise to get it.

When you are participating in a meeting, come to it *prepared*. Take an active role and keep an open mind.

Working at improving your communications in all of these areas benefits everyone. As you become more concerned with how others think and feel, relationships often improve. You might find yourself becoming a better listener too, thanks to the preparation and thought that you're now putting into your communication efforts.

▶ **WHAT YOU CAN DO** → *You can improve your communication skills if you . . .*

1. Become aware of the internal and external roadblocks that make communication break down—things such as background noise, stray thoughts, language, and perceptions.

2. Take time to think through your ideas, simplify your message, speak clearly and carefully, and review points. These actions will help make your conversations clear.

3. Pay attention to the other ways in which you communicate—in writing and in meetings. Strive to express yourself clearly and completely.

Effective communications depend upon an exchange of meaning and understanding between management, supervisors, and employees—with first-line supervisors in the key position.

ACTION PLAN:

PRAISE AND CRITICISM

For some supervisors, handing out praise to their subordinates is easy and enjoyable. But they have a tough time when it comes to criticizing a worker's poor performance. Other supervisors have no qualms about pointing out someone's mistakes, but have trouble praising a worker for a job well done. In either case, there are ways to improve your communication skills so that you can . . .

Achieve the Right Balance

Deciding whether someone has done a good job or a bad job is a pretty simple matter. After all, performance criteria exist in every kind of job. So meeting those standards—or failing to—should be the way employees are judged. But how and when do you communicate that judgment?

In general, you should:

- Use *praise* to boost better than average performance into outstanding achievement.

- Use *criticism* to spark better performance.

Keep in mind that there is a right way and a wrong way to communicate your judgment to workers. The wrong way is to blame a person for not performing up to par. The right way is to praise employees for their accomplishments and criticize constructively.

How to Use Praise

Probably the best use of praise is to boost good performance into consistently above-average work. But unwarranted praise is an insult to your people. If you give the impression that you are pleased with barely adequate job performance, you are only encouraging employees to keep on pleasing you—with barely adequate work.

The lesson is clear—save your praise for praiseworthy events. Properly used, it will stimulate others to improved performance as well as boost the worker you praise.

Follow these simple guidelines and you'll use praise effectively:

★ **Keep praise appropriate to the achievement.** Regardless of how you word it, effective praise always means "I'm proud of you" to the people who receive it. Unless praise reflects justifiable pride, it belittles both the worker and the achievement.

"You handled that job very nicely, Paul" is effective praise for a simple job done well on the first try. But if you repeat the praise for the second and the third performance of the same simple job, it reflects a lack of any real appreciation of the worker's ability. You'll lose credibility if you overpraise your employees.

★ **Combine praise with recognition.** Whenever you feel that a few workers have made outstanding contributions or someone has come through with a record performance, praise them publicly. This can be done through company publications or a group meeting.

But lavish praise for a spectacular achievement will seem like an empty gesture unless you combine it with some form of recognition. This might be a promotion, a delegation of more authority, or a special award.

★ **Use praise as a lure, not as a prod.** Never try to use praise of an employee's good performance to spur others. This creates strong resentment against the employee who should be a positive influence.

Also, if others get the feeling that your praise is actually camouflaged criticism of them, then instead of inspiring them to do better work, it will backfire—and performance all along the line will slacken.

Rather than point out that others should try to imitate an unusually good performance, just let them see that it is recognized and appreciated. They'll make their own judgment as to the value of doing a good job.

How to Use Criticism

Constructive criticism can be an effective way to inspire better performance. This requires that you approach a situation in a positive manner. Instead of saying, "You're doing that job all wrong," you'll get better results if you say, "Try doing the job this way and let me know if it works any better."

Taking this approach allows the individual being criticized to focus on the criticism itself—rather than on personal feelings of anxiety or hostility.

Ideally, the employee will view the criticism as a potential source of valuable information and will ask for specific ways to correct the situation. When circumstances are not so ideal and the employee appears to feel personally attacked by your criticism, stick to the facts and refrain from personal innuendo.

Any time you criticize an employee, there are certain steps that should be followed. These are:

1. Choose an appropriate time and a private place.
2. Make certain that what you're criticizing can be changed.
3. Avoid threats and accusations.
4. Make certain the person understands your criticism and the reasons for it.

In addition, be as specific and constructive as possible when giving criticism. If you're going to get the results that you want, you have to communicate clearly and precisely.

Don't expect your people to be mind readers. If you take this approach, you could find yourself in a situation like the following one.

Breaking the Backlog

Supervisor Dave Fabian didn't know exactly how to handle Laura Turner, one of his new assemblers. She had shown promise during her training period, but once she was cut loose on her own, her work didn't measure up.

Soon assemblies started to pile up at her workstation. It was obvious to Fabian that Turner knew the job; she just wasn't doing it fast enough.

Finally, he confronted her. "If your work doesn't improve, I'll have to let you go."

The employee seemed surprised at this news. "Just tell me what to do," she pleaded.

"You have to start producing more assemblies every day," Fabian said. "If you just do that, everything will be OK."

The following week, Turner began producing more work. She routinely turned out three or four more assemblies than she had earlier.

Unfortunately, Fabian had been looking for her to produce eight to ten more units per day. He dreaded having to discuss the problem with her again, but he knew she'd have to boost her production to break the backlog his department was facing.

Round Two

"I hate to say it," he began, "but I've still got some problems with your output."

"What do you mean? Didn't you say that all I had to do was up my output?" Turner asked.

"Yes, but..."

"And haven't I increased my production rate?" she continued.

"Yes, that's true, but..."

"Then I don't see what the problem could be," the employee declared.

"The problem is I need ten more units a day from you," Fabian said.

"Well, why didn't you say so?" Turner asked. "If that's all you want, then that's what I'll do."

The very next day, Turner produced ten more units than she normally did. The day after that, and every day thereafter, her rate remained as high.

Getting the Results You Want

Getting the performance improvements you want *can* often be as simple as telling employees exactly the results you are looking for. You have to be concrete and specific, though. A general criticism of their work tells them very little.

Laura Turner didn't know where she stood with her supervisor. His criticism of her work was so vague that she didn't know what was expected of her. But once Supervisor Fabian spelled out his expectations, she rose to the challenge.

Most employees don't mind being criticized as long as it's done constructively and they get details on how to improve. And when employees are doing a good job, they need to know that you've noticed their efforts so that they will keep on doing good work.

▶ **WHAT YOU CAN DO** ➡ *You can make effective use of praise and criticism if you . . .*

1. Use praise to boost achievement, but be sure to keep your comments appropriate to the achievement.

ACTION PLAN:

_____

_____

> **2.** Try to combine public praise with some form of recognition: an award, a promotion, or additional authority.
>
> **3.** Let employees make their own judgment as to the value of doing a good job—instead of asking them to imitate another employee's good performance.
>
> **4.** Criticize workers in private, being careful to communicate your expectations as specifically and positively as possible.
>
> *You'll inspire above-average performance when you show a genuine interest in your people and use praise and criticism effectively.*

GIVING EFFECTIVE ORDERS

Your chief job is to get things done—not only by yourself but also by the people you supervise. The kind of results you get depends upon your ability to give directions that enable employees to work intelligently and effectively. In essence, that means you must . . .

Make Yourself Understood

Orders too often are not properly carried out when they are given to the wrong people, in the wrong way, or at the wrong time. You don't have to have a knack for analyzing bothersome situations to know that a lot of irritation and confusion is caused by misunderstanding instructions.

It is up to you to see that the message does get across. How do you accomplish this? Simple. Any order you give to your employees should be based upon the following six rules:

1 Make your order clear and complete. Keep your instructions as simple as possible, but be sure to include all the facts an employee needs to complete the job quickly and efficiently.

For instance, if you tell a machinist, "Be careful with this job; we need a close fit," he might say to himself, "I'm always careful," and think no more about it.

A more effective approach would be to say: "Fred, see the close tolerance specified for this part? Be sure to hold it because there's a very close fit between this and the mating part. If the fit's sloppy, the whole piece will have to be scrapped."

2 Make your order fit the person. Be certain that the worker you give the order to has the experience to complete it. Can you depend on this employee to do the best possible job—and do it on time? Ask yourself if more than one person should be assigned to the order or if close supervision will be necessary.

3 Make your order businesslike. Neither you nor your worker should be conscious of personalities when any order is given. Facts and circumstances dictate that a job must be done and that you are the one who is in the position to effect it—no more and no less.

In addition, present your orders positively. Many times employees do exactly what they are told *not* to do because the order is phrased in the negative. For example, if you want a certain form, say so. Don't bother mentioning any forms that aren't to be used.

4 Establish a team approach. If you depend on

your position of authority, you *may* get obedience, but it will be of the unthinking variety that will actually weaken your department in the long run.

Obedience based on willingness and understanding is the kind that produces top results in productivity and efficiency. By always stressing the cooperative "team" approach, you can make your orders more effective.

5 Use the right type of order. You can give an order in a variety of ways, and you'll find it effective to use different approaches to fit particular employees or situations. Most frequently, you will find that a request works best if you have established a nonauthoritarian climate.

True, a request carries almost the same weight as a direct command. But a request makes the receiver feel that his or her cooperation is being *asked for* rather than demanded—so you're more likely to get it.

Another type of order that is even more dependent on initiative and cooperation of subordinates is the suggestion. The order is merely implied, but it frequently brings a positive response from conscientious workers.

The direct order should be used with care. It may be necessary to stress the urgency of the situation in times of emergency or in dealings with employees who don't respond to any other type of order. But more often than not, issuing orders is the least effective way to get them obeyed.

6 Time your order correctly. Orders normally should not be given just before lunch or quitting time; they'll most likely be forgotten. And unless it's urgent, an order should not be given to an employee who is feeling harassed, rushed, or preoccupied.

Imagine the following scenario: You're hard at work on a report that has to be finished by tomorrow morning. Your immediate superior strides into your office and drops a batch of forms on your desk. You are told that you are to stop what you are doing and take care of this new task.

No matter how important those forms might be, you are almost certain to feel at least some irritation at being interrupted. The more often you are interrupted, the greater the irritation. Keep this fact in mind when issuing your own orders.

Think It Through

Almost nothing will undermine employees' confidence in their superior faster than the supervisor who issues orders without thinking ahead. It's all too easy to leave out important details, or even to give wrong instructions to employees, if you don't think your order through. Here is a good example of what can happen:

Supervisor Charlie Rogers led his newest employee, Ralph Bell, to the two long wire-coating machines and explained his duties to him: "When the hopper on either machine gets below the halfway mark, fill it from these bags of granules. The machine melts them down and coats the wire with hot plastic.

"Oh, yes, throw in a scoop of these brown flakes each time, too," he said, pointing to a bag. "You can shout for Donna Horton down at the far end of the machines if you need any help. Any questions?"

Bell shook his head.

As Rogers walked back to his office he said to himself: "He shouldn't have any trouble. It's really a simple job."

Two hours later, Donna Horton came storming into Rogers' office. "Charlie, why didn't you tell that new worker how to do the job? I was away for a few minutes getting my knife sharpened, and when I got back, both wire coaters had run dry because he goofed up feeding them. I'll lose at least a half an hour getting back in operation!"

"What did he do wrong?" Rogers asked.

"He let the hoppers go empty while he was looking for the flakes," she replied.

Shouldering the Blame

Rogers realized he had left out a vital piece of information when he gave his directions to the new employee.

"Sorry, Donna, it's my fault," said Rogers. "I didn't tell Bell those flakes are only leftover plastic coatings cleaned out of the machines at night and reprocessed. I should have told him that we add them to the new granules so there won't be any waste of material."

"That's right, Charlie," said Horton. "When he ran out of the flakes, he could have just used the fresh granules in the bags. It would have saved me a good chunk of production time if he had done that."

With this incident, Rogers relearned something: You can't expect workers, especially new ones, to act intelligently if they aren't aware of all the facts.

The best way to be sure that workers understand instructions is to ask them to repeat the order. Of course, they might be able to repeat your words without really knowing what they're supposed to do. If you suspect this to be so, ask questions that will test their understanding.

Remember, the art of issuing orders isn't an inborn skill, it has to be learned. It takes tact, thought, and ingenuity to give instructions that give you the results you desire.

> **WHAT YOU CAN DO** → *You can avoid misunderstandings when giving directions if you . . .*

1. Give clear and complete instructions and fit your order to the person.

2. Explain the instructions in a businesslike manner, being careful to phrase your order in positive terms.

3. Act as a leader, not a dictator. Stress the team approach to get top results.

4. Communicate your orders in a variety of ways, tailoring your approach to the employee, the task at hand, and any extenuating circumstances.

5. Take special pains to think through your order and give complete directions to all employees, especially newcomers.

6. Ask questions of employees to make certain they understand exactly what is expected of them.

Telling people what to do—and how to do it—is a fact of everyday life for most supervisors. That's why it's essential that your instructions get understood the first time around.

ACTION PLAN:

_____
_____
_____
_____
_____
_____
_____
_____
_____
_____
_____
_____

COMMUNICATING COMPANY POLICY

Communicating company rules is one of your most important responsibilities as a supervisor, but it can also be one of the toughest. Many of these rules may be cut-and-dried, but human behavior rarely is. Thus, enforcement can be . . .

A Hard Line to Toe

As a supervisor you must play on two teams at the same time—with your work group and with the management group you report to. You owe it to both groups to make sure your interpretation of company policy is correct and your communication to others is clear.

Just what is company policy, anyway? Of course, it will differ from organization to organization, but it ususally includes not only the rules and regulations concerning personnel policies but all the various directives from management as well.

Naturally, in order to effectively communicate company rules and regulations, you must understand them yourself. But what do you do when a policy has not been clearly communicated to supervisors, so that you are left to interpret it in your own way?

Consider the following case in point:

In the milling and grinding department, when a worker asks supervisor Herb Bradford for a new tool, Bradford tells that person to get several so that he or she won't have to keep running to the toolcrib. But in the drill press section, when Janice Landis is asked for a new drill, she looks over the old one and usually says, "There's plenty of life in this drill. Sharpen it—that's what we have grinders for."

These two supervisors are interpreting company policy, though they probably are not conscious of it. What Herb Bradford is saying is that it's the policy of the company to be generous in issuing tools. On the other hand, Janice Landis is telling her workers that the company expects them to get the most possible use out of their tools and that everyone should practice economy.

Differences of opinion like these can lead to dissatisfaction among workers. So, whenever a situation exists where company policy is not clear, seek an official ruling so that there will be consistency throughout the workplace. Once you attain agreement, you may even find a new spirit of cooperation between departments.

Understanding Is Believing

You don't need to be able to quote each rule verbatim, but it's vital that you fully comprehend the fundamental points of the policies you are communicating. If your department has an employee or supervisor manual, review it periodically. Ask yourself several questions while boning up on company regulations:

- **How does the policy read?** Is it clear and direct, or are there some nebulous areas? Should you consult your superior for clarification?

- **How is the policy being used?** Does management demand that you implement the rule to the letter, or does it allow room for interpretation or exceptions?

Some policies are in the best interest of employees and the company, and you can't make exceptions. Other areas may be situations where you are allowed to use your experience and knowledge about specific employees to implement the policy in different ways. You must be able to make an educated decision whether to permit it.

Ask yourself, "Is this something I have the ability to grant within my own area?" That's the issue you have to be able to handle.

- **What is the intent of the policy?** Comprehending exactly why a policy has been outlined will improve your sense of conviction, and thereby aid you in supporting it with enhanced effectiveness.

For example, if you have a no-smoking policy, that is to maintain a healthy environment for employees. It is a benefit to people. Similarly, a locked-door policy is for security—to provide a safer environment.

Help Your People to Understand, Too

Once you feel you have a strong handle on the whys and wherefores of company policies, you must convey them clearly to your staff. Merely stating that "rules are rules" will create resentment. Your people need to understand the reasons behind rules, just as you do.

Explain to your people the purpose of policies and why you are implementing them. Don't just state rules that may seem arbitrary to employees. For example, if several workers are peeved because you've told them they may not smoke in a certain area, have a meeting with them and openly discuss the issue. Explain that the company has outlined the rule to maintain a healthier workplace, and provide information about secondhand smoke and other smoking perils to help support your point.

Handing Down New Rules

It is also your job to communicate any new policy that management has instituted or resurrected. Your first step is to tell your subordinates about it. Obviously, if workers don't know the rules, they can't comply with them. Here are some steps that should prove effective when you're handing down new rules:

▶ **Publicize the rule.** Memos, notices, and announcements should make it clear to all workers that the rule is in effect.

▶ **Meet individually with employees.** Explain what the new regulation is and why it was created. Ask employees for suggestions to prevent infractions. And remember, don't be too quick to lower the boom. It takes time for workers to get used to new policies.

♦ **Enforce regulations objectively.** The rules go for everyone, regardless of race, religion, national origin, sex, age, or disability.

♦ **Keep necessary records** to show that work rules have been equally applied and enforced.

♦ **Take a firm stand.** It's up to you to show employees that you are committed to rule enforcement.

When You Don't Agree

You'll probably run into several company policies or rules that you do not agree with. Probably the worst thing you can do is explain a policy by saying, "I know this sounds crazy and I don't like it any more than you do, but this is the way the front office wants it."

Anytime you make a statement like that, you're asking for trouble. It would be impossible for the workers to comply willingly, and you could find yourself in deep trouble.

A much more sensible way to treat a regulation or policy that you disagree with is to first explain it to your employees without comment. If the policy seems to have outlived its usefulness or is unrealistically harsh in light of changed conditions, you might then seek to improve the situation.

Change Is in the Air

Policies and procedures need to be continually reviewed and updated. Times change and products change. All these things need to be looked at regularly, and it is a supervisor's responsibility to let managers know if things aren't working. Some policies benefit from rewriting.

If this is the case, communicate what the problem is that you are having. You can do that through your management chain, or you can call your company's personnel or human resources department. Many companies have personnel administrators who are liaison persons.

As a supervisor, you're on the front line and can point out problems. If you see abuse of a policy, you have a responsibility to point that out. A policy that no one is following is far better off being changed.

▶ **WHAT YOU CAN DO** → *You can communicate and enforce company policy effectively if you ...*

1. Seek an official ruling whenever a policy is unclear. In this way, each supervisor won't be left to interpret the rule in his or her own manner.

2. Review your employee or supervisory handbook periodically to brush up on company rules.

3. Convey to your people not only the rules but also the reasons behind the rules.

4. Take care when handing down new rules to enforce them slowly, clearly, and fairly. Keep records to confirm your enforcement, and stand firm.

5. Tell the proper people when a policy seems unfair, too harsh, or no longer useful.

When it comes to interpreting company rules, recognize your responsibility to your employees and your managers, and take steps to keep both groups informed.

ACTION PLAN:

_____
_____
_____
_____
_____
_____
_____
_____
_____
_____

THE VALUE OF LISTENING

Do you know how to listen? Don't be too quick with your answer. The fact is that many supervisors don't know how to listen effectively. Simply hearing what's said isn't enough. Listening well requires interpretation, evaluation, and response. If you haven't given much thought to listening in the past, now is your chance to . . .

Improve Your Listening Habits

Even though listening is one of a supervisor's most important tools, it is often completely neglected. Whenever you are preoccupied with your own thoughts, you're probably giving only superficial attention to conversation with your workers. That means you could be missing valuable information.

Obviously, it pays to become a better listener. But is it something you can learn to do? Certainly, *if* you have empathy and trust.

You must want to understand the speaker and trust that his or her message is important enough to take up your time. That doesn't mean you have to agree with the speaker, just that you are trying to understand the point being made.

Breaking the Sound Barrier

Many things can interfere with the listening process. But knowing what these barriers are can help you overcome them. Among the problems are:

- **Jumping to conclusions.** This can happen when the subject matter is too basic and also when it's too complicated. You might feel you are an expert on the subject being discussed, so you jump to conclusions about what the speaker will say next.

- **Distractions.** These can be auditory, such as the noise from a machine or repeated interruptions from the telephone. They can also be visual. Suppose that during a conversation, you see someone walk past, someone whom you've been trying to reach. Without interrupting the speaker, you might mentally shut off the conversation as you start thinking about the other person.

- **Prejudices.** If we are completely turned off by the way a person looks, dresses, or behaves, it's easy to decide that the person's message is unimportant. In the same way, many of us find ourselves not listening to other people simply because we don't like them personally.

- **Sense of self.** Sometimes people are so eager to tell their side of the story that they block out what the speaker is really saying. This is especially likely to happen when you disagree with the speaker about an issue.

- **Emotions.** Certain words can carry an emotional impact and make us react in certain ways. For instance, "unfair" and "fault" are two words that put us on the defensive. When words such as these are used, people tend to *stop* listening and tend to *start* lacing their boxing gloves.

Listen to "How" as Well as "What"

How a person says things is sometimes just as important as the words used. Here's a case in point:

Tom Carey was upset. He had just found his personal micrometers in another worker's toolbox. They were expensive instruments and meant a lot to Carey. Of course, he was told, "I just borrowed them for a minute. I meant to return them," but Carey wasn't so sure that was the truth. He decided to tell his boss about it.

When Carey got to his supervisor's office, he blurted out, "Russ, I've got to talk to you." But that's as far as he got. Russ Simpson was hard at work on his monthly production report, so he interrupted with "Wait just a second."

Carey stood and cooled his heels for 5 minutes, becoming more agitated all the time. Finally he got a chance to tell his story. He finished his account with an ultimatum: "If anything else turns up in his toolbox, there's going to be real trouble."

Unfortunately, Simpson heard very little of what Carey said. Carey was a constant complainer, and Simpson was tired of listening to his tirades. So he ended the interview as quickly as possible and said: "You can see how busy I am, Tom. I can't get mixed up in every little argument. Everybody forgets to return stuff once in a while. Just forget about it."

The next week, Simpson had to suspend both Carey and the other operator for fighting.

Dangers of Selective Listening

It's a natural reaction to want to tune out the person who gripes continually. But many times we prejudge people who have gripes and decide they're full of hot air even before they speak.

Ever since you became a supervisor, you've no doubt been warned about the problems that can be created by showing favoritism. That's why you are very careful in meting out discipline and work assignments.

But there's another, more subtle kind of favoritism that you can fall prey to. It's the practice of listening to some employees and not others. In other words, some people can always get your ear, whereas others find that you're too busy or too impatient to give them your full attention.

Open the Door to Communication

Follow these steps and you'll improve your listening and discover a whole world of useful information:

★ **Pay attention.** Don't let your thoughts intrude on what other people are saying. Keep your mind on their words, and think about your own problems when you're alone.

★ **Repeat what you've been told—briefly.** If you follow this rule, you'll force yourself to pay attention to the speaker. When you do restate the information, keep your tone neutral. Remember, you're not trying to convince the other person of your conclusions, you're trying to get his or her ideas.

★ **Avoid preconceived ideas.** One of the most effective ways to close your mind to new ideas or methods is to take the stance that something is not true because it's contrary to what you "always knew." Evaluate the speaker's idea or information on its own merits.

★ **Consider the source.** To get the full meaning of a message, you frequently have to interpret it. If you know the speaker—when he or she is biased or inclined to overstatement—you can get a clearer meaning.

★ **Use self-discipline.** Never let anger or sympathy influence your understanding of what a person says. Differentiate between facts and feelings. If you react emotionally to a statement, you lose your objectivity.

★ **Really want to listen.** Don't just pretend to be interested in what you're being told. Stop doing other things (such as reading or fumbling with papers). Show your interest by asking questions when the other person has stopped talking.

★ **Listen full time.** Instead of thinking about what you're going to say, pay close attention to what the other person is trying to tell you. Don't interrupt. You can talk when he or she finishes.

Good listening habits can help you make sound decisions. Relationships in your department—and between departments—can also improve. Listening can also keep disagreements from growing into larger, and potentially more damaging, confrontations.

▶ **WHAT YOU CAN DO →** *You'll develop better listening habits and improve your communication if you . . .*

1. Have trust and empathy for the speaker's feelings. You must want to understand the speaker and trust that his or her message is important.

2. Recognize the barriers that inhibit listening—barriers such as distractions, emotions, prejudices—and work to deal with these successfully.

3. Listen to how something is said as well as what is said.

ACTION PLAN:

_____

_____

_____

_____

_____

_____

4. Avoid selective listening and learn to suppress personal feelings that can color your judgment.

5. Concentrate on becoming a more effective listener by paying attention to every speaker, avoiding preconceived notions, using self-discipline, and considering the source.

Learn to recognize how important listening is to you and your job—you can't get ahead without it.

FEEDBACK: A COMMUNICATION ESSENTIAL

Perhaps the single most important technique in better communications is feedback. That's because it can tell you if you are communicating as well as you think you are. Feedback can help you learn what is being understood by the person to whom you're talking. Is your message getting through? Do you have the whole picture? To find out . . .

Ask For Feedback

Although some supervisors might regard feedback as just a lot of idle chatter, most recognize its value—in many aspects of supervision. The ideas, suggestions, and observations of your subordinates can help make your job—and theirs—easier and more comfortable.

Feedback can help you solve problems in your department, keep morale high, and increase productivity. You can elicit feedback in several different ways:

1 Keep people informed. If you are free with your information, you are far more likely to get people to be open with you as well. Don't play "I've got a secret."

2 Treat people as you want to be treated—as individuals. Employee feedback is more spontaneous when workers know they're being treated as individuals with certain skills and needs. They need to know when they are putting out good work as well as when their performances need polishing. If people hear from you only when you have something negative to say, you are not likely to get the kind of feedback that you want.

3 Hold meetings. Especially when there are changes to be made, involve workers by giving them a real chance to make some input.

4 Ask for information. Your people can provide you with the necessary data to justify such items as new equipment. And when they do need something for their work, be sure to follow through on their feedback as quickly as possible.

5 Be approachable. It's often difficult for employees to approach a superior simply because of the aura of authority about the position. Make it easy on your people by keeping a high profile. Make it a point to get out on the floor and talk to your workers informally.

Get the Whole Truth

Of course, getting employees to give you feedback is only half of the battle. Often, people will tell you only what you want to hear—even though you need honest feedback to make informed decisions. If this seems to be happening, your questioning skills may be the reason. Ineffective questioning can hinder honest feedback.

The way in which you phrase and deliver a question reveals your feelings about your employees.

193

Thus, your questions can convey criticism or disapproval whether you intend it or not. In turn, these negative messages can intimidate employees and create tense situations.

There are, however, ways to effectively question people—ways that will help you get the whole truth. Here are some examples of effective questions:

- **Open/direct questions** usually begin with who, what, where, when, or how. They imply respect for the employee and invite opinions. "Tell me, how do these directives look to you?" "Do you have any ideas about how we can complete this project with three employees on vacation?"

- **Planted-answer questions** imply the direction you want the person's answer to take. You may already have arrived at the answer, but need some support to back up your solution. "How about using this approach to do the job?" "Don't you think this outline needs additional work?"

- **No-feeling questions** are based on reason and elicit no emotion. "What procedures did you follow?" "How would you tackle this problem?"

- **Off-the-hook questions** allow employees to refuse a request without losing face. "There has been a change in the schedule—our deadline has been moved up to next week. I don't suppose you would want to put in an extra hour or two this week?"

Now, here are some examples of ineffective questions—questions that should *not* be used with your employees:

▶ **Disagreeable questions** are phrased in such a way that they assume the employee agrees with the supervisor—regardless of the worker's true feelings. This type of question can reduce the employee's self-confidence and create resentment. "None of your ideas have worked out. What makes you think you could come up with a decent solution?"

▶ **No-way-out questions** drive the employee into a corner. "As I see it, this is the only solution. What do you think?"

▶ **Ill-feelings questions** create negative feelings in the worker. "You know we've tried this approach several times before, so why do you insist on doing something that obviously won't work?"

▶ **Trick questions** are traps to get employees to agree with you because they're left with little or no choice. "What should we do with this work schedule: Implement it, or put in some long hours revamping it?"

Remember, questions can imply many things to many people. For that reason, few queries are as simple as they seem. But being able to "telegraph" appropriate messages can help you get honest feedback.

Attention to Signals

Asking the kind of questions that elicit more than "yes" or "no" answers can help you get feedback. There are other signs to look for that will tell you how and if your message is getting across.

The first essential for maximum feedback, of course, is face-to-face communication. Only then can you tell if your people understand, agree, are sympathetic, feel hostile, or are just confused. The feedback comes not only through the receivers' words but also through their behavior.

You should watch for expressions of puzzlement, anger, or comprehension that may flicker across their faces. Gestures and other physical actions can reveal impatience, animosity, lack of enthusiasm, or agreement.

The point is, most people tend to respond to these signals subconsciously. But if you make it a point to watch and respond deliberately, you may be amazed at how much better you and your employees understand one another.

▶ **WHAT YOU CAN DO** → *You can use feedback to boost morale and solve problems faster if you . . .*

1. Use various methods to elicit ideas and information from your people. For instance, it helps to be open and approachable, to hold meetings, and to treat employees as individuals.

ACTION PLAN:

_____

_____

_____

2. Ask open-ended and nonthreatening questions. This kind of question will help you obtain the quality and the quantity of information that you are after.

3. Avoid questions that conceal employees' real thoughts or put people on the defensive. These queries are never constructive.

4. Use face-to-face communication in order to "read" a person's response. Feedback is revealed not only in words but also in behavior.

You can never hope to know everything that's going on, but feedback from employees can take some of the pressure off and make everyone's job a little easier.

CLOSING DOWN THE RUMOR MILL

Rumors can have a profound effect on productivity in your department. When employees are busy worrying over unfounded bad news, celebrating imagined good news, or simply spending their time spreading rumors, their work may not be up to snuff. That's why you must be constantly on the alert for ways to . . .

Prune the Grapevine

There are two types of rumor that can have a negative impact on your department. One is the "wish-fulfullment" rumor, which can keep employees guessing about a real or imagined benefit they think they are going to receive in the near future. The other, more common, problem-provoking rumor is the "apprehension" tale. Here, employees worry about something that will make their jobs tougher or eliminate the positions altogether.

Who's in the best position to stop rumors before they get out of hand and affect departmental productivity? In most cases, it's you, the first-line supervisor. Because you already have built-in lines of communication with your people, you can ease their fears and correct their misconceptions better than anyone else in your organization.

It Starts With Prevention

If you can keep damaging rumors from getting started in the first place, that's a big plus. But to do that, you must recognize that rumors often start with *you*. Surprised? You shouldn't be.

After all, as a supervisor, your words are automatically invested with a certain amount of authenticity. Your people have a predisposition to believe what you say to them. So if they misinterpret something you say, or if you pass along information that is less than accurate, there's a good chance the rumor mill will start grinding again. So, weigh carefully what you say *before* you say it.

It's especially important to watch what you say when your company is planning a change in the organization. If your firm is planning a move, an expansion, or a layoff, you should wait until the final decision has been made before you let the news slip to employees.

Mum's the Word

Just as you shouldn't discuss company plans before they're finalized, you should never discuss the performance of individual employees with other members of your workforce. If your observations are negative, word could get back to the person being discussed, which could set him or her to worrying about whether some sort of discipline—or dismissal—is imminent.

One positive step you can take to prevent rumors is to give your workers factual, important information to talk about—such as ways to improve productivity. If you do, they'll be less likely to waste time speculating about the rumors that are flying around.

So as soon as you receive a piece of information that will affect employees, make it a point to pass the facts on to them.

Track Down the Source

Of course, you're not the only source of rumors in your department, and even the best preventive measures on your part won't keep rumors from being spread from time to time. That's why it's a good idea to keep an ear out so that you'll know which rumors are making the rounds. After all, if you don't know what kind of misinformation your employees are passing around, you can't put a stop to it.

When you do discover a rumor that is harming productivity, your next step should be to locate where the rumor arose in the first place. By asking workers and other supervisors, you can probably pinpoint just who is spreading stories.

Once you've discovered who the rumor-spreader is, sit down with him or her and outline the problems that can occur when gossip is spread. Then, if the rumor is something that affects all employees (such as a layoff or company closing), call a group meeting to clear the air and set your people straight.

Case in Point

To gain a better understanding of how rumors can adversely affect a department, take a careful look at this case study:

Supervisor Roger Shaw was taken aback by a question put to him by Jane Gallagher, one of his employees.

"My curiosity has gotten the better of me," she admitted with a smile. "Would you mind telling me how much of a bonus we're actually getting?"

"Bonus?" asked the confused supervisor. "What are you talking about?"

Gallagher plunged ahead, but with a lot less assurance. "Word has it that the company is doing so well we're going to get a bonus this year. Isn't that true?"

"Not to my knowledge," said Shaw. "I don't know where that story came from, but it's absolutely not true. These are hard times. Very few companies can afford to give bonuses, and we're certainly not one of them. I suggest you go back and tell whoever told you that rumor that he or she should stop spreading falsehoods."

The matter was dropped.

Not the Best Approach

On the surface, it may seem that Shaw has squelched this rumor. But there are several flaws in his approach. For one thing, he hasn't backed up his denial with any concrete facts. So his statement runs the risk of being held up for scrutiny along with the rumor, and employees may not make the right decision when they try to decide which story is the more accurate of the two.

Also, Shaw hasn't made an attempt to investigate where the rumor came from so that he can put a stop to similar episodes in the future. And he hasn't called his employees together as a group to clear the air. Instead, Shaw has sent one employee around to straighten things out.

That's the real problem. Chances are that by the time the story is disseminated to the general workforce, distortions will take place in the original statement. The result? More rumors may be sparked as a result of Shaw's denial. Unfortunately, that's exactly what happened in this case.

The Distorted Story

Passing Shaw's denial about the bonus through the grapevine resulted in a serious distortion of what he had said. This was brought home to him when he walked into his office a week after his conversation with Gallagher to find most of his employees assembled there.

"What's going on here?" asked Shaw, noting the look of concern on the employees' faces.

"You tell us," said John Vitale, a veteran employee. "There's a rumor that the company is about to go under, and that we'll be shut down in a month."

"First, that's simply not true," answered Shaw. "Second, I'd like to know once and for all who's been starting these rumors."

Vitale looked surprised. "I don't know about any other rumors, but I heard that this story about the company closing came right from you. You supposedly told someone that the company was going through tough times, and money was hard to come by. I just assumed the story was valid, since you said it."

Then Shaw recalled his conversation with Jane Gallagher. "Well, that's not exactly what I said. I just said the rumor about bonuses wasn't true. But I can see how the story may have been distorted as it was passed along."

Shaw thought for a moment and then addressed his workers again. "Tell you what—I'll take some time this afternoon to find out exactly what's going on with the company's financial status. Then we'll have a departmental meeting tomorrow to get everything straightened out."

Now Shaw is beginning to understand the importance of stopping rumors, and he's chosen an approach that will help keep rumors from negatively affecting productivity in the future.

They Look to You

It's only natural for your employees to look to you for information about their company and their jobs. In most cases, they understand that of all the people in the department, you're the person who is best informed and stands the best chance of getting to the bottom of a puzzling question.

Supervisors who make a concerted effort to present information to their employees in a timely fashion stand the best chance of seeing the rumor mill grind to a screeching halt.

▶ **WHAT YOU CAN DO** → *Rumors have a way of negatively affecting the productivity of any work group. To keep gossip from causing disruptions . . .*

1. Fill your employees in about any moves that affect them. But make sure you have all the facts straight before you call them together.

2. Watch what you say. Be careful not to let any information about personnel slip during an idle conversation.

3. Talk with rumor-spreaders to let them know that their activities have a harmful impact on the productivity of others.

4. Listen to the grapevine to find out which rumors are being spread so that you can put a stop to them.

Keep rumors under control by keeping your people informed. That will provide the additional benefit of keeping both morale and productivity at high levels.

ACTION PLAN:
_____
_____
_____
_____
_____
_____
_____
_____
_____
_____
_____

HOW TO HOLD MEETINGS THAT WORK

Thousands of meetings occur every day in the business world. Conducted properly, meetings are invaluable. Well-planned meetings can go a long way toward improving production, quality, and morale in your department. But the trick is to make your meetings . . .

Short and Productive

You've no doubt been to the kind of meeting that drags on and on without serving any useful purpose—and you know how uninspiring such meetings are. In fact, you may even have vowed that you would never hold that type of meeting yourself.

How long should a meeting be? Let the topic dictate the length of the meeting. Ten minutes will probably do if you're giving a routine rundown of safety regulations plus a pep talk on the importance of working safely. Fifteen minutes for such a topic may well be unjustified interruption of production.

In contrast, when you talk about subjects such as a new piece of equipment or subsequent reassignment of jobs, the meeting should be longer. As a general rule, however, even sessions like these shouldn't exceed 30 minutes.

How to Plan the Meeting

It's essential that you plan ahead and cover all the bases. Planning will give you control over the session. And the better you plan, the more effective you'll be at winging it when something unexpected happens. Thoroughly planning a meeting means doing the following:

★ **Defining your purpose.** Is the main purpose to offer new information to the group, to draw ideas from them, or to solve problems? Will it be a motivational session to increase productivity or to remind people of goals? Be specific about your objectives, and decide exactly what you want people to know by the end of the meeting.

★ **Selecting key people.** Ask yourself, who really needs to attend? By limiting attendance, you ensure the kind of input you want and save valuable time.

★ **Dividing your time.** It's a smart idea to divide your meeting into two sections: your presentation and a question-and-answer period. Say the meeting runs 15 minutes. Allot about 10 minutes to yourself and use the rest of the time for questions and answers.

These last 5 minutes are important. By the questions and comments, you can tell how clearly you have gotten your information across. At the same time, you can gauge people's reaction to your message. Finally, this period allows people to participate in the meeting—and not to be just "talked at."

Guiding the Discussion

Once your preparation is complete, you'll still need to project a strong leadership image in order to pull everything together. When it's time for the meeting to begin, stand up and take control. Stand where everyone can see you, and speak loudly enough to be heard by everyone in the room.

Too often, meetings degenerate into an unorganized group of people holding private discussions. While you don't want to be a dictator, you must take charge to guide the meeting to a successful conclusion. To keep order, follow these six steps:

1 Call the meeting to order. State the purpose of the meeting. Be brief and to the point as you begin the meeting. Pare away the word fat and irrelevant ideas.

Example: "I'm sorry to say that I've noticed in the past month that the locker room has been cluttered with towels, newspapers, sandwiches, and so forth. I think what we ought to do is to try to keep it cleaner." You can reduce this to: "The locker room is a mess. We've got to keep it cleaner."

2 Set the scene. Don't immediately start with the details. That can confuse a lot of people. Instead, remind the group of related situations or discussions: "You may remember that last month we had a situation like this. At that time we decided to . . ." Give some brief history about the problem, what has already happened, and any assumptions that exist.

3 Clarify and integrate comments. During the course of the meeting, restate a speaker's comments to help the group keep track of what is said and to let the speaker clear up any possible misinterpretations. "As I understand you, Mary, you feel that supervisors and employees aren't aware of each other's problems."

Then, when new ideas are presented, link them to those that are already accepted by the group: "Bob's idea for circulating weekly progress reports fits in nicely with our commitment to improving communications."

4 Provide additional information. Drawing on your thorough preparation, provide any additional information the group may need to make a decision or to solve a problem: "One fact we have to consider before coming to a decision is . . ."

5 Answer all complaints on the spot—if you can. Otherwise, promise to investigate. Don't try to bluff your way out of a hot corner, or you'll be labeled a supervisor who doesn't know what you're talking about.

6 Summarize and assess. Offer a strong concluding statement whenever the group completes discussion of a topic, and also at the end of the meeting. Last but not least, poll everyone to make sure that solutions were satisfactory and that no other issues need addressing. This last step will ensure that the meeting has achieved its objectives.

Dealing With Dominators

It's important to let everyone who attends the meeting have the opportunity to speak. However, meetings often become dominated by certain personalities. These are the people who won't stop talking, who disagree with everything, or who bring up a completely unrelated subject just to complain.

Fortunately, there are steps you can take to control such people. One way is to have all participants take a break. While everyone is on break, talk with the person who is dominating the session. Ask him or her to allow others to speak. If the person is still uncooperative, request that he or she remain quiet or not attend the rest of the meeting.

You can also direct questions and comments away from the dominant personality and at other individuals. The key is to not let the dominator run the meeting; once that happens, you'll find it difficult to regain control and the meeting will fail in its objectives.

Tending to Taciturn Types

The opposite personality is the taciturn employee who tends not to say anything at all. This person will sit and listen for the entire meeting, but will contribute little. Ironically, such individuals often can contribute much to meetings. Therefore, you must accept the onus of getting these people to speak.

One of the most effective ways to accomplish this is to direct a question or comment towards them. The point is to make them want to talk without coercion. Forcing them to speak can cause them to feel even more inhibited.

Three Tools You Can't Do Without

Knowing how to hold a meeting is critical for a successful outcome, but other factors also influence a meeting's effectiveness. These essentials include choosing the proper *facilities*, having on hand the necessary *equipment*, and providing needed *supplies*. Let's take a look at each item:

■ **Facilities.** Holding a meeting in a small room with a great number of people is a surefire equation for failure. If people are cramped into a small room, the temperature rises, and so do the tempers of participants. So, make sure the room you select is roomy enough to accommodate the number of people who will attend.

Crowded conditions do not make for a successful meeting, and neither does lighting that is too weak or too strong. Poor lighting can cause participants to fall asleep or lose attention while strong illumination causes considerable eye fatigue. Check the level of lighting in your meeting rooms before the actual date of the gathering.

■ **Equipment.** Nothing can wreck a meeting more quickly than having little or no equipment. An excellent way to encourage the successful execution of a meeting is to make available at least one of these items: chalkboards, whiteboards, easels, videocassette players, and overhead projectors.

People often remember better that which they have seen, and these items will allow participants to actually visualize your points. Words alone are not always enough to describe technical processes. Diagrams can be, and frequently are, used to show clearly the interrelationships between components of a system.

■ **Supplies.** Of course, the best equipment is useless if insufficient supplies exist to support it. So, make sure your meeting room is equipped with ample supplies. This means having on hand sufficient quantities of marker pens, chalk, projector bulbs, easel paper, and videocassettes.

Such supplies should be conveniently available so that employees do not have to disrupt the meeting to find what they need. If any disruption occurs, it distracts participants and breaks their attention. But having the supplies readily available will contribute to a smooth and efficient meeting.

Most employees, of course, are somewhere in between the dominant and the taciturn personalities. Most are willing to speak, but yield to the other person who wishes to talk. Recognize that fact and encourage interaction.

Your Role as Referee

Even the best leader can find it difficult to maintain a dignified discussion. Many times, meetings result in heated disputes. Once that happens, the dialogue between people deteriorates. This situation is especially apt to occur when more than one dominant personality attends your meeting.

At such times, you'll have to assume the role of referee. That means asking that the dispute be settled outside the meeting. If the argument continues, conclude the meeting and reschedule it.

Meetings are important communication tools. But they must be conducted properly if they're to serve a purpose. By thoroughly planning for the meeting, guiding the discussion, and assuming control, you can achieve the results that you want.

▶ **WHAT YOU CAN DO** → *You can make your meetings short and productive if you . . .*

1. Plan ahead. Take the time to define what your purpose is, who should attend, and how you should divide your time.

2. Guide the discussion. After calling the meeting to order, be sure to start slowly, link and clarify comments, answer all complaints, and summarize topics.

3. Take a poll. At the end of the meeting, check with participants to make sure the meeting has achieved its objectives.

4. Control the group. Keep dominant personalities under control while encouraging taciturn individuals to contribute.

5. Keep tempers in check. Settle any arguments outside the meeting.

By thoroughly planning for a meeting, guiding the discussion, and assuming control, you can be sure your session is useful and informative.

ACTION PLAN:

_____
_____
_____
_____
_____
_____
_____
_____
_____
_____
_____
_____

MEMBER OF THE MEETING

By now, running meetings may be second nature to you. You know how to direct a group discussion, illustrate your points, and keep people's attention. You may even consider yourself a very good group leader. But remember, sometimes . . .

The Shoe Is on the Other Foot

Supervisors who are accustomed to leading their own meetings sometimes don't give much thought to sessions run by others. If you're a member of your company's safety committee or an ad hoc group formed to study the pros and cons of a particular change in company policy, you may look upon your participation as an "extracurricular" activity—something you're doing for the good of the company rather than for yourself.

If you go into group meetings with this type of attitude, your role is likely to be a passive one. Sure, you'll put in your two cents worth from time to time just to let the rest of the group know you're committed to exploring the issue at hand. But many supervisors simply don't put the same kind of energy into being a group *member* as they put into being a group *leader*.

This is where many supervisors make a big mistake. They see their roles as leaders in *active* terms and their roles as participants in more or less *passive* terms. But the ability to be a good group member is just as important as the ability to hold a fruitful meeting with your own employees. Why? Because a meeting is only as effective as its participants, and the group leader is powerless without their support.

Anatomy of a Group Member

There are certain characteristics that all group members share. First, a good group member isn't afraid to assume the responsibilities that go with the role.

These responsibilities include not only participating in discussions and fact-finding efforts, but also speaking up when the group is going off on a tangent or missing the point, or volunteering to pursue the aims of the group in whatever way is necessary after the meeting has adjourned.

What other characteristics do valuable group members have in common? One is the ability to listen. This is such an obvious point that it's often taken for granted. Yet, supervisors who are in the the habit of running meetings (rather than participating in them) have a tendency to use the time while someone else is speaking to prepare what they are going to say next.

This is a dangerous practice for two reasons. First, it's usually obvious to the speaker that you're not paying attention; and second, you may miss hearing a point that could change your own presentation.

Active listeners sit at attention and hang on every word. Sitting at attention doesn't mean you have to be perched on the edge of your seat. But you'll listen better if you sit up reasonably straight, look directly at the speaker, and refrain from fidgeting or interrupting. Now, let's take a look at some of the other characteristics you'll need to be a valuable participant.

Keep an Open Mind

No one appreciates the group member who comes into a meeting with a particular opinion about the subject and refuses to budge when contradictory ideas are presented. It may be that what takes place during a meeting will fail to change the opinions you had on coming into it, but you owe it to the other group members—and to yourself—to display an open-minded attitude.

The best way to maintain an open mind is to refrain from making premature evaluations of the facts and opinions being presented. When others get up to speak, don't immediately start to summon up arguments against them in your mind. Wait for them to finish, and let others in the group join in the discussion.

Be Ready to Take Part

The most worthless member of all is the one who sits idly by, doodling on a pad or staring out the window while the other members share constructive ideas and hammer out solutions. It's often a tip-off that the individual hasn't done any homework on the issue.

Let's say you are attending weekly conferences where you are supposed to be learning all about the new incentive plan that will soon go into effect. The subject is complicated, and you have to learn it well enough to be able to explain it to your own people.

But have you done your homework? Have you read the information sheets and other materials you were given before the meetings? If you haven't, you are shortchanging not only your people but yourself as well.

Unprepared, you won't be as likely to understand all that you hear; and, worse, your questions are likely to be superficial and uninformed—making you look silly as well as giving others the opinion that you are uninterested.

Let Your Defenses Down

When someone criticizes your ideas, it's a natural reaction to take the criticism personally and get defensive. But defensiveness is a real drawback to the group discussion and problem-solving process.

It makes it difficult for anyone else to say something negative—no matter how justified—for fear of further wounding your ego. In short, it tends to close off discussion on a matter that may be of central importance, simply because no one wants to take a chance on getting you more upset.

Criticism of your ideas is not the same thing as criticism of you personally, so there's really nothing to get upset about. Accept criticism of your ideas as just another point of view. Take a few moments to think through what's been said and to weigh its merits.

Playing the Devil's Advocate

A good group participant knows how to spur on the discussion instead of dragging it down. A meeting in which all the participants agree can be just as unproductive as one in which no one seems to agree on anything.

Playing the devil's advocate doesn't mean you have to stir up strife where none exists. But if everyone else is quick to agree that a particular course of action is called for or that a certain idea is great, you may be able to get them to examine their reasoning a little more closely by pointing out some potential problems they may not have considered.

It's just a way of forcing the others to double-check their own thinking and of making sure none of the less obvious points have been overlooked by the group.

Turn "Mine" Into "Ours"

When you're a member of a group, you have to sacrifice a certain amount of your individuality. This holds true especially when it comes to presenting your ideas. It takes skill and practice to get the group to think of your idea as something they all had a hand in; but if you succeed, you'll see your ideas being adopted more and more.

A good way to get the group thinking along your lines is to draw on the comments that have already been made when it's your turn to present an idea. For example: "Donna already mentioned that we should be especially sensitive to how employees react to this new policy, and Jim added that most opposition will come from older workers. I couldn't agree with them more, and that's why I think we should do such and such."

In one fell swoop you've presented your idea, summoned support for it, and made it sound as though you're merely putting the finishing touches on an idea that the group as a whole has helped to mold.

Be Considerate

What all these points add up to, essentially, is "be considerate." You wouldn't want others to interrupt you during a meeting or not take your point of view seriously. So there's no reason for you to do the same to them.

What you should do is make a brief presentation of the points you consider most important, and then sit down and listen to what the others have to say. If another member says something that strengthens or changes your own ideas, don't jump to your feet to follow up. Wait until everyone has had a chance to speak. You may hear other information that will change your view once again.

Getting your own points across concisely while listening carefully to the comments of others will make you a valuable member of any group. And if other participants in your discussions notice how you conduct yourself and begin to emulate you, your meetings will really get results.

▶ **WHAT YOU CAN DO** → *You can be a key part of successful meetings if you . . .*

1. Take an active role. Contribute your ideas freely and give good reasons in support of them.

2. Accept the responsibility that goes with being a group member. Do your homework prior to the meeting, be willing to listen, and keep an open mind about what others are saying.

ACTION PLAN:

_____
_____
_____
_____

> **3.** Accept constructive criticism. Don't take what people say personally or light into them because of it.
>
> **4.** Play devil's advocate. Point out potential problems that may have been overlooked.
>
> **5.** Tie everyone else's ideas to your own. That way you'll be sure to draw a lot of support for your own position.
>
> *You owe it to your company—and to yourself—to be as good a group member as you are a meeting leader.*

WRITE TO BE UNDERSTOOD

Many people can get their points across in person, but blanch at the thought of having to express themselves on paper. They think that writing is something that can be done only by Shakespeare. But writing is merely a matter of saying what you have to say and assuring that you'll be understood. To do this, start by . . .

Facing the Blank Page

Oh, no! you think. They've just given me a plum assignment, but I have to write a report for the department head. I won't know what to say or how to say it. Writing is just so hard.

No one ever said that writing was easy; it's a challenge even for the people who do it every day. All of us have known how difficult it is to face a blank page. On the other hand, all of us have also been forced to read reports and letters that are boring, wordy, and full of misspellings and cloudy meanings.

So you can see why it's important for everyone in the business world to improve his or her writing skills. As a reader, you don't want to be bored or confused by someone else's poor writing; and as a writer, you don't want to be the one who works hard at writing a report that bores and confuses others.

What you need to know, then, is how to meet your readers' needs and make yourself understood. If you remember the following tips, you can accomplish all of this and more.

Keep Your Reader in Mind

When you sit down to write, what is your first response? More than likely you stare at the page and wonder how you will ever fill it. This is a common response, but remember, no one expects you to write "the great American novel." That's not your goal. Your goal is to serve your readers—and yourself—by:

- Focusing on relevant information that you want to tell and they want to know.

- Making your writing brief and easy to read so that your readers will understand it rather than toss it aside in frustration.

In other words, you should strive to be read and understood. You can succeed in this if you apply the following guidelines:

1 Judge readers' reactions and plan accordingly. Before you write, stop and think about what the reader needs to know. Why are you writing this letter, report, or memo? What should happen as a result of it?

If, for instance, you're writing to your department

head, ask yourself, *What does the boss need from me? Do I have information that will help solve a problem?* If you don't have anything specific to offer, there's probably no point in writing.

Advance thinking is perhaps the most difficult part of writing. But if you don't take this first, crucial step, chances are good that your message will be confused or vague—simply because you have not thought it through.

2 Keep it short and to the point. Many people try to inflate their own importance by writing memos and letters that are too long for the message they are trying to convey. Instead, simply say what you have to say. Long-winded introductions and beating around the bush will only distract readers and waste their time.

To this end, use words that convey your message. "This is to inform you that we'll send you the materials by Friday" is more clearly stated as: "We'll send you the materials by Friday."

3 Make it visually attractive. If you have a lot to say, break up the copy by using subheads to introduce new topics, and "bullets" to highlight key points. You might also include a concise one- or two-page summary. That way you'll get your major points across even if the reader doesn't have time to go over the entire piece. Often, the summary may be all you need to send. If your readers need more information, they can ask you for it.

Sound Like Yourself

Once you've decided what you want to say, how you're going to say it, and what it will look like on the printed page, go ahead and write. Then go back over your work, paying close attention to the tone of your message. Your writing should reflect your personality, your way of conducting business, and your relationship to the reader.

As a supervisor, you may regularly be writing in a style that is authoritative—a style that clearly says, "Do it or else." However, this style is likely to make employees angry and may actually decrease productivity, so the hard-line approach should be used with care.

On the other hand, weak writing—writing in which you never take a firm stand—suggests to clients, employees, and superiors that you lack authority or are chronically indecisive. Therefore, you should use directness but balance it with respect for your reader. Using "you" and "I" fairly equally is one way to make readers feel you have a genuine interest in their concerns.

Also check your writing for a negative attitude. Even if your message isn't cheerful—say there's been a problem with a customer's order, or you have to tell employees that you're revoking a previous privilege—strive to keep your tone as upbeat as possible. State facts briefly and clearly, and offer positive alternatives.

Ask Direct Questions

What was the last direct question you asked? Did you get an immediate response? As you can see, starting off with a question can focus your writing and get your readers' attention.

If you're writing a letter of persuasion, for example, a question can immediately create involvement for the reader. If you've been asked to serve on a community fund-raising program, asking a question such as "Do you remember when we worked to...?" can help establish reader rapport.

Questions can be equally effective at the end of the message. Asking "May I count on you?" avoids an overly aggressive closing that might defeat your purpose. You also will have avoided common closings such as "Thank you in advance for your cooperation."

Avoiding Old Saws, Twice-Told Tales

Business writing is notorious for using some phrases so often that they lose all meaning. Over the years, most supervisors have become so accustomed to business clichés that they believe these expressions *should* be used. In reality, however, there is no such thing as "business" English, there's just *good* English.

Years ago, business writing was extremely formal, and impersonal phrases such as "at your earliest convenience" were found in almost every business communication. So these expressions became overworked until they become phrases that were used out of habit with no particular concern for their appropriateness.

What readers really want is a message with a sense of action. Phrases such as "in this matter" and "said date" are lazy, overstuffed words that sound like legal prose and clutter your writing. If you find yourself writing "please be advised that," strike it out and begin with the next word. Replace "under separate cover" with "separately"; instead of "at your earliest convenience," write "soon." In other words, *keep it simple*!

The point here is that true communication does

not take place unless your reader *understands* exactly what you are trying to say.

The Overall Impression

As a final tip, remember that you are a person writing to other persons. So take the simplest, clearest, warmest approach possible. Tell your readers only what they need to know, keep your writing brief and to the point, adjust the tone, and weed out clutter and cliches.

The result will be the most readable piece you've ever written, and you might even find that you've come to enjoy writing.

▶ **WHAT YOU CAN DO** → *You can write business letters, memos, and reports that get your points across if you . . .*

1. Realize that your goal is not to write "the great American novel," but merely to be read and understood.

2. Take some time before you write to decide what your readers need to know.

3. Keep your writing short and to the point, simply saying what you have to say.

4. Analyze the tone of your writing to be sure it doesn't offend your readers.

5. Weed out worn-out expressions that get in the way of what you want to say.

By using these pointers, you'll improve your writing skills and assure that you are understood.

ACTION PLAN:

_____
_____
_____
_____
_____
_____
_____
_____
_____
_____

BEFORE YOU INTERVIEW

Interviewing prospective employees is a time-consuming business. Because it takes so much time, some busy supervisors may be tempted to dive right into the process, without planning ahead. But in order to make the best use of your time, it's essential that before *you begin your interview, you take certain . . .*

Preliminary Steps

On the surface, hiring a new employee seems to be an easy proposition. But it's actually very involved: Successful interviewing is the result of careful analysis of the open position, coupled with detailed examination of the applications you receive.

Why is conscientious planning so important? Because it will improve your chances of making a correct hiring decision—one you can feel truly comfortable with. Planning enables you to select the most skilled, productive person available to fill the position.

Job analysis is one of the most important components of the employment process. Analysis involves determining the level of performance the job requires and the type of person who will best fill it. What this means, of course, is that you need to create a job description if one doesn't already exist.

Writing or revising a job description isn't a difficult task. A helpful source of information is your company's personnel department, which can probably supply you with some sample job descriptions to use as guidelines.

Begin by writing up a job specification worksheet describing the duties that will be performed by the new employee. Be sure to talk to other people at your company who hold positions similar to the one to be filled. They may be able to provide you with some ideas about job duties that you have overlooked.

Get Your Priorities in Order

As you list the qualifications for the job, how can you separate those that are essential from those that are "nice-to-haves"? A simple worksheet with two headings—"musts" and "wants" can be a useful tool.

The "musts" column should include all the qualifications the employee simply must possess in order to carry out the job. The "wants" column should include those qualifications that you would like the worker to possess, but that aren't absolutely essential for success in the position.

Once you've completed both columns, go over the "musts" column once again and put the items in a prioritized order. Then you'll know what qualifications you should *really* be looking for, and you'll have a truer picture of the kind of person you'll need to fill the job.

The Final Worksheet

Once you've completed the "musts" and "wants" worksheet, you know the qualifications you should be looking for. But there are some questions that remain unanswered. For instance, how are you going to measure the skills you have listed? What *specific* knowledge will the employee need to carry out each task? After hiring, how much time should the employee be allowed to become proficient?

To answer these questions, draw up a final worksheet that summarizes all aspects of the job and its qualifications. This record will allow you to organize, on one or two sheets of paper, everything that is important about an available position and the person who will fill it.

Keep in mind that job descriptions must accurately reflect the work performed by employees. If they don't, your company could end up in courts—facing a discrimination suit under the Equal Pay Act.

In court, job descriptions can help you justify differences in pay between employees. Or they can be used by suing employees to show that the responsibilities of certain jobs are not substantial enough to justify the disparity in pay.

To ensure your job descriptions work for—not against—you, make them up-to-date and accurate. Include the following information on your final worksheet:

▶ **Job classification.** State the job title and to whom the employee will report.

▶ **Duties.** Describe the tasks you've outlined on the job specification sheet and the means of doing them. Include occasional duties, but make sure you specify the relative importance of those duties. If they're not vital, say so.

▶ **Working conditions.** Elaborate on any unusual working conditions and equipment used.

▶ **Skills, education, and training.** Include vocational and on-the-job training, as well as any special knowledge or experience required. Be specific.

▶ **Performance standards.** Write down how well the person is expected to perform each task. For example, how many errors are allowable in the job? Also, specify how much time the employee will have to reach the desired level of skill proficiency.

▶ **Hours and shifts.** State whether the job is full-time, part-time, or temporary.

What's the Use?

By now you may be thinking to yourself, *What's the point of all this paperwork? It's just going to bog me down.* In fact, "all this paperwork" is going to help you immensely as you begin to make a hiring decision.

The first part of your hiring decision isn't the job interview; it's deciding whom to interview in the first place. In most cases, the number of applications you receive for a position will far outweigh the number of people you want—or have time—to interview. You'll have to decide which people you should invest some time in talking to.

So as you sift through the applications that come across your desk keep in mind your final worksheet with its lists of duties, skills, and required knowledge. Then assess each job candidate's strengths and weaknesses as they stack up against those requirements.

Some Constructive Questions

Once you've determined whom you will interview, you have to decide *what* you're going to ask them. Again, the job description and the worksheets you drew up earlier can give you some guidance as you formulate your questions.

What kinds of questions should you prepare? They should be specific and should relate directly to the duties and skills required for the job. You may want to go so far as to write down the questions and have them handy during the interview to keep the discussion on track.

Aside from the usual queries about past experience and qualifications, you may find that questions that require the applicant to make a self-evaluation will prove helpful. For example:

- How do you feel you can contribute to this department?
- What do you hope to gain by working here?
- What do you feel are your outstanding qualities—and what are some of your problem areas?
- How well do you get along with co-workers and supervisors?

Tread Carefully

The questions listed above are the ones you can and should ask. But there are some questions you *can't* ask, since they may result in a discrimination suit against your company. Courts have held that an interviewer may not ask about an applicant's:

- **Religion.**
- **Race.**
- **Marital status.**
- **Age.** (But you may ask if the applicant is over the minimum legal age.
- **Military experience.** But you may ask about experience included in an employment history.
- **Memberships in clubs or social organizations.** You can ask if the applicant belongs to any union, professional, or trade organizations.
- **Arrest record.** But you can ask if the person was ever *convicted* of a crime if the crime is reasonably related to the job.
- **Physical disabilities.** You may ask about those that would have a direct bearing on the applicant's ability to do the job.

This list is by no means complete, and it's sure to change and expand as more court decisions on discrimination are handed down. So the wise supervisor would do well to stay up-to-date on such changes and keep them in mind as he or she formulates the job specification worksheet and selects the questions that will be asked during the interview.

▶ **WHAT YOU CAN DO** → *Effective hiring begins long before the first interview takes place. To ensure that you make the right decision . . .*

1. Analyze the position thoroughly so that you can draw up a job description. Consider the duties that the job will entail, and decide what skills the successful applicant must possess.

2. Use the job description to evaluate the applications you receive. Make arrangements to interview those who come closest to meeting your requirements.

3. Draw up a list of questions to use during the interview. It will help you keep the discussion on track.

4. Learn which questions are considered discriminatory

ACTION PLAN:

_____
_____
_____
_____
_____
_____
_____

and be sure not to ask them during the interview.

If you follow these steps, you'll be able to staff your department with the kind of people you need—knowledgeable, skilled, productive workers.

INTERVIEWING FOR BEST RESULTS

Poor job candidates fall into two basic categories: those who aren't qualified for the job and those who are qualified but just wouldn't fit well in your department. How can you avoid hiring either type? The answer lies . . .

Right in Your Lap

To build an effective workforce, you have to obtain good employees who have the potential to develop and improve. And in order to get these people, you must know how to interview. The job interview is your key to hiring the right person for the job.

Naturally, you want to find out all you can about the qualifications and aptitudes of the people you interview, but it's equally important that they be given enough information to determine if the job is right for them. Just as a candidate must try to sell you on his or her talents, you must try to sell the benefits your company offers to attract good candidates.

Review your applicant file in advance so that you are familiar with each candidate you will be interviewing. Knowing how much experience the applicant has will tell you what the person is looking for in your company. For example, people considering entry-level positions are often looking to get on board with a good company in which they can advance.

More experienced candidates will want to go with a front-runner, the best company they can find. That's why you must make it a point to know what growth and compensation the company can provide in the future. Of course, you may have to do a little research to have this information at your fingertips.

Importance of Time and Place

Once you've done your homework, you're ready to interview. Your first consideration is place. It should ensure privacy. Surroundings should be businesslike, yet relaxing. There's enough stress on a job seeker without adding real or imagined distractions and interruptions.

While timing of interviews is usually a matter of mutual convenience, a good general rule is to avoid scheduling interviews late in the day. Too frequently you have last-minute things to do that may lead you to shortchange the applicants. Be careful to leave enough time for both of you to discuss thoroughly the points that should be covered.

Setting the Tone

The tone for the entire interview is set at the beginning of the talk. Initiate a handshake, look the interviewee in the eyes, and make pleasant small talk. This is an important ritual—don't jump right into business.

These first few minutes of the interview are the most important. If things go wrong then, it will be very hard to set them right. It's your job as interviewer to establish rapport.

Let the candidate know that the interview is not meant to cause stress. It is simply an opportunity to get and give information. Making this clear will set a relaxed tone for the entire interview.

Gathering the Facts

After you've set the tone, it's time to explore the candidate's job history, skills, career objectives,

208

and motivation. To do this, you must be able to stimulate productive answers, answers that will give you a good idea of what the interviewee is like and what his or her needs are.

That means you should always ask open-ended questions, those that cannot be answered with a simple yes or no. Closed questions tend to make interviewees feel they're being interrogated. In response, they give brief, uninformative replies. If you do get an answer you feel is incomplete, ask the candidate to elaborate. Some key phrases to prompt further information are:

- "Tell me about . . ."
- "Describe your experience . . ."
- "What have you done regarding . . ."
- "Elaborate upon . . ."
- "Explain what you mean by . . ."

These are all phrases that will open up a person's conversation and help you gather the information that you need. Be careful, however, not to be too talkative. Your purpose is to analyze the applicant's qualifications. Let him or her do most of the talking. Just say enough to promote an exchange of ideas.

Key Questions

Just as it's important to know *how* to phrase questions to get the answers you need, you also have to know *what* questions you should ask.

Here are five key questions to help you determine whether or not a job candidate and your company are right for each other:

1 Why should I hire you? You're looking for what the candidate can do for your department and the company. The candidate's answer should tell you:
- if he or she has set goals and expectations
- if the person has a solid knowledge of what he or she can do
- if the job seeker knows how to apply his or her abilities to your department's needs

This question will help you identify skills that show a match between the applicant's background and your needs. The key is to find skills that can be used to your company's advantage once the person hired gains experience.

2 What contributions can you make and what are your aspirations? A good answer will contain a candidate's game plan of projected career growth with your company. Is the person looking to settle in and be comfortable, or is he or she looking to move up to bigger challenges?

3 Why did you leave your last job? If the candidate didn't get along with a former boss, was the boss similar to you in methods or temperament? Do some digging to find out why the person didn't hit it off with his or her last boss.

Job-hopping used to be a black mark, but that stigma has faded somewhat. Don't let job-hopping alone put you off. The person might have left the last job because the company went bankrupt. And remember, job-hopping is different from just being unable to hold down a position.

4 Why do you enjoy this particular type of work? Look for answers that center on challenge, variety, responsibility, growth, and application of skills. Anything that indicates a person is in the field to learn and grow is a positive response.

5 What irritates or frustrates you? If you find that the three things that frustrate an applicant are present in your department, why hire the person?

Be wary of people who complain about previous employers, supervisors, or co-workers. They may be chronic malcontents, who will complain about you if you hire them.

Job and Company Focus

This can be a touchy stage if you have strong doubts that you will hire the interviewee. But if you're seriously interested in an applicant, discuss company needs and objectives with him or her. Ask if there are any questions about the company.

The response can tell you a great deal about how motivated the applicant is. A highly motivated person, for example, will have done some preliminary research and at least have enough facts at his or her disposal to ask a few intelligent questions. This knowledge shows the candidate is serious about establishing a career at your firm—not just getting any job until something better comes along.

Throughout the interview, focus on the similarities and differences between the applicant's qualifications and the company's needs and objectives to help you determine how he or she might fit in as an employee.

Closing Ritual

Bring the interview to an end by summarizing what has been said. Briefly sum up the company's requirements for the job and the applicant's qualifications. This will have the psychological effect of tying up loose ends and setting the stage for a graceful dismissal of the interviewee.

If you are interviewing several applicants, give yourself at least a 10- to 15-minute break before each to jot down your impressions of the person you've just interviewed. Note their answers to key questions and such observations as "He flinched slightly when asked if he worked well as part of a team." These notes will prove very useful when you make your final decision.

> ▶ **WHAT YOU CAN DO** → *To make each interview a productive, informative one...*
>
> 1. Thoroughly research your company and your department. This knowledge will enable you to put your company in the best possible light during the interview.
>
> 2. Choose the appropriate time and place. Select a private and relaxing environment for the interview, and don't schedule it too late in the day.
>
> 3. Set a relaxed, inviting tone. Don't jump into business right off the bat, but take a few minutes to talk informally with the candidate and put that person at ease.
>
> 4. Explore the applicant's job history, skills, and needs by asking key questions that demand more than a yes or no response.
>
> 5. Communicate your company's needs and objectives, and ask if the person has any questions.
>
> 6. Close the interview by summing up the requirements of the job and the applicant's qualifications. Take a few minutes to write down your impressions of the candidate.
>
> *Finding the proper fit between company, department, job, and candidate is a challenging task. But you can succeed if you know how to interview effectively.*
>
> **ACTION PLAN:**
> _____
> _____
> _____
> _____
> _____
> _____
> _____
> _____
> _____
> _____
> _____
> _____
> _____
> _____
> _____

INTEGRATING NON-ENGLISH-SPEAKING EMPLOYEES

If your department is representative of the American "melting pot," it will sooner or later include employees who have recently immigrated to the United States. Despite the obvious differences in language and culture, these workers are highly capable and eager to do a first-rate job for you. You can do a great deal to help them to become fully productive by . . .

Helping Them to Assimilate

When a new hire is new to the country as well as to the company, you may need to take special steps to help the employee successfully assimilate. The main point to remember is to start delegating right away so that the new hire feels he or she is trusted. Don't be overly cautious and hold back on assigning tasks.

The employee may just be starting to develop work and English-language skills. If you hesitate to let the person join the mainstream of work activity, the person's language and work skills may actually begin to deteriorate.

Toppling Language Barriers

Allow use of a worker's native language during training, if possible. Obviously, if you or an experienced member of your department is familiar with the new hire's native tongue, you may use your common language from time to time if it will help you to more effectively convey information. English must be stressed, but don't be disappointed if bilingual workers occasionally slip back into their native tongue or if you must rely on other bilinguals to translate.

Encourage Frequent Queries

Many workers may be hesitant to ask questions when they don't fully understand your instructions, for fear of appearing slow-witted. As a result, they may feign understanding. This is a special problem for employees with minimal knowledge of English.

To alleviate such difficulties, encourage such workers to ask questions whenever they're in doubt. It's worth your time to encourage workers to ask questions routinely so that you don't confuse any language shortcoming with ordinary on-the-job problems.

Begin Criticism on a Positive Note

You can help alleviate some of their work-related anxiety by taking a positive approach to correcting errors. Sometimes, when this type of worker sees the supervisor coming toward him or her, it raises feelings of doubt or fear.

So, try to use the fewest negative terms possible. For example, it's better to say "I prefer that you do the job like this" rather than "You're doing that wrong." Then the criticism doesn't sound like a reprimand and isn't taken personally.

It's Worth Your Effort

The increasingly international nature of business and industry calls for more American supervisors to work with employees from other cultures. You can get these workers to respond positively if you are patient and willing to trust their abilities.

In addition to cultivating their skills, you'll learn to create a more cooperative work environment and improve intradepartmental cooperation.

▶ **WHAT YOU CAN DO** ➡ *You can help workers who are new to your company and the country if you...*

1. Are patient and tactful with workers who are just learning the English language, and ask others in your department to do the same.

2. Encourage them to routinely ask questions about job assignments and anything they don't understand.

3. Take a positive approach when criticizing. This will help to reduce any job anxiety they may be feeling.

Employing workers from diverse cultures provides opportunities to encourage communication.

ACTION PLAN:

CHAPTER SEVEN
DEVELOPING YOURSELF AS A SUPERVISOR

RISING TO CONTINUOUS CHALLENGE

During the course of your employment you've developed a number of talents and skills. You get the job done well and on time. You have a good rapport with your people and your peers. Now, you can rest on your laurels, right? Wrong. Remember, it takes continuous challenge to maintain...

A Keen Edge

Your value to the company and to yourself depends on your ability to accept changes and new methods. After all, growth and change are the sustaining forces of all living things. You and your job need that sustenance, too.

Most supervisors who rise to the top say that their current success is primarily due to their willingness to accept challenges. But if you sit back and take it easy, it won't be long before you realize that you are becoming stale, bored, and uninspiring to your employees—and yourself.

Portrait of a Plateau

What can you do if job stagnation has already set in? The first thing to do if you suspect you are on a career plateau is to realize the situation you are in, says Jim Wellington, manager of organizational development at Arizona Public Service Co. (Phoenix).

There are a number of symptoms that suggest you're stuck where you are, he explains. They involve:

▸ **Your image.** If you're a good supervisor who's going places, you're often asked your opinion by various people—your boss, your peers, your subordinates. If they stop coming to you for advice, that's a sign that you need to make some changes.

▸ **Your attitude.** "If you're bored, if you hate to go to work, often exhibit temper and generally have problems with self-esteem, that's a sure sign of a plateau," says Wellington. "You need new challenges."

How do you get new challenges? One important way, says Wellington, is by being visible. "Visibility is the key," he says. "Unless someone recognizes your work and knows what you can do, good work alone won't necessarily get you ahead."

In most organizations your best bet in gaining visibility is a mentor. This is someone who is acquainted with your skills and takes an interest in you. This person should be able to speak for you at critical times, such as when a new job assignment or some special project is in the works.

Who Should Your Mentor Be?

If you show consistently good work, chances are that you'll attract the notice of more than one person. Wellington sees nothing wrong with having more than one mentor. You get that much more visibility.

Wellington's view is that the best mentor to have is your boss. This is the person who reviews your work and is in a position to know best what you can do.

"And once you have a boss as a mentor, he or she will always be there, even when you move on," says Wellington. "This will be a person who knows you and can speak favorably about you."

One thing you should never do, however, is try to outshine a boss who's not the best. "Try to make your boss look as good as possible," he advises. "It can only hurt you if the boss looks bad.

"Then, too, as you work your way up with the support of mentors, you also want to help out others," Wellington suggests. "The time will come when you become the mentor."

How? By becoming expert in what you do and making that expertise visible through actions and performance, and by generously sharing your expertise and judgment with whoever is smart enough to ask.

Get on the Right Track

Career stagnation is an acute problem today—one that often accompanies mergers and downsizing of departments. So, even if you aren't on a plateau right now, you should always be looking for growth opportunities. Here are some ways you can keep stagnation at bay:

- **Keep your eye out for special assignments and projects.** Look for chances to assist your superiors or for temporary vacancies that need to be filled. These small challenges will give you the chance to learn new skills and the confidence to take on greater responsibilities.

- **Overcome your fear of change.** When presented with a challenging opportunity, it's natural to feel "green" at first. You may feel reluctant to take on new responsibilities simply because you're unfamiliar with the skills that will be required.

But you have to be willing to tolerate this initial discomfort if you're going to grow in a career. So, accept the challenges that are presented to you. You can only become proficient through *doing*.

- **Direct the course of your career.** Although challenges can be good for your career, you don't have to accept every offer that is presented to you. There may be times when change can do you more harm than good.

For example, if you're offered a position in another department, but are sure that you want to remain where you are, you would be wise to refuse this particular challenge. You may recognize that your own department offers myriad stimulating opportunities. Or, you may want to become a specialist by building on your knowledge in your current area.

- **Be willing to further your education.** In many industries, promotions are often contingent on education credentials. But if you choose to go back to school, you should be ready to apply what you've learned. It's one way of showing management that you are committed to your career.

- **Recognize that professional growth is continuous.** Even when opportunities aren't available, excitement and enthusiasm for your industry or field can continue to fuel your career. Learn all that you can about productivity improvement techniques and sound supervisory practices. In turn, you'll continually challenge your performance.

What's Holding You Back?

Some people, despite their best efforts, and even the good words of a mentor or two, still can't seem to get ahead. In this case, it could be that you're just a little too combative with peers.

Be competitive in your performance, but don't get into a peer's turf; if you do, let that person know why. Don't forget the team building aspect of work. If you try to get ahead at the expense of others and have relationship problems with peers, you're not going to make it.

When you get into someone else's territory, do it by way of trying to help. It's hard for someone to get upset when you're trying to help them. Blowing out the other person's candle does not make yours burn brighter.

How about it? Have *you* risen to all of the challenges presented by your company? Remember, instead of resting on your laurels and maintaining the status quo, keep rising to the challenges presented you. This will enable you to keep discovering new aspects of your job *and* yourself.

> **WHAT YOU CAN DO** → *To stay inspired and in top form, you need to...*

1. Recognize a career plateau. Then, strive to rise above it by gaining visibility through a mentor, preferably your own boss.

2. Take on new responsibilities and assignments. Overcome any fear of change that stands in the way of a challenging opportunity.

3. Realize that you don't need to take on every challenge that comes your way. Only you can decide if a change will do you more harm than good.

4. Be committed to your career. That may mean going back to school or learning new skills on the job. It always means being enthusiastic about your field or industry.

5. Remain competitive, but don't try to get ahead at the expense of others.

Being the best supervisor you can be will pay off for you in terms of loyal, hardworking people and recognition from your peers and superiors.

ACTION PLAN:
_____
_____
_____
_____
_____
_____
_____
_____
_____
_____
_____

PLANNING YOUR ADVANCEMENT

Planning is at the core of every supervisor's job. The purpose of planning, of course, is to utilize your time in the most efficient way possible—as well as to prevent emergencies. But in addition to planning how to do your job, you should also . . .

Prepare for Promotion

The first question you must ask yourself is: *Do you really want a promotion or would you rather remain a first-level supervisor?* Most supervisors will probably respond, *Of course, I want a promotion. Why wouldn't I?*

If that is your answer, then there are some other questions and considerations that naturally follow. But believe it or not, there *are* people who just aren't suited to be in the position of supervising others. So, before you go to the trouble of making yourself promotable, perhaps you ought to consider what you may be in for:

★ **Are you prepared for the different types of responsibilities in the next higher level?** Have you observed and studied what your boss actually does? Are you convinced you are qualified to perform those functions?

★ **Have you recognized that a promotion will probably result in your supervising supervisors**—instead of hourly personnel? Remember, while you will still see nonsupervisory employees on the job, your communication with them is likely to be through someone else.

★ **Are those who make promotional decisions aware that you are interested in advancement?** Have you discussed this in performance reviews? Have you made it known through your interest and participation in a wide spectrum of assignments and responsibilities?

If you answer "yes" to these questions, then you should have a planned approach to achieve your promotion objective. The supervisor who talks about wanting to get ahead, but never takes any concrete steps toward that goal, won't go anywhere in the organization.

Learn How to Promote Yourself

How exactly can you plan for promotion? While there are no hard-and-fast rules, most supervisors agree that getting ahead is often a matter of *self promotion*. Marketing yourself doesn't mean you should blow your own horn every chance you get.

Instead, think of yourself in a sales situation. You are selling your talents and abilities to management. And your sales pitch will either open the doors to advancement or close them.

Think about it. You sell your appearance, your personality, and your talents every day—whether you realize it or not. And this daily sales pitch can land you a promotion.

But first you must perfect your pitch and channel your energies toward advancement. How can you do this? Concentrate on increasing your visibility, polishing your leadership skills, and recognizing opportunities when they present themselves.

Increasing Your Visibility

To promote your candidacy for advancement, you need to set and achieve specific goals within your present position. Demonstrating what you can do is essential for moving ahead. But you should also concentrate on increasing your visibility so you'll be foremost in management's mind when opportunities arise.

Here are some ways to make yourself visible:

★ **Make your department look good.** Employees will appreciate your giving them credit, and will respond accordingly. Their support will show management that you can inspire team spirit. And just as every coach gets acclaim for the team's victories, you'll receive credit for your department's successes.

★ **Take committee assignments seriously.** Committees are the most common forum for discussions and decision-making. You can often sell ideas or recommendations by leading or being a member of a committee. And your effective performance on a committee makes you very visible to management.

★ **Be prepared for meetings.** Whether you're leading the meeting or just participating, be prepared to contribute. Study the agenda and decide which items are of primary interest to you. Focus your active participation on these topics, instead of every matter that comes up during the meeting. The *quality* of your contributions will make a far more positive impression than their quantity.

Polish Leadership Skills

In addition to increasing your visibility, strive to develop a polished leadership style. Becoming the most capable leader you can be will help you succeed in your present position, as well as increase your promotion potential.

One way to accomplish this is to tailor your leadership style to your immediate superior's personality. You don't have to become your boss's clone, but you should be aware of his or her preferences. This means avoiding traits that annoy your boss. Here is a sampling of traits that bosses commonly find irritating:

- Procrastinating and failing to meet deadlines.

- Passing the buck on problems and refusing to take responsibility.

- Claiming to understand how to do something and then doing it wrong.

- Lacking initiative and drive.

- Failing to deliver on assignments and commitments.

An effective leader also possesses superior communication skill. This ability is highly prized by management because people who can speak, write, and listen well can persuade and influence others. In fact, except for integrity, no item ranks higher among the desired characteristics for supervisors and managers than direct and open communication.

And don't disregard such communication skills

as reading and note-taking. Brief but understandable reminder notes from meetings and tours through the work area are valuable aids to planning and communicating.

Recognizing Career Opportunities

Career opportunities are not handed to supervisors on a silver platter. You have to learn how to recognize *and* act on them. In many cases, it's the person who seizes the moment who will advance in the company.

Do you recognize opportunity when it knocks? Here are some advancement possibilities you may not have considered:

1 You get a new boss. Reporting to a new boss can be an opportunity—if that person perceives you in a positive light. Make it clear that you want to make your new boss successful. Developing a strong alliance of trust and mutual support can sow the seeds of a rewarding future.

2 You are given a high-visibility project. Nothing draws the attention of the top brass as quickly as a supervisor who tackles a big project successfully. If you have completed a project that puts you in the limelight, be at your best while others are watching you.

3 You complete a training course. If you go through such a course, it may qualify you for bigger and better things. Look for training opportunities that provide you with skills for positions of additional prestige and authority.

4 You are ready to assume a new role. If your company is expanding into new areas or is introducing new products or services, that may spell an opportunity for you. Look for the chance to take a leadership role in a new division.

Possibilities for advancement may also arise from negative factors, such as being passed over for a promotion or being assigned a new job that seems less prestigious than your previous one. When this happens, discuss the situation with your superior and find out why the decision was made. This dialogue could change an opinion or open the door for new opportunites.

▶ **WHAT YOU CAN DO** → *Once you've decided you want to rise in your company, take steps to . . .*

1. Market yourself. We are all salespeople, whether we acknowledge it or not. Every day we sell our appearance, our character, our talents, and our ideas.

2. Increase your visibility. Do everything you can to make your department shine, take committee assignments seriously, and prepare for every meeting you attend.

3. Perfect your leadership style. Avoid traits that bosses find irritating and polish communication skills.

4. Recognize opportunity when it knocks. Possibilities for advancement can arise out of change, high-visibility projects, and even negative situations—such as being passed over for a promotion.

Advancement doesn't just happen. You have to take an active role in following your career aspirations. This takes commitment, hard work, and a strong belief in your talent.

ACTION PLAN:

_____
_____
_____
_____
_____
_____
_____
_____
_____
_____
_____
_____

MANAGING THE SPECIAL PROJECT

Being selected to lead a special project is quite a feather in your cap. It shows that management has faith in your skills and is confident of your ability to follow through. Perhaps the project was a brainchild of your own. Or maybe management assigned the topic. Either way, this is an exciting chance to exercise your creativity and ...

Boost Your Department Track Record

A special project can give you the chance to improve the company's productivity record as well as that of your department. It might be your opportunity to select and install new, more effective equipment or to introduce an employee participation program. It certainly will enrich your job by demanding that you use your supervisory skills in a new way.

What's so different about handling a temporary assignment? As a *supervisor,* you are responsible for getting the daily work done. As a *project leader,* you are the "change agent"—the person who comes up with long-term improvement ideas, develops a project plan, and motivates people to put the plan into practice.

Maybe you'll be heading a team of colleagues. Or maybe you'll be enlisting the aid of your workers. In any case, certain skills are essential—or else the project will never get off the ground. Here are the key skills you will need:

- **The ability to balance project and company objectives.** Be sure your objective supports your company's mission. Too often, supervisors come up with ideas that will improve the productivity of their department—not realizing that the plans will hamper efficiency in another section of the company. Or their plans call for expensive adjustments—changes management isn't willing to make. Your plan must balance the project objectives with the company's overall goals.

- **The desire to delegate.** Unless the project is very small, you can't do it all yourself. You must be willing to assign tasks and guide colleagues and workers toward the project's goal—without assuming their responsibilities yourself.

- **The ability to promote the project.** If you want people to help your project along, you must "talk up" your plan. Discuss it with other supervisors and managers and explain how it will benefit their departments. And let workers know why the change will make their jobs more meaningful.

- **The willingness to watch, listen, and learn.** Project leaders don't sit in their office and wait for project results to come in. They move among their team members, listening and watching for hidden problems.

Map Out a Plan

No project will get off the ground without a specific target—a statement of what you want to accomplish and how you'll know when you've accomplished it. These goals must be specific: If your objectives are foggy, you won't be able to assign tasks to other people. Nor will you be able to recognize when each assignment has been completed. In short, you need a plan.

The only way to make large projects manageable is to attack them in logical and progressive increments. Everything must be conquered one step at a time. A well-written project plan lists every task and activity to be completed, and helps you tackle the steps. Here's how to develop your plan:

▶ **Estimate how long each part, subpart, and the project as a whole will take.** Allow "cushion" time for unforeseen problems. Remember, you have other responsibilities—your regular assignments and supervisory duties—and so do the people who will be helping you. Also allow for vacations, holidays, and illness.

▶ **Spell out what supplies you'll need.** What service, materials, or money will you need, and from whom and when? If you'll need computer time, for example, list this; you'll need to get clearance for it ahead of time.

▶ **Divvy up the project tasks.** With objectives in hand, organize the project into parts, which you will later give to team members—the people who will assist you in the special assignment. Draft descriptions of what will be expected of members and what help you'll provide.

♦ **Set "final acceptance criteria."** These are guidelines that spell out what needs to be done and how people will know when they've completed it. The criteria serve as benchmarks for determining what, if anything, stands in the way of achieving your project's goals.

Project Ambassadors

Occasionally, you may be asked to handle a project on your own. In other cases, however, management will ask you to gather colleagues and/or employees to act as assistants.

Selecting your team poses a special challenge. In a sense, the members will be your "project ambassadors." Thus, it's essential that you line up people who fully support the project and who are eager to make it work.

But how do you select your team associates? By locating people with these key characteristics:

★ **Qualifications.** Look for individuals who have expertise in the areas your project touches.
★ **Time.** Expertise alone won't help you if the person's work schedule conflicts with the team's. So make sure each person has the time to pitch in more than a few hours' work.
★ **Ownership.** It's smart to select people who will somehow benefit from your plan. The people who will ultimately be affected by the plan have a vested interest in making it work well.

Once you have selected your members, meet with each candidate individually. Discuss the project, ask for feedback, and make sure the candidate really is interested and has the time to devote to the assignment. Each potential member should understand:

- What his or her assignment will be
- Why it is important
- How it is to be accomplished
- When it's to be completed
- How it's to be reported
- Whose assistance will be needed

Set due dates for both progress reports and completion of the individual assignments. Ask for weekly progress reports from each team member, and hold team meetings every two weeks to discuss progress, solve problems, and set new directions if necessary.

Keep in mind that you'll need to use different skills during different phases of the project. In the early phase, you must be adept in finding team members, planning goals, and delegating jobs. When work is in full swing, you must be a motivator and an expediter. And when the assignment nears completion, you must be able to insist on deadlines, tie up loose ends, and make a well-organized final report.

How to Keep Energy High

As the project moves along, you also need to pace yourself. Being a project leader *and* a supervisor can be a bit stressful. Naturally, you want to excel on the project, yet you can't ignore your supervisory responsibilities. Your employees will need as much attention as they have received in the past—and maybe a bit more, if the project dramatically affects them.

How can you cope with all these demands and still keep your energy high? Follow these strategies:

■ **Find relaxing work.** You can "relax" with work projects that are challenging, creative, and satisfying—but that don't involve immediate deadline pressure. Often, these jobs are ones you've been successful with in the past. Thinking about them keeps your attitude positive.

■ **Remember the broad picture.** Keep your overall goals in mind and separate them from more tedious, detail-oriented tasks. When you can concentrate on these goals and relate your daily work to them, you'll work more efficiently. And you'll be able to give your project the attention it needs to improve both your department's and your company's track record.

▶ **WHAT YOU CAN DO** ➡ *As project leader, you are ultimately in control of—and responsible for—the shape your project finally takes. To make your project a success . . .*

1. Sharpen your planning and motivation skills so as to

ACTION PLAN:

_____

_____

help the project get off the ground—and stay there.

2. Establish a timetable and some benchmarks for indicating when the project is complete.

3. Select as project assistants people who have the qualifications, time, and interest to see the project through. These people will be your "project ambassadors," so they should be as excited about the project as you are.

4. Take steps to ensure that you—or your team members—don't burn out before the assignment is finished.

Being a project leader is demanding. But it's also an exciting opportunity to use your creativity and to show management how you can shine.

HARNESS YOUR CREATIVITY

Creativity is a prized possession in the business world. Creative supervisors can analyze complex situations and find appropriate solutions. They can run a more productive department and manufacture a better product. Do you count yourself among the creative idea developers? You should. Believe it or not, everyone has . . .

Creative Capacity

Most people have a creative capacity but don't use it in their daily worklives. Some think that creativeness takes too much time. Others feel that their ideas won't work, and so they kill ideas before they have a chance to develop. And still other people believe that their job is simply to manage people and make sure they meet production deadlines.

Certainly, you can't neglect those deadlines and production schedules. Nor can you spend all your time daydreaming about ways to improve the department. Nonetheless, as a supervisor, you have a responsibility to cultivate improvements in your department and in your company. That's part and parcel of being a member of the management team. To make these improvements, you need to strengthen—and use—your creative skills.

What Is Creativity?

Creativity is the ability to take things that seem unrelated and put them together. It expands choices instead of limiting possibilities. Developing ideas through creativity provides more alternatives for solving productivity problems in the company.

Opportunities for creativity always exist—in new ways of organizing the work, methods to boost quality, techniques for motivating employees. There is always a better way. And if you learn to channel your creative energy, you can find that better method.

Obstacles to Creativity

Why do people limit their creativity? Usually, it's because they hold themselves back in some way. They fall victim to some of these idea defeaters:

★ **Hard-line thinking.** Hard-line thinkers only look for one or two solutions to a single problem. They don't understand that it's important to look at many options. When supervisors use this approach, they say, "If this idea looks good in the beginning, let's go for it; if not, let's discard it." Such people are looking for a quick fix. They don't give more complicated ideas a chance, and so they end up killing a potentially good idea for the future.

★ **Inability to deal with ambiguity.** Proceeding in an orderly way from point to point is safe. Living with ambiguity—letting your imagination wander, allowing major jumps in your thinking—is creative.

The creative supervisor learns to feel comfortable in uncertain situations. This involves freeing yourself to think and examine potential ideas without any restrictions. Some supervisors are fearful that solutions will not emerge from disorder. They need to learn to trust ambiguity and know that order will return.

★ **Idea killers.** These are typical responses to original ideas. All are negative. They are the quickest way to stifle initiative, because they translate to "Don't bother; that idea can't possibly work." People who use idea killers undermine their own creative potential as well as the potential of co-workers.

Idea killers include statements like:

- "We tried that last year and it didn't work."
- "Somebody else can do it better."
- "We're on the wrong track."
- "That will cost too much."

Maybe a similar idea has been tried before, or maybe another person could do the job better. But that doesn't mean that the problem can't be solved. Idea killers are blanket negatives that don't leave room for exploration. When you hear a response like that, you automatically give up.

Thus, the first step in boosting your creativity lies in recognizing the obstacles to innovation and removing them. Resolve not to let your fears get in the way of developing productivity or quality-improvement strategies.

Develop an Idea Bank

Okay, you've resolved to remove the obstacles that hinder your imagination. What's next? Start an idea bank.

Ideas can be put in a bank just like money. An idea bank is a place where you jot down all the thoughts, ideas, and wild notions that go through your head. Forget about restrictions or limitations. Whenever you see something you'd like improved in the company, or spot a technique that might cut a production step, write it in your idea bank. Some supervisors carry a notepad, transferring ideas to the bank when they get back to the office.

To generate ideas for your bank, try these exercises:

■ **Make analogies.** Study the way scientists or artists have solved similar problems. Or maybe you could gather some ideas from nature. Try to adapt these approaches to your situation.

■ **Ask "what if" questions.** Every time you come up with an obstacle to solving a problem, ask yourself "what if" questions to remove the obstacle. For example: "We can't streamline this process because we'd have to move too many workstations." "What if we moved a door instead of a station?"

Some of the ideas in your bank may seem silly, but it's surprising how often these flash ideas can be used a few weeks or months down the road. If your boss asks you to streamline the work process, for example, you can look through your bank and pull together the thoughts you've saved over the months. One of them may be just the thing your boss was looking for. Or with just a little more thought, a wacky idea might spark a practicable solution.

Five Steps to Follow

Once you establish an idea bank, ideas can be pulled at any time to be developed. Here are five steps to help you examine and apply these improvement ideas:

1 Define your problem. To begin, you must first decide what issue you want to address. If there is a problem you want to solve, make sure you understand it thoroughly. Without a clear goal, the best answer may elude you.

2 Explore your options. Once you've selected some ideas from your bank, examine them to see if they warrant further attention. Be careful not to dismiss any strategy automatically. At this stage, ideas should be nurtured, not killed, so there shouldn't be anything that prevents an idea from getting consideration.

3 Develop the ideas further. After the exploratory phase, some ideas will demand further investigation. This is what happens in this next phase.

Ask yourself, "What will be the ramifications of this idea? Can I get some of my people to put a few hours into it? What are the possible risks?" Following this line of questioning, your plan starts to firm up.

4 Start a limited project. Once evidence has been gathered on your ideas and research has been started, certain ideas will be viable and others won't. Put the unworkable ideas back into your bank, and turn your attention to the idea that looks the strongest.

Set aside some time and energy to investigate that idea. If it involves polishing the work flow, for example, talk with your boss about setting up a trial run in one part of the department. This limited project will be a test. If the plan works, you can convert the whole department later. If it doesn't, you won't have wasted much time or money.

5 Begin the "Go" project. Ideas that pass the limited project phase successfully become "Go" projects: plans that you're willing to support 100 percent of the way. Make your presentation to management, explaining what results your pilot plan produced and what resources you'll need (if any) to make the idea work on a larger scale.

At this phase, be sure to congratulate yourself. Whether or not your plan gets the green light from upper management, you should feel proud of your creative effort.

Innovation Everywhere!

Where can you apply your innovative ideas? To just about every part of your job. You can dream up better ways of managing your time, or new strategies to get employees concerned about safety. You can eliminate quality problems, or find ways to polish your department's productivity record. All this is yours if you learn to harness your creativity.

That's why it is smart to have a strategy to get results from your ideas. If you're willing to harness your creative notions and develop them carefully, you'll be able to achieve original and lasting results for any supervisory problem you face.

▶ **WHAT YOU CAN DO** → *It's your job to keep improving department operations. To make innovation part of your everyday management skills . . .*

1. Recognize your creative potential. Everyone can be a creative idea developer—including you.

2. Locate and eliminate idea defeaters—those negative attitudes that stymie your imagination.

3. Develop an idea bank. Write down all the improvement ideas, thoughts, or wild notions that pop into your head. Turn to this bank whenever you have a problem to solve or a challenge to meet.

4. Consider tapping your employees' expertise. Why not teach your employees how to be creative, too?

Your company's competitive edge depends on its employees' ability to develop innovative ideas. The supervisor who can contribute fresh ideas helps the company grow.

ACTION PLAN:

_____
_____
_____
_____
_____
_____
_____
_____
_____

WINNING THE RACE AGAINST TIME

Time is a commodity that, once wasted, cannot be replaced. The further you rise in your company, the more critical it is to recognize that time is money and must therefore be managed. That's why, as a supervisor, you must learn to . . .

Make the Most of Every Minute

Supervisors either run their jobs or let their jobs run them. To determine if you're running your job, ask yourself: "Do I have too much to do?" If you find that the only honest answer is "yes," your problem is most likely poor time management.

Here are some more questions that will help you see whether you need better planning to improve your use of available time:

● **Do you work overtime to catch up?** If you think that working overtime just to keep up with your regular work load will create a good impression, you may be kidding yourself. It could have the opposite effect. You may earn the reputation of being a poor planner and be looked upon as inefficient.

● **Are you spending too much time at your desk?** In trying to keep up with your paperwork you may find that you're neglecting another important part of your duties—supervising operations on the floor. Plan your paperwork so that you can get maximum results from the time you have to spend at your desk.

● **Do you find yourself making guesses because you don't have accurate data on hand?** If you don't have time to anticipate emergencies, you soon find yourself in a vicious circle: You do not plan; therefore, emergencies overtake you, and you're so busy getting out of hot water that you have no time to plan ahead. Planning properly in the first place will enable you to foresee some emergencies and be ready for them.

Getting Your Priorities Straight

What's the key to effectively managing your time? Priority setting. A good way to keep your schedule under control is to prepare a daily priority list.

Devising such a list is simple. Decide what must be accomplished first and what can wait until later. Set priorities for each task you need to accomplish during the day. Your list will enable you to complete tasks in a timely fashion, rather than jumping from one job to another, hoping to somehow finish them all.

When composing your priority list, take into account your personal habits and tailor your list accordingly. For example, if you know you are most productive in the morning, put high-priority tasks at the top of your list. On the other hand, if you do your best work just after lunch, you may want to schedule your most important tasks for this time.

Keep in mind that different supervisors have different reasons for losing control of their time. Perhaps you're a compulsive telephone answerer. Or maybe you're constantly distracted by drop-in visitors—or a window with a view. Being aware of the habits and distractions that eat into your time is the first step in eliminating them.

A Trio of Time-Wasters

Do you know what eats into your time? If you don't, there's a sure way to find out. Keep a log of your activities for the next few days. Write down everything that you do on a sheet of paper—from chats on the floor with other supervisors to time spent answering questions from workers.

Try to fill out the log as often as every 15 minutes, if possible. You should not let more than an hour pass without filling out your log. This may seem time-consuming in itself, but what you'll learn from the log will make it all worthwhile.

And just what will you learn? You'll discover what time-wasters are keeping you from staying on schedule. Here are some of the most common ones:

▶ **Meetings.** Many supervisors find themselves attending sessions that are poorly constructed, too long, and nonproductive. The first question to ask yourself when invited to a meeting is whether your presence is actually required. You may be able to skip the session and get a brief rundown of what took place later.

Of course, if you are running the meeting yourself, you'll have more control. To avoid time-wasting, prepare a specific agenda, control and direct the discussion, and set a time limit. When the limit has been reached, adjourn the session.

▶ **Telephone calls.** Some supervisors are enslaved by the telephone. They allow random calls to break their chain of thought or interrupt their work. Frequently, the time is spent talking to subordinates, peers, and outsiders on issues that often could be delegated, addressed in a meeting, or avoided altogether.

If you find yourself in this boat, a solution might be to screen telephone contact or to leave a specified time of day when calls will be received and made.

▶ **Interruptions.** When your work is interrupted by employees, peers, or superiors for work-related reasons, you shouldn't begrudge the amount of time you spend to deal with whatever prompted the interruption. If you're really pressed for time, however, you can ask the person to come back at a more convenient time.

But there's another form of interruption that's more annoying—other supervisors who just want to pass the time of day. A little light conversation never hurt anyone, but when it harms your ability to carry out your job in a timely fashion, you have to put a stop to it.

A good way to get someone who interrupts you to keep it short is to stand up when the person approaches, and remain standing until he or she moves on. It's also a good idea to mention your work load as often as possible, and to keep your own answers polite but brief. If the person still doesn't catch on, you may have to come right out and say something like, "I've got a lot of work to do, so why don't we pick this up another time?"

The Most Common Problem

Paperwork is an annoyance to many supervisors—so much so that they avoid doing it as long as possible. Then, when it *must* be done, it gets rushed along and often isn't completed properly. Here's how paperwork hampered the efforts of one supervisor to do her job effectively:

Supervisor Sandi Becker had been dreading this moment all day: Her boss, Paul Ross, was approaching her with an expression that showed he was anything but pleased.

"Sandi, you promised me that report on your department's output two days ago, but I still haven't gotten it," he complained. "What's the holdup?"

"Well, some of my people haven't gotten all the information I need to me yet," she answered. "So naturally, I couldn't put the report together for you."

"Great. I hope you realize that your report is just part of *my* report to top management, and you're making *me* fall behind schedule. Now, get your report together by the end of the day—and no excuses."

Overpowering Paperwork

How can you balance your need to complete paperwork with your need to carry out other supervisory duties? Although Becker doesn't know it yet, she's stumbled on one of the first rules of overpowering paperwork. Here are steps you can take to bring your paperwork under control:

1 Give people firm deadlines. If you rely on others to get you information, you must relay to them a sense of urgency about getting back to you, the same sense of urgency your superiors have imparted to you. To ensure that others supply you with the material you need, agree on a deadline with them and follow up shortly before that date to remind them you still need the information—on time.

2 Do paperwork at the same time every day. Setting aside a portion of each day to handle reports and forms creates a good habit that lets you keep paperwork under control.

3 Eliminate unnecessary paperwork. Begin by getting out samples of the forms you are required to send to other departments and your superiors. Do any of them request the same information? If so, suggest that all people needing that information refer to the single form you will be supplying in the future.

You may even come across paperwork that you regularly fill out, but which no one uses. (This often happens when a change in personnel has taken place at upper management levels.) If so, you can remove that particular piece of paperwork from your list of obligations.

4 File only essential information. A file drawer is a convenient place to forget about items of paperwork you just don't know how to dispose of. It might be a good idea to go through your files and throw out documents that date back to more than a year or two unless management has specifically requested that you keep them.

And once you've gotten the deadwood out of your files, don't start in again. Every time you're tempted to file something, ask yourself if it's truly necessary. You'll soon find that paperwork is no longer the annoyance you thought it was.

Now that you've discovered which time-wasters cut into your time, you must make a commitment to eliminate them. Once this is accomplished, you'll be able to complete all your supervisory tasks in an orderly fashion.

▶ **WHAT YOU CAN DO** → *If you find that you have too much to do, and too little time to do it, you should . . .*

1. Devise a daily priority list so that you complete your most important tasks when you are most effective.

2. Become familiar with the habits and time-wasters that are cutting into your time by logging your activities every fifteen minutes for several days.

3. Take steps to get paperwork under control. This means establishing deadlines, doing paperwork at the same time every day, streamlining redundant paperwork, and purging your files.

These steps will enable you to effectively manage time once and for all.

ACTION PLAN:

_____
_____
_____
_____
_____
_____
_____
_____

LESS STRESS

As a supervisor, there's a lot of responsibility resting on your shoulders. You have to keep productivity and quality high, ensure worker safety, complete forms and reports on time, and attend to the myriad other duties you're expected to carry out. With so much to do, it's little wonder that many supervisors find the stress of their position . . .

A Little Overwhelming

It was late Friday afternoon, and Supervisor David Bentley was up to his eyeballs in paperwork. Completing routine obligations during the week had left no time for filling out daily forms, so he had to get them out in the remaining few hours before they were due to his boss. To make matters worse, needed supplies had run out in the middle of the morning, and Bentley had had to make a rush order to get some for his employees.

The supervisor was only halfway through the forms he had to finish when he was approached by Tom Foster, one of his employees. "Do you have any of those medical claim forms?" asked Foster. "I need to put in for my doctor's appointment last Wednesday."

Bentley threw up his hands in frustration. "Can't you see I'm busy!" he shouted at the employee. "I swear, you people pick the worst times to bother me with your stupid requests. If you had half a brain in your head, you'd know by now that the claim forms are kept in the cabinet over there."

The Damage Done

As David Bentley will soon discover, one outburst made under stress can damage your relationship with all your employees. After all, what do you think is going to happen when Foster goes back and tells his fellow workers about his face-off with the supervisor? While Bentley may have been perfectly reasonable and cordial in the past, his people are likely to be wary when they are around him in the future.

In fact, their wariness may lead them to avoid the supervisor, robbing the department of new ideas and creating an "us versus them" atmosphere. The situation could feed on itself, causing supervisor-employee relationships to deteriorate further. That could culminate in increased turnover as workers seek to desert the sinking ship.

The stress that Bentley was under clouded his thinking; instead of thinking of his employee as an interruption in his work, he should have realized that dealing with employees is *part* of his work.

But such outbursts are a routine symptom of stress. And rather than deal with individual episodes, the best approach is to control your stress, rather than having your stress control you.

Goal-Setting to Reduce Stress

To control stress, you must consider both the physical and mental aspects of your life, both in and out of the workplace. First of all, consider how you react while under stress. Do you tend to snap at your employees and fellow supervisors? Do you tune everyone else out? Do you cave in under the pressure?

A positive reaction to stress is to set a goal, one that will result in your alleviating the stressful situation. David Bentley, for instance, can set a goal of completing his daily reports an hour before he goes home each day. This will eliminate the stress he feels on Friday afternoon—assuming he achieves his goal, of course. To enable him to achieve that goal, Bentley should commit himself to doing only one thing at a time.

When you're swamped with work and are juggling three or four different things, stress is sure to follow. However, choosing one aspect of your job and working on it to the exclusion of everything else can be helpful. You'll have to make room for any emergencies that come up, naturally, but single-mindedness is likely to help you complete one chore in a timely fashion so you can move on to the next before you fall behind. Keep in mind that eliminating stress is often a process of small steps.

Put Things in Perspective

Probably the most important step you can take in controlling stress is to place your job and its role in your life in perspective. Do you work to live, or do you live to work? If your answer is the latter, then you are setting yourself up for some major-league stress on the job. Every little setback at work will seem like the end of the world to you, and the people who work for and with you will be subjected to undue stress by your overreaction.

A proper perspective is one that recognizes that your supervisory job is an important part of your life—but that it is just a part, nonetheless. Make time in your personal life to gear down from the stress of work, and develop outside interests that will let you forget about the pressures you face on the job, at least temporarily.

To that end, here are some steps you can take when the pressure is on:

1 Conserve your energy. Your body has only so much energy at its disposal on any given day. Like an automobile, it will conk out if the energy it needs runs short. That's why it's important to use only enough energy to do the job at hand.

For instance, when showing an employee how to perform a task, don't do the work *for* the person over and over again. Demonstrate once or twice, be available for questions, but don't burn up all your energy hovering over the employee and doing the job for him or her. That way, if a stressful situation arises late in the workday, you'll still have the physical resources you need to handle it.

2 Use breathing as a tranquilizer. One of the best tranquilizers is one of the most natural—breathing properly. When people are under pressure, they often constrict their chest muscles, or even hold their breath. This, in turn, creates even more tension. It's a good idea to practice good breathing techniques. Once you establish them, they can become second nature when you're under stress, and can help calm you down.

What are proper breathing techniques? When you inhale, you take in healthful air. When you exhale, your respiratory system removes waste products. Therefore, you should strive to increase the time of exhalation to twice that of inhalation. This provides for optimum lung expansion, which allows you to breathe deeper and, in turn, helps you to relax.

3 Take a vacation without moving an inch. When stress is building, take 10 minutes or so for a mental vacation. Close your eyes, breathe deeply, and picture yourself in a relaxing setting. Your mental picture can be a secluded cabin in the woods, a deserted beach, or a flower-filled meadow—whatever you find most peaceful. Once you have the setting fixed in your mind's eye, insert yourself into the scene. Imagine the things that you see and hear around you.

How can this mental exercise help your physical state when you are under stress? After the first 5 minutes or so, true relaxation produces specific physiological changes and can stimulate the immune system. By "relaxing" during your mental vacation, you ensure that you will still be relaxed when you return to the stressful situation you are faced with.

Learning to Cope

It's important to remember that using these techniques won't *eliminate* stress from your life; stress is the unavoidable reaction to any demand made upon you.

What these techniques *will* do is allow you to cope with the stress that's a natural part of your job. You will be less likely to fall victim to the physical and mental strains of work pressure, and will be better able to control your emotions so they don't boil over when the heat is on.

That means, ultimately, that the stress you're feeling won't turn into stress for your employees. When they see you keeping an even keel under pressure, they'll strive to do the same.

▶ **WHAT YOU CAN DO** → *To keep stress under control, you must . . .*

1. Recognize when you are reacting to stress negatively. When your response seems out of proportion to the problem you are faced with, you are probably allowing stress to affect your supervisory performance.

2. Set reasonable goals for yourself. You can create your own stress if you try to accomplish too much in too little time.

3. Go on a mental vacation when stress builds to an overwhelming point. In your mind's eye, take yourself away to a relaxing setting. When you set to work again, you'll be refreshed and ready.

You may not be able to avoid stress altogether, but taking these steps can help you fight back against the potentially dangerous consequences of allowing pressure to build.

ACTION PLAN:
_____
_____
_____
_____
_____
_____
_____
_____
_____
_____
_____

CONCLUSION

SELF-APPRAISAL: GAUGING YOUR EXPERTISE

Every six months or once a year, most supervisors review their employees' job performance. The purpose of this appraisal is to let each person know where he or she stands, to record progress, or recognize trouble spots. Reviews like these encourage an employee's self-development.

But what about you? Do you get a chance to appraise your performance? "Sure," you say, "my boss and I have a heart-to-heart once a year. I'm doing okay."

Being satisfied with "okay" can have its drawbacks, however. It may be why some supervisors are passed over for promotions, are assigned routine projects or are constantly faced with lackluster productivity. For these reasons, you need to take steps to develop yourself into the best supervisor possible. To achieve this goal, an honest appraisal of your strengths and weaknesses is in order. And the best person to do this is *you*.

An honest evaluation of your performance is not going to be easy. Most supervisors find it hard to be objective about their own talents—tending to either overestimate them or play them down.

Because it's tempting to take your skills for granted, you need a standard by which you can accurately gauge your level of supervisory expertise. The best way to do this is with the following quiz. It will help you determine your strengths and weaknesses in the key supervisory areas: leadership, cost control, training, safety, human relations, communication, and personal development.

Circle your response to each question below. Then, compare your answers to the answer key on page 230 and add your score. This number will tell you how you are doing as a supervisor.

---

1. Which of the following qualities is *not* considered an attribute of an effective leader:

A. Fairness
B. Aggressiveness
C. Competence
D. Salesmanship

2. What's the best way to arrive at a decision?

A. Gather information, analyze it, weigh the pros and cons, and then choose the best course of action.
B. Think back to similar situations, and follow the precedent.
C. Trust your instincts; they've never failed you in the past.
D. Poll other supervisors to see what they think should be done.

3. When delegating assignments to employees, it's wise to spend a little time deciding who should do what. This means asking yourself:

A. Who wants more responsibility.
B. Who can spare the time.
C. Who would gain the most growth.
D. All of the above.

4. The best way to deal with chronic lateness on the part of your employees is:

A. Head it off before it becomes a problem by explaining the importance of being on time.
B. Threaten dismissal the first time an employee is late.
C. Ignore it. A few minutes of missed work here and there won't hurt your department.
D. Give offenders a lighthearted lecture on tardiness.

5. Employee theft is a serious drain on company profits. You may think that employee theft can't happen in your department. But studies have shown that the percentage of employees who steal from employers is:

A. 17 percent
B. 25 percent
C. 33 percent
D. None of the above

6. What is one of the best ways to eliminate unnecessary overtime?

A. Make production schedules well in advance.
B. Be on the lookout for individual employee problems.
C. Give rush jobs top priority.
D. All of the above.

7. The first step in training a new hire should be to:

A. Personally choose a seasoned employee to conduct the training.
B. Divide the material into easy segments.
C. Determine what specific skills you want the new person to learn.
D. None of the above.

8. Which of the following is *not* an acceptable training method:

A. Demonstration
B. Lecture
C. Sink-or-swim
D. Written instructions

9. It's a good idea to let experienced employees train new hires because:

A. It helps relieve your busy schedule.
B. It puts trainees at ease.
C. It boosts the experienced employee's morale.
D. All of the above

10. Job safety is a critical issue. What percentage of accidents and injuries on the job can a competent supervisor eliminate?

A. 85 percent
B. 50 percent
C. 27 percent
D. None of above

11. Which of the following causes the most on-the-job accidents and injuries:

A. Human failure (unsafe acts)
B. Mechanical failure (unsafe conditions)
C. Catastrophes (acts of nature)
D. Failure to enforce safety rules

12. Which of the following statements about horseplay is *not* correct?

A. Related injuries can lead to workers' comp claims and lawsuits.
B. Employees who engage in horseplay compromise their own safety.
C. Horseplay serves a useful purpose in the workplace since it releases tension without risk.
D. Nearly 25,000 workers are injured "fooling around" on the job each year.

13. You can deal effectively with disputes between workers by:

A. Ignoring them and waiting for them to blow over.
B. Firmly disciplining the involved parties.
C. Taking one person's side to simplify matters.
D. Listening to both sides and remaining objective.

14. When a major change is about to take place in the department, you should:

A. Tell your people at the last minute so as not to disrupt work.
B. Explain that inefficient past methods warrant the change.
C. Include workers in the process of implementing the change.
D. Let your crew figure out how best to deal with it.

15. When conducting employee evaluations, you should:

A. Rely on "gut" personal feelings.
B. Stick to the positive, and avoid bringing up faults.
C. Give the worker a chance to respond to your comments.
D. All of the above.

16. Listening is one of the most important supervisory skills. Which of the following will *not* help you be a better listener?

A. Briefly restate what you have been told.
B. Keep your mind on what the speaker is saying.
C. Avoid reacting emotionally to what is being said.
D. Pretend to be interested in what you're being told—even if you're not.

17. When handing out praise to your employees, you should remember to:

A. Keep praise appropriate to the achievement.
B. Tie public praise to a concrete form of recognition.
C. Use praise as a lure, not as a goad.
D. All of the above.

18. Pruning the grapevine is an important part of your job. When you have information that may concern your employees, you:

A. Keep it to yourself. Even if they will be affected by the information, you tell as little as possible. After all, they don't make the decisions.
B. Pass on the facts as soon as you know them—as long as it affects their jobs and is not confidential.
C. Tell only a carefully selected and trusted few employees about company business.
D. None of the above.

19. When you're hard at work and someone interrupts you, you keep the conversation short by:
A. Standing up. Then remain standing up until he or she leaves.
B. Fidgeting—and stealing glances at your watch every few seconds.
C. Shouting "Can't you see I'm busy!"
D. Putting your work aside—a little light conversation never hurt anyone.

20. Visibility is one of most important traits an up-and-coming supervisor can possess. Which of the following is a good way to make yourself visible:

A. Come to every meeting prepared to take an active role.
B. Take committee assignments seriously.
C. Make your department look good every chance you get.
D. All of the above.

HOW DO YOU RATE?

The Answer Key

Compare your anwers with the following key. Give yourself one point for each correct answer and zero for each incorrect answer.

A total score of 17 or more means your supervisory know-how is sharp. A score from 8 to 16 is average and means there is room for improvement.

Notice that the answers are grouped into categories. Pay close attention to how you've scored in each of these areas. This will help you pinpoint areas in which you might improve.

For further review, the page numbers after each answer tell you where in the book the particular topic is discussed.

LEADERSHIP

1. B ( )
2. A ( )
3. D ( )

COST CONTROL

4. A ( )
5. C ( )
6. D ( )

TRAINING

7. C ( )
8. C ( )
9. D ( )

SAFETY

10. B ( )
11. A ( )
12. C ( )

HUMAN RELATIONS

13. D ( )
14. C ( )
15. C ( )

COMMUNICATION

16. D ( )
17. D ( )
18. B ( )

SELF-DEVELOPMENT

19. A ( )
20. D ( )

INDEX

—A—

Absenteeism, *40-42*, *102*
Accidents and injuries
  how to be prepared for emergencies/
    disasters, *121-24*, *157*, *159*
  how to prevent, *110-21*
  unsafe acts and, *110-11*, *113-14*, *118-21*
  unsafe conditions and, *111-12*, *114-15*, *116-18*
  what to do when an employee is injured, *108-9*,
    115, *117-18*
Advancement, planning your, *214-16*
Age Discrimination in Employment Act (ADEA), *175*, *179*
Arizona Public Service Co., *212*
Assistant, your
  action plan for improving skills re selecting, *18-19*
  grooming a potential successor, *18*
  importance of selecting, *16-17*
  as trainer, *97*
  training of, *18*
  what to look for in selecting, *17*
  where to look in selecting, *17-18*

—B—

Barnard, Tennan, *101-3*
Barnes, Wiley, *104-5*
Beckwith, Philip, *32-34*
Binney and Smith, *32*
Boss, building a productive relationship with your
  action plan for improving skills re, *137-38*
  giving input to your boss, *137*
  honest communication, *7*
  mentor, your boss as, *213*
  rules to follow, *136-37*
  seeking input from your boss, *74*, *178-79*
  what not to do, *135-36*
Bryant, Kendred L., Jr., *127-129*
Burlington Industries, *127*

—C—

Change
  employee adjustment to, *149-52*
  overcoming your fear of, *213*
Civil Rights Act of 1964, *171*, *179*
Coaching of employees, *85-86*, *88*
Coleman, Ron, *69-71*, *72*
Colussy, Connie, *98*
Communication, effective
  action plans for improving skills re, *183*, *185-86*, *188*,
    190, *192-93*, *194-95*, *197*, *200*, *202-3*, *205*, *207-8*,
    210, *211*
  barriers to, *181-82*
  company policy, communicating, *188-90*
  criticism, use of, *184-86*, *201-2*, *211*
  as important for your advancement, *215-16*
  interviewing prospective employees, *205-10*
  listening, importance of, *191-93*
  meetings, *183*, *193*, *197-203*, *215*
  non-English-speaking employees and, *210-11*
  orders, giving, *186-88*
  praise, use of, *184-86*
  rumors, how to deal with, *195-97*
  speaking the language of your employees, *9*, *182*
  steps to ensure, *182-83*
  written, *183*, *203-5*
  See also Input
Complaints from employees, dealing with, *144-46*
Cost control
  absenteeism and, *40-42*
  action plans for improving skills re, *34*, *37*, *40*, *42*,
    49, *52-53*, *55*, *58*, *61*, *64-65*, *68*
  energy conservation and, *65-68*
  input from employees and, *32-33*, *35-37*, *44*, *45*
  materials handling and, *59-61*
  preventive maintenance to limit downtime, *55-58*
  productivity and, *33*, *50-53*
  quality and, *53-55*
  responsibility of employees and, *33*
  stock control and, *33-34*
  tardiness and, *37-40*
  theft and, *62-65*
  turnover and, *43-45*
  unnecessary overtime and, *46-49*
Counseling of employees, *85-86*, *88*, *165*, *178*
Co-workers, dealing with former, *6*
Crisis, conquering a, *19-21*
Criticism
  action plan for improving skills re, *185-86*, *211*
  non-English-speaking employees and, *211*
  of your ideas, *201-2*

—D—

Dayton Power & Light Co., *4*
Decision-making
  action plans for improving skills re, *12*, *16*, *18-19*
  bad decisions, *11-12*
  principles of, *10*
  promotions and, *15-19*
  steps essential to correct, *10-11*
Delegating, effective, *12-14*
Department of Refuse Removal (Orlando), *3*
Disabled employee(s)
  action plan for improving skills re, *160*
  blind, *157*
  definition of a, *156*
  discrimination and, *158-59*
  evacuating, in an emergency/disaster, *122*, *159*
  hearing-impaired, *157*
  how to integrate, *156-60*
Discipline, *160-63*, *178*
Discrimination
  action plan for improving skills re, *176*
  company policy and, *190*
  disabled employees and, *158-59*
  examples of, *174-75*
  firing an employee and, *176-80*
  how to avoid, *174-76*
  interviewing prospective employees and, *207*

older employees and, *175, 179*

—E—

Emergencies/disasters, how to be prepared for
  action plan for improving skills re, *124*
  assessing risks, *121, 123*
  evacuating disabled employees, *122, 159*
  setting up guidelines, *123-24*
Employee Retirement Income Security Act, *179*
Employees
  absenteeism and, *40-42, 102*
  accepting responsibility for your, *7*
  accidents and injuries, *107-16, 116-18*
  adjustment of, to change, *149-52*
  balancing work loads and, *21-23*
  coaching of, *85-86, 88*
  complaints from, *144-46*
  conflicts among, *147-49*
  cooperation from, *8-10, 51-52, 130, 164*
  counseling of, *85-86, 88-89, 165, 178*
  dealing with former co-workers, *6*
  disabled, *122, 156-60*
  disagreeable tasks and, *22-23*
  discipline and, *160-63, 178*
  firing of, *176-80*
  getting to know your, *130-32, 142-43*
  goal-setting and, *29-31, 87*
  input from your, *7, 23, 32-33, 34-37, 44, 45, 128-29, 151, 155, 193-95*
  input to your, *7, 22, 31, 39, 51-52, 59-60, 67-68, 150-51, 165*
  interviewing prospective, *205-10*
  motivating, *29-31, 51-52, 103-5, 112-15, 119*
  non-English-speaking, *210-11*
  older, *153-55, 175, 179*
  performance evaluation, *163-66, 185*
  performance problems, *128, 141-43, 167-70, 171, 178, 185*
  planning and needs of, *25*
  preventive maintenance and, *56-57*
  productivity and, *22, 33, 50-53, 164, 171*
  promotion decisions and, *15-19*
  quality and, *53-55, 73-74, 164*
  recognition and, *138-41*
  requests from, *9*
  responsibility of, cost control and, *33*
  safety and, *101-26, 164*
  setting a good example for, *7, 39, 53, 93*
  sexual harassment and, *170-73*
  speaking the language of, *9, 182*
  substance abuse and, *167-70, 177*
  tardiness and, *37-40*
  theft and, *62-65*
  training of, *18, 22-23, 59, 69-100 108, 117, 119, 124-26, 151, 154-55, 165, 210-11*
  turnover and, *43-45*
  See also Human relations
Employment-at-will, *176-80*
Energy conservation, *65-68*
Equal Employment Opportunity Act, *179*
Equal Employment Opportunity Commission (EEOC), *171, 174*
Equal Pay Act, *175*
Evaluation, performance
  action plans for improving skills re, *166, 185-86*
  benefits of, *163, 165-66*
  counseling interview and, *165*
  criticism, effective use of, *184-86, 211*
  frequency of, *163-64*
  methods of, *164*
  praise, effective use of, *184-86*
  what not to do, *164-65*
  what should be evaluated, *164*
Evaluation, productivity, *22, 50-52, 164*

—F—

Fair Labor Standards Act, *179*
Feedback. See Input
Firing an employee
  action plan for improving skills re, *180*
  discipline before, *178*
  employment-at-will and, *176-80*
  exit interview, *179-80*
  how not to handle, *177, 179*
  input from your boss and, *178-79*
  justifiable reasons for, *177, 178, 179*
  recordkeeping and, *178*

—G—

Goal-setting, *29-31, 87*
Gray, John, *73-75*
Grefe, Peter, *32-33*

—H—

Heimburg, Dave, *3-4*
Hensley Construction Co., *127*
Hipp, Bob, *4*
Hiring. See Interviewing prospective employees
Human relations
  action plans for improving skills re, *129-30, 131-32, 135, 137-38, 140-41, 143, 146, 149, 152, 155, 160, 162-63, 166, 170, 173, 176, 180*
  building a productive relationship with your boss, *7, 74, 135-38*
  complaints from employees, *144-46*
  conflicts among employees, *147-49*
  cooperation with other supervisors, *132-35*
  disabled employees, *122, 156-60*
  discipline, *160-63, 178*
  employee adjustment to change, *149-52*
  firing an employee, *176-80*
  flexibility and, *151-52, 164*
  getting to know your employees, *130-32, 142-43*
  how to approach, *127-30*
  how to avoid discrimination, *174-76*
  input, *7, 22, 23, 31, 32-33, 35-37, 44, 45, 51-52, 59-60, 67-68, 128-29, 150-51, 155, 165*
  performance evaluation, *163-66, 184-86*
  performance problems, *128, 141-43, 167-70, 171, 178*
  recognition, *138-141*
  sexual harassment, *170-73*
  substance abuse, *167-70, 177*

—I—

Input
  action plan for improving skills re, *37*
  boss, from your, *74, 178-79*

232

boss, to your, *137*
employees, from, *7, 23, 32-33, 35-37, 44, 45, 128-29, 151, 155, 193-95*
employees, to, *7, 22, 31, 39, 51-52, 59-60, 50-51, 165*
how to encourage, *34-37, 193*
Interviewing prospective employees
action plans for improving skills re, *207-8, 210*
closing ritual for, *209-10*
discrimination and, *207*
job analysis/description and, *205-6*
preparation for, *205-8*
questions not to ask, *207*
questions to ask, *207, 209*

—J—

Job analysis/description
for hiring, *205-6*
for training, *79-81*

—K—

Kleinheider, Leon B., *127, 128*

—L—

Leadership
action plans for improving skills re, *5, 7, 9-10, 12, 14, 16, 18-19, 21, 23, 26, 29, 31*
aggressive, *8-9*
assertive, *8-9*
authoritative, *4*
conquering a crisis, *19-21*
decision-making, *10-19*
delegating, *12-14*
democratic, *4*
goal-setting, *29-31, 87*
as important for your advancement, *215-16*
laissez-faire, *4*
learning from other supervisors, *6-7, 74*
motivating employees, *29-31, 51-52, 103-5, 112-15, 119*
passive, *8-9*
people-oriented, *4-5*
planning, *24-26*
promotion decisions, *15-19*
qualities needed for effective, *3*
reviewing your performance, *7*
scheduling, *26-29*
setting a good example for your employees, *7, 39, 53, 93*
speaking the language of other supervisors, *9*
speaking the language of your employees, *9, 182*
styles of, *3-5, 8-9*
taking a fresh approach, *6*
task-oriented, *4-5*
trainer, you as, *97*
Leber, Bob, *69-72*
Legal issues
action plans for improving skills re, *176, 180*
company policy and discrimination, *190*
disabled employees and discrimination, *158-59*
employment-at-will, *176-80*
how to avoid discrimination, *174-76*
older employees and discrimination, *175, 179*
recordkeeping and, *175-76, 178, 190*
sexual harassment, *170-73*

—M—

Maintenance, preventive, *55-58*
Materials handling, *59-61*
Meetings
action plans for improving skills re, *200, 202-3*
effective communication at, *183, 193, 197-203*
preparation for, *198, 201, 215*
safety, *102, 108*
steps to take in guiding discussion, *198-99*
as time-wasters, *222-23*
tools essential for, *199*
when you are a group member, *200-203*
when you are in charge, *197-200*
Mentor, acquiring a, *212-13*
Motivating employees
to be concerned about safety, *103-5, 112-15, 119*
goal-setting as a way of, *29-31*
to improve productivity, *51-52*

—N—

National Labor Relations Act, *179*
Non-English-speaking employees, *210-11*

—O—

Occupational Safety and Health Act, *179*
Older employees
discrimination and, *175, 179*
how to use experience of, *153-55*
Orders, giving effective, *186-88*
OSHA (Occupational Safety and Health Administration), *105-7*
Overtime, how to deal with unnecessary, *46-49*

—P—

Paperwork, how to deal with, *223-24*
Parma Company, *101-3*
Performance
evaluation, *163-66, 185-86*
problems, *128, 141-43, 167-70, 171, 178*
PERT (Program Evaluation and Review Technique) method, *27-28*
Planning, *24-26*
Policy, communicating company, *188-90*
Praise, effective use of, *184-86*
Productivity
action plans for improving skills re, *52-53, 143*
cost control and, *33, 50-53*
evaluation of, *22, 50-51, 164*
motivating employees to improve, *51-52*
performance problems, *128, 141-43, 167-70, 171, 178*
sexual harassment and, *171*
Promotion, preparing for your, *214-16*
Promotion decisions
action plans for improving skills re, *16, 18-19*
grooming a potential successor, *18*
promoting from outside the department, *15-16*
promoting from within the department, *15*
reasons why promotions can backfire, *15*
selecting an assistant, *16-19*

—Q—

Quality
  evaluation of, *164*
  how to improve, *53-55, 73-74*

—R—

Recordkeeping, importance of, *175-76, 178, 190*
Rhodes & Associates, *181*
Rumors, how to deal with, *195-97*

—S—

Safety
  absenteeism and, *102*
  action plans for improving skills re, *103, 105, 107, 109-10, 115-16, 118, 120-21, 124, 126*
  cost of working unsafely, *109*
  eliminating hazardous acts, conditions, and attitudes, *107-10*
  employee judgment and, *101-2*
  evacuating disabled employees, *122*
  evaluation of an employee's safety record, *164*
  guidelines, *101*
  horseplay and, *118-21*
  how to be prepared for emergencies/disasters, *121-24, 159*
  how to build awareness, *103-5*
  how to prevent accidents and injuries, *110-21*
  machine hazards, *116-18*
  management commitment to, *101, 102-3*
  meetings, *102, 108*
  motivating employees to be concerned about, *103-5, 112-15, 119*
  OSHA and, *105-7*
  outside resources and, *102*
  steps to improve, *104-5*
  training and, *101-2, 108, 117, 119, 124-26*
  unsafe acts, *110-11, 113-14, 118-21*
  unsafe conditions, *111-12, 114-15, 116-18*
  what to do when an employee is injured, *108-9, 115, 117-18*
Sandstrom, Jeannine, *181-83*
Scheduling, *26-29*
Self-development
  action plans for improving skills re, *214, 216, 218-19, 221, 224, 226*
  advancement, planning your, *214-16*
  challenges, *212-14*
  creativity, harnessing, *219-21*
  mentor, acquiring a, *212-13*
  paperwork, how to deal with, *223-24*
  self-appraisal quiz, *227-30*
  special projects, managing, *217-19*
  stress, how to deal with, *224-26*
  time, making effective use of, *222-24*
Sexual harassment, *170-73*
Shur-Lok, *32*
Skills, Inc., *73*
Stress, *74, 224-26*
Substance abuse
  action plan for improving skills re, *170*
  as grounds for firing an employee, *177*
  recognizing the problem, *167*
  ruling out other causes, *167-68*
  what to do about, *168-70*
Successor, grooming a potential, *16-18*
Supervisors, other
  cooperation with, *132-35*
  learning from, *6-7, 74*
  speaking the language of, *9*

—T—

Tanner Industries, *104-5*
Tardiness, how to deal with, *37-40*
Theft, how to deal with, *62-65*
Time, making effective use of, *222-24*
Training
  action plans for improving skills re, *72, 75, 78, 82, 84, 88, 93-94, 96, 100*
  assessing needs re, *78-82*
  coaching, *85-86, 88*
  continuing education, *97-100, 213*
  costs and, *94-96*
  counseling, *85-86, 88, 165, 178*
  cross-, *87, 119*
  developing employee trainers, *89-94, 97*
  disagreeable tasks and, *22-23*
  employee reluctance and, *98, 99*
  goal-setting and, *87*
  instilling self-confidence in trainees, *73-75*
  instructor's checklist, *91*
  job analysis chart, sample, *80-81*
  job requirement breakdown card, sample, *79, 81*
  in materials handling, *59*
  methods of, *71*
  non-English-speaking employees, *210-11*
  older employees as trainers, *154-55*
  orientation, *76-78*
  outside, *71-72, 97-99*
  preparation tips for, *70*
  progress report, sample, *81-82*
  rules for, *151*
  safety and, *101-2, 108, 117, 119, 124-26*
  seizing the opportunity for, *69*
  selecting trainers, checklist for, *90*
  steps to effective, *69-71*
  stress and, *74*
  tips on sending employees for, *98*
  value analysis of, *95-96*
  written instructions for, *82-84*
  you as trainer, *97*
  of your assistant, *18*
  your continuing, *213*
Turnover, *43-45*

—U—

Union Electric Co., *69*

—W—

Wellington, Jim, *212-13*
Work loads, balancing, *21-23*
Written communications, effective, *183, 203-5*